Research and Development in Expert Systems IV

THE BRITISH COMPUTER SOCIETY WORKSHOP SERIES
Editor: P. HAMMERSLEY

The BCS Workshop series aims to report developments of an advanced technical standard undertaken by members of The British Computer Society through the Society's study groups and conference organizations. The series should be compulsive reading for all those whose work or interest involves computing technology and for both undergraduate and post-graduate students. Volumes in this Series will mirror the quality of papers published in the BCS's technical periodical *The Computer Journal* and range widely across topics in computer hardware, software, applications and management.

Some current titles:

Current Perspectives in Health Computing
Ed. B. Kostrewski

Research and Development in Information Retrieval
Ed. C.J. van Rijsbergen

Proceedings of the Third British National Conference on Databases (BNCOD3)
Ed. J. Longstaff

Research and Development in Expert Systems
Ed. M. A. Bramer

Proceedings of the Fourth British National Conference on Databases (BNCOD4)
Ed. A. F. Grundy

People and Computers: Designing the Interface
Eds. P. Johnson and S. Cook

Expert Systems 85
(Research and Development in Expert Systems II)
Ed. M. Merry

Text Processing and Informational Retrieval
Ed. J. C. van Vliet

Proceedings of the Fifth British National Conference on Databases (BNCOD5)
Ed. E. A. Oxborrow

People and Computers: Designing for Usability
Eds. M. D. Harrison and A. F. Monk

Research and Development in Expert Systems III
Ed. M. A. Bramer

People and Computers III
Eds. D. Diaper and R. Winder

Research and Development in Expert Systems IV
Ed. D. S. Moralee

Research and Development in Expert Systems IV

Proceedings of Expert Systems '87, the Seventh Annual Technical Conference

of the British Computer Society Specialist Group on Expert Systems,

Brighton, 14-17 December 1987

Edited by D. S. Moralee

Knowledge Engineering Group,
Unilever Research Laboratory, Merseyside

The right of the
University of Cambridge
to print and sell
all manner of books
was granted by
Henry VIII in 1534.
The University has printed
and published continuously
since 1584.

Published by

CAMBRIDGE UNIVERSITY PRESS

on behalf of

THE BRITISH COMPUTER SOCIETY

Cambridge

London   New York   New Rochelle

Melbourne Sydney

Published by the Press Syndicate of the University of Cambridge
The Pitt Building, Trumpington Street, Cambridge CB2 1RB
32 East 57th Street, New York, NY 10022, USA
10 Stamford Road, Oakleigh, Melbourne 3166, Australia

First published 1988

Printed in Great Britain by Redwood Burn Limited, Trowbridge, Wiltshire

Library of Congress cataloguing in publication data available

British Library cataloguing in publication data
British Computer Society. *Specialist Group on Expert Systems. Technical Conference (7th : 1987 : Brighton)*
Research and development in expert systems IV: proceedings of Expert Systems '87, the Seventh Annual Technical Conference of the British Computer Society Specialist Group on Expert Systems, Brighton 14-17 December 1987.– (The British Computer Society workshop series).

1. Expert systems (Computer science)
I. Title   II. Moralee, D. S.   III. Series
006.3'3   QA76.76.E95

ISBN 0 521 35551 6

Contents

Preface

The papers in this volume were presented at the seventh Expert Systems conference organised by the British Computer Society Specialist Group on Expert Systems.

On behalf of the Program Committee, I would like to thank all those who took part in refereeing the papers for this conference. They provided excellent advice under tight time pressures. Particular mention should be made of the contribution of Dr Nigel Shadbolt, for his work and support as overall Conference Chairman for ES87, and also of the main Organising Committee.

The successful production of these proceedings (and the ES87 conference) is in large measure due to the professionalism, advice, assistance and constant reminders from the staff at Conference Clearway.

INTRODUCTION

D S Moralee
Knowledge Engineering Group
Unilever Research Laboratory
Merseyside

Expert Systems is a topic which continues to interest both the academic world and the industrial/commercial world. Each has a different emphasis - on the one hand the academic seeking understanding of basic problems, and on the other hand the industrial/commercial workers seeking to exploit the technology either as products in the market place or as effective internal information systems. Both communities have much to learn from each other, and one of the major successes of the Alvey initiative has been the further progress made in bringing these communities together.

Since its inception in 1981, the British Computer Society Specialist Group on Expert Systems has encouraged this sharing of ideas and experience between academia and industry, between researcher and exploiter. A major part of this activity has been through the annual conference organised by the group. Now in its 7th year, this conference continues to act as a forum for the two communities - the 'Call for Papers' this year explicitly encouraged a broad mix of papers, on theoretical topics, on technique development and on applications experience.

This volume is the fourth volume in the series 'Research and Development in Expert Systems' and it contains the refereed papers accepted for the 1987 conference. In addition to these refereed papers, three invited papers were presented and are included in the volume. These invited papers were from Alan Bundy (Edinburgh University), Richard Young (MRC Applied Psychology Dept) and Robin Muir (Rolls Royce Ltd).

The papers are presented in the book in the order in which they were given at the conference - the reader will have little difficulty in identifying the theoretical, technique and application categories.

The papers cover many important aspects of current Expert Systems work - in particular they address theoretical topics, practical techniques, real applications of Expert Systems and discussions of issues of importance to the future development of the subject. The applications cover a wide spectrum of commercial and industrial interest - from tax consultants, insurance and town planning, to hydrocarbon exploration and drilling.

The expert systems field continues to attract interest and investment from industry and commerce. The papers in these proceedings provide a good indication of the practical results which can be obtained from the use of Expert Systems technology, describe methods for eliciting knowledge and developing applications, introduce a number of issues which are important for the future development of the subject, and discuss recent theoretical work.

The number of papers submitted this year was the highest yet, giving the Program Committee and the Referees a difficult job in reducing the papers to the present number - which is the maximum which can be presented without recourse to parallel sessions. This, in addition to the Tutorial papers and the Fringe papers presented at the conference, is further indication of the continuing activity and development in this subject.

How to Improve the Reliability of Expert Systems

Alan Bundy

Department of Artificial Intelligence
University of Edinburgh

Abstract

Reliability is likely to become an increasingly important issue for knowledge engineers. Without assurances of reliability they will be restricted in the scale and scope of the expert systems they can build and will not be able to capitalise on their current success. The key to greater reliability is a sound theoretical foundation for current and new knowledge engineering techniques — making knowledge engineering a proper engineering science. We illustrate the kind of theoretical work that is required with a few case studies, in the areas of search control, fault diagnosis and learning.

Acknowledgements

I am grateful for conversations on the topics of this paper with Richard O'Keefe, Aaron Sloman, Robert Inder, Roberto Desimone, Bill Sharpe and Mike Uschold. I would also like to thank Bill Sharpe and Hewlett Packard for allowing me to work on this paper in the ivory tower of their Bristol Research Laboratory away from the hubbub of university life. Some of the work described here was funded by SERC grant GR/44874.

1 Introduction

The UK expert system community has been very successful in the development of small scale, commercial, rule-based, expert systems. A typical example is a fault diagnosis system for a piece of specialised hardware, consisting of a set of less than 100 rules, running on a PC, in one of the many commercial shells. Part of the success consists of the unexpected (to me anyway) discovery of a large number of commercially interesting problems which yield to such a simple mechanism.

UK knowledge engineers have also been active in building much larger expert systems, with hundreds or even thousands of rules. In addition, they have experimented with alternative knowledge representation and reasoning techniques, e.g. frames, objects, semantic nets, etc. This use of large scale expert systems and of alternative and/or multiple knowledge representations has been more typical of the US market, but both are becoming more important here.

I pay tribute to the success of UK knowledge engineering, but in this paper I want to look beyond it and see what we need to do now in order to lay a solid foundation for future success. To see what might be required in the future we must first explore the limitations of existing systems. The main limitation I will focus on is the unreliability of current expert systems. This is an important topic in its own right, but assumes greater importance in the context of the shift to both larger scale and to alternative and mixed knowledge representations. Unreliability often increases as the system gets larger; large collections of rules are more likely to be inconsistent, incomplete or to interact in unpredicted ways, because it is harder for humans to check them 'by hand'. Unreliability is also likely to increase when alternative knowledge representation formalisms are used, because these new formalisms are often poorly understood or are combined in poorly understood ways.

2   Unreliability

What do we mean by the term *unreliable* as applied to an expert system? It is a catch-all term, and can include any of the following overlapping phenomena.

- **Fragility** (non-robustness): The system may fail in unexpected ways.

- **Unpredictability**: The user either cannot specify the circumstances under which the system will produce an answer or cannot specify the type of answer that will be produced.

- **Brittleness** (non-flexibility): The system cannot deal with problems on which it has not been previously tested.

- **Discontinuity**: The system gives very different output in response to similar input.

All of these phenomena are undesirable in a commercial product. In a real time situation, unreliability can cause chaos. In a life critical situation, unreliability can be fatal. Even in more mundane situations, unreliability can cause expensive mistakes and lead to users rejecting the product. The unreliability of expert system shells and toolkits makes it difficult for a knowledge engineer to decide whether a particular tool will help solve the current problem; thus it is difficult to advise customers whether their problems are soluble by current techniques or to predict whether a knowledge engineering project will be successful. Thus reliability is a very desirable feature both for suppliers and users of expert systems.

Contrast the situation of expert systems with more mature branches of engineering. Before building a bridge, a structural engineer makes a number of drawings and carries out elaborate calculations. These calculations enable the engineer to predict the behaviour of the bridge under a wide variety of stresses. As a result the engineer can say, with confidence, that for a specific range of loading and weather conditions the bridge will behave robustly, predictably, flexibly and continuously. If the engineer does not carry out these calculations or does so inaccurately, and the bridge falls down, then he/she is guilty of professional negligence (*cf* the Tay Bridge disaster).

3   Causes of Unreliability in Expert Systems

There is not, yet, the same tradition in the field of knowledge engineering. In fact, there is a common assumption that analogous assurances of reliability could not be given; that algorithms do not exist on which analogous calculations could be based; that the heuristics on which expert systems are based lead to an inherently unreliable product.

I will argue that this is wrong. It is possible to base expert systems upon techniques which lend themselves to the giving of reliability assurances. Some work of this kind already exists and I will outline it below.

However, it is true that existing knowledge engineering practice leads to unreliable products. For instance, the following practices are of that kind.

- The mixing of control and factual information in the same rule.

- The attachment of arbitrary procedures to rules.

- The use of multiple knowledge representation formalisms without a clear understanding of their relationship to each other.

- The use of "uncertainty factors" without a clear understanding of their meaning.

- The incremental development of systems by patches and hacks, and without consideration of the whole system.

- A lack of theoretical understanding of the techniques used in the system's development.

The last of the these points, *a lack of theoretical understanding*, is a generalization of the others. We will use it below as a summary of the causes of unreliability.

This kind of bad practice is encouraged by existing expert system shells, toolkits and knowledge representation systems. For instance, most expert system shells provide a facility for attaching numbers to rules and facts to represent "uncertainty", but few explain what these numbers mean. Many alternative interpretations are possible. This may cause the numbers to be used differently by different knowledge engineers and users, leading to a clash of expectations about the expert system and, hence, to unreliability.

Suppose an expert system for crime detection is investigating the murder of Mary. When it asks a witness whether John hated Mary, the witness can choose a range of options between 1, meaning "no", and 5, meaning "yes". What would an answer of 3 mean? The system's designer may have intended 3 to mean a mild form of hate. The rules of the system will embody this meaning and draw appropriate inferences from it. However, the witness might use 3 to mean that someone hated Mary intensely, but that it might not have been John. Consequently, the expert system may fail to suggest a culprit for Mary's murder or may suggest an innocent person.

Most toolkit systems (e.g. ART, KEE, LOOPS, etc) offer a range of different knowledge representation formalisms, e.g. rules, frames, objects, semantic nets, isa hierarchies, procedures, but no account of the relationship between them. The user of the toolkit is faced with the difficult choice of choosing an appropriate representational formalism. The representational scopes of the formalisms overlap considerably. For instance, a relationship of membership between an element and a set may be represented as a predicate in a logical assertion, an arc in an isa hierarchy or a slot in a frame. However, the toolkit may not be capable of translating between equivalent representations. So if a mixture of formalisms is used the toolkit may not be able to combine the knowledge effectively. More confusing still, the toolkit may translate between the formalisms only some of the time, so that the user is unable to predict when two pieces of knowledge will be effectively combined and when they will not, [Inder 87b]. At the root of the problem is a lack of theoretical understanding of the relationship between the formalisms, for instance, is the slot in a frame merely syntactic sugar for a logical assertion or is it something subtly different?

4 Resolution: A Model of Propriety

Among this collection of, mostly unreliable, knowledge-engineering techniques, one family stand out as a model of respectability and reliability: the techniques of logical deduction used in automatic theorem proving and logic programming, e.g. resolution. The reliability of resolution-like, deduction techniques is given by their semantics, and by the soundness and completeness theorems that accompany these semantics. How does this work?

The semantics of a logical formalism is a systematic way of assigning meaning to its expressions. The semantics of predicate calculus (*aka* first order logic) was invented by Tarski. Since then semantics have been given for other types of logic, e.g. by Kripke for modal logics. Each symbol of the logic is of a particular kind, e.g. constants, variables, functions, predicates, etc. An *interpretation* of predicate logic consists of a set of objects, called the *universe*, and some *mappings* on this universe. The constants of the logic refer to particular objects in the universe, the variables range over the objects, the functions refer to mappings from objects to objects, and the predicates refer to mappings from objects to truth values. Interpretation independent mappings are associated with the logical connectives and quantifiers, e.g. the implication arrow, $\longrightarrow$; the conjunction symbol, &; and the universal quantifer, $\forall$. Tarskian semantics uses these mappings to calculate the references of complex expressions from the references of their sub-expressions.

So, for instance, we might choose the set of real world objects as the universe. We might associate with the predicates *gun* and *weapon*, mappings from each object, *o*, in this universe to the set $\{true, false\}$ such that $gun(o)$ is *true* if and only if *o* is a gun and $weapon(o)$ is *true* if and only if *o* is a weapon. Under this interpretation the complex expression:

$$\forall X \; gun(X) \longrightarrow weapon(X)$$

is forced to have the reference *true*, since in the real world all objects that are guns are also weapons.

An expert system rule or fact can be regarded as a formula of (predicate) logic if it can be interpreted as having a (Tarskian) semantics. In a knowledge base, consisting of a set of such logical formula, we would obviously want them all to have the same semantics. It is up to the author of a knowledge base to say what universe its variables range over, what its constants refer to, and what mappings to associate with its functions and predicates. A reference can then be calculated for each formula in it. The author of the knowledge base will almost certainly want the reference of each formula in it to be *true*. An interpretation in which each member of a knowledge base is *true*, is called a *model* of that knowledge base. If a formula is *true* in every model of a knowledge base, then it is called a *logical consequence* of that knowledge base.

The pay-off of this investment is that any formula, C, deduced by resolution from a knowledge base, K, will be a logical consequence of K. This is the soundness theorem of resolution. In addition, every logical consequence of K can be deduced by resolution from it. This is the completeness theorem of resolution.

What this means to the user of a resolution-based expert system shell is that it is possible to have some weak form of prediction about the behaviour of the system. To get the benefit the user must try to write *true* rules and facts according to some specific assumptions about what objects exist in the universe and what the other symbols in the knowledge base mean. The user should add sufficient rules and facts to the knowledge base so that only the intended interpretations are models of all of them. The shell will then be guaranteed to draw all and only those conclusions which are true in all these models. This does not prevent the user being surprised at some of the conclusions which are true in these models, but it does curtail some of the wilder flights of inference to which expert systems are prone.

The user can also use resolution to test if the knowledge base is inconsistent. If it is inconsistent then it will have no model, i.e. there will be no circumstance in which all the rules and facts are simultaneously *true*. In this case resolution is guaranteed to be able to deduce *false* from them. So to test for inconsistency, resolution can be set loose on the knowledge base: if it deduces *false* then the knowledge base is inconsistent; if it does not, then the knowledge base is consistent. Unfortunately, there is no time limit to how long this might take - you could wait a long time and still not be sure whether *false* has just not been deduced yet or never will be.

The theory underlying resolution thus makes possible some procedures, analogous to the bridge builder's calculations, which enable certain predictions to be made about the behaviour of an expert system. Consider what reliability assurances are made possible by these calculations.

- **Robustness**: The system will not fail to deduce a conclusion if it is a logical consequence of the knowledge base.

- **Predictability**: The user can specify that the system will deduce a conclusion if and only if it is a logical consequence of the knowledge base.

- **Flexibility**: The system can deduce any logical consequence of the knowledge base, even though the user has not tested this deduction in advance.

- **Continuity**: If two similar knowledge bases both share the same models, then the same conclusions will be deduced from them.

Thus the burden of reliability assurance is shifted from the procedure of deduction to the semantic concept of logical consequence. These assurances fall a long way short of what we would like. They still leave a large burden on the user in designing a knowledge base with just the intended models and, hence, just the intended logical consequences. They give no assurances about the amount of effort required to deduce a logical consequence. In addition, they only apply to a situation in which logical deduction is being applied to a knowledge base. They do not apply to other kinds of reasoning, e.g. learning or inference involving uncertainty However, they are a start. In the next section we consider how they might be strengthened and extended to other kinds of reasoning.

5 Does this Idea Generalise?

In order to develop similar kinds of reliability assurance for expert systems based on other knowledge engineering techniques we must first develop similar kinds of theoretical frameworks. But before we can do this we have to define the other knowledge engineering techniques in question. The resolution family of logical deduction techniques is not just unusual in having a clear theoretical framework, but is also unusual in being clearly defined.

Basic AI research can be seen as the attempt to develop a loose collection of computational techniques of which resolution is one, [Bundy 86]. New techniques are often developed using exploratory programming, and AI researchers have not been diligent in separating them clearly from the program in which they were invented, nor in analysing their theoretical properties, nor in using such an analysis to extend and generalise them. The Catalogue of Artificial Intelligence Techniques, [Bundy 84], is an attempt to identify, informally define, and catalogue AI techniques. Mathematical logic is one of the most promising mathematical tools for the formal definition, analysis and extension of these informally defined techniques.

A major aspect of the formal analysis of knowledge engineering techniques is the classification of the different kinds of knowledge used in them. For instance, when using exploratory programming, knowledge engineers often include both factual and control knowledge in the same rule. However, a resolution-style analysis of the semantics of the rule is concerned only with its factual content; in order not to confuse the analysis it is necessary to separate off the control knowledge, e.g. into a separate meta-level (see section 5.1 below). This separation buys considerable computational advantages; it makes possible a simpler semantics which simplifies the tasks of the automatic inference and learning of both factual and control knowledge, [Bundy 81].

Similarly, a theoretical analysis of uncertainty cannot be given without separating the different kinds of uncertainty that the knowledge engineer may entwine into the same value. In the example above we saw that an uncertainty value of 3 applied to the fact "John hated Mary" is ambiguous; it could be modifying either its intensity or the identity of the hater (or hatee). If the fact were represented by the logical formula $hate(john, mary)$[1] then the ambiguity can be represented by considering the uncertainty value as applying either to the predicate *hate* or to the constant *john* (or *mary*).

In addition to all this, there are the more obvious ambiguities about just what the value 3 means in terms of reduction of intensity or doubts about someone's identity, etc. Sometimes this kind of ambiguity can be clarified by interpreting an uncertainty as a probability. For instance, a value of 3 (out of 5) applied to the rule:

$$hate(M, V) \ \& \ possess(M, W) \ \& \ weapon(W) \longrightarrow kill(M, V)$$

might mean that person M will kill person V in 60% of the cases in which M hates V and possesses a weapon W. Note that this probabilistic interpretation is not available if the uncertainty value is taken as a measure of the intensity of the hate or the doubt about the identity of someone.

Teasing apart the different kinds of knowledge used in expert systems makes it easier to develop procedures for reasoning with the different kinds of knowledge. We are then in a position to strengthen existing reasoning procedures and to develop new ones. We are also in a position to classify users's tasks according to the kind of knowledge they involve and give a prediction about which techniques, if any, are appropriate to their solution.

The sort of work that needs to be done is best illustrated by examples of existing work employing this methodology. In the following sections I will give some examples of such work. This is not meant to be an exhaustive list: it is limited by available space and my own ignorance.

5.1   Proof Plans for Guiding Inference

A major problem with automatic inference techniques is the *combinatorial explosion*: the number of possible inference paths that an expert system must explore grows exponentially or worse with the number of inference steps. When attempting a non-trivial inference, the expert system becomes bogged down in the possibilities. The usual answer to the combinatorial explosion is the provision of a heuristic, search control mechanism. A heuristic is a rule of thumb which is not guaranteed to work, but often does. Heuristics suggest which paths to explore first. For instance, if you are trying to prove a conjecture in which there are two or more occurrences of a term then at some point you must apply a rule or fact which reduces those occurrences to one or zero. Such rules can be identified syntactically and it is worth trying to apply them before other rules.

The design and selection of heuristics has been relegated by most workers to the realm of 'art form'. This is unfortunate. The provision of good heuristics is crucial to the success of an expert system afflicted with the combinatorial explosion, i.e. any system whose rules create many choice points during inference and in which the inference is deep. Without such heuristics the expert system will be unable to draw the required conclusion within a reasonable time, but will be bogged down in unpromising parts of the inference process. In order that the user can predict whether the expert system is going to succeed in a reasonable time, it is necessary to promote the provision of search control from 'art-form' to 'science'.

My own research group has been exploring how this might be done. We have chosen the domain of mathematics because it contains many deep and highly branching, deductive inferences, which cause large combinatorial explosions. However, experienced mathematicians have developed sophisticated techniques for controlling their search for a proof.

---

[1]In this paper we adopt the Prolog convention that words starting with a capital letter represent variables and those that do not represent constants, so we have to represent the constant "John" as *"john"*.

We have tried to represent this search control knowledge using a logical formalism, which we call a *meta-logic*, with its own declarative semantics. To use it to control the search for a proof we make deductions with it; a process that we call *meta-level inference*, [Bundy 81]. The universe of the meta-logic consists of the expressions and proof strategies of the area of mathematics in which we are trying to prove theorems: the *object theory*. Meta-level inference analyses the object-level conjecture to be proved and finds an appropriate proof strategy, which it then applies.

Recently, we have been trying to capture the concept of a proof plan using these techniques. Mathematicians, when trying to prove a conjecture, often have a plan of how to proceed. Such a proof plan should have the following properties:

- **Usefulness**: The plan should control the search for a proof.

- **Expectancy**: The use of the plan should carry some expectation of success.

- **Incertitude**: On the other hand, success cannot be guaranteed. (Most interesting mathematical theories have no decision procedure. A proof plan which was always successful would amount to a decision procedure.)

- **Patchability**: If the plan should fail it should be possible to patch it by providing alternative steps for the failing ones.

If our representation of proof plans can capture the correct balance between 'expectancy' and 'incertitude', then we can provide a tool for predicting whether an expert system will succeed in a reasonable time. Necessarily, such a tool would not be perfect, but it would give as good a prediction as it was possible to give, and it could be used to localise the possible causes of failure.

We see a proof strategy as consisting of a program of proof tactics, [Gordon 79], where each proof tactic is a procedure for performing a small part of the proof, e.g. collecting several occurrences of an equation unknown into one, [Bundy 81]; unfolding a recursively defined function, [Darlington 81]; applying mathematical induction. Note that some tactics may fail, causing failure of the whole strategy. For instance, a tactic for collecting two occurrences of a term into one may work by applying a rule drawn from a suitable set. Thus the two occurrences of the term *john* in the goal *hate(john, john)* may be collected by applying the rule:

$$depressed(D) \longrightarrow hate(D, D)$$

backwards to produce *depressed(john)*. On the other hand, the attempt to collect the *john*s in *possess(john, john)* might fail because no suitable rule was available.

A proof method is a meta-level specification of a proof tactic. It contains a *precondition* and an *effect*. Both are descriptions in the meta-logic: the precondition describes the expression that the tactic applies to, and the effect describes the expression that the tactic produces if it succeeds. An example of the method for collection is given in figure 1.

A proof plan is a meta-level specification of a proof strategy, i.e. it is a kind of super-method. It is so constructed that the preconditions of each of its sub-methods are either implied by its preconditions or by the effects of earlier sub-methods. Similarly, its effects are implied by the effects of its sub-methods. The original conjecture should satisfy the preconditions of the plan; the effects of the plan should imply that the conjecture has been proved. Executing a proof plan consists of running each of its tactics according to the program it specifies. A proof plan can either be hand coded by the system builder, or the techniques of automatic program synthesis can be used to construct it.

This representation meets the specification given above, point by point, as follows:

- **Name**: *collection(Term)*
- **Input**: *Before*
- **Output**: *After*
- **Preconditions**: $occ(Term, Before) = B$
- **Effects**: $occ(Term, After) = A$ & $A < B$
- **Tactic**: a program for applying collection rules and facts

Figure 1: Proof Method for Collection

- **Usefulness**: As the tactics run they will each perform a part of the object-level proof.

- **Expectancy**: If the conjecture meets the preconditions of the plan and each tactic succeeds then the effects of the plan will be true and the conjecture will be proved.

- **Incertitude**: However, a tactic may fail, causing failure of the plan.

- **Patchability**: Since the preconditions and effects of a failing tactic are known, program synthesis techniques may be (re)used to patch the gap in the plan with a subplan.

5.2   Abduction for Diagnosing Causes of Effects

In the diagnosis of faults in machines or diseases in people, we are interested in working from the observed symptoms to discover their underlying causes. This process may be applied recursively: working from symptoms to their immediate causes, then to the causes of these causes, and so on until we reach something we can regard as a fault/disease.

Since Mycin, the classic way to automate this process has been by using production rules of the form:

IF $effect_1$ is present
AND $effect_2$ is present
$\vdots$
AND $effect_n$ is present
THEN *cause* is present with likelihood c

In Mycin, and many other expert systems, these rules are used backwards, i.e. from suspected diseases to observed symptoms. This is a little technical detail that is irrelevant to the discussion below, but has the potential to confuse it totally. Please pay attention only to the direction of the chain of implications, which is from effects to causes, even if this chain is constructed in reverse.

IF/THEN production rules like this seem very similar to logical implication rules. Translating the above production rule into the logical rule:

$$effect_1 \text{ \& } effect_2 \text{ \& } ... \text{ \& } effect_n \longrightarrow cause \tag{1}$$

seems like a good way to put it onto a firm theoretical foundation.

Unfortunately, the semantics of this logical rule gives us some trouble. The causal link runs in the opposite direction; causes cause effects, not vice versa. This suggests that the logical implication also runs from right to left, that is, if a particular cause is present then some particular combination of effects will also be present. This would be represented, logically, as:

$$cause \longrightarrow effect_1 \ \& \ effect_2 \ \& \ ... \ \& \ effect_n \tag{2}$$

It is not at all obvious that rule 1 holds, i.e. that the presence of this combination of effects implies the presence of this cause. The effects may be due to some other cause or combination of causes.

For instance, if we think that a cause of person B possessing an object P is that B bought P then the type 1 representation is:

$$possess(B, P) \longrightarrow buy(B, P)$$

whereas the type 2 representation is:

$$buy(B, P) \longrightarrow possess(B, P)$$

There is clearly something wrong with the type 1 representation; it is possible to possess something without buying it, for instance someone might give it to you or you might steal it.

This lack of logical implication in rules of type 1 is one reason why, from Mycin onwards, knowledge engineers have felt it necessary to attach uncertainty values to production rules; the uncertainty expresses the lack of strict logical implication from the effects to the causes. If we use logical implications running in the opposite direction, from causes to effects, then we can dispense with such uncertainty values [2].

Unfortunately, if we use implications running from causes to effects then we cannot use deduction (as Mycin effectively does) to deduce what faults/diseases are causing the symptoms observed. The process of conjecturing hypotheses that might imply a given fact is called *abduction*, [Kowalski 79]. But for a formula to be regarded as the fault/disease causing a symptom, it is not enough that the fault/disease logically imply the symptom; some additional conditions must be met. Cox and Pietrzykowski, [Cox 86], have recently specified some candidate additional conditions, which define what they call *fundamental* causes. Here are their definitions:

C is a cause of E with K, where K is some knowledge base, if and only if:

- $C \ \& \ K \longrightarrow E$ must hold, i.e. C together with K must 'account for' E.

- C is a formula, with no free variables, consisting of some quantifiers followed by a conjunction of negated and unnegated propositions. The idea is that C represents some concrete situation. We do not want to count as a cause anything that is vague, so we do not want to allow disjunction, for instance. Compare the concept of mental model from cognitive science, [Inder 87a].

C is a fundamental cause of E with K if and only if it is a cause of E with K and it is:

- **Consistent:** $C \ \& \ K$ must have a model. We do not want C to be a cause of E just because it is inconsistent with K and, therefore, the conjunction of them implies everything [3].

---

[2] Unless, of course, we require them for some other reason, e.g. to express partial ignorance about the effect of a cause or the cause of an effect.

[3] In more recent work this condition has been relaxed somewhat, but the new condition is rather more complex, and so I have omitted it from this elementary discussion.

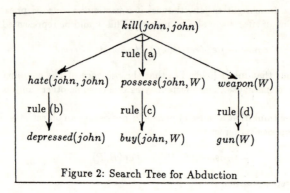

Figure 2: Search Tree for Abduction

- **Non-trivial**: $C \longrightarrow E$ does not hold. We do not want the connection between C and E to be a tautology, we want it to involve some knowledge from K in an essential way.

- **Basic**: Every consistent cause of C is trivial. We do not want C to itself have a cause. This condition makes C be the ultimate cause, e.g. the actual fault or disease.

- **Minimal**: For all causes, C' of E, $C \longrightarrow C'$ implies $C \longleftrightarrow C'$. We do not want C to have any extraneous material; we want it to be the simplest formula consistent with the other conditions.

In addition, Cox and Pietrzykowski have developed a procedure for conjecturing fundamental causes given their effects. This works with rules of the form 2, and is an alternative fault/disease diagnosis technique to the Mycin one of using deduction on rules of the form 1. The basic idea of the Cox-Pietrzykowski abduction procedure is to apply resolution to $K \& E$ and look for dead-ends in the search space. These dead-ends are sure to be basic causes. They are then processed in various ways to ensure that they are also consistent, non-trivial and minimal. This procedure may fail to terminate, either in the generation of dead-ends or in the test for consistency. However, if it does terminate then the soundness and completeness of resolution can be used to show that it generates all and only the fundamental causes of an effect. It can also be easily adapted to find basic causes that fail to be fundamental, e.g. are not consistent or minimal.

For example, let K be the knowledge base:

(a) $hate(M,V) \& possess(M,W) \& weapon(W) \longrightarrow kill(M,V)$
(b) $depressed(D) \longrightarrow hate(D,D)$
(c) $buy(B,P) \longrightarrow possess(B,P)$
(d) $gun(G) \longrightarrow weapon(G)$

Let E be the symptom $kill(john, john)$, i.e. John commits suicide. To find the fundamental cause of this suicide, we first run a process of deduction on E using K. This generates the search tree given in figure 2.

The last line of figure 2 is, taken together, a dead-end. It is consistent with K, non-trivial and minimal. It needs to be processed into the logical form of causes to give:

$$\exists W \; depressed(john) \& buy(john, W) \& gun(W)$$

i.e. the fundamental cause of John's suicide is that he was depressed and bought a gun. This would not satisfy a psychiatrist, but it is the poverty of the knowledge base that is at fault not the abduction procedure

This theoretically based work on abduction puts it on a similar footing to deduction. The user of the abduction procedure has some account of what the procedure finds, i.e. fundamental causes, and some assurance that it will find them. When it fails to do so it fails for good reasons, i.e. the essentially undecidable nature of the problem, and not because of some kludge in the program.

We have seen that one form of uncertainty has been taken out of the diagnosis process: the uncertainty associated with the lack of logical implication in the Mycin-type rules. As a result the fundamental causes produced by the abduction procedure are not ordered by uncertainty values. If meaningful uncertainty values could be associated with the rules then the abduction procedure could easily be adapted to incorporate this 'feature'. These uncertainty values would be essentially 'cleaner' than the Mycin ones in that they would not be associated with the lack of logical implication, but would reflect only the remaining sources of uncertainty, e.g. ignorance about the precise causes of effects, the probability of an effect following a cause, or whatever.

The only ordering of causes implicit in the abduction procedure is a partial one generated by the conditions met by each cause, e.g. a fundamental cause is better than one that is not minimal. It would be interesting to experiment with additional conditions: including some domain specific ones, and consider the orders implied by them. For instance, some logical expressions might be preferred as causes either because they describe faults more likely to occur or because they describe more concrete situations.

It would also be interesting to classify the rules in the knowledge base according to whether they represented causal links, and to invent additional conditions in the definition of fundamental cause requiring causal and non-causal rules to be used differently, e.g. in the deduction of E from C and K. For instance, rules (a) and (c) above seem to express a causal link, whereas (b) might be considered part of the definition of *depressed* and (d) is taxonomic information. The derivation of E ought to use at least one causal rule. Possibly, there are other requirements.

5.3   Explanation-Based Learning

One of the most exciting areas of recent research in automatic learning is the development of explanation-based learning (EBL) techniques. EBL techniques learn a target concept by generalising an example. This involves separating the incidental features of the example from the essential ones. Similarity-based learning techniques do this by comparing many examples and discovering the features common to all of them. In contrast, EBL techniques usually work from a single example of a piece of reasoning in which the target concept plays a central rôle.

A number of recent researchers have put explanation-based learning on a formal basis, [Mitchell 86,KedarCabelli 87,DeJong 86]; in particular, they have given an account of EBL in terms of logical deduction. We summarise this below.

Mitchell has stated the EBL problem as follows:

Given:

- **Target Concept**: A high level description of the concept to be learned, but at the wrong level of description.

- **Training Example**: A description of a particular example of the concept at the right level of description.

- **Domain Theory**: What we have above called a knowledge base. This can be used to relate the right to the wrong levels of description via a deductive chain.

- **Operationality Criteria**: A description of what counts as the right level of description, typically the listing of 'ok' predicates, etc.

Determine:

- **Partial Definition**: A partial definition of the target concept at the right level of description.

The basic idea of the procedure is to find a deductive chain linking the training example to its partial definition at the right level of description, to generalise this chain abstracting away the example specific aspects, and then to use this generalised chain to construct the required definition of the target concept.

An example will illustrate this. We will use the same knowledge base as for the example in section 5.2 above[4]. Suppose the training example is:

(e) *depressed(john)*
(f) *buy(john, gun1)*
(g) *gun(gun1)*

and the target concept is $kill(X, Y)$, i.e. we want to learn part of the operational definition of killing from a particular example of killing.

The first step is use the knowledge base to discover why the training example is an example of killing. This is done by deducing

$$\exists X, Y \ kill(X, Y)$$

from the knowledge base and the training example. The derivation is represented by the proof tree in figure 3. The arcs of the proof tree are labelled with both the rule or fact names and the substitutions required to apply the rules. Read T/X as T is substituted for X.

The second step is to generalise this proof tree. Any uses of the training example and substitutions associated with such use are deleted from the tree. The remaining substitutions are applied to the formulae in the tree. This gives the generalised tree in figure 4.

The third step is to apply the operationality criteria to decide which predicates in the tree are at the right level. Suppose we decide to allow: *depressed, buy, gun* and *weapon*. We must choose a horizontal slice through the tree which involves only these predicates. Such a slice is marked by a double line in figure 4. We then conjoin the formulae joined by this line and form an implication between them and the formula at the root of the tree. This gives:

$$depressed(B) \ \& \ buy(B, G) \ \& \ weapon(G) \longrightarrow kill(B, B)$$

---

[4]In fact, this knowledge base was first developed by DeJong, [DeJong 86], to illustrate EBL.

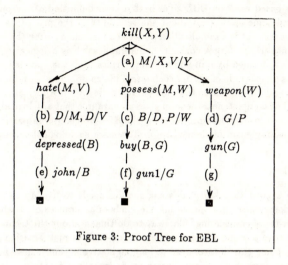

Figure 3: Proof Tree for EBL

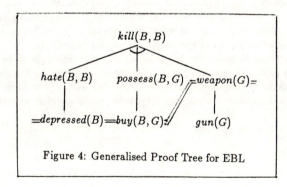

Figure 4: Generalised Proof Tree for EBL

which is the partial definition of the target concept required. In fact, it is a partial definition of a special case of the killing concept, namely suicide.

This theoretically based work on EBL gives both a clear definition of the purpose of this learning technique and some assurances about the reliability of the procedure. The partial definition of the target concept is an implication between a formula meeting the operationality criteria and an instance of the target concept. This implication is a logical consequence of the knowledge base; it is formed by unifying a chain of rules from the knowledge base and in programming terms is an example of *partial evaluation*, [Safra 86]. The soundness theorem of resolution gives the required guarantee that the partial definition is a logical consequence of the knowledge base. The completeness theorem gives a guarantee that any logical consequence of the appropriate logical form can be produced by the EBL procedure, in particular, that an appropriate training example can be defined to produce each such logical consequence.

6   Conclusion

In this paper I have argued that knowledge engineering needs to live up to its name and become a proper engineering science: providing the kinds of assurances of reliability that are normal in other branches of engineering. The way to do this is to put the techniques used to build expert systems onto a sound theoretical basis. The tools of mathematical logic appear to be a good basis for doing this, but we need to be imaginative in their use — not restricting ourselves to deductive inference, but investigating other aspects of reasoning: search control, abduction, learning, uncertainty, alternative knowledge representation techniques, etc.

This theoretical work is normally seen as being the province of academic researchers, but it need not be exclusively so. In any case, the success of the theoretical work is of crucial importance to applied researchers, in industry and elsewhere; without it they will not be able to build reliable expert systems.

The interaction is not all in one direction; applied researchers have important feedback to provide on the utility of existing knowledge engineering techniques 'in the field'. Basic researchers are particularly interested in the *failures* of current techniques, so that they may be improved. Unfortunately, such failures are usually poorly described in the literature, if they are described at all. We need a change of attitude among knowledge engineers, so that the failure of an expert system is not seen to reflect badly on its designers, but to be a valuable result of an experiment with particular knowledge engineering techniques.

'Failure' is usually taken to mean the failure of a particular technique to be useful for a particular task. I also want to draw attention to failures of reliability, e.g. the user's failure to predict just what tasks the technique can succeed on. We will need to know about both kinds of failure if we are to build the reliable, large-scale, wider-ranging, expert systems of the future.

References

[Bundy 81]   A. Bundy and B. Welham. Using meta-level inference for selective application of multiple rewrite rules in algebraic manipulation. *Artificial Intelligence*, 16(2):189–212, 1981. Also available as DAI Research Paper 121.

[Bundy 84]   A. Bundy, editor. *Catalogue of Artificial Intelligence Tools*, Springer-Verlag, 1984. Second Edition.

[Bundy 86]   A. Bundy. *What kind of field is AI?* Research Paper 305, Dept. of Artificial Intelligence, Edinburgh, 1986. To appear in the Proceedings of the Workshop on the Foundations of Artificial Intelligence, New Mexico, 1987.

[Cox 86]   P.T. Cox and T. Pietrzykowski. Causes for events: their computation and applications. In J. Siekmann, editor, *Lecture Notes in Computer Science: Proceedings of the 8th International Conference on Automated Deduction*, pages 608–621, Springer-Verlag, 1986.

[Darlington 81]   J. Darlington. An experimental program transformation and synthesis system. *Artificial Intelligence*, 16(3):1–46, August 1981.

[DeJong 86]   G. DeJong and R. Mooney. Explanation-based learning: an alternate view. *Machine Learning*, 1(2):145–176, 1986.

[Gordon 79]   M.J. Gordon, A.J. Milner, and C.P. Wadsworth. *Edinburgh LCF - A mechanised logic of computation.* Volume 78 of *Lecture Notes in Computer Science*, Springer Verlag, 1979.

[Inder 87a]   R. Inder. *The Computer Modelling of Syllogistic Reasoning using Restricted Mental Models.* PhD thesis, Dept. of Artificial Intelligence, Edinburgh, 1987.

[Inder 87b]   R. Inder. The state of the ART. *Airing*, (1):8–14, February 1987. Available from AI Applications Institute, Edinburgh.

[KedarCabelli 87]   S. Kedar-Cabelli and L.T. McCarty. Explanation-based generalization as resolution theorem proving. In P. Langley, editor, *Proceedings of the 4th International Machine Learning Workshop*, pages 383–389, Morgan Kaufmann, 1987.

[Kowalski 79]   R. Kowalski. *Logic for Problem Solving. Artificial Intelligence Series*, North Holland, 1979.

[Mitchell 86]   T.M. Mitchell, R.M. Keller, and S.T. Kedar-Cabelli. Explanation-based generalization: a unifying view. *Machine Learning*, 1(1):47–80, 1986. Also available as Tech. Report ML-TR-2, SUNJ Rutgers, 1985.

[Safra 86]   S. Safra and E. Shapiro. *Meta Interpreters for Real.* Report CS86-11, Deapartment of Computer Science, The Weizmann Institute of Science, May 1986.

CLINTE: Coopers & Lybrand International Tax Expert System.

John F.J.Gleeson & Malcolm L.J.West

Coopers & Lybrand Associates,
Plumtree Court,
London EC4A 4HT.

ABSTRACT:

CLINTE is an operational expert system in the volatile financial domain of
international taxation. The paper introduces the domain, describes the
knowledge acquisition techniques employed, the design and development
criteria and, finally, a scenario illustrating the functionality available
to the end user. CLINTE uses a blackboard architecture to apply both
national and international tax planning strategies and regulations to
partial corporate models. It attempts to optimise the tax position of
corporations within the bounds of user defined constraints. This has major
implications for forward planning, mergers and acquisitions and financial
management.

Keywords :

Rule-based, Knowledge Acquisition, Partial Models, Interactive Graphics,
International Tax.

1. INTRODUCTION

CLINTE, Coopers & Lybrand International Tax Expert, was developed over the
course of the last year by the Knowledge Engineering Group at Coopers &
Lybrand Associates with the help and cooperation of the Tax Group. Versions
of CLINTE are currently running on Symbolics and TI Explorer, however, the
possibility of delivering versions on other machines such as the PC, are
being examined.

This paper describes the background to CLINTE by introducing the
complexities of the domain of international taxation and describing the
knowledge acquisition process which was used to scope the system and derive
the expertise which form the knowledge bases of the system. This is
followed by a discussion on the design of the system, which begins by
expressing the need for flexibility in the implementation. CLINTE relies
on a model based approach incorporating corporate and international models.
The user interacts with these models through a sophisticated graphical
interface while the various knowledge bases manipulate the models through
a blackboard type interface. These models, the interface and the
architecture are described. The functionality of the system is illustrated
by means of a scenario of system use. The paper concludes by describing
some of the possible future developments and identifying the major
conclusions from the development to date.

2. BACKGROUND

2.1. Multinationals and Tax

The taxation of multinational corporations is extremely complex due to a number of factors. The first of these is the sheer size and diversity of many large multinational corporations. It is not unusual for multinational corporations to consist of over 500 companies based in over 100 countries. Some of the larger corporations run into thousands of companies. These companies may be nested in several levels of ownership. Some subsidiaries may be wholly owned and others partially owned. Various groups of companies in the corporation may function as single units, trading amoungst themselves as well as externally. Very often trading of this type will be international.

The second factor element of complexity is introduced by the variety of countries in which these companies are located. The tax laws applicable, their extent and their interpretation within each country must be considered. The location within a country is often important; for example a company based in Berlin will have special status under West German tax laws. The nature of a company's business may also be of importance; for example manufacturing companies based in Ireland are subject to corporation tax at the rate of 10% rather than the normal 50%.

Once the company has been taxed locally, the dividends must be routed back through the intermediate companies to the parent company. When these funds are paid across international borders, a dividend witholding tax may be applied. The ownership structure of the corporation then becomes important if the tax is to be minimised.

2.2. Nature of Experts

Good international tax experts, like all good experts, are a scarce resource. As such they are usually required to solve the particularly complex and difficult tax cases which arise in large multinational corperations. Often tax experts are called in only when a problem arises. It appears that in many cases tax experts do not have the opportunity, or are not available to play a full role in forward planning. As a result many problems or undesirable situations arise which could have been avoided. More importantly many opportunities to reduce the total tax burden of a corporation are lost. The size and complexity of multinational corporations is often restrictive, as analysing and reviewing the total structure could absorb tax experts for a considerable length of time. Such experts are rarely available to do a full review of a corporation, instead they are called upon to review a particular group of subsidiaries. Even attempting to restructure a small group of companies can be difficult as a variety of possibilities may have to be explored, with application of laws, regulations and calculations for each possible structure. As the number of companies being considered grows, this task grows more and more difficult.

Capturing the tax experts strategic knowledge and automating the application of tax regulations, inorder to allow quick and easy reviews of large corporations in their entirety, was the motivation for developing CLINTE.

2.3. Knowledge Acquisition

The primary technique applied for knowledge acquisition in the early stages involved recording conversations between tax experts and two knowledge engineers working together. Initially these conversations were quite general and covered a wide range of issues relevant to international taxation. As these conversations progressed, the important aspects of taxation of multinational companies became apparent and more importantly, the techniques which the tax experts apply to organisation and planning started to emerge. These recordings were then transcribed and analysed both by the knowledge engineers involved in the sessions, and by secondary knowledge engineers. This analysis identified the areas in which expert systems might be most usefully employed within the overall tax planning and management operation. The nature of the expert's knowledge also started to become apparent, and from this ideas were developed about how the system might be implemented to support and organise the knowledge.

A prototype system was implemented and detailed knowledge acquisition in particular areas of international tax planning was carried out. Much of the detailed factual "knowledge" needed for the system was available in various reference books on tax. This information formes the basis of the International Tax Calculator which will be described later. The tax experts were used to provide the planning strategies which should be applied to various types of company structures. This knowledge was acquired by working through a series of scenarios. These scenarios also provided useful examples for system testing at various stages of implementation.

Once the system reached a satisfactory level of sophistication, the tax experts were asked to review it. A series of reviews provided several refinements to the knowledge, adjustments to how the system applied tax laws and also a number of useful comments on the user interface and use of the system.

3. PRELIMINARY DESIGN

3.1. Design Methodology

The tax position of multinational corporations is dynamic because of a number of factors. One is that the nature of the corporation changes over time as the markets etc change. Another is the changes that can occur within and between the various countries where the corporation has or could have a presence. Because of the need for ease of maintenance and the potential complexity of the completed system it was a major requirement to produce a flexible and modular system. The modular structure can be seen from Fig 3.1 whereby the modelling of the corporation and the world have been separated as much as possible so that the corporation model can exist independently of the world model. Also, the knowledge base has been modularised by compartmentalising the rules into rule sets which reason about a certain aspect of the problem, the whole being controlled by the meta-knowledge represented in the control rules. In addition, the rules that perform the tax calculations as they apply to companies within the corporation structure have been packaged as a separate entity and are activated when required.

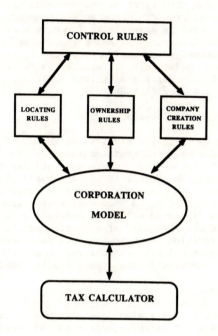

Fig. 3.1

3.2. The Corporate Model

The corporate model in general is a partial instantiation of a hierarchy of
companies. This hierarchy forms a tree, the root of which is the parent
company of the corporation and as such controls all those companies beneath
it in the tree. Each company in the tree is an instance of an object that
has a large number of attributes that define its major operation, its
financial state, its location (ie. how it relates to the International
Model) and any other special information about the company. Typically,
within the model of the corporation any number of attributes and links
between objects may be left undefined. The effect of defining them is to
impose a set of constraints upon the system in order to restrict the
reasoning process so that worthless alternatives are not tried (for
instance, so that the system does not try to move a manufacturing
subsidiary for tax reasons when the cost of the move would be prohibitive).
Indeed, in the general case the corporation can be completely unstructured
in order to remove all the constraints and allow the system to produce an
optimal structure of control and location between subsidiaries.

Within the reasoning process it is the corporate model which is the dynamic
data which is continually upgraded and reassessed in the light of new
information as it is gleaned.

3.3. The International Model

The International Model describes the world as it applies to the tax
position of multinational corporations. The model comprises of a set of
modular descriptions of the possible countries including their tax rates,

any special status, any special regional benefits etc, and a set of
relationships between them (such as the dividend withholding tax which is a
tax payable on transferred dividends across boundaries between subsidiary
and owner). This model is essentially fixed in that the knowledge bases
use the data in the international and corporate models to reason about and
rationalise the corporate model. However, it is possible to effect changes
to the International Model quite trivially via the interface provided to
the system so that the user can postulate the effect of a 5 point reduction
in UK corporation tax, for instance.

3.4. The Modelling Tools Interface

It was decided early on that a significant amount of effort should go into
the development of a powerful graphics interface which would take the
internal representation of the dynamic data and format it into a meaningful
display to the user. The result is an icon-based, mouse-menu-driven
interface which displays company structures as graphical trees displaying
one of the numeric values via a thermometer-type icon next to the icon for
each company. The displayed value can be changed at any time which allows
the user to choose the parameter of significance across the whole
corporation. In addition, each company can be described from a menu and
edited if required or quickly restructured in an unrestricted manner.
Furthermore, the countries in the system can be remodelled in a similar way.

3.5. Knowledge Bases

The Knowledge Bases in the system have been modularised by defining them in
terms of rule sets which all have access to the model. The rule sets are
split by function so that, for instance, the rules that suggest possible
locations for companies exist separately from those that suggest parents
for unparented companies. The decision about which rule to fire at any
time in the inference is made by the meta-knowledge contained in the
control rules. These rules are essential to the efficient running of the
system since they can stop potential combinatorial explosion by tending to
fire rules that restrict inference before those that increase it. For
instance, there is no point in attempting to calculate an optimal location
for a company before firing a rule (typically shallow) that provides a set
of reasonable alternatives to use for the calculation.

3.6 The Inference Engine

The rules in CLINTE are forward-chaining and are driven by assertions that
are made into the corporate model. The assertions are made indirectly by
the user as the corporation is defined via the graphical interface. When a
rule is triggered it is added to an agenda which keeps a record of all the
rules that are ready to be used along with the reason why they have been
activated. The position in which the rule is placed on the agenda is
determined by the meta-knowledge.

The inference engine takes a rule at a time off the agenda and fires it.
Of course, this will typically update the world model and cause more rules
to be added to the agenda. Whenever this happens the meta-knowledge
maintains the integrity of the agenda by retracting from it those rules
whose reasons are no longer valid and prioritising the rest.

In addition to this forward-chaining agenda based inference there is also the use of active values. These are used in 2 ways; firstly, they are used to maintain the integrity of the graphical description of the corporate model by updating the hierarchy displayed where necessary; secondly, they are used in the object representation to maintain consistent collective financial data, such as the total dividend from a company's subsidiaries, with the individual parts.

4. System Functionality

In the scenario a sample corporate structure will be built up, the international tax calculation facilities will be demonstrated and finally the system will be used to suggest locations and parents for new companies which are being added to the corporate structure.

4.1. The User Interface

The CLINTE user interface consists of five "windows" as shown in Fig 4.1. These are the command menu window at the top, the company structure graphics window, the country icon window, the company icon window and the system command window at the bottom.

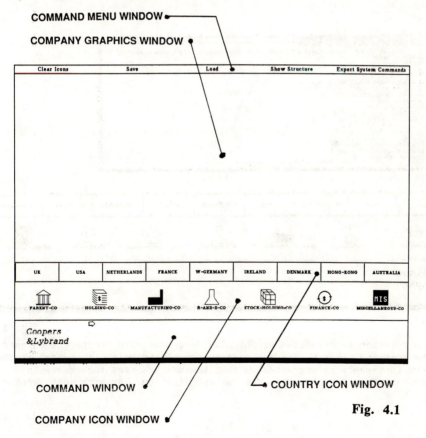

Fig. 4.1

4.2. Modelling Corporations

A corporation is described by the user as a hierarchy of functional units which are nominally called companies. A company is a unit that has a set of attributes which can be set by the user. Models of corporations may be built up by selecting company types (using the mouse) from the company icon window to create instances of them. The only information the system requires at creation time is the company name for which the user is prompted.

The system provides a menu which allows the user to specify a location for this new company. The system also provides various financial details relevant to international tax.

Once created the attributes may be set, providing financial information about the company and giving it a name, a location and, if applicable, a parent company. The attributes are input, in general, via a template menu as shown in Fig 4.2.

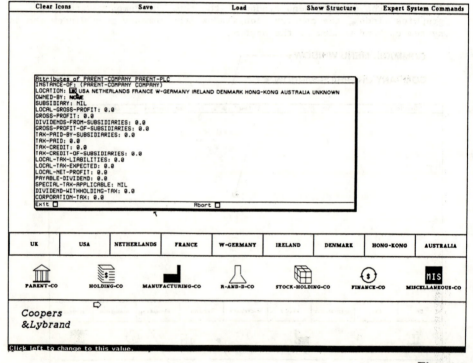

Fig. 4.2

The corporation is displayed graphically as a tree with the parent company at the root and its subsidiaries beneath it. The display is changed as the tree is incrementally augmented so that the user can see the ownership constraints that are placed on the tax optimisation. As with most aspects of the system if the user selected not to define ownerships then the system would be able to consider a range of possible parent-subsidiary relationships in order to optimise the tax position. A typical corporation structure is shown in Fig 4.3. Each icon in the structure has a "thermometer" associated with it which is used for displaying one of the various numeric values which are held as attributes of the company. The attribute selected to be displayed can be set globally by the user. Notice that the initial value is zero because the thermometer is controlled by an active value which delays updating the screen until inferencing takes place.

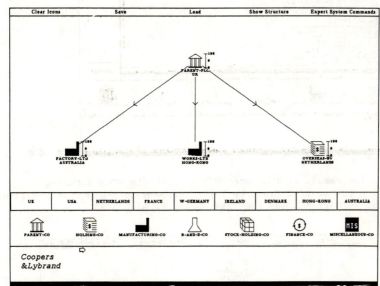

Fig. 4.3

4.4 Tax Optimisation

The underlying tax expert system can now be run by selecting the option from the command menu. The tax expert system makes all the necessary international tax calculations and the corporate tax calculations for each company in each country. In this example the thermometers represent the payable dividends of each of the companies. For Parent-plc the figure of 1313 represents the total funds which are available for payment to the shareholders.

If we look at the attributes menu in Fig 4.4 for Factory-Ltd we can see that all the financial details relating to the taxation of that company have been updated. These include the corporation tax payable in Australia of 46%, the dividend for the withholding tax payable between Australia and the UK of 15%, the various tax deductions and the payable dividend and tax credit which may be passed on to the parent company in the UK.

The ownership of this company may be changed by selecting one of the other companies on the list as the new owner or by removing the constraint altogether. This allows us to experiment with the company structure and evaluate the tax advantages or disadvantages of any alterations made.

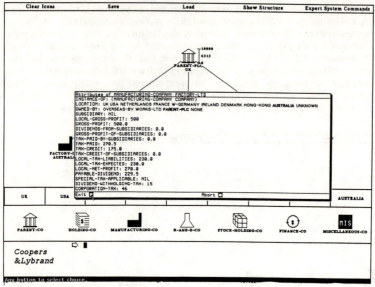

Fig. 4.4

Fig 4.5 shows the result of the ownership of both the manufacturing companies being transferred from the Parent company to the Overseas Holding company in the Netherlands and the taxes being recalculated.

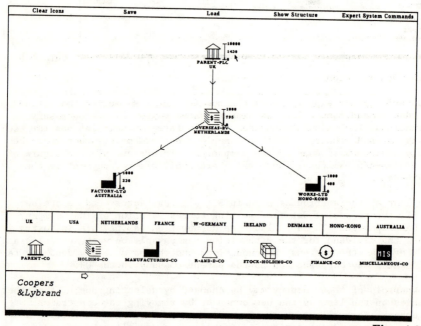

Fig. 4.5

The funds now payable to the shareholders of the Parent company in the UK
is 1430 as opposed to 1313 for the previous corporate structure. This
represents a 9% rise in the funds. This rise is due to the dividends of
the 2 manufacturing companies being mixed in the Netherlands. The high tax
paid by the manufacturing company in Australia is offset by the low tax
paid by the other manufacturing company in Hong Kong. This means that full
advantage may be made of the tax already paid when the funds are returned
to the UK.

Along with doing international tax calculations, the system attempts to
give the user advice on various aspects of corporate structure.

In the case in Fig 4.6 it is assumed that the company wishes to create a
new R&D subsidiary but does not know where this should be located
geographically or how it should be Parented within the group. The system
will locate this new company Ideas-Ltd geographically and within the
corporate structure in the optimum position for tax.

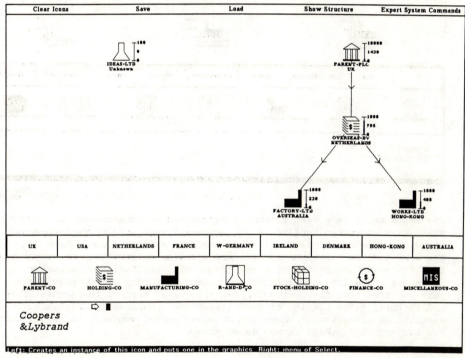

Fig. 4.6

The result is shown in Fig 4.7. The system automatically locates Ideas-Ltd
in France. This is because France offers large tax incentives to R&D
companies locating there. The system has also made Overseas-BV the owner
of this new subsidiary company thus routing the profit back to the parent
company in the UK via the Netherlands. This means that the low tax paid by

this new company may be used to offset high taxes from other subsidiaries
of this Netherlands company thus optimising the overall tax situation. The
system knows about various company types and locations which suit them.

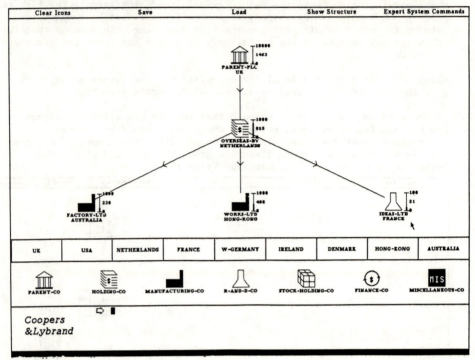

Fig. 4.7

Ideas-Ltd could have been given a location but no Parent and the system
would have attempted to give it the optimum Parent within the corporate
structure. Alternatively, a second corporate structure could have been
provided and the system would have attempted to absorb this new corporation
into its structure as either a new branch of subsidiaries or a number of
companies added into the existing corporate hierarchy. This provides a
very powerful tool for evaluating the effects of mergers and acquisitions
and optimising the results of such operations. An example of a mergers and
acquisition situation is where the UK based parent company, is taking over
New Corporation, a West German based group.

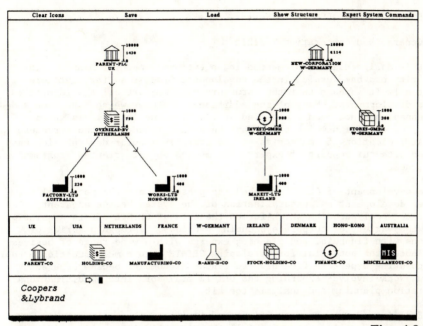

Fig. 4.8

When the expert system is run, a new corporate structure is proposed and the associated payable dividends displayed.

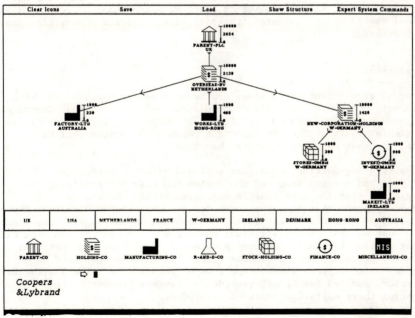

Fig. 4.9

5. POSSIBLE FUTURE DEVELOPMENTS

5.1. Generalised Corporation Toolkit

CLINTE is designed and implemented in an extremely modular manner. This modularity has been useful in the development process so far, but more importantly it appears that the structure will support all the identified future developments. Many of the additional features which have been added or planned, had not been identified at the time the initial design was done. The ease with which these have been integrated into the structure is a clear indication of the merits of the strictly modular design which was adopted with the support of expert systems and object oriented programming techniques.

As the development of CLINTE reached its present state the potential for further development and generalisation of the system became apparent. The corporate model paradigm which formes the core of CLINTE offers a solution to a wide variety of corporate planning problems. Through a series of sessions with financial and planning experts with a wide range of business experience, the potential for developing CLINTE into a multifunctional tool incorporating expertise from diverse financial domains became apparent. Current work involves expanding the CLINTE framework into a multinational corporation planning and analysis toolkit.

CLINTE is intended to form the first module of a full multinational corporation expert toolkit. The full toolkit will allow policy and decision makers to optimise and evaluate their corporate structure and organisation from a variety of different points of view. Other modules which are currently being examined or experimented with include evaluation of corporate loans, interest payments along with geographical locations and personnel availability, markets, transportation, equities, securities and foreign exchange.

6. Conclusions

A number of significant conclusions can be made on the basis of the work carried out. One which has already been discussed involves the advantages of the modular implementation techniques for supporting further development and system evolution. This is important because the system will be expanded to cover many topics other than taxation.

The knowledge acquisition techniques employed were successful in identifying the initial scope of the system and also for providing the strategic and planning expertise incorporated within the system.
It became apparent that financial experts use a variety of different types of "knowledge". At the lowest level they apply laws and regulations which might almost be described as "factual knowledge". In conjunction with this somewhat shallow knowledge they use a deeper form of knowledge based on experience, previous cases etc. Sometimes this knowlege is based on subtleties or interpretations of the laws or regulations. The blackboard architecture adopted for CLINTE provided an elegant framework for segregating these differing types of knowledge.

Perhaps the most significant conclusion which can be drawn to the work done in the CLINTE project, is that expert systems techniques are useful and effective in the domain of corporate modelling, planning and advanced decision support. The success and popularity of the system with financial experts illustrates this point.

LOKE

A Drill Bit Selection System

by

T. Sørensen and O. Nordhus
STATOIL, P.O.Box 300, N-4001 Stavanger, Norway

Abstract

LOKE is a knowledge based system developed to help the drilling
supervisor to choose a proper drill bit for the next run. The
purpose of the system is to reduce drilltime by improving the drill
bit selection process. The system is developed by means of
Teknowledge's shell M1 and the programming language C, and is used
in drill-operations in the North Sea. Some experience from the
development and use of the system, is presented in this paper.

1. Background

Statoil, the Norwegian State Oil Company, wished as a part of its
R&D efforts, to develop a knowledge based system to investigate if
these techniques could be used to reduce operational costs. The rig
cost in exploration wells is approximately 170 000 USD per day. By
reducing the drill-time a considerable amount of money can be saved.
One of the factors that influence drill-time is the drill bit. (Moore
1986.) A bad choice can easily increase drill-costs by several hundred
thousands of dollars.

In addition to have a potential for economic savings, it was
important to choose an area where Statoil had long experience, expertise
and a lot of written material. Bit selection called LOKE was
therefore chosen. LOKE is one of the "Gods" in the old norwegian
mythology that followed Tor and Odin on their travels. He was their
advisor. Often Loke gave them good advice, but sometimes the advice
was really bad. The reason for giving the system this name was,
however, that it is possible to find the letters LOKE from the
Norwegian equivalent to Drill bit selection.

The system is meant as a decision support system to be used by
the drilling supervisor on exploration rigs. He chooses the bits
to be used. This choice is based on prognosed lithology, drill
bit records from the equivalent wells (correlated wells) and from
the performance of the bit in the hole (figure 1.0.a). The problem
is to choose a bit with the best combination of tooth length,
structure, bearings and gauging for the prognosed lithology. A lot
of different bits exist. These are classified by a code (IADC coding),
which make the choice independent of the manufacturers. The system
choice results in an IADC code, not in a bit from a special manufacture.

LOKE is at the moment, limited to:
- Vertical exploration wells (not deviated wells)
- 12 1/4" bits
- Rock- or insert-bits (not diamonds or
  polycrystalline-bits).
- Knowledge from the Norwegian continental shelf

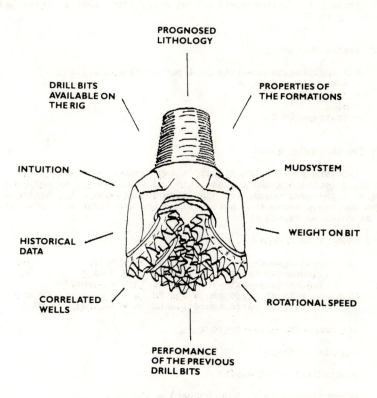

FIGURE 1.0.A FACTORS INVOLVED IN DRILL BIT SELECTION

2. Construction

2.1 Tools

The system is developed by means of Teknowledge's expert system
shell M1 (the C-version). For calculations, screen dialogues and data
retrievals we have developed special routines written in C. This is
to reduce response-time and to make the system more user-friendly.
To make the system available on drill-rigs, LOKE is installed
on an IBM PC AT.

2.2 System design

The application consists of 4 parts (figure 2.2.a):
- A knowledge base
- A data base
- M1
- Routines in C

2.3 The knowledge base

The main part of the system is experience or knowledge in
drilling technology and the selection of drill bits. By making a
lot of interviews (chap. 2.3 Knowledge acquisition), the builders
(the knowledge engineers) have refined the knowledge and reformulated
it as rules or facts:

Example of a rule:

```
if    rop-judgement        for RU in W = low          and
      (length-judgement    for RU in W = high          or
       length-judgement    for RU in W = normal)
then analysis of performance for RU in W = poor  cf 80 and
     analysis of performance for RU in W = normal cf 50.
```

cf. means certainty factor.

Example of facts:

grading (1) = not-used.

bit-evolution ((1, 1), harder) = (1, 2) .

One difference between a shell and traditional programming
languages, is that the knowledge is not a part of the code, but
is placed in a separate file called the knowledge base. This makes
it suitable for rapid prototyping during the knowledge acquisition
and easy to modify in the maintenance phase.
M1 uses variables in rules and facts (RU and W in the above
examples). This reduces the knowledge base significantly.

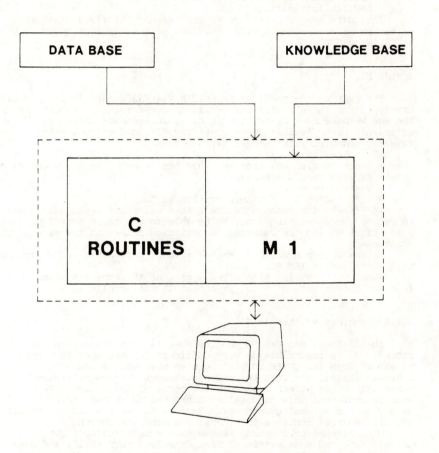

FIGURE 2.2.A SYSTEM CONFIGURATION

2.3.1 The data base

    Loke is using the following information:
    - Manufacturers drill-bit data (for each type bit, the
    IADC coding and min. max values for ROP and RPM)
    - Historical data for the correlated wells.
    - Drillability data.
    The data base consists or several sequential files that can
either be maintained by special routines written in C or by an editor
as EDLIN or SIDEKICK.

2.3.2 M1.

    The root of the shell M1 is EMYCIN via KS300, and it is specially
developed for the PC. Earlier versions were written in PROLOG, but
the one we have used is written in C. This has made it more
efficient, more flexible, more user-friendly, and increased the
capacity compared with the earlier versions.
    M1 is used to:
    - Reach conclusions from the knowledge-base by backward chaining.
    - Explain conclusions.
    - User-interface.
    - Interfacing the routines written in C.
    The reason for choosing a shell to develop the application, was
to reduce the developing-time, to be able to use rapid prototyping as
a technique during the knowledge acquisition phase and the ease of the
maintenance.
    M1 was chosen because we found it to be a flexible and efficient
tool installed on IBM PC.
    Fancy user-interface is often a part of the expert systems, but
this was determined not to be important in this application.

2.3.3 Routines written in C

    The dialogue between M1 and the user is by questions on the
screen. It is impossible or very difficult for the user to correct
an answer when the ENTER button has been pressed. Because the
users in Statoil are used to screen dialogues, it was determined
essential to use screen dialogues for parts of the system. To be
able to implement this, special routines had to be made in a
traditional programming language. Because M1 has a built in facility
to call external routines in C, this language was chosen.
    Traditional programming languages are more suitable for
calculations and data retrieval from databases than shells and other
languages for knowledge based system. For those parts of the
application we also used C.
    By using C in addition to M1, the application appears as efficient
and user-friendly.

2.4   Knowledge acquisition (K.A.)

The K.A. was made in 3 steps:

1. An introduction to drilling techniques for the
   builders (knowledge engineers).
2. Interviews of drilling supervisors, geologists and
   drilling engineers.
3. Use of rapid prototyping.

The introduction to drilling techniques consisted of studying
books and papers. In addition the project's user-coordinator,
explained the drilling process and other aspects regarding the subject.
Without him we doubt that the project would have been successful.
He has a drilling background and knows the drilling personnel. By this
he was able to get in touch with the people we wanted to interview.
     Before the first interview, as much information as possible was
gathered concerning one spesific well. The drilling supervisor was
told that we were going to drill a well and he was to choose the bit.
Any information he needed, he had to ask for. By doing this it was
clarified which information is essential in the bit selection process.
     The supervisor then used the information to select a bit.
The bit selected was then compared with the choice done at the rig.
To get a better understanding of the reasons for the choice, questions
as reasons for different choice, how would the bit performance be, and
which bit would be the best etc., was raised. Other wells were
selected and new interviews made.
     This process was repeated with other drilling supervisors, and by
confronting them with other views of the problem, it was easy to get
to an agreed view in most of the cases. However sometimes it was
impossible to come to an agreement. To settle these cases, we had a
"Superexpert", who's views was put into the system. The disagreements
were noticed for use during the prototyping process.
     The knowledge from the interviews, was coded as facts and rules
in the M1's syntax. By using these prototypes in the interviews, and
comparing results, new discussions occured and resulted in new
knowledge or a more varied view of the knowledge. This iterative
process continued until we had a prototype which selected the drill
bits that was decided correct, for the wells we had picked out as
test-wells.
     In a cooperation between builders and drilling supervisors, the
system was then tested on other wells which had not been discussed
during the development phase. The advice given by the system was
so good that it was not necessesary to change the knowledge base.
     The system was then declared as the first production version
and is now used on drilling rigs in the North Sea. In addition we
are continuing the work with checking the system's advice against
what happened in the old wells.
     The main problem encountered during the knowledge acquisition
phase, is that it is impossible to know which bit would have done
the best job. We only have weak indication for judging a drill bit
selection as poor or good.

3. How the system works

    The system is meant to co-work with the drilling supervisor as an
experienced colleague. Communication is made by the key-board and
screen. The drilling supervisor has decided to change the bit. While
the bit in the hole is moving up to to the surface (trip out), he
normally orders two or three bits to be put on the drill-floor. When
the bit is out of the hole and graded (TBG grading), the final
selection will be done. The system goes through the same sequence.
Before the bit is graded, it gives one recommendation based on the bits
used in the correlated wells and another based on the prognosed
lithology and the performance of the bit tripping out. After the old
bit is graded, it will give one advice mainly based on the performance
and grading of the old bit and prognosed lithology.
    The system will start by analyzing the last run (figure 3.0.a).
The result of this analysis will be to characterize this run as poor,
normal, or good. This is done by taking the following factors into
account:
    - Average rate of penetration (ROP)
    - Drilling time
    - Weight on bit (WOB)
    - Rotational speed (RPM)
    - Trends in penetration rate
    - Lithology
    - Correlated wells
If the run is rated poor, the system will try to find the causes. From
the prognosed lithology it will decide if these causes will last.
If so, it will find remedies for the causes in the next run.
    The system's choice for the next run is based on:
    - The drill bit used in the last run
    - The drill bits used in the correlated wells.
    - The prognosed lithology for the next run
    - The lithology in the correlated wells
    - Possible remedies for avoiding the eventually
      poor performance of the last run.

4. LOKE's Behaviour

    The system is developed by using old wells in the knowledge
acquisition phase. After the system was declared to be a production
version, LOKE has been tested on several other old wells. To do
these tests, it is necessesary to involve drilling experts to find
out what really happened while drilling. One of the supervisors
in the project team took part in these tests. Preliminary
conclusions are:
    - LOKE chooses more or less the same bit as was chosen
    - LOKE's choice is not rated poorer than the actual choice
    - For one selection, LOKE's choice was certainly better
      than the actual one.
    The system is now used on the Tommeliten field in the North Sea.
The wells are for production and this means that most of the wells
are deviated. One of the system's assumptions, is the limitation
of non-deviated wells. Another problem is that the system cannot
handle polycrystalline bits. These are used on the location.
Although some of the assumptions are violated, the system seems to
behave properly.
    Preliminary conclusions are:
    - LOKE has chosen many of the used bits
    - For some very good runs, LOKE's choice is not as

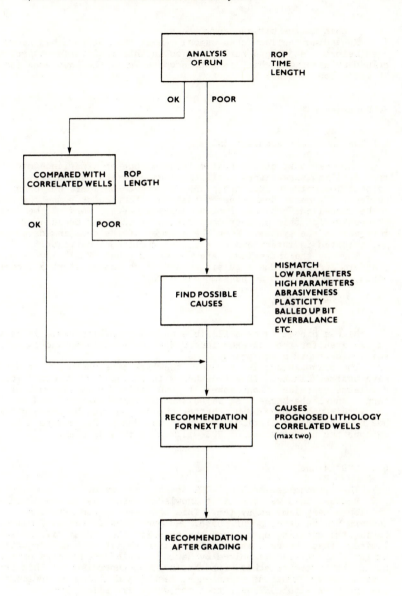

FIGURE 3.0.A BLOCK DIAGRAM OF THE SYSTEM

good as the bit chosen.
Regarding the last conclusion: A bit that Statoil had never used before, is doing a real good job in this field. The experience gained by using this bit, is not incoporated in the knowledge base. It will soon be done.

5. Experience

5.1 The knowledge acquisition.

The main part of the system is knowledge or experience gathered from drilling supervisors, drilling engineers and geologists. Cooperation between this group and the system builders has been perfect. It never has happened that an interview or a meeting had to be cancelled, because of other "more important work" to be done. The reason for this perfect cooperation is probably because of interest in the system. Even the manager of the drilling department participated in interviews as a former drilling supervisor.
The way the interviews were performed (chap. 2.3), gave a good platform for knowledge acquisition and if we had to start all over again, we would choose the same methodology.

5.2 The tools.

M1 has proved to be a flexible and easy tool to use. It is easy to use even for the non-experienced knowledge engineer and is well suited for rapid prototyping.
The disadvantage is, however, the lack of structure. It doesn't have control blocks. This together with the lack of graphics for knowledge representation, makes it unsuitable for maintenance of larger knowledge-bases. S1 is now on the IBM PC market, and we think this would have been a better choice. An even bigger problem has been memory limitations. This is not due to M1, but to DOS. We hope the new versions of DOS will solve this problem.

5.3 LOKE in use

The bit choices made by LOKE so far, are good.
Because this was our first knowledge based system, we decided to develop a very limited system. This has been a good strategy concerning the development phase. However, the system is limited. During the drilling operations the need for the system will be so limited, that the existence of the system easily "can be forgotten". So far this problem is solved by having knowledge engineers on the rig, using the system together with the drilling supervisors. This is also a good way of gathering experience, teaching drilling supervisors to use and work with LOKE as a tool for drill bit selections.
Probably LOKE will be extended. By this in addition to the above mentioned introduction, we assume the drilling supervisors will use the system on their own.
The user-interface is not very fancy. However, the users are satisfied, and they are normally able to use the system without any help from the system-builders. The most important improvement of the system, would be to explain in a user-understandable language, why a conclusion is drawn. This is not difficult to do in M1. However,

because of the limitation in memory size, we are not able to do this
without reducing the knowledge base considerably.

References

Harmon, P & King, D. (1985). EXPERT SYSTEMS
Artificial Intelligence in Business.
New York: John Wiley & Sons, Inc..

Framentec SA. (1986). M.1 Reference Manual Version 1.3.
Paris: Framentec SA.

Moore P.L. (1986). DRILLING PRACTICES MANUAL.
Tulsa, Oklahoma: PennWell Publishing Company.

Adams N.J. & Charrier, T. (1985). Drilling Engineering.
A Complete Well Planning Approach.
Tulsa, Oklahoma: PennWell Publishing Company.

APPLYING EXPERT SYSTEMS TO EXPLORATION FOR HYDROCARBONS

Tom Reynolds, John Moody and Clive Smallman

Research and Development Division
British Gas plc
Engineering Research Station
Newcastle upon Tyne NE99 1LH

Reference E.593

Abstract

DELIA (Demonstration Expert Log Interpretation Assistant) was constructed as part of a feasibility exercise to ascertain how expert decision aids might be applied to exploration for hydrocarbons (oil and gas). It assists in the derivation and selection of various parameters used in the evaluation of lithology via electronic well logs.

This paper presents an overview of the problem domain, details of the system architecture, and discusses the frame based knowledge representation formalism with examples.

1. Introduction

Expert systems are beginning to be applied to many areas of human endeavour. Hayes-Roth et al (1983), characterised ten types of system. These were condensed to four typical tasks by Reichgelt and van Harmelen (1986): interpretation; prediction; design; and monitoring.

In searching for natural energy reserves, such as gas, oil and, more recently, nuclear power sources, many companies have turned to various types of expert system for assistance in the evaluation of the quality of new finds. For example, PROSPECTOR (Gashnig (1980)) was used in the evaluation of the US government's uranium resources. Relevant to the application to be discussed herein, is the Dipmeter Advisor (Smith (1984)). Both of these systems involved facets of each of the tasks mentioned above. However, their chief role was in the interpretation of data.

DELIA is a system which assists a human expert in the analysis of hydrocarbon well log data. This assistance includes a data validation phase which deals with noise in data signals, and the derivation of parameters used in analysis of the logs.

This system has been developed on a Sun-2/120* computer using the POPLOG programming environment to manipulate a frame-based knowledge representation scheme. Extensive use has been made of interactive, high resolution graphics, in order to provide a familiar user interface to the log analyst.

*(Sun is a trademark of Sun Microsystems Inc.)

2. The Problem Domain

2.1 Well Logging and Formation Evaluation

The discovery and recovery of hydrocarbon deposits requires knowledge of subsurface structures - composition, origin, geometry, etc. It is the objective of wireline logging of exploration wells to record sufficient data to enable log analysts, the domain experts, to estimate accurately the location (depth) of natural porosity of the rock and the fluids (hydrocarbons or water) contained therein.

Logging is an expensive operation which is usually performed by specialist companies. Typically this involves the winching of several sensors, coupled together in "toolstrings", from bottom to top of a well at constant speed. Each tool or sensor records data at (typically) 6 inch intervals. This is recorded (after some preprocessing) on tape at the surface, along with other information (stored in a "header file") which may be needed to assist subsequent interpretation, eg geographical location, bit size, etc.

As logging can take place over depth ranges of several thousands of feet, the volume of data produced can be enormous. Multiple logging runs using different toolstrings may be necessary to record a comprehensive set of data which will permit full evaluation of the formation.

In addition to the raw data tapes, the logging company will supply plots over depth of the readings for each sensor. These are known as "mnemonic" plots and are identified by unique mnemonics (eg TENS = tension, GR = gamma ray, PEF = photoelectric factor, etc). These plots are the primary source of information used by the log analyst during the interpretation process.

Once the analyst has mentally constructed a hypothesis about the formation under consideration, he can investigate the accuracy of it by providing parameter estimates for a log interpretation package such as ULTRA*. This complex suite of software mathematically reconciles the actual tool responses with those that would theoretically be expected, based on the parameters proposed by the log analyst, to provide a measure of "goodness of fit". Iterative modification of certain parameters follows until an acceptable hypothesis is formulated.

In this context, there are two problems which have been addressed within DELIA - the log quality control (LQC) of the raw data and estimation of the parameters to be used by ULTRA.

2.2 Log Data Quality Control

During the logging process, various situations can arise which may degrade or invalidate the data. These include problems with noise, problems with the physical uniformity of the well wall (rugosity) and depth alignment when several logging runs have taken place. The severity and implications of these problems varies, but all should be addressed to make accurate interpretation possible.

The log analyst can identify the existence, and to a large extent, the severity, of poor data by pattern recognition of characteristic features on one or more of the mnemonic curves.

*(ULTRA is a trade mark of Cetis, Paris, France)

2.2.1 Tool sticking

Whenever the toolstring sticks, data continue to be recorded as if they were collected at 6 inch intervals as before. This situation will continue until the wireline tension increases to a point where the toolstring forcibly frees itself and correct logging recommences. During this period, all depth-related data are unreliable. The degree of this unreliability depends on the duration and severity of the stick.

The analyst is able to identify problems with tool sticking by a visual inspection of the tension (TENS) mnemonic. Typically this rises uniformly while the tool is stuck and rapidly returns to normal when it becomes free again. This pattern/feature on the TENS curve is known as a "tension ramp".

2.2.2 Sensor failure and noise

Sensor failure will result in the recording of inaccurate data and failure to log data results in the recording of null values. In some instances it is possible to estimate what the correct readings should have been, or what the absent values might have been, by a combination of interpolation and deductive techniques. The complexity of this reconstitution and the reliability of the inferred data depends on the particular mnemonic and circumstances at the time of logging. In some cases absent values are left as such, and are handled appropriately within the program suite.

For example, the short and long-spaced sonic tools, each of which comprises 2 transmitters and 2 receivers, measure the time required for a compressional sound wave to travel through 1 ft of formation and are particularly susceptible to noise. The information is recorded as 4 transit times (mnemonics TT1, TT2, TT3, TT4) and a derived "delta t" mnemonic (DT or DTL) which are essential to the estimation of formation porosity.

Low signal levels in the sonic tool can result in the detectors missing a first signal and triggering on subsequent arrivals, giving rise to overlong sonic measurements. This phenomenon is known as "cycle skipping". Mechanically induced noise may result in the detectors triggering too soon, resulting in shortened sonic measurements. This is known as "noise triggering".

The analyst is able to identify sonic problems by visual inspection of the sonic mnemonics. Reconstitution of bad DT or DTL values is often possible by using variations in the equations which originally combined the TT data to calculate them.

2.2.3 Rugosity

For a variety of reasons, the wall of the well may exhibit physical irregularities - collectively known as "rugosity". These irregularities primarily affect the responses obtained in tools which rely on the smooth contiguity of the measurement tool and wall. Where the wall is too rough or has caved in, any measurements taken are suspect.

For the detection and quantification of rugosity, the analyst usually needs to cross-correlate characteristic features on several mnemonics, and this can be a time-consuming and demanding task. Typically of interest are the caliper (CALI), bulk density correction factor (DRHO) and micro resistivity (MSFL) mnemonics.

The credence which can be placed in data recorded over rugose regions is dependant on the level of significance of the rugosity and the mnemonic itself. The log analyst must rely upon a great deal of expertise and subjective assessment for this.

2.2.4 Depth matching

When several logging runs have been performed, it is possible that the depth reference points are not identical for each log. This will result in the recorded data being offset, which could lead to interpretation problems - particularly where it is necessary to cross-reference and compare mnemonics from different logs.

Depth matching is a technique which attempts to overcome this problem by identifying a common reference point and aligning all mnemonic data to it. The natural gamma radiation of the formation (GR mnemonic) is used as the well "fingerprint" and is recorded with every log. Assuming that GR will remain constant over time, the analyst will perform depth matching by recognising the same significant features of the GR curve of different logs, noting the amount of shift needed to align them.

2.3 Estimation of ULTRA Parameters

ULTRA is a comprehensive log interpretation package. The analyst supplies, in the form of parameters, a model of the formation and the software finds a mathematically optimal solution by attempting to reconcile the analyst's model with the actual logged data. This optimisation is made with respect to the interpretation unknowns, ie porosity, lithology and saturations.

There are over 600 ULTRA parameters. It is desirable to provide reasonable estimates for a large proportion of them in order to obtain an acceptable optimal solution. It is unlikely that such a solution will be obtained in one pass, and iterative refinement of the parameters (in the light of intermediate results from ULTRA) will be necessary. The sources of information used by the analyst to arrive at a set of estimates include past experience, analysis of the log data, other relevant data recorded at the time of logging, best default options, and so on. These sources may be contradictory, but must be reconciled and prioritised sensibly and consistently.

3. Structure of DELIA

DELIA is an interactive tool which is intended to be used by the log analyst (expert) only. It allows him to superimpose his judgement on all recommendations, and to reject or modify the advice of the system at all times. The idea is to leave the expert in control whilst simultaneously removing the more mundane, repetitive and time consuming tasks.

3.1 Functional Requirements

In the context of the problem domain, the functional requirements of DELIA are:

i)   To support basic manipulation of log data.
ii)   To interact with the analyst, both graphically and textually.
iii)   To extract information from the data (ie do a numeric to symbolic
       transformation).
iv)   To manipulate and make inferences on symbolic data.
v)   To allow the analyst to examine and modify the knowledge bases in a
       simple manner.

3.2 System Architecture

        The functional requirements have led to the development of
DELIA in a highly modular fasion. The knowledge based modules are
implemented in POPLOG and the other software in C under UNIX*. A more
detailed description of these modules follows. (Figure 1 shows a simple
representation of the architecture.)

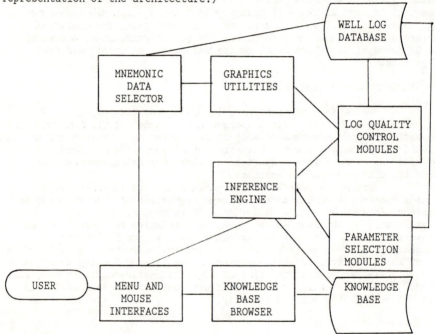

Figure 1:   System Architecture

        At the kernel of the system is a general purpose backward
chaining inference engine written in PROLOG (under POPLOG) which
manipulates a number of knowledge bases sequentially during a
consultation session. Information for these knowledge bases is supplied
by "messenger routines" (conventional data analysis software written in
C) by direct interaction with the log analyst. This is one of the key
concepts of the system design - the separation of the problem solution
into feature recognition on the raw data and higher level manipulation of
these symbolic representations.

*(UNIX is a trademark of AT&T)

Great emphasis has been placed on the user interface, which accounts for a large proportion of the total software. The analyst is accustomed to working in a graphically biased environment and DELIA attempts to provide all the facilities necessary to support this.

The knowledge base browser allows the user to examine or edit the contents of a knowledge base without requiring detailed knowledge of the internal representation. It includes an explanation facility which supports pseudo-natural language access via keywords, and is implemented in POP-11. A teaching facility exists to interactively extend the scope of the keywords or to customise the user dictionary. The editor is written in POP-11 and guides the user as far as possible to provide the necessary information to build, remove or modify existing knowledge. The user responses are restructured into the internal representation required by the inference engine.

Whenever changes are made to the structure of the knowledge base integrity and consistency checking are performed which prevent contention elsewhere. For example, if an additional attribute is added to a frame, then all existing facts based on that frame will be amended to include the attribute with value set to "unknown".

An important benefit of the modularity of the system has been the ability to iteratively prototype individual modules without seriously affecting other unrelated ones.

3.3 Knowledge Elicitation

The major source of expertise in DELIA is an experienced well log analyst. He is both knowledgeable and eloquent, and is extremely enthusiastic about DELIA. Due to these three factors it has been possible to rely on loosely structured interviews for eliciting information. These interviews were largely based on looking at and analysing specific examples. There are several specialist texts (Rabia (1985), Desbrandes (1985)) which give excellent background information, along with several journal papers.

Following initial elicitation of information, rules are derived, tested and amended, using the familiar iterative cycle common to most expert system developments.

It is fortunate that the expert is easily able to verbalise his approach to problem solving. As yet no recourse has been made to more structured techniques (Gammack and Young (1985)), although these may be required to increase the "depth" of the knowledge in the system, at a later stage of development.

3.4 Overall Solution Strategy

An example of the methodology employed by DELIA for dealing with the constituent problems of LQC and ULTRA parameter estimation is given in section 5.0. The overall solution strategy, regardless of the well under consideration, is a sequential process as follows:

i)   Identify tool sticks on individual logging runs by searching for tension ramps on TENS mnemonics.
ii) Flag all mnemonics as corrupt over ranges of tension ramps.
iii) Depth match logging runs.
iv) Identify sonic problems by analysing behaviour of TT mnemonics.

v)   Identify rugosity problems by combined analysis of DRHO, MSFL and
        CALI mnemonics.
vi)   Flag RHOB, MSFL, ILM and PEF mnemonics as corrupt over rugose
        depth ranges.
vii)   Flag TT mnemonics as corrupt over depth ranges identified in (iv)
        and reconstitute DT by alternative formulae where possible.
viii)   Identify formation type and depth range.
ix)   Analyse supplementary log data (eg header files).
x)   Perform data reduction by mnemonic "zoning", ie the production of
        typical values which are applicable over depth ranges.
xi)   Generate depth-related ULTRA parameter estimates from all
        available sources of information.
xii)   Reconcile conflicts/inconsistencies in ULTRA parameter estimates,
        where there are alternative sources of derivation, and output a
        list of values.

        In reality the log analyst does not follow such a
well-structured and sequential methodology. He will tend to jump between
LQC and parameter estimation in an ad hoc manner as the situation
demands, principally because the LQC aspect is so time consuming and
uninteresting that he will attempt to keep it to the absolute minimum.
Since DELIA can handle LQC in a much more automatic and efficient manner,
with minimal demands on the log analyst, no attempt has been made to
mimic this ad-hoc solution strategy.

4. Knowledge Representation

        In carrying out his task it was found that the log analyst
makes use of many [attribute, value] relationships. Often he will "link"
several of these relationships in order to form a concept:

                [concept-1,
                        [attribute-a, value], and
                        [attribute-b, value], and
                        ....
                        [attribute-z, value]]
e.g.
                [gamma-ray
                        [reading, 38.0], and
                        [top-depth,0], and
                        [bottom depth, 1000.0], and
                        [source, gamma-ray-log]].

This type of concept formation is heavily inclined towards frames.
Hence, this was the representation scheme chosen.

4.1 Knowledge Bases

        The inference engine is capable of supporting several
distinct knowledge bases. A knowledge base consists of metarules, rules,
facts and object oriented modules.
        The modularity of DELIA extends to the knowledge bases so
that only knowledge relevant to the particular sub-problem under

consideration (eg rugosity) will be manipulated at any one time. This partitioning of the knowledge bases leads to greater clarity and also reduces the search space that the inference engine has to deal with.

4.2 Metarules

Metarules are the highest level of knowledge representation and are interpreted and acted upon sequentially. They therefore define, by their order, the solution strategy of a knowledge base module.
Their structure is:

```
meta_rule (name, num_execs,
        [action, description, weight],
        [cond_list])
```

where _name_ is a unique identifier for the rule; _num-execs_ is 'once' or 'all' to specify either the first found occurrence of facts satisfying the condition list, or all such facts; _action_ is any one of 12 instructions which invoke external processes (e.g. 'process'), carry out frame construction and manipulation (e.g. write-frame), or communicate with the user (e.g. 'output'); _description_ is additional information required by an action (e.g. process name); _weight_ (0-100) is assigned to an action which updates a fact - the actual certainty factor of the action is a combination of this weight and the individual certainties of the condition list clauses; and _cond-list_ is a list of frame-based or symbolic clause which must be "satisfied" for the action to fire.

Example:

```
meta_rule (fire_rampspotter,
        [once, process, 'rampspotter.x', 100],
        [always]).
```

will unconditionally execute the messenger routine "rampspotter" once only.

4.3 Rules

Rules have the same basic structure as metarules but can be placed in any order within the knowledge base. They are similar in form to production rules.
A rule is fired when another rule or metarule requires information which does not exist in the current knowledge base, but which could possibly be obtained or inferred by the actions of the rules. In this way the knowledge base usually expands as a consultation progresses.
Their structure is:

```
rule (name, [action, description, weight], [cond_list])
where slot names are as for meter-rules.
Example:

rule (ask_analyst_for_bitsize,
        [tell_me, bitsize, 100],
        [[bitsize, [value, =, unknown]]]).
```

will ask the analyst to provide a value for the bit size if it is
currently unknown.

4.4 Facts

Facts are the most fundamental knowledge structure and can be
of two distinct types - symbolic or frame based.
Symbolic facts take the form:

fact (name, certainty, [source]).

Where name is a unique fact identifier, certainty is a
measure of belief that the fact is true and source gives the origin of
the fact and a list of rules which have modified it.
Example:

Fact (always, 100, [default]).

Frame based facts take the form:

fact (name, certainty, [source], [attr_list]).

Where name is the frame upon which the fact is based - a
frame description must exist; certainty and source are as for symbolic
facts; and attr-list is a list of values corresponding to those in the
frame description.
Example:

fact (formation, 100, [analyst], [9757.0, 9884.0,
rotliegende]).

indicates that the analyst has provided information (with absolute
certainty) that the Rotliegende formation exists from 9757 to 9884 ft
based on the frame:

frame (formation, [top_depth, bottom_depth, type]).

4.5 Object Oriented Modules

The knowledge representation described so far can become
unwieldy when attempting to manipulate facts in a complex manner
(eg combining several overlapping TT facts to decide when the DT mnemonic
can or cannot be reconstituted). For this reason, an object oriented
approach (using POPFLAVOURS - an integral part of POPLOG) has been taken
to handle some of the more difficult knowledge manipulation.
Instead of defining procedures which manipulate data, data
objects (their attributes and way in which these may be accessed or
changed) are defined. These objects can store data in their attributes,
or they can handle "messages" which request information on or changes to
their status. The descriptions of how objects handle messages are known
as methods.

Hierarchies of objects can be defined which inherit characteristics from those at higher levels.

For example, a "feature" on a mnemonic curve is a generic term (a "mixin") for objects which always possess start depth and end depth attributes. A "blip" is a specific instance of a "feature" which also possesses a size attribute. (The start and end depths are inherited from the "feature").

The similarity between objects and frame based facts allows conversion from POP-11/PROLOG form into POPFLAVOURS form and vice versa. This in turn facilitates the integration of POPFLAVOURS modules into the knowledge representation formalism already described.

The encapsulation of rules as methods within the objects has the effect of reducing the search space during inferencing. Only methods which are appropriate to any particular object will manipulate those objects. As a consequence of this, the knowledge representation provided by POPFLAVOURS creates a black-box environment in which the programmer can make use of a set of manipulation utilities without needing to know the details of their implementation.

5. Generating Ultra Parameter Estimates

As a specific example of the knowledge representation and inferencing method, consider a simplified overview of the derivation of an ULTRA parameter estimate, based on the Gamma Ray mnemonic.

As noted in section 2.2.4 depth matching of log runs is achieved using Gamma Ray (GR) data. This is because the GR measurement provides a good "fingerprint" to resolve the location of different lithologies. Indeed the GR curve is sometimes used as a measure of the clay content at any depth.

It is necessary to determine the upper and lower bounds on GR values over a given formation. GRMIN and GRMAX are used to provide estimates of the GR activity of pure sand and pure shales respectively.

It is not sufficient to obtain these directly from the GR log. Instead the expert will look for cross over points in the graphs of formation density and porosity. Where the maximum separation occurs, so the GR value at the corresponding depth is GRMIN.

DELIA searches for a maximum on the density-neutron separation (DNS) mnemonic to establish GRMAX.

Two sets of facts are generated from zoned information. Facts of type "gr" have slots "start_depth", "end_depth" and "value". Facts of type "dns" have the same slots. Where "dns""value" is greater than 0, so a maximum is defined. The "gr" "value", which covers the same depth range, represents a possible value for GRMIN; the possibles are of type "min gr", with "start depth", "end_depth" and "value" attributes. This is represented so:

```
rule(generate_min_gr,
      [write_frame,
          [min_gr,
              [start_depth, =,
                    [gr, start_depth]],
              [end_depth, =,
                    [gr, end_depth]],
              [value, =,
                    [gr, value]]], 100],
  [
      [dns,
          [value, ≥, 0]], and,
      [gr,
          [start_depth, ≤,
                [dns, start_depth]],
          [end_depth ≥,
                [dns, end depth]]]]]).
```

This is done for all possible combinations of "gr" and "dns"
facts. The true MINGR is established by sorting the set of "min_gr"
facts, to establish the smallest value.
        Unfortunately, the calculation of GRMAX is not so straightforward.
In some formations pure shale does not lie in discrete layers.
Consequently, it is infeasible to pick a value directly from the GR
curve. However, when there is less shale present, the accuracy of the
parameters describing it is less critical and interpolation can be used.
        Therefore, derivation of these GR boundaries is not simply a
matter of numerical calculation. It requires feature spotting and
analysis.

6. Multi-language Programming

        In implementing DELIA, a number of programming environment
and language requirements were identified. Good graphics capability,
reasonably fast numeric computing, suitability for artificial
intelligence programming, potential for portability and reasonable
costs.
        It was apparent that no one language could hope to meet all
of these requirements. FORTRAN is exceptional for "number crunching" and
graphics work. C is useful for graphics, is reasonably strong
numerically speaking, and is exceptionally portable. Neither C nor
FORTRAN are favoured by the AI community; although expert system
construction in either is not infeasible.
        Pure LISP and PROLOG are seldom mentioned for their numerical
capability. Neither are they considered suitable for graphics work (on
non-specialist hardware). With hindsight the specialist AI workstations,
with their object oriented operating systems and programming environments
might appear to have been the obvious choice; however when this project
was initiated this selection was too expensive and complex to
contemplate.
        Consequently, a compromise was chosen. C could support
graphics and numerical work, whilst POPLOG offered a good interactive
programming environment, including PROLOG, LISP and POP-11, for AI

programming. This, together with a Sun Workstation, met all of the requirements, although a little ground work was required in terms of windowing. Also quite significant use was made of UNIX shell scripts for file handling and data retrieval.

POP-11 and PROLOG deal with all of the expert systems side, with a blend of procedural and declarative styles to suit the requirements. For example, the inference engine was written in PROLOG whilst the knowledge base browser made use of POP-11's procedural style. To date no use has been made of POPLOG Common LISP, as most of what you can do in LISP is easily achieved in POP-11. Also, the Common LISP implementation was poor at the outset of the project.

Out of this has grown a sophisticated menu driven system. There are some performance problems with the existing hardware configuration, but it is envisaged that any such problems would be resolved if the system were resident on Sun-3 hardware.

The strengths of each programming language has been used to advantage to address problems to which they are best suited. This has been beneficial in that it has forced modularity into the system, with well defined interfaces between the various modules.

One of the more innovative ideas in the implementation has been the use of POPFLAVOURS, POPLOG's version of the object oriented paradigm, as an integral part of the knowledge representation.

7. Conclusions

At the time of writing, knowledge pertaining to one formation type alone has been encoded completely. ULTRA parameter derivation relating to this type is also complete.

The system is being extended to encompass the derivation of more ULTRA parameters, and to include knowledge which will cover more formation types. Iterative refinement of parameters is not yet incorporated, but this will be addressed.

At present DELIA is purely a prototype. It was the original intention that the major deliverable from this work would be a software specification, rather than a live system. At present this still remains the case.

The intended users are log analysts. At the present time, DELIA's use is confined to the development team and the expert.

In terms of "quality", the system has been received enthusiastically by the expert. It has also received a favourable response from a software engineer specialising in geologically oriented work.

Multi-language programming has been found to be a vital element in the success of the project to date. The complexity of the problem forces the use of several languages, each being used where they are best suited. This is exemplified by the separation of the problem into feature recognition in data, using conventional programming, and manipulation of these features (at a higher level of abstraction) by an expert system shell.

The object oriented paradigm is without doubt very useful. In this case it improved the efficiency of some aspects of DELIA by an estimated order of magnitude.

To date no work on the manipulation of certainty factors has been undertaken, primarily because of the complexity of condition lists. A suitable method of combining certainty measures in these lists is not clear.

REFERENCES

Desbrandes, R (1985). Encyclopedia of Well Logging. Paris: Editions Technip.

Gammack, J G and Young, R M (1985). Psychological tools for eliciting expert knowledge. In Research and Development in Expert Systems, ed. M A Bramer, pp 105-112. Cambridge: Cambridge University Press.

Gashnig, J (1980). An application of the PROSPECTOR system in the D.O.E's national uranium resource evaluation. 1st Conference of the American Association for Artificial Intelligence, pp 295-297.

Hayes-Roth, F., Waterman, L A and Lenat, D B (1983). An overview of expert systems. In Building Expert Systems, eds. F Hayes-Roth, D A Waterman and D B Lenat, pp 3-29. Cambridge MA: Addison Wesley.

Rabia, H (1985). Oilwell Drilling Engineering, London: Graham & Trotman.

Reichgelt, H and van Harmelen, F (1986). Criteria for choosing representation languages and control regimes for expert systems. The Knowledge Engineering Review, 1, (4), pp 2-17.

Smith, R G (1984). On the development of commercial expert systems. The AI Magazine, 5, (3), pp 61-73.

Acknowledgements

The authors wish to thank British Gas for permission to publish this paper.

David Camden, of the British Gas Exploration Department, is our enthusiastic and knowledgeable expert, to whom we are more than grateful. Dr Ian Whiteley made valuable suggestions on our first draft. Thanks also to David Larkin who completes the ERS team.

SATISFYING DISJUNCTIONS OF CONSTRAINTS BY SPECIALIZED RESOLUTION

Sam Steel
Dept Computer Science, University of Essex
Colchester, CO4 3SQ, UK

Abstract

Constraint satisfaction problems in which there may be disjunctions between constraints have been little studied; yet they do turn up. A way of handling disjunctive constraints is proposed in detail. It uses a form of theorem proving analogous to resolution theorem proving, except that it is used as an affirmation proof procedure, and treats literals about set membership in specialized ways.

1. Introduction and general proposal

The idea of constraint satisfaction is well known. There are boxes (often called variables or units). There are fillers (often called values or labels) that can go in boxes. There are rules (constraints) about what fillers can go in which boxes simultaneously. One has to find a filler for each box such that none of the constraints are violated. If a constraint mentions just one box, it is said to constrain the domain of that box. For instance, suppose there are two boxes Wine and Dish. Conventional etiquette demands

        fish(filler(Dish)) -> white(filler(Wine))

I shall write "Box" for "filler(Box)" in future (which though unsound will not matter for my purposes); and all predicates will take a single tuple as an argument. So etiquette now dictates

        fish(<Dish>) -> white(<Wine>)

There are methods of constraint satisfaction: but they have difficulties with disjunctions of facts about boxes. Before discussing this, I shall describe this paper's proposal.
        First, a seemingly trivial point: there are two ways of expressing a constraint.
- By a predicate. The box is a term in a sentence (other than as below) such as

        greater_than(<Box1 Box2>)

- By a set

        <Box1> e { <1> <2> <3> <4> }
        <Box1 Box2> e { <1 5> <2 3> }

Of course, set membership is a predicate, and the second can always be expressed as a form of the first:

           Box1=1 v Box1=2 v Box1=3 v Box1=4

but this is not always most convenient. I say why not later.
           "Resolution theorem proving" is of course the use of a uniform
proof procedure that employs the resolution rule of inference. The
proposal I am making is to do constraint satisfaction using the same proof
procedure, but with some extra rules of inference besides resolution. All
facts about the fillers of boxes, data and constraints, are to expressed
in conjunctive normal form (cnf). If, just for now, one calls the use of
these rules "extra-resolution", then this process is to be done:

```
if      the empty clause has been derived
then    stop. the constraints are contradictory and so unsatisfiable
elseif  the extra-resolution of some pair of clauses has not been tried
then    if      that pair of clauses extra-resolves
        then    factor the extra-resolvent
                if      the extra-resolvent is implied by another clause
                then    discard it. It constrains no box.
                else    for      every clause C
                        do       if the extra-resolvent implies C
                        then     discard C
                        end
                add the extra-resolvent to the clauses
else    stop. the clauses present are the strongest description of the
        fillers of the boxes compatible with the constraints, the  data,
        and the inference rules used.
```

           The proof procedure is here being used as an affirmation (not
refutation) proof process, unlike its usual use. The empty clause is bad
news, not good.
           To get a definite set of fillers for the boxes, one can wrap
that process in this loop:

```
accept the initial constraints and data
loop
           run the above process
           if      the filler of every box is uniquely determined
           then    exit with success
           elseif  the empty clause has been derived
           then    exit with failure
           else    make an arbitrary choice of the filler of some box,
                   compatible with the clauses extant
           end
endloop
```

           Here is a simple example. The two boxes are "dish" and "wine".
The constraints are:

           wine e {hock sauterne claret moselle}
           dish e {salmon mullet}
           dish e {salmon sole trout} -> wine e {hock moselle}
           dish e {mullet} -> wine e {tokay}

           Here they are in cnf:

```
1          wine e {hock sauterne claret moselle}
2          dish e {salmon mullet}
3          -(dish e {salmon sole trout}) v wine e {hock moselle}
4          -(dish e {mullet}) v wine e {tokay}
```

Here are the deduced clauses, saying what clauses were clashed to produce them:

```
5 (2,4)         dish e {salmon} v wine e {tokay}
6 (1,5)         dish e {salmon}
7 (6,3)         wine e {hock moselle}
```

At the end of the run, the only clauses still in the database - all the others having been subsumed - are:

```
6          dish e {salmon}
7          wine e {hock moselle}
```

2. Why disjunctive constraints matter but aren't handled

I have just given a sketch of the method I propose. Why is it needed when there is already a lot of work on constraint satisfaction methods? Because I found (while working on Allen-style planning, as in (Allen & Koomen 1983)) that I needed to represent constraints such as

```
relation( finish(int1), start(int2) ) e { =, < }
v
relation( finish(int2), start(int1) ) e { =, < }
```

which are of the form

```
(box1 e Set1) v (box2 e Set2)
```

or, even more abstractly,

```
P(box1) v Q(box2)
```

Such disjunctive constraints are, as far as I can see, impossible to represent in the machinery that eg (Mackworth & Freuder 1985) or (Nudel 1983) consider in their reviews of the various sorts of machinery available for constraint satisfaction. In (Mackworth & Freuder 1985), though predicates constraining fillers of boxes, or of pairs of boxes, such as

```
P(box1) <=> A(box1) v B(box1)
```

```
Q(box1,box2) <=> C(box1) v D(box2)
```

are perfectly possible, disjuncts of constraints on *different* boxes are not. Similarly, in (Nudel 1983) the set of binary (and in principle n-ary) predicates expressing compatibility between fillers of pairs (or n-tuples) of boxes is imagined as a table all of whose entries are simultaneously true. There is no opportunity for disjunction.

The algorithm in (Haralick & Shapiro 1979) can handle such disjuncts, since it considers a relation R which can, if it must (and here it must), describe all legal complete sets of <box,filler> pairs. However, building the relation R may be elaborate and counter-intuitive. For instance, the constraints

         a e {p q}
         b e {s t}
         c e {v w}
         (a e {p}) v (b e {s})

will have to appear (though this is not precisely Haralick & Shapiro's notation) as something not conveying the same intuitive impression at all:

         <a b c> e { <p s v> <p s w> <p t v> <p t w> <q s v> <q s w> }

        In fact, the systems such as those reviewed by Mackworth, Freuder and Nudel can in principle be modified to handle disjunctive constraints. As Mackworth and Freuder (1985) say

> ... it is most unlikely that a polynomial time algorithm exists for solving general constraint satisfaction problems (CSP). Accordingly the class of network consistency algorithms was invented. These algorithms do not solve a CSP completely but they eliminate once and for all local inconsistencies that cannot participate in any global solution. These inconsistencies would otherwise have been discovered repeatedly by any backtracking solution. One role for network consistency algorithms is as a pre-processor for subsequent backtrack search.

        Haralick and Elliot (1980) review ways of doing such pre-processing. Crudely, what happens in them is that the ordinary backtrack algorithm at some point stops, considers the choices it has made and has still to make in the light of the constraint information it has, and decides to fail, succeed or continue. If disjuncts are to be permitted in the constraint information, the pre-processor will have to look at what follows from each possible way of choosing among the disjuncts. I know of no work done on this. So it seems worth looking at a method adapted to disjunctions.

3. Why and how is resolution departed from?

        The big problem with resolution is the number of clauses that get generated. Much of this paper is about ways of preventing that that are specially adapted to constraint satisfaction problems. The main way is: to do lots of subsumption checking (as mentioned above); and to use extensional (set) statements of what fillers can fill a box instead of many equalities and inequalities. For instance, suppose there are two clauses

         box1=1 v box1=2 v box1=3 v box1=4
         box1=3 v box1=4 v box1=5 v box1=6

To suppose that anyone would use the clauses -(1=2), ... and pure resolution to continue is to erect a straw man. Suppose instead one had added to ordinary binary resolution

```
      A v B              C v -B
      -----------------------------
             A v C
```

a specialized form

```
A v X=J        C v X=K        J, K are semantically different
------------------------------------------------------------------
             A v C
```

Even so, the clauses above can be resolved 13 ways, producing 13 resolvents. None subsumes any other. None is the useful conclusion

> box1=3 v box1=4

But from the same data given as sets

> box1 e {1 2 3 4}
> box1 e {3 4 5 6}

and some set theory, one gets immediately

> box1 e {3 4}

But unfortunately that inference is not the sort of clash resolution needs. Can this be cured?

     I will back off and consider the proof procedure abstractly. It is given by stating what actions can legally be done to the sentences currently asserted (the logic issue), and which legal action should be done to the sentences (the control issue).

     These actions are not inferences, though saying when they may be done may refer to ¦-, the inference relation. But of course ¦- is not decideable, and even if it were, it would be circular to have a test for entailment as a sub-part of a proof procedure. What one really wants is an easy test of whether A ¦- B which is sound even if not complete.

     A proof procedure like resolution theorem proving (RTP) involves doing four sorts of action described below: removing falsity from a clause; clashing; subsumption; factoring.

     X, Y ... are disjuncts (perhaps empty) of literals. A, B ... are literals. I, J, K ... range over tuples. # is falsity. Theta is a substitution.

3.1 Removing falsity

     Since X v # -¦¦- X, literals known to be false can be dropped from a clause. In ordinary RTP, # is never introduced into a clause. With set literals, however, the literal

> I e {}

may crop up, and can be dropped if it does.

3.2 Clashing

     Clauses are combined to produce a new clause. In RTP, the action on two clauses is

```
if        A v X  is present
          B v Y  is present
          A Theta, B Theta ¦- #
then      add    X Theta v Y Theta
```

But if A and B can be set literals, one can still do something very
similar:

```
if        A v X  is present
          B v Y  is present
          A, B ¦- C
then      add    X v Y v C
```

(One can see the clashing step for resolution as

```
if        A v X  is present
          B v Y  is present
          A Theta, B Theta ¦- #
then      add  X Theta v Y Theta v #
```

with a falsity removal step done at the same time.)
          The simplest set literal clashes are:

A	B	C
I e Set1	I e Set2	I e intersection(Set1,Set2)
I e Set1	-(I e Set2)	I e difference(Set1,Set2)
-(I e Set1)	-(I e Set2)	-(I e union(Set1,Set2))

But this isn't enough. One may have literals giving information about
permissible or impermissible combinations of fillers of boxes, such as

          <box1 box2> e {<1 2> <1 3> <2 5>}

To combine such literals one also needs these rules

A	B	C
<IJ> e Set1	<JK> e Set2	

          <IJK> e {<LMN>¦ <LM> e Set1 &   <MN> e Set2 }

```
<IJ> e Set1 -(<JK> e Set2)
```

          -(<IK> e { <LN> ¦ All M (<LM> e Set1 -> <MN> e Set2) })

          or equivalently

          -(<IK> e {<LN>¦ includes({M¦<MN> e Set2},{M¦<LM> e Set1})}])

Proof: Suppose rule is unsound. So conclusion false while premises true.
So   All M (<IM> e Set1 -> <MK> e Set2)
So   <IJ> e Set1 -> <JK> e Set2
But   -(<JK> e Set2)
So   -(<IJ> e Set1)
So contradiction. []

        For symmetry, one might consider the clash of

    -(<IJ> e Set1)   -(<JK> e Set2)

but nothing useful follows.
        One can give rules for the extensions of more than two boxes.
For instance, suppose one has

        <abc> e {<2 1 3> <4 3 8> <4 2 7> <5 1 9>}
        <cdb> e {<3 5 1> <7 9 2> <8 5 3>}

This can be reshaped as

        <a<bc>> e {<2 <1 3>> <4 <3 8>> <5 <1 9>>}
        <<bc>d> e {<<1 3> 5> <<2 7> 9> <<3 8> 5>}

from which, by one of the rules above, one can derive

        <a<bc>d> e {<2 <1 3> 5> <4 <3 8> 5>}

which can finally be reshaped as

        <abcd> e {<2 1 3 5> <4 3 8 5>}

The rule that permits reshaping is

        T1 e Set -¦¦- T2 e { T2 ¦ T1 e Set }

Proof:
"U e { V ¦ P }" is true iff "P"[V:=U] is true, so
"T2 e { T2 ¦ T1 e Set }" is true iff "T1 e Set"[T2 := T2] is true.
But "T1 e Set"[T2 := T2] is syntactically identical to "T1 e Set". []

        One of the reshapings above is done by

    <cdb> e {<3 5 1> <7 9 2> <8 5 3>}

    <<bc>d> e { <<bc>d> ¦ <cdb> e {<3 5 1> <2 7 9> <3 8 5>} }

    <<bc>d> e {<<1 3> 5> <<2 7> 9> <<3 8> 5>}

        Predicate literals can't be re-shaped, or at least I can't see
how to do it.
        An extra refinement in clashing is to reject out of hand any
attempt to clash identical set literals. These will always clash, but they
will always produce themselves as a result. So any resolvent including it
will be worthless, since it will be subsumed by both its parents.
        Sometimes boxes may be constrained by both sorts of constraint:

```
            greater_than(<IJ>)
            <IJ> e {<1 2> <5 3> <5 7> <9 4>}
```

In general, no easy inference can be made with such a mixture, unless the predicate has a decision procedure. Arithmetic predicates (greater_than etc) are the commonest such predicates. To clash mixed literals, use the predicate as a filter on the set.

A	B	C
P(I)	I e Set	I e { L ¦ L e Set & P(L) }

Nothing follows from

        P(I),   -(I e Set)

and no generality is gained by letting P(I) be negative.

One can't generalize to the case where the literals describe different tuples in quite the same way as before, because nothing follows from

        P(<IJ>),   <JK> e Set

but one can filter the set if the predicate constrains a sub-tuple of the tuple:

A	B	C
P(I)	<IJ> e Set	<IJ> e { <LM> ¦ <LM> e Set & P(L) }

3.3 Subsumption

If a clause in the DB entails (subsumes) one already there, the general algorithm given at the beginning demands that one remove the one subsumed.

```
if      X present
        Y present
        X ¦- Y
then    remove Y
```

Set literals complicate this slightly, since one needs to be able to show that this clause

        I e {1 2 3}   J e {7 8 9}   v   K e {15 16 17}

is subsumed by

        I e {1 2}   v   J e {7 8}   v   K e {15 16}

By using associativity and commutativity of v, and the facts

```
        A v X ¦- B v Y    if  A ¦- B  and  X ¦- Y
        X ¦- Y            if  X is the empty disjunct
```

one can reduce testing implication between clauses to recursion and the testing of implication between literals. The conditions for A ¦- B are:

```
A              B
---------------------------
X              X Theta        always

I e Set1       I e Set2       if includes(Set2,Set1)

-(I e Set1)    -(I e Set2)    if includes(Set1,Set2)

I e Set1       -(I e Set2)    if intersection(Set1,Set2) = {}
```

In general, -(I e Set1) never implies I e Set2.
Literals may also have to be reshaped, since literals describing different sets may subsume each other. Eg

$$<IJ> e \{<1\ 6> <1\ 7> <1\ 8> <2\ 7> <2\ 8>\}$$

subsumes

$$<I> e \{<1> <2> <3>\}$$

The general rules are

```
A              B
---------------------------
T1 e Set1      T2 e Set2       if includes(Set2,{ T2 ¦ T1 e Set1 })

-(T2 e Set2)   -(T1 e Set1)    if includes(Set2, { T2 ¦ T1 e Set1 })
```

Proof:
Using rule about reshaping from above

```
T1 e Set1
-----------------------
T2 e { T2 ¦ T1 e Set1 }      includes(Set2,{ T2 ¦ T1 e Set1 })
------------------------------------------------------------------
T2 e Set2
```

and its contrapositive. []

Here are some rules about conditions under which a set literal easily implies a predicate literal, and vice versa. (Again, P must have a decision procedure, and the set may have to be reshaped.)

```
A              B
---------------------------
I e Set        P(I)           if { L ¦ L e Set &  P(L) } = Set

P(I)           -(I e Set)     if { L ¦ L e Set &  P(L) } = {}

<IJ> e Set     P(I)           if { <LM> ¦ <LM> e Set &  P(L) } = Set

P(I)           -(<IJ> e Set)  if { <LM> ¦ <LM> e Set &  P(L) } = {}
```

3.4 Factoring

Because clashing is binary, factoring has to be considered. For instance, the clash of these clauses

```
box1 e Set1    v    box2 e Set2
box1 e Set3    v    box2 e Set4
```

produces a clause

```
box1 e intersection(Set1,Set2)  v  box2 e Set2  v  box2 e Set4
```

with more literals than it need. If possible, many literals are replaced by a single equivalent literal.

```
if        A v B v X  is present
          A v B -¦¦- C
then      delete  A v B v X
          add   C v X
```

In general the question is, if A, B are literals in a clause, when can one easily find a C that is equivalent to A v B ? The easiest case of this is when A ¦- B, because then A v B -¦¦- B.

```
if        A v B v X  is present
          A v B -¦¦- B
then      delete  A v B v X
          add   B v X
```

We already have a table of when the obvious cases of one literal entailing another - it is exactly the table used in subsumption. There is however one set of special cases:

A	B	C
I e Set1	I e Set2	I e union(Set1,Set2)
-(I e Set1)	-(I e Set2)	-(I e intersection(Set1,Set2))
I e Set1	-(I e Set2)	-(I e difference(Set2,Set1))

4. Conclusions

Constraint satisfaction problems with disjunctive constraints are a real problem. They can be handled by the theorem-proving process proposed in this paper.

It would be good to see the relation between this approach and others already extant made clearer. In particular, much is known about the complexity of the other approachs, and nothing about the complexity of this one.

Acknowledgements

I want to thank Edward P K Tsang for the many very useful

discussions about the relation between planning and constraint
satisfaction I have had with him.

References

Allen JF, Koomen JA (1983). Planning using a temporal world model. IJCAI-83

Haralick RM, Elliot GL (1980). Increasing tree search efficiency for
constraint satisfaction problems. Artificial Intelligence 14 (1980) 263-313

Haralick RM, Shapiro LG (1979). The consistent labeling problem: Part I.
IEEE Trans on pattern analysis and machine intelligence PAMI-1(2) 1979

Mackworth AK, Freuder EC (1985). The complexity of some polynomial network
consistency algorithms for constraint satisfaction problems. Artificial
Intelligence 25 (1985) 65-74

Nudel B (1983). Consistent-labeling problems and their algorithms: ...
Artificial Intelligence 21 (1983) 135-178

INFERENCE AND THE CONCEPTUAL GRAPH KNOWLEDGE REPRESENTATION LANGUAGE

Michael K. Jackman
Rutherford Appleton Laboratory,
Informatics Division,
Chilton,
Didcot,
OXON OX11 0QX

Abstract

The conceptual graph knowledge representation language (CGKRL) is a general language for knowledge based systems. It includes an explicit representation for the hierarchical organisation of knowledge, known as the type hierarchy. The use of a type hierarchy means that fewer rules need be encoded to represent some area of expertise, and therefore search space is smaller and computation potentially more efficient in any inference process. Underlying the inference process is a matching operation known as the maximal join. In this paper the basic elements of the CGKRL are presented and the maximal join operation and its use in inference are explained.

0. Introduction

The conceptual graph knowledge representation language (CGKRL) is a powerful language for representing knowledge (Sowa, 1984). It can represent all the propositions of first order logic, as well as those of higher order and modal logics. One of the advantages of this language over some other knowledge representation languages (KRLs) is that there is a hierarchical organisation of knowledge. This means that fewer rules need be written to represent some area of expertise and so search space can be smaller and computation more efficient in some inference process.

This paper is divided into five sections, as follows. First, the basic elements of the CGKRL are presented. Second, the use of hierarchical organisation of knowledge in reducing the number of rules required to represent knowledge is explained. Third, an explanation is given of the fundamental operations which may performed on conceptual graphs, and how they are used in defining a partial ordering. This partial ordering is intimately related to notions of truth maintainence. Fourth, the maxim join operation is described and how this is related to the partial ordering for conceptual graphs, and therefore to truth maintainence. Finally, requirements for a matching operation in inference are specifie and it is shown how a variation of the maximal join satisfies these requirements.

1. A brief overview of the conceptual graph approach to knowledge representation

1.1 The conceptual graph

The basic concepts of the conceptual graph structure may be illustrated by an example. Figure 1 shows the graphical form of a conceptual graph for "a dog is eating a bone".

Figure 1 - a dog is eating a bone

There are a number of fundamental elements - concepts, conceptual relations and directed arcs. Conceptual relations, and their directed arcs, show the roles that the various concepts play in building up other concepts, or elements of knowledge. Concepts are represented by a label inside a rectangle, while a conceptual relation is represented by a conceptual relation label inside an ellipse. Directed arcs link relations to concepts. Concepts are not allowed to be directly linked to other concepts; similarly, relations may not be directly linked to other relations. A conceptual graph may consist of just one concept. However, since conceptual relations always have at least one arc, then there must always be at least one concept in a conceptual graph. Relations may have any pre-specified number of arcs, but generally have two. If a relation has n arcs, then by definition, the nth arc points away from the relation, while the rest point toward the relation. On the other hand, a concept may have any number of arcs pointing toward and/or away from it.

The concepts represented in figure 1 are known as "generic" concepts. In each case, no particular individual is being referenced. In order to refer to the extensions of concepts, some notation is added to the basic conceptual graph. In particular, there is a "referent field" along with the type label inside the box for a concept. While Sowa (1984, 1986) shows how to represent various kinds of "referent" we shall only be concerned here with simple referents.

To make a unique reference a "reference marker" is used - with each specific object being referred to having its own unique reference marker. The convention is that normally, each of these referent markers has the "#" sign followed by some unique number. So, in order to show a reference to a particular individual, we enter the referent in the referent field for the concept. Therefore, in a concept box we have the concept label, a colon denoting the start of the referent field, and then the referent itself. A simple example is shown in figure 2, which shows the conceptual graph for "the dog is eating the bone".

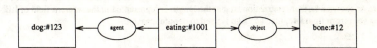

Figure 2 - The dog is eating the bone

Each of the objects dog and bone are specific objects in the world, as is also the specific eating event. In this particular example, then, we are referring to some specific dog (referent #123) and some specific bone (referent #12) taking part in some specific eating action (referent #1001).

It is often the case that we use names to refer to individuals. In a given context, this name may be unique. This allows us to use a name as a referent label to a particular object. Figure 3a shows a conceptual graph for "Spot, the dog, is eating a bone". Assuming the name to be unique, we may use the representation in figure 3b. It should be noted that one is merely invoking a shorthand version - one can always go in reverse from 3b to 3a. Furthermore, when using a name as a referent the "#" sign is not used - the letter string on its own is used. When a name is explicitly inserted into its own concept box, the letter string is enclosed in quotes. This is necessary since we wish to differentiate between a letter string which is used as a type label for a concept, and a letter string which is used as a name. It is possible that the same letter string could be used as a type label and as a name. Enclosing the letter string in quotes when it is used as a name avoids the ambiguity.

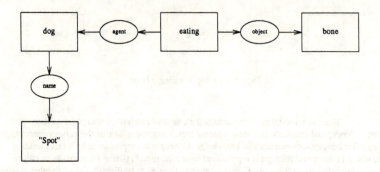

Figure 3a - Spot, the dog, is eating a bone

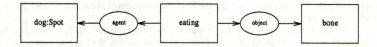

Figure 3b - Spot, the dog, is eating a bone

The notation for referring to the extensions of concepts can be extended further. Consider the concept of "a bar of length 24 cms". While this may refer to any number of bars, in some sense it can be regarded as a sort of "in between" concept - i.e. it is not just a bar, nor is it a particular bar. Sowa has extended the notation for naming to allow reference to these kinds of entities. Figure 4a shows the full representation of "a bar of length 24 cms.". Figures 4b and 4c show the corresponding shorthand notations. Figure 4b shows the effect of using the name from Figure 4a in the referent field of MEASURE in Figure 4b. Figure 4c shows a further contraction so that the length is represented in the referent field of LENGTH. As can be seen from figure 4c, the "@" sign is used to denote measure.

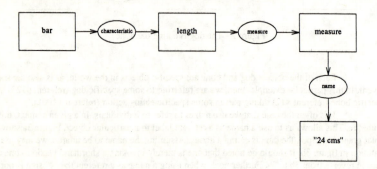

Figure 4a - a bar of length 24 cms (full representation)

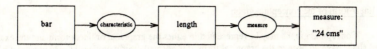

Figure 4b - a bar of length 24 cms (shorter representation)

Figure 4c - a bar of length 24 cms (shortest representation)

1.2 Knowledge structures in the CGKRL

The full CGKRL allows for various kinds of knowledge structures - meaning that different kinds of knowledge can be encoded in different ways. Briefly, these are:

1. type definitions — A concept may be defined in terms of necessary and sufficient conditions. A type definition is a conceptual graph which represents this kind of information.

2. prototype — Generally, we have some notion of what a typical object is like. For example, a typical bird may be a bit like, but not quite like a robin. A prototype for a concept is again a conceptual graph. However, it represents default information about a typical entity of that type.

3. schema — Wittengstein observed that it was not always possible to give Aristotelian definitions of concepts. For example, the only way we can understand the concept of a game is to be aware of the different ways in which we talk about games. In this case, the concept of a game involves a set of schema representing each of the different aspects about games - each schema being represented by a conceptual graph.

4. individuals — Any KRL will need to represent information about particular individuals. In the CGKRL this is a conceptual graph which is an aggregate of all the associated information about the given individual. It is a kind of "record" of some particular entity in the world.

5. canonical graphs — Most would agree that the sentence "green ideas sleep furiously" is semantically anomalous. Therefore, in a KRL there needs to be some way of "disallowing" such concepts. Canonical graphs are graphs which show which concepts may be related to which other concepts by various relations. Therefore, to rule out this example, there would be no canonical graph which had IDEA as an AGENT of SLEEP, etc.

6. propositions — The category of propositions is essentially the category which represents knowledge which allows the system to perform valid inferences. It is therefore a means of representing the set of rules which apply in a given knowledge system.

1.3 The linear form of the conceptual graph

Conceptual graphs may be represented in either the graphical or linear form and the examples presented so far have all been in the graphical form. It is normally fairly obvious how to construct a linear form from the graphical form, although some additional notation is required. The basic approach can be illustrated with the concept "Spot, the dog, is eating a bone":

    [dog] -
       (name) → ["Spot"]
       (agnt) ← [eating] → (obj) → [bone].

or, in shorthand form:

    [dog: Spot] ← (agnt) ← [eating] → (obj) → [bone].

If a conceptual graph has cycles, as in "a man is looking at his foot", then variables need to introduced to show specific links:

    [man: *x] ← (agnt) ← [look] → (obj) → [foot] → (partof) → [man: *x].

Finally, graphs which reference other graphs and include co-reference links such as "John sees a hammer with which, he believes, Fred hits Mary", have the following form:

    [John] -
       (agnt) ← [see] -
                    (obj) → [hammer:*x],
       (agnt) ← [believe] -
                    (obj) → [proposition: [Fred] -
                             (agnt) ← [hit] -
                                    (obj) → [Mary]
                                    (inst) → [hammer:*x]].

2. The hierarchical organisation of knowledge

2.1 The type hierarchy

Consider the concept of a bird - a bird is a type of animal. Similarly, the concept human is also a type of animal. This is hierarchical knowledge. The importance of hierarchical organisation of knowledge has been discussed, amongst others, by Woods (1986).

In order to represent type hierarchy information, a set of type labels are defined. In fact, they are the labels which appear inside the boxes and ellipses which represent concepts and conceptual relations. In order to represent the hierarchical information, we define what is known as a "partial ordering". Specifically, if we know that a human is a type of animal, then we write the following:

HUMAN < ANIMAL

Similarly, since we know that bird is a type of animal, we write:

BIRD < ANIMAL

The "<" symbol is therefore used to represent the fact that some concept is an example of a subcategory of another concept. It is an ordering since we know that human is a subcategory of animal, but not vice versa. The "<" symbol represents this information. It is a partial ordering, since for some concepts we cannot write the "<" symbol between them. For example, there is no ordering between HUMAN and BIRD; HUMAN is not an example of a subcategory of BIRD, and vice versa.

The set of type labels, and the partial ordering that exists between them is known as the type hierarchy. Also, we call the type HUMAN a "subtype" of ANIMAL, and the type ANIMAL a "supertype" of HUMAN, since HUMAN < ANIMAL.

2.2 A type hierarchy reduces the search space during inference

A type hierarchy reduces the number of rules that need be explicitly represented in a knowledge based system - and therefore reduces the search space in any inference process. This can be seen by considering some fairly simple examples.

Suppose we have in our system the fact that human beings, dogs and monkeys are mammals, robins, pidgeons and eagles are birds, and mammals and birds are animals. Suppose further that represented in the system is the fact that all animals breathe oxygen. In the Peano-Russell notation we would represent these facts/rules as:

$\forall x$ HUMAN_BEING(x) $\Rightarrow$ MAMMAL(x)
$\forall x$ DOG(x) $\Rightarrow$ MAMMAL(x)
$\forall x$ MONKEY(x) $\Rightarrow$ MAMMAL(x)
$\forall x$ ROBIN(x) $\Rightarrow$ BIRD(x)
$\forall x$ PIDGEON(x) $\Rightarrow$ BIRD(x)
$\forall x$ EAGLE(x) $\Rightarrow$ BIRD(x)
$\forall x$ MAMMAL(x) $\Rightarrow$ ANIMAL(x)
$\forall x$ BIRD(x) $\Rightarrow$ ANIMAL(x)
$\forall x$ ANIMAL(x) $\Rightarrow$ $\exists y,z$ ANIMAL(x)$\wedge$BREATHE(y)$\wedge$OXYGEN(z)$\wedge$AGENT(x,y)$\wedge$OBJECT(y,z)

On the other hand, in the CGKRL this would be represented as:

HUMAN_BEING < MAMMAL, DOG < MAMMAL, MONKEY < MAMMAL
ROBIN < BIRD, PIDGEON < BIRD, EAGLE < BIRD
MAMMAL < ANIMAL, BIRD < ANIMAL

if
[ANIMAL:*x]
then
[ANIMAL:*x] <- (AGENT) <- [BREATHE] -> (OBJECT) -> [OXYGEN].

In Peano-Russell notation inference would involve a search space of nine "rules" - in the CGKRL, the equivalent search spaces consists of just one rule, plus a type hierarchy.

We do not gain anything in terms of what inferences can be drawn - we have only reduced the potential search space. With large type hierarchies this saving in search space is likely to be very significant.

Of course, the point needs to be made that, although the search space has been reduced, we need to show that the operations used to perform inference are efficient. There are two elements to this. First, there is a type hierarchy. Second, we necessarily require a more complicated matching operation than is required for the "flat" organisation of knowledge - a matching operation which takes into account the type hierarchy. It is relatively straightforward to set up an efficient encoding of the type hierarchy. However, defining a good algorithm for the matching process is more difficult, though not impossible.

3. Deriving graphs from other graphs - a partial ordering for conceptual graphs

Sowa (1984) defined a number of operations for deriving graphs from other graphs. These operations are important since they define a "partial-ordering" for conceptual graphs. A partial-ordering is related to the notion of "truth maintainence", "specialisation" and "generalisation". Given graphs g1 and g2 such that g2<g1, then g2 will correspond to a more specialised situation in the world than g1. (This is generally true - but there is one important exception which is discussed below). Conversely, g1 will correspond to a more general situation in the world than g2. In other words, whenever g2 is true, then so will be g1 - but the converse is not necessarily the case.

The partial ordering is fundamental in the CGKRL system since it underlies the definition of the matching operation for graphs. In fact, in any type hierarchy language, one will always need to define a partial ordering for that language before one can define the matching operation for the inference process.

The partial ordering is defined in terms of a set of "canonical formation rules", and these are as follows:-

copy   a graph g2 may be an exact copy of a graph g1

restrict   for any concept c in a graph g1, type(c) may be replaced by a subtype; if c is generic, its referent may be changed to an individual marker. These changes are permitted only if referent(c) conforms to type(c) before and after the change.

join   if a concept c in a graph g1 is identical to a concept d in a graph g2, then a graph g3 may be obtained by deleting d and linking to c all the arcs of conceptual relations that had been linked to d.

simplify   if conceptual relations r and s in a graph g1 are duplicates, then one of them may be deleted from g1 together with all of its arcs.

Given the set of canonical formation rules, we can say that if a graph g2 is derivable from a graph g1 by the application of any of the rules, then g2 is a specialisation of g1 - conversely, g1 is a generalisation of g2. We write g2≤g1. (According to Sowa (1984), we should only be able to write g2=g1 when g2 has been derived from g1 by the application of the copy rule. But, it should be noted that the canonical formation rules, as stated, have a "bug". The rules are such that given a graph g1 it is possible to derive g2, and given g2 it is then possible to derive g1 - and this is possible without using the copy operation. Given that we require a partial ordering for graphs to be related to truth maintainence, this would create havoc for any matching operation in the inference process. However, since this problem is easily corrected it will not concern us here).

It was stated that for two graphs g1 and g2, if g2<g1 then g2 generally corresponds to a more specialised situation than g1 - i.e. g1 may be true when g2 is not true. There is one important exception to this. Suppose we have a type hierarchy with PERSON < INTELLIGENT-ENTITY, and PERSON < ANIMAL. Suppose further that we know [person:#100] is valid - i.e. there is an individual #100 who is a person. Then for the following graphs:

g1   [animal:#100] <- (agent) <- [eat] -> (object) -> [food].

g2   [intelligent-entity:#100] <- (agent) <- [eat] -> (object) -> [food].

g3   [person:#100] <- (agent) <- [eat] -> (object) -> [food].

we have g3 < g2 and g3 < g1. Nevertheless, the three graphs have exactly the same truth status. This is simply because #100, being a person, is also necessarily an intelligent-entity (in this system) and an animal.

A matching operation for a type hierarchy language will take advantage of the fact that graphs may have the same truth status even though one is a "specialisation" of the other.

4. The maximal join operation

The maximal join attempts to join graphs on "common parts". In the CGKRL the "common parts" of two graphs are formally defined as the (least) common generalisations of the two graphs.

In the following example, the letter "r" will be used to denote relations, and "c" to denote concepts. Suppose we have the following type hierarchy:

$c^1_1 \cap c^2_1 = c_1, c^1_1 < c^0_1, c^2_1 < c^0_1$
$c^1_2 \cap c^2_2 = c_2, c^1_2 < c^0_2, c^2_2 < c^0_2$
$c^1_3 \cap c^2_3 = c_3, c^1_3 < c^0_3, c^2_3 < c^0_3$

and we wish to join the following graphs:

g1.a $[c^1_1] -> (r1) -> [c^1_2] -> (r2) -> [c^1_3]$.

g1.b $[c^2_1] -> (r1) -> [c^2_2] -> (r3) -> [c^2_3]$.

Then the generalisations of these two graphs are:

g0.1 $[c^0_1]$ -> (r1) -> $[c^0_2]$.

g0.2 $[c^0_3]$.

as shown by using the canonical formation rules. It can also be shown that there are no specialisations of g0.1 and g0.2 which are still generalisations of both g1.a and g1.b. The following two graphs are then the only two maximal joins of g1.a and g1.b:

g2.a $[c_1]$ -> (r1) -> $[c_2]$ -
                              (r2) -> $[c^1_3]$
                              (r3) -> $[c^2_3]$.

g2.b $[c_3]$ -
                    (r2) <- $[c^1_1]$ <- (r1) <- $[c^1_2]$
                    (r3) <- $[c^2_1]$ <- (r1) <- $[c^2_2]$.

It can be seen that a maximal join does not join on everything that it is possible to join since the following graph, which is the result of such a process, is not a maximal join:

      $[c_3]$ -
                    (r2) <- $[c_2:*x]$
                    (r3) <- $[c_2:*x]$ <- (r1) <- $[c_1]$.

Furthermore, a maximal join need not be a graph which is merely a greatest common specialisation of two graphs since the following is also not a maximal join:

      $[c_1]$ -
                    (r1) -> $[c^1_2]$ -> (r3) -> $[c^1_3]$
                    (r1) -> $[c^2_2]$ -> (r2) -> $[c^2_3]$.

This example shows, then, that the maximal join produces graphs which are not as specialised as they could be (i.e. everything joined), nor are they as general as they could be (i.e. joining on just a single concept). (If the two graphs had the same number of concepts and relations, and everything possible that could be joined was joined, then we would have a variation of unification). Formal definitions for the maximal join are given in Sowa (1984).

5. A matching operation for inference using conceptual graphs

5.1 Requirements for a matching operation

In order to perform inference it is necessary to have a matching operation - this is true of any language. For languages with a type hierarchy the notion of a partial ordering is very important and forms a guide for the matching operation. There are a number of ways in which the matching operation can be developed but we shall consider a method based on that of Fargues et al. (1976) and Rao and Foo (1987). While this was developed in the context of conceptual graphs it should be noted that the method applies to any typed language where a partial ordering on the expressions of the language has been defined.

Suppose g1 and g2 are two expressions in the language (in this case conceptual graphs) which represent some facts about the world. Furthermore, suppose that g2 represents either a goal in some inference process or, equivalently an antecedent of some rule. Suppose further that g1 represents some consequent of a rule or, equivalently, some fact against which we wish to match g2. Since g1 and g2 are generally different graphs, we will need to find a g3 which is the result of the match of g1 and g2. The partial ordering now becomes important. Now, g2 will always be true when some specialisation of g2 is true, so the match g3 will be such that g3 ≤ g2. Furthermore, since g1 will in turn be matched with other expressions, then we require g3 ≤ g1. However, while we wish to derive a g3 such that g3 < g1, we do not want the truth status of these two graphs to be different. The reason for this is straightforward. Given that g1 may be a fact, and that g3 refers to a more "specialised" situation, then if g3 has a different truth status it may not actually be true in the given facts available to the system. On the other hand, if the truth status of g3 is the same as that of g1, then g3 will always be true when g1 is true.

Therefore, the important question is: how do we ensure that the matching operation gives a g3 which has the same truth status as g1?

Observe that if we replace any type in g1 with subtypes such that the referents in the subtypes are the same as the referents in the types they have replaced, then we have not altered the truth value of g1. This was shown earlier. For example, with the graphs:

g1   [animal:#24] -> (attribute) -> [feathers].
g2   [bird:#24] -> (attribute) -> [feathers].

g2 will be true, if g1 is true, so long as #24 is actually an individual of type bird. (Replacing types with no specific referents with subtypes is more tricky - however, the same general principle holds).

This suggests that one way of ensuring that g3 has the same truth status as g1 is to require that g3 is derived from g1 by replacing types of g1 with subtypes.

One way of producing this result is to insist that every concept and relation of g2 matches a concept and relation of g1 (but not necessarily vice versa). In the CGKRL the matching operation involves replacing a matching pair of concepts with their maximal common subtype. (Relations are not typed in the present form of the CGKRL). Hence, it follows that g3 must necessarily have the same truth status as g1 - which is what we require.

One final point should be noted. The expression g3 is such that there is no other expression g3´ such that g3 < g3´. In other words, it is the most general expression in which all the subcomponents of one expression have been matched with subcomponents of another expression. Since g3 < g2 and g2 may be true when g3 is false, then making g3 the most general such expression will mean that this will occur the minimum of times. So, in finding a successful match, the inference process will maximize the chances of proving the goal.

5.2 The role of the maximal join in inference

The role of the maximal join in inference can be illustrated with a very simple example. Consider the following set of graphs:

Fact   [person:#100] -

                        (status) -> [hungry]
                        (attribute) -> [thin].

Rule   if:
        [intelligent-entity:*x] -> (status) -> [hungry].
        then
        [intelligent-entity:*x] <- (agent) <- [seek] -> (object) -> [food] -> (attribute) -> [quantity:@ large].

Goal   [animal:#100] <- (agent) <- [seek] -> (object) -> [food].

Suppose we further have that:
        PERSON < MAMMAL
        PERSON < ANIMAL
        PERSON < INTELLIGENT-ENTITY

The goal is equivalent to asking whether the animal, which is the individual #100, will seek food. In order to find out whether this is true, we need to match the goal with the consequent of the rule. The matching operation we use in this case is a restricted form of the maximal join in which the whole of the conceptual graph corresponding to the goal is matched with some part of the consequent of the rule. If we do the restricted form of the maximal join we get the graph:

        [person:#100] <- (agent) <- [seek] -> (object) -> [food] -> (attribute) -> [quantity:@ large].

since PERSON is the maximal common subtype of INTELLIGENT-ENTITY and ANIMAL. We now attempt to match the antecedent of the rule with the only fact. However, the antecedent and the consequent share a concept which is linked by a co-referent link. So, the actual graph we need to match is:

[person:#100] -> (status) -> [hungry].

We now find the maximal join of this graph with the only fact in the system and get:

[person:#100] -

(status) -> [hungry]
(attribute) -> [thin].

Hence, we can conclude that the goal is satisfied.

While this example is very trivial the importance of the whole process should not be over-looked. In any real application there will be a large number of rules and facts. By using a type hierarchy, the number of rules and facts will be kept at a minimum. Therefore, in searching rules and facts for poten-tial matches, the search space will be considerably reduced. This reduction in search space will be be mag-nified since every time a match is found, the rules and facts have to be searched again for the next match.

6. Concluding remarks

It has been shown how the CGKRL, in having an explicit type hierarchy, results in a smaller search space in any inference process. However, the expressions in such a language require a special matching operation for the inference process. A matching operation based on the maximal join, and which can fulfill this requirement has been described.

References

Fargues, J. et al. (1986) Conceptual graphs for semantics and knowledge processing. IBM Journal of Research and Development, 30, 70-79.

Rao, A. S. and Foo, N. Y. (1987) Congres: Conceptual graph reasoning system. Proceedings of IEEE, 87-92.

Sowa, J. (1984) Conceptual Structures: Information processing in mind and machine, Addison-Wesley, Reading, Mass..

Sowa, J. F. (1986) Notes on conceptual graphs.

Woods, W. A. (1986) "Important issues in knowledge representation," Proceedings of the IEEE, vol. 74, pp. 1322-1334.

A THEORY OF FUZZY FRAMES

Ian Graham
Logica Financial Systems Ltd.,
64 Newman Street,
London W1A 4SE

Peter Llewelyn Jones
Creative Logic Ltd.,
Brunel Science Park, Kingston Lane,
Uxbridge, Middx UB8 3PQ.

Abstract

The theory of Fuzzy Frames is developed with examples. It is related to existing notions in knowledge representation and fuzzy mathematics, and a number of applications are suggested.

1. Introduction

In this paper we introduce a new computational method of representing uncertain and certain knowledge which we have developed as a generalisation of the frame notion introduced by Minsky [8]. Since our generalisation uses, in an intrinsic way, the theory of fuzzy sets due to Zadeh [15], it is natural that we choose to designate our generalised objects 'fuzzy frames'. We hope, in this paper, to lay the basis for the future development of the theory of fuzzy frames, and to show how they may be applied in knowledge engineering applications.

To begin with we review briefly the existing theory of frames (variously called 'schema', 'units', or 'scripts' in the literature [1,3,4,8,11,18,19]) and the, perhaps less familiar, machinery we require from fuzzy set theory. In the sequel to this paper [21] we explore some of the intriguing questions which our theory raises, some of its problems and suggest topics for further research. In doing this we have cause to compare our approach with the fuzzy quantifiers of Zadeh [16,3,5], truth maintenance systems and nonmonotonic logic [7,10]. We suggest that Fuzzy Frames offer a unified framework for the representation of both certain and uncertain knowledge about objects, and, in a sense to be explained, generalise fuzzy relations and *a fortiori* relations.

2. Representing knowledge about objects

In terms of knowledge engineering, there are many ways to represent knowledge; as productions, by logic, in procedures, etc. These formalisms are usually better at expressing particularly suitable types of knowledge; about causality, relationships, methods, etc. See [2,3] for a more complete treatment. The forms of knowledge representation which seem to best capture knowledge about objects and their properties are those which are generally referred to as semantic networks and frames. In this paper we concentrate on these. Often such knowledge is uncertain, and usually some additional mechanism has to be introduced to model the uncertainty. This can be done by assigning certainty factors or probabilities to the rules or their atomic clauses, or through the use of some truth maintenance procedure, depending on the type of uncertainty involved. Here we concentrate of the kinds of uncertainty which can be readily modelled with fuzzy sets, but, in principle, our arguments should apply to stochastic problems equally well.

2.1 Semantic Networks and Frames

A semantic network consists of a set of nodes and a set of ordered pairs of nodes called 'links', together with an interpretation of the meaning of these (See [14]). In the terminology of Winston [13] we will restrict ourselves to describing this interpretation using a *descriptive semantics*; that is, a set of

statements describing the interpretation. Terminal links are called 'slots' if
they represent properties (predicates) rather than objects or classes of objects.
A *frame* is a semantic net representing an object (or a stereotype of that
object) or a class of objects, and will consist of a number of slots and a
number of outbound links. Consider, for clarification, the frame for a toy brick
shown in figure 2.1 in the form of a network. It may also be represented in a
tabular form as follows.

> <u>Brick-12</u>
> IsA: Brick, Toy
> Colour: Red

A collection of frames forming a semantic network will be referred to in
this paper as a 'framebase'. In the above example, there are implicitly frames
for Brick and Toy.

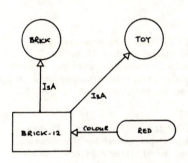

Figure 2.1: A Semantic Network

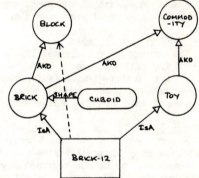

Figure 2.2: Inheritance of Properties

Figure 2.2 illustrates the inheritance of properties into slots as shown
also in the form of frames below.

> <u>Brick</u>   <u>Toy</u>
> IsA: Block, Commodity   IsA: Commodity
> Shape: Cuboid

Frames can inherit properties through IsA links, so that Brick-12 inherits the
Shape slot's value from Brick in this case, as well as those properties of toys,
commodities and blocks which offer no contradiction. Some authors, including
Winston, make a distinction between IsA links, which connect individuals to
classes, and AKO (a kind of) links, which connect classes. This has relevance for
attempts to reduce frame systems to first order logic, such as found in Hayes
[4], but need not concern us here. We follow the tradition of FRL [11] and use
IsA to stand for both. In any case, Touretzky [12] has argued that such attempts
founder when the frame systems permit multiple inheritance (see below).

2.2 Property Inheritance

Inheritance of the type described provides computer systems with a method
of reasoning with implicit facts. Various frame based languages have been
implimented; FRL, KRL [11,1,19]. Most of these systems however suffer from
various problems. They usually have no formal semantics, they are not good at
reasoning about exceptions (nonmonotonic logic) [12,7,10] and they cannot handle
partial inheritance, either in the sense of partially inheriting a property or of
inheriting a combination of partially true properties. Other authors have,
discussed partial inheritance, but from a different point of view. An example is
[6]. The programme begun with this paper aims to remedy all these defects
within a single unified framework and, additionally, unite the theory with the
relational model of data.

Touretzky [12] points out that nonmonotonic or default logics, while possessing a formal semantics, are hopelessly general for practical purposes because they do not have the facility of inheritance systems to reason with implicit data.

We assert here a sort of duality between logics that add extra operators, such as L and N in modal logics and M in nonmonotonic logics, and those that expand the truth space, such as many valued, fuzzy and probability logics. An example of the latter, which we exploit in this paper, is fuzzy logic with Zadeh's fuzzy quantification given the Σ-Count interpretation of his test-score semantics [16,5]. We will show informally later how the mechanisms of Fuzzy Frames can be used to model this logic and compare this approach with that of nonmonotonic logic.

A certain amount of the machinery of fuzzy logic will be required, and we introduce this as briefly as possible.

3. Basic Fuzzy Set Concepts

The concept of a fuzzy set is due to Zadeh [15] and involves the relaxation of the restriction on a set's characteristic function that it be two valued. This section gives a fast summary of the techniques of fuzzy set theory which we require later in this paper. This is merely to fix terminology, and is not intended as a tutorial. Fuller explanations can be obtained from [3] or [5].

3.1 Fuzzy Sets

A fuzzy set is a function λ whose codomain is the unit interval. It may be interpreted as a linguistic value over the variable represented by the domain. For example, if the domain represents wealth (over an arbitrary interval scale) we can introduce fuzzy sets to stand for the imprecise linguistic terms 'rich', 'comfortable' and 'poor' as illustrated in the diagram in Figure 3.1. Fuzzy sets are conveniently represented pictorially in this way. They may also be represented as vectors of truth values.

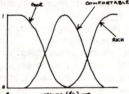

Figure 3.1: Some Fuzzy Sets

There are several fuzzy logics. In the standard one which we adopt here the operations of the propositional calculus are defined for fuzzy predicates as follows.

$$\lambda \text{ AND } v = \min(\lambda,v)$$
$$\lambda \text{ OR } v = \max(\lambda,v)$$
$$\text{NOT } \lambda = 1 - \lambda$$

Implication is then defined in the usual way, by $(\lambda \Rightarrow v) = (\text{NOT } \lambda) \text{ OR } v$.

Given a term set of permissible linguistic values, it is possible to extend it using the propositional operators and operations known as hedges. As an example the hedge 'very' is often defined by:

$$\text{VERY } \lambda = \lambda^2$$

Thus, expressions such as 'very rich or not very poor' receive an interpretation as a fuzzy set. This has evident utility in knowledge representation, and this is explored in many other works (cf. [3]).

3.2 Rules of Inference

Given these basic definitions it is possible to approach the problem of representing inexact inferences with fuzzy sets. The two kinds of statements we

wish to use are assertions of the form 'X is A' and rules of the form 'If X is
[not] A [and/or X' is ...] then Y is B'. X, X' and Y stand for objects and A and B
stand for fuzzy sets. Simple syllogisms such as

    X is A
    <u>If X is A then Y is B</u>
    Y is B

are handled as follows. The extension in the cartesian product of all linguistic
variables appearing as assertions is computed and the intersection E taken. This
fuzzy set is interpreted as an elastic constraint on the solution. Next, taking
each consequent clause separately, the maximum value of E is used to determine
the truth of the antecedent, so that the fuzzy set B is effectively truncated at
this level. The resultant, truncated fuzzy set is the value of Y. When
generalised, this method is known as the compositional rule of inference. This
rule will be used in this paper, although others have been suggested.

3.3 Defuzzification

    In case it is not convenient to work with fuzzy sets as output values, the
result may be 'defuzzified' to return a scalar value. There are a number of ways
this can be accomplished. We will need to know about two. The 'mean of maxima'
(or maximum) method involves returning the scalar in the domain of the
resultant fuzzy set which is the arithmetic mean of its maxima. The 'centre of
moments' (or moments) method returns the average of all domain values weighted
by their truth in the output fuzzy set. The appropriateness of these methods in
different applications is discussed extensively in [3].

    If a fuzzy set is required as output but some regularity in its form is
desirable, then a method known as linguistic approximation may be invoked. This
involves the predefinition of an allowed 'term set' of fuzzy sets over the
domain. In the case of fuzzy numbers (fuzzy subsets of the real line) an
example term set might be {tiny,small,medium,large,huge}. The term set may be
extended by fuzzy set operations (e.g. to include 'not very small'). Linguistic
approximation returns the term 'closest' to the resultant fuzzy set, according to
some stated measure of distance.

3.4 Fuzzy Quantifiers

    Fuzzy quantifiers are represented by words such as 'most', 'almost all',
'some' and so on, as opposed to the crisp quantifiers 'for all' and 'there
exists'. They often occur implicitly in natural language. Thus, 'birds fly' may be
interpreted as 'most birds can fly'. Zadeh [16] introduces rules of inference and
a formal semantics for such statements. His test-score semantics interprets
quantifiers as elastic constraints on a family of fuzzy relations, which are
regarded as entities. This structure is viewed as a test which scores according
to the compatibility of the quantifier with the objects in the world (the
database). A typical rule of inference for this system is

    Q_1 A are B
    <u>Q_2 (A and B) are C</u>
    $Q_1 * Q_2$ A are (B and C)

where the Q's are fuzzy quantifiers, interpreted as fuzzy numbers, and $*$ stands
for the product of fuzzy numbers. For example this justifies the syllogism:

    Most (about 90%) birds can fly
    <u>Most (about 90%) flying birds have feathers</u>
    At least many (about 81%) birds have feathers

Of course there are other rules of inference. The exact meaning of the test
scores depends on the measure used for the cardinality of a fuzzy set. The
usual one is the Σ-count measure, which is to say the arithmetic sum of the
grades of membership (the integral in the continuous case). More details may be
found in [5].

This completes the presentation of the minimal set of concepts from fuzzy set theory which we shall require in this paper.

4. Fuzzy Frames

We now come to the main new results of this paper. First, we extend the notion of a frame to that of a fuzzy frame in two ways. First, by allowing slots to contain fuzzy sets as values, in addition to text, list and numeric variables. Second, we allow inheritance through IsA slots to be partial. Later we will generalise in a third dimension by allowing frames to contain more than one 'tuple', or set of slot values, to facilitate the representation of possible worlds or time-variant objects. To explain the advantages and mechanics of fuzzy frames it is preferable to use an example, rather than to develop the formal mathematics. In doing so we will introduce a syntax similar to that used in Leonardo III [18].

Consider the following (toy) problem. You are faced with the problem of estimating the safety implications following on the purchase of various leisure items. Frames give us a way of representing knowledge about and data concerning objects or concepts. The most natural way to analyse (remembering that we are thinking of building a computerised advisor here) the problem is to list the objects involved. Suppose they include a dinghy and a hang-glider among a number of others. These objects are types of more general objects, and have associated with them various properties. Figure 4.1 shows how we can represent our knowledge about some objects interesting in this context using fuzzy frames. We will now consider nine of these frames, in each case annotating them with explanation of the syntactic convention, on the way to a solution of the problem.

Notice in the figure, incidentally, the syntactic provision for defaults and backward chaining demons (IfNeeded procedures). Forward chaining demons would be dealt with similarly.

First, consider the most general concept of a commodity. Our general knowledge about commodities can be summarised in the following structure.

```
F1   Commodity
     IsA         :Object
     Uses        :undefined [list]
     Owner       :undefined [text]
     Cost        :undefined [fuzz]
     Necessity   :undefined [fuzz]
     Utility     :high [fuzz]
     Safety      :high [fuzz]
```

Here the IsA slot points to another frame, in this case the most general one possible. Commodity is a fuzzy frame in two respects. First, the degree of property inheritance from the frame(s) in the IsA slot may be specified as a number between 0 and 1 in square brackets after the name. In this case no value is given and the default value of [1.00] is assumed. Secondly, the other slots may contain fuzzy sets (vectors of truth values) as values. The bracketed expressions indicate the type of the value; either [fuzz], [real], [list] or [text]. The fuzzy sets used in the Commodity frame may be represented as follows:

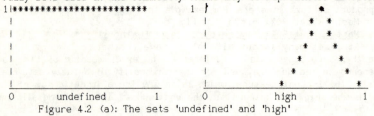

Figure 4.2 (a): The sets 'undefined' and 'high'

```
F1    Commodity
      IsA        :Object
      Uses       :undefined [list]            FIGURE 4.1
      Owner      :undefined [text]         Some Fuzzy Frames
      Cost       :undefined [fuzz]
      Necessity  :undefined [fuzz]
      Utility    :high [fuzz]
      Safety     :high [fuzz]


F2    Vehicle              F3   Toy
      IsA        :Commodity      IsA         :Commodity
      Uses       :(travel,pleasure)  Uses    :(pleasure)
      Keeper     :undefined [text]  Keeper    :child
      Necessity  :high            Necessity  :low
      Safety     :high            Safety     :undefined [fuzz]
      Utility    :high            Utility    :high
      Cost       :high            Cost       :low


F4    Borrowed-object             F5   Dangerous-object
      IsA        :Object               IsA        :Object
      Lender     :undefined [text]     Safety     :minimal
      Keeper     :undefined [text];default=finder
      Cost       :mimimal [fuzz]


F6    Dinghy                      F7   Hang-glider
      IsA        :Vehicle [0.4],       IsA        :Vehicle [0.05],
                  Toy [0.6],                       Toy [0.7],
                  Dangerous object [0.1]           Dangerous object [0.9]
      Safety     :undefined          Safety :undefined
      Cost       :undefined          Cost   :undefined
      Draught    :3 [real];IfNeeded=depth-calc


F8    Car                         F9   Toy-car
      IsA        :Vehicle [0.9],       IsA        :Vehicle [0.3],
                  Toy [0.6],                       Toy [0.9]
                  Dangerous object [0.1]  Cost     :undefined
      Safety     :undefined          Safety :undefined
      Cost       :undefined


F10   Book                        F11  Magazine
      IsA        :Dangerous-object,    IsA        :Book [0.5],
                  Toy [0.6]                        Toy [0.3],
      Cost       :undefined                        Borrowed object [0.5]
      Safety     :undefined          Safety :undefined
                                     Cost   :undefined


F12   Dinghy-123                  F13  Hang-glider-765
      IsA        :Dinghy             IsA        :Hang-glider,
      Draught    :undefined                      Borrowed object
      Safety     :undefined          Safety :undefined
      Cost       :undefined          Cost   :undefined
```

Now for some slightly less general fuzzy frames representing specific types of commodity.

```
F2    Vehicle                    F3    Toy
      IsA       :Commodity             IsA       :Commodity
      Uses      :(travel,pleasure)     Uses      :(pleasure)
      Keeper    :undefined [text]      Keeper    :child
      Necessity :high                  Necessity :low
      Safety    :high                  Safety    :undefined [fuzz]
      Utility   :high                  Utility   :high
      Cost      :high                  Cost      :low
```

The Toy frame will inherit the value 'high' for Safety, since the slot contains 'undefined'; the uniform fuzzy set on the interval scale. The other slots are unaltered. Inheritance occurs based on the immediately superior frame only and then only when the 'child' has an undefined value. In certain applications, such as database ones, it may be preferable to allow inheritance into even those slots which contain defined values. In such a case the inheritance mechanism is modified in such a way that the intersection (minimum) of the fuzzy sets in the parent and child is taken. This corresponds to what we choose to designate the *Fuzzy Closed World Assumption*. That is, if the values assigned to slots represent immutable knowledge about the state of the world and the constraints it imposes, we would not wish to permit a contradictory reassignment that ignored the influence of the value in a parent. The distinction between the two control strategies is analogous to the one between rules and assertions in fuzzy production systems (see Graham & Jones Chapter 6 [3]).

Two more frames representing general classes of objects must now be discussed. They are:

```
F4    Borrowed-object            F5    Dangerous-object
      IsA       :Object                IsA       :Object
      Lender    :undefined [text]      Safety    :minimal
      Keeper    :undefined [text]
      Cost      :minimal
```

Here we may wish to consider the sad possibility that a borrowed object, such as a book, may pass from *meum* to *tuum* without the transition being too noticable. Thus, in the case of the borrowed magazine in frame F11, only 0.5 of the ownership properties of F4 may be inherited. In particular, the inheritance mechanism attaches a 0.5 certainty factor to the Lender and Keeper values (if they are known) The mechanism for fuzzy slots is that the fuzzy sets (minimal in this case) are truncated at the 0.5 level. Returning to the mainstream of our argument, two new fuzzy sets have been introduced, so we give their definition pictorially, as before.

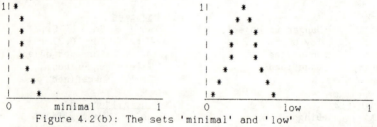

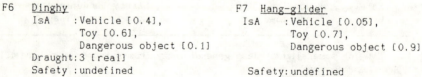

Figure 4.2(b): The sets 'minimal' and 'low'

```
F6    Dinghy                           F7    Hang-glider
      IsA    :Vehicle [0.4],                 IsA    :Vehicle [0.05],
              Toy [0.6],                             Toy [0.7],
              Dangerous object [0.1]                 Dangerous object [0.9]
      Draught:3 [real]
      Safety :undefined                      Safety:undefined
      Cost   :undefined                      Cost  :undefined
```

Now we come to the frames describing fairly specific items in the scheme. For example, the ones shown above as F6 and F7.

We now have to understand how the undefined slots in the lowest level frames (representing individuals) for Dinghy-123 and Hang-glider-765 may be filled. Notice first that we have a non-fuzzy slot for Draught, and multiple inheritance from higher levels. Let us look at the Safety slot of Dinghy first.

Since a dinghy is a vehicle the slot inherits 'high', but as this is only true to the extent 0.4 the fuzzy set is truncated at this level. It also inherits the value 'minimal' from Dangerous-object, but only to degree 0.1. The inheritance path from Commodity via Toy gives the value 'high' in degree 0.6. These fuzzy sets are combined with the union operator as shown in Figure 4.3(b). If this were the final result of some reasoning process the resultant fuzzy set would be defuzzified (in this case with the mean-of-maxima operation) to give a truth or possibility value for the term 'safe'. Alternatively linguistic approximation could be applied to return a word corresponding to a normal, convex fuzzy set approximating the returned value. In a different application the moments defuzzification method might be applied. This is a control decision in the same category as the fuzzy closed world assumption, and, we feel, should be left to the discretion of the user or systems designer. The other diagram in Figure 4.3(b) shows the fuzzy set for the dinghy's cost. In the absence of evidence to the contrary, Dinghy-123 inherits both these values.

Cost here is being interpreted as the cost that one might be willing to bear, and thus the cost of a dinghy purchased just for fun ought, normally, to be low. The case of the safety slot of Hang-glider is a little more interesting. The diagrams in Figure 4.3(a) illustrate the text.

Here, the Safety slot inherits the union of the fuzzy set minimal from Dangerous-object [0.9] and high from both vehicle [0.05] and Commodity (via Toy) [0.7]. Applying the operation of union or disjunction to these three fuzzy sets (we of course exclude 'undefined' from this process) to represent the view that IsA attributes are *alternative* viewpoints from which the object may be viewed, we arrive at a resultant fuzzy set. Defuzzification then gives a value close to zero (or the linguistic approximation 'minimal'). Thus the system is able to deduce correctly that a hang-glider is a very dangerous toy along with the unsurprising conclusion that it doesn't cost much to borrow one in the case of Hang-glider-765.

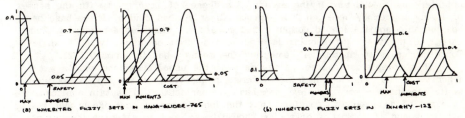

(a) INHERITED FUZZY SETS IN HANG-GLIDER-765   (b) INHERITED FUZZY SETS IN DINGHY-123

Figure 4.3: Inheritance of Fuzzy Properties

Clearly, the reason we have adopted the view that a hang-glider is only a vehicle to a small extent is that one usually thinks of a vehicle as a safe-ish means of getting from A to B and, indeed, back again. This is not independant from our assumptions about dangerous objects. This warns of a possible design problem for fuzzy framebases. However, there is a further problem. If, as is quite reasonable, a survey showed that most people actually gave a higher value, say 0.95, to the 'toyness' of a hang-glider, then the result would be quite different under the maximum rule of inference, and quite counterintuitive: Hang-gliders would be highly safe. The apparently counter-intuitive nature of this

result - which, incidentally only has noticable, serious consequences under the
moments rule - could be due to the incompleteness of our example semantic
model. We suggest a way round this problem in the sequel [21], couched in terms
of a theory of normal - or non-redundant - forms for fuzzy frames. Currently,
the topic of design criteria for fuzzy semantic models is undergoing research,
but remains only partially solved.

To put matters right temporarily, let us now explore an example which does
conform to intuition more closely than the one chosen above to explicate the
syntax and semantics.

Immortal	Mortal	Man
IsA:Category	IsA:Category	IsA:Mortal
Goodness:high		Goodness:fair
Intellect:omniscient		Intellect:average

Apollo	Lucifer	Socrates
IsA:Man[0.4],	IsA:Immortal	IsA:Man,Immortal[0.2]
Immortal[0.9]	Goodness:low	Intellect:bright
Goodness:undefined		Goodness:undefined

Philanthropist	JohnpaulgettyIII
IsA:Man,	IsA:Philanthropist
Immortal[0.1]	Goodness:undefined
Goodness:high	Fame:undefined
Fame :high	Intellect:undefined

In this case the inheritance mechanism enables us to infer that John Paul
Getty III is a nice chap who'll be remembered for quite a while, because philan-
thropists are usually famous. Apollo, on the other hand, inherits average
intelligence as the epitomy of manliness and omniscience from his godliness. We
know from our Homer that Apollo was in fact only wise on occasion, and this is
reflected in the returned fuzzy set for his intellect, whose linguistic approximation is something like 'bright' if we use the moments rule. Apollo's goodness
is also reduced by his manliness. In the absence of a richer structure or, in
other words, more knowledge and information, we can only deduce average intelligence for John Paul Getty III, although he might be remembered by posterity as
brighter due to the magnifying effect of a degree of immortality (in the sense
of living in memory here) on intelligence. Clearly, this kind of frame base has
considerable application to computerised models of commonsense reasoning. Zadeh
refers to the type of reasoning implied here as that of 'usuality' [17], while
Touretzky calls it 'normative' reasoning (he means 'what is normal') [12].

This example, of course, raises many of the usual questions about
inheritance that we find in crisp systems. In addition, we are led to ask what
would happen in a more complex framebase. In particular, in certain applications
it might be necessary to consider that the inheritance of god-like properties by
offspring and offspring of offspring should be subject to attentuation but not
to complete exception (e.g. Leda, Europa, etc.). In that case we would want to
invoke the fuzzy closed world assumption. A classical example of this assumption
may be found in the Book of Common Prayer: '... visit the sins of the fathers
upon the children unto the third and fourth generation'. The other question
raised here, as compared with the previous example, is the evident comparability
of the categories represented by the IsA links. This suggests that well designed
framebases should evince this property. We have more to say on the soundness of
designs in [21].

For some reason it is apparent that the moments method of defuzzification
is the more appropriate one in the example deductions we have discused here.
This is because we were dealing with the usuality of properties which are

subject to combination in reaching a 'balanced view', rather than ones which
contribute to either/or decision making. There could be problems if we had mixed
objectives in our use of the framebase. We would at least have to type the IsA
links were the two strategies to be required over the same framebase.

We have thus presented, via a couple of very simple examples, the basic
theory of fuzzy frames and explained its logic of inheritance. We now justify
our efforts by presenting a more practical example.

Consider the problem faced in allocating a marketing budget among the
various activities which could lead to higher sales of a product. It is part of
the folk-lore of marketing that different types of product will benefit from
different allocations. Suppose that the methods at our disposal are: Advertising;
Promotion; Sales Training; Packaging; and Direct Mail.

Now, suppose that we compare the allocation ideal for breakfast cereals
with that for package software. Advertising, promotions and packaging are
clearly all useful, but there isn't much point in direct mailing cereal consumers
and the degree of training required by the salesmen isn't usually considered to
be high. Thus, in the existing situation we might well represent the allocation
of resources in the following matrix of percentages. Warning to marketing
executives: These figures are not meant to represent a truly effective strategy!

	Adverts	Promotion	Sales Training	Packaging	Direct Mail
Breakfast Cereal	30	50	5	15	0
Package software	10	5	15	20	50

In the case where knowledge is expressed inexactly we can readily replace
these numbers by fuzzy numbers as follows.

	Adverts	Promotion	Sales Training	Packaging	Direct Mail
Breakfast Cereal	about a third	about half	hardly any	a little	none
Package software	less than a little	hardly any	a little	about a fifth	about half

What we have here is two fuzzy relations, for Breakfast-cereal and
Package-software. Presumably they can be regarded as part of a larger database
of products; in fact product *classes*. Viewing them as classes prompts us to
write them down as fuzzy frames and ask about inheritance through IsA links. To
see that inheritance (of the properties under consideration) may be partial,
consider the fuzzy frame representing the class of commodities called Vending-
machine. A vending machine may be viewed as office furniture, catering equipment
or even as packaged food depending on the marketing approach taken. Fuzzy
Frames give a natural way to build a description of this problem and suggest an
implementation which is able to combine evidence and reason with exceptions.

Figure 4.4 shows how the combined partial inheritance of fuzzy (i.e.
linguistically expressed) allocations from general classes of products may be
used to infer an allocation for specific types of product. All slots are fuzzy
and undefined slots are left blank.

Another possible practical application is to 'dotted line' relationships in
organisations, where the responsibilities of certain specialists to technically
related parts of an organisation may override or mingle with those of the
formal reporting hierarchy. One application of the framebase is to assist with
the decision as to whom should be consulted when the specialist is asked to
work overseas for a year. Another concerns the construction of formal models of

the sort of loose-tight properties of organisations referred to by Peters and Waterman [9].

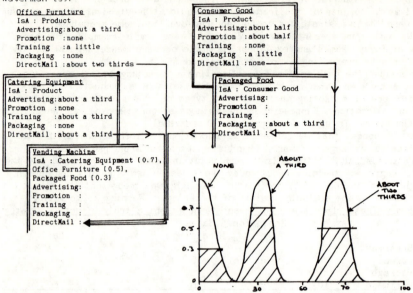

The resultant fuzzy set for Direct Mail

FIGURE 4.4   How to sell vending machines

In yet another example of a fuzzy framebase, we can now explore their application to one of the classical problems in inheritance, using non-standard quantifiers instead of nonmonotonic logic. Touretzky discusses (and dismisses) this approach by reference to the work of Altham [20], but seems to be unaware of Zadeh's more encouraging results for the representation of fuzzy quantifiers and their inference properties [16,17,5,3].

Zadeh's theory of dispositions and fuzzy quantifiers and test score semantics [16,17,5,3] lets us express one of the classical motivating problems of nonmonotonic logic as 'Most birds can fly'. This can be neatly expressed with fuzzy inheritance. Here is the framebase.

Flying-animal
IsA: Animal
Can-fly:true [fuzz]

Tweety
IsA: Bird [1], Penguin [1]
Can-fly: ?

Bird
IsA: Flying-animal [0.9]
Wings: 2

Penguin
IsA: Bird
Can-fly:false [fuzz]

The fuzzy sets involved are illustrated in Figure 5.1. The answer is that Tweety is a bird and can't fly. So far this is the same result as that suggested in McDermott and Doyle [7] – but we can do better: Penguins do sort of fly (they make fluttering movements when diving or running) and the fuzzy set shown in Figure 5.2 preserves this information in a way.

A possible generalisation springs to mind at this point. The numerical factor representing the degree of inheritance could be replaced by a linguistic variable (a fuzzy set or fuzzy number). This would mean that the truncation of inherited fuzzy sets would itself be fuzzy. We could call such objects 'Ultrafuzzy Frames' or '2-Fuzzy Frames'. However, finding a formal semantics then becomes much harder, and we suspect that the practical value of such a theory would be severely limited by its complexity. In fact, this generalisation would correspond much more closely to the interpretation of fuzzy quantifiers given in section 3.4. where fuzzy quantifiers are represented as fuzzy numbers. The inheritance mechanism of 2-fuzzy frames could indeed be modified to exploit the inference rules of approximate reasoning (e.g. the intersection-product syllogism given in 3.4). This is being investigated.

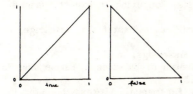

CAN TWEETY FLY?

MAXIMUM RULE: NO.

MOMENTS RULE:
    NOT VERY MUCH.

Figure 5.1 The fuzzy set 'true' is given by x=x; 'false' by x=-x

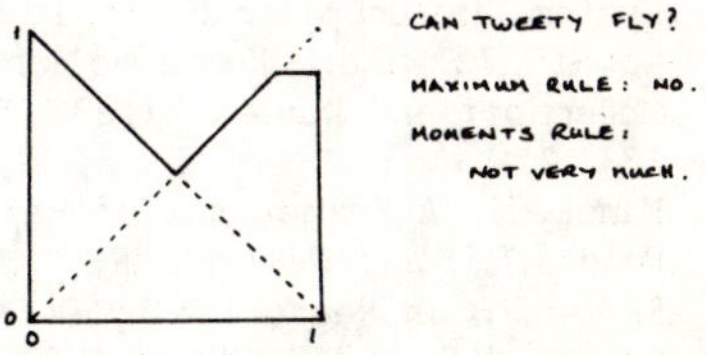

Figure 5.2 Fuzzy set for the compatibilty of the statement 'Tweety can fly'

It does look as if we can interpret a fuzzy link as a most/some type fuzzy quantifier. In the hangglider/toy example this is not the most natural interpretation. IsA links may be used (or mis-used) for a variety of conflicting purposes. A good design theory would force us to state the interpretation of the inheritance links and not mix them up. An alternative is to permit fuzzy frames to have a number of 'typed' inheritance links. Then inheritance could take place through a manifold of different networks. This too is under investigation. Fuzzy frames are not alone in raising general problems in terms of property inheritance. We have begun to look at some of these in [21].

This paper is the first in a series of papers on Fuzzy Frames. In it we have informally defined the syntax and semantics of fuzzy frames. This makes it possible to move on to the stage of implementation and application of this form of knowledge representation. A formal syntax is in preparation. It is our belief that there are a tremendous number of opportunities for the application of fuzzy frames. Of course, it may be argued that these applications can be addressed by other technologies, but none that we can think of offer simultaneously the advantages of naturality of expression in a unified representational formalism to the extent that fuzzy frames do. We have suggested several candidate applications. Among the most difficult of the others which suggest themselves is the application to the interpretation of natural language statements. We hope that other, more academic, researchers will take this up as a research topic. Our interest is in the practical knowledge engineering issues.

The authors would like to thank Gail Swaffield, of Thames Polytechnic for a number of helpful comments on the early drafts of this paper.

References

1.   Bobrow,D.G. and Winograd,T., An Overview of KRL, in [2]
2.   Brachman,R.J. and Levesque,H.J. (1985) Readings in Knowledge Representation, Morgan Kaufman
3.   Graham,I. and Jones,P.L.K. (1987) Knowledge Uncertainty and Decision: Fuzzy Logics in Expert Systems and Decision Support, Chapman and Hall
4.   Hayes,P.J., The Logic of Frames, in [2]
5.   Kandel,A. (1986) Fuzzy Mathematical Techniques with Applications, Addison Wesley
6.   Khan,N.A. and Jain,R. (1986) Explaining Uncertainty in a Distributed Expert System, in: Coupling Symbolic and Numerical Computing in Expert Systems, Kowalik,J.S. (Ed.), North Holland
7.   McDermott and Doyle,J. (1980) Nonmonotonic Logic I,Artificial Intelligence 13(1,2)
8.   Minsky,M., A Framework for Representing Knowledge, in [2]
9.   Peters,T.J. and Waterman,R.H. (1982) In Search of Excellence, Harper and Row
10.   Reiter,R., On Reasoning by Default, in [2]
11.   Roberts,R.B. and Goldstein,I.P. (1977) The FRL manual, AI Memo. No. 409, MIT Artificial Intelligence Laboratory
12.   Touretzky,D. (1986) The Mathematics of Inheritance Systems, Pitman
13.   Winston,P.H. (1984) Artificial Intelligence, Addison-Wesley
14.   Woods,W.A., What's in a Link, in [2]
15.   Zadeh,L.A. (1965) Fuzzy Sets, Information and Control 8
16.   Zadeh,L.A. (1982) A Computational Approach to Fuzzy Quantifiers in Natural Languages, University of California (Berkeley) Mémo. UCB-ERL M82-36
17.   Zadeh,L.A. (1985) Syllogistic Reasoning in Fuzzy Logic and its Application to Usuality and Reasoning with Dispositions, IEEE Transactions SMC-15 No.6
18.   Leonardo Reference Manuals (1987) Creative Logic Ltd., Uxbridge
19   KEE Reference Manuals (1985) Intellicorp Inc., California
20.   Altham,J.E.J. (1971) The Logic of Plurality, Methuen
21.   Graham,I. and Jones,P.L.K. (1987) A Theory of Fuzzy Frames II, BUSEFAL 32

SCHUBERT'S STEAMROLLER IN A NATURAL DEDUCTION THEOREM PROVER

Nick Davies,
AI Group,
GEC Research,
Marconi Research Centre,
Gt Baddow,
Chelmsford, CM2 8HN,
UK.

Abstract

We present the solution of Schubert's Steamroller in a
natural deduction theorem prover. Schubert's Steamroller has become
well-known as a challenging puzzle for theorem provers and until recently
no automated solution had been found. Our natural deduction theorem
prover incorporates a number of techniques for improving its efficiency
in finding a proof. The research reported here is part of the Alvey-GEC
funded project "Socrates: A Flexible Toolkit for Building Expert
Systems". Socrates provides tools and an environment for building expert
systems. Socrates' underlying reasoning mechanism is a natural deduction
system using many-sorted logic which exploits the techniques used in our
theorem prover. Thus the solution of Schubert's Steamroller provides an
interesting test of the feasibility of Socrates' approach to inference.

1. Introduction

We present the solution of Schubert's Steamroller in a
natural deduction theorem prover, the first proof of this problem found
by such a system.

Schubert's Steamroller has become well-known as a challenging
puzzle for theorem provers and until recently no automated solution had
been found, although the problem has now been solved using resolution
based theorem provers (Walther 1984). Our natural deduction theorem
prover incorporates a number of techniques for improving its efficiency
in finding a proof.

The research reported here is part of the Alvey-GEC funded
project "Socrates: A Flexible Toolkit for Building Expert Systems".
Socrates provides tools and an environment for building expert systems.
Socrates' underlying reasoning mechanism is a natural deduction system
using many-sorted logic which exploits the techniques used in our theorem
prover. Thus the solution of Schubert's Steamroller provides an
interesting test of the feasibility of Socrates' approach to inference.

We begin by describing Socrates' logic-based approach to
expert system development. We then discuss the solution to Schubert's
Steamroller, showing how various features offered by the Socrates system
which we have exploited in our program help in the solution.

2. The Socrates system

The motivation for attempting a solution to Schubert's

Steamroller in a natural deduction system was to provide a testbed for the Socrates system.

With many current expert system tools and shells, there are doubts over the semantics and soundness of knowledge representation schemes and their inference mechanisms. As has been argued elsewhere (see, for example, (Hayes 1977)), the main advantages in using logic for knowledge representation are that it provides formally defined, well understood semantics and a set of sound inference rules.

The use of logic as the basis for the knowledge representation scheme of the Socrates toolkit provides a specific, three stage process when specialising the toolkit to a particular expert system application. The three stages are as follows:

(i) Logical Language Declaration: at this stage the knowledge representation language to be used to represent the knowledge is defined. The logical predicates, constants, functions and connectives of the language are declared.

(ii) Declaration of Inference Rules: the next step is to declare the logical inference rules which can be applied to the logical language statements to construct a proof. Some of the inference rules, however, are hardwired into the knowledge base retrieval mechanism.

(iii) Declaration of Proof Strategy: one must now define how the inference rules are to be used in practice. This step is essentially that of defining a meta-level interpreter.

The system uses natural deduction (Bledsoe 1977) rather than refutation as its means of theorem proving. There are several reasons why natural deduction is preferable as a theorem-proving mechanism in the context of expert systems. Firstly, the logical propositions which represent the knowledge are more easily understood since there is no requirement to convert them to a normal form as in resolution systems. Secondly, the proof development is also easier to follow: resolution theorem provers usually employ just one inference rule, whereas a natural deduction system has a set of inference rules which are intended to model the reasoning steps humans use to develop proofs. Both these factors improve the comprehensibility of an expert system's reasoning and help in the construction of natural explanation facilities. Another advantage is that it is easier for the user of such a system to identify heuristics to control the problem-solving process.

Of course, the availability of a large number of inference rules has a potential disadvantage in terms of computational tractability, since the search space when seeking a proof becomes larger. In Socrates, this problem is tackled in four ways, as described below.

The search space can be reduced by removing some inference rules from the system. In the context of expert systems, this loss of completeness is not a disadvantage but rather, by using a well-chosen set of inference rules, helps to focus the theorem prover.

A further reduction in search space is achieved by the use of meta-level knowledge to guide the exploration of this space. Meta-level knowledge here is a proof strategy which controls the application of inference rules in the attempt to construct a proof of a given goal.

Efficiency is also improved by the use of a sorted logic. This reduces the complexity of the formulae in the knowledge base, thus

reducing the number of potential inferences at each stage of a proof
(Cohn 1985). The sorted logic used is of the restricted quantification
type. A taxonomy of sorts is declared and quantified variables are given
a sort, which defines the subset of the domain of individuals over which
they can range. So the first order predicate calculus (FOPC)
proposition:

(all (x)(man(x) ⇒ mortal(x)))

becomes

(all (x:man)(mortal x)), where 'man' is now a sort.

Similarly, if 'bird' were a sort, the FOPC proposition

(exists (x)(bird(x) ∧ cannot_fly(x)))

becomes

(exists (x:bird)(cannot_fly x)).

(Throughout the remainder of this paper, we use a
'Polish-style' prefix notation for logical propositions in our sorted
logic. In this notation, connectives, predicates and functions appear at
the head of a list, the tail of which is the list of arguments to which
they apply).
Another optimisation we have adopted is to embed certain
inference rules into the many-sorted unification algorithm which is used
as the knowledge base retrieval mechanism.
The knowledge base is required to represent propositions in a
logical language. This involves making a series of declarations of
predicates, functions, connectives and sortal information, which specify
the definition of well-formedness in the representation scheme.
Incorporated into the declaration of connectives is the facility for
specifying their commutativity and associativity. The inference rules we
have included in the retrieval mechanism exploit the commutativity and
associativity properties of logical language connectives and sortal
information on variables.
We also include the following inference rules to deal with
quantificational reasoning:

• universal elimination *(all (x:T) (p x)) ⊢ (p a)*
for any constant *a*, of sort *T'*, where *T'* is a subsort of *T*

• existential introduction *(p a) ⊢ (exists (x:T) (p x))*
for any constant *a*, of sort *T'*, where *T'* is a subsort of *T*

• quantifier interchange
(exists (x:T1) (all (y:T2) (p x y))) ⊢
     (all (y:T2) (exists (x:T1) (p x y)))

The automatic application of these inference rules in the
unifier reduces the number of inference steps performed by the
interpreters in a proof.

As an interesting test of the feasibility of these ideas, the solution of Schubert's Steamroller, a notoriously difficult problem for automated theorem provers, was attempted in a program using the four techniques just discussed. We will show how each of the four techniques are exploited in the solution. The program reported here uses the logical language declaration and retrieval mechanism of Socrates (Davies et al. 1987). The inference rules and proof strategy are 'hard-wired' Lisp code: that is to say, there is no declarative representation of these in the current program. It is nevertheless a simple matter to add and remove inference rules from the system since they are explicitly (albeit procedurally) represented in the theorem prover. Work is continuing on the declaration of inference rules and proof strategy (Reichgelt and van Harmelen 1986). It is expected that the declarative representations will compile for efficiency into Lisp code looking similar to the current program.

3. Schubert's Steamroller in a restricted quantification logic

The problem below is taken from (Walther 1984). It was first proposed by L. Schubert and is known as Schubert's Steamroller. It has become well known as a problem which humans can solve after some thought, but which is difficult for automated theorem provers to solve because of the huge search space it generates.

Wolves, foxes, birds, caterpillars, and snails are animals, and there are some of each of them. Also there are some grains, and grains are plants. Every animal either likes to eat all plants or all animals much smaller than itself that like to eat some plants. Caterpillars and snails are much smaller than birds, which are much smaller than foxes, which in turn are much smaller than wolves. Wolves do not like to eat foxes or grains, while birds like to eat caterpillars but not snails. Caterpillars and snails like to eat some plants. Therefore there is an animal that likes to eat a grain-eating animal.

Recently, a number of authors (Cohn 1985; Walther 1984), have reported success using resolution theorem provers and many-sorted axiomatisations. As far as we are aware, no natural proof has yet been found by an automated theorem prover.

An axiomatisation of the problem in standard first order predicate calculus is:

$$(exists\ (u\ v\ w\ x\ y\ z)(w(u) \land f(v) \land b(w) \land c(x) \land s(y) \land g(z)))$$
$$(all\ (x)((w(x) \lor f(x) \lor b(x) \lor c(x) \lor s(x)) \Rightarrow a(x)))$$
$$(all\ (x)(g(x) \Rightarrow p(x)))$$
$$(all\ (x)(a(x) \Rightarrow (all\ (y)(p(y) \Rightarrow eats(x,y))$$
$$\qquad\qquad\qquad \lor (all(y)((a(y) \land mst(y,x) \land$$
$$\qquad\qquad\qquad\qquad (exists(z)(p(z) \land eats(y,z)))) \Rightarrow eats(x,y))))$$
$$(all\ (x\ y)((c(x) \land b(y)) \Rightarrow mst(x,y)))$$
$$(all\ (x\ y)((s(x)) \land b(y)) \Rightarrow mst(x,y)))$$
$$(all\ (x\ y)((b(x) \land f(y)) \Rightarrow mst(x,y)))$$

```
(all (x y)((f(x) ∧ w(y)) ⇒ mst(x,y)))
(all (x y)((f(x) ∧ w(y)) ⇒ ~eats(y,x)))
(all (x y)((g(x)) ∧ w(y)) ⇒ ~eats(y,x))))
(all (x y)((b(x) ∧ c(y)) ⇒ eats(x,y)))
(all (x y)((b(x) ∧ s(y)) ⇒ ~eats(x,y)))
(all (x)(s(x) ⇒ (exists(y)(p(y) ∧ eats(x,y)))
(all (x)(c(x) ⇒ (exists(y)(p(y) ∧ eats(x,y)))
```

We are trying to prove:
(exists (x y)(a(x) ∧ a(y) ∧ (all(z)(g(z) ⇒ (eats(x,y) ∧ eats(y,z)))))))

          In order to recast this into our sorted logic, we must first
declare a sort hierarchy. The sort hierarchy used, which is effectively
a taxonomic representation of the animals and plants occurring in the
problem, is shown in Figure 1.

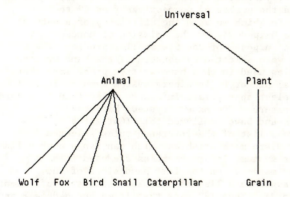

Figure 1.   Sort Hierarchy

Our new (sorted) axiomatisation is:

1. *(all (a1:animal a2:animal p1:plant p2:plant)*
   (∨ (eats a1 p1) (⇒ (∧ (mst a2 a1) (eats a2 p2)) (eats a1 a2))))
2. *(all (f:fox w:wolf) (mst f w))*
3. *(all (b:bird f:fox) (mst b f))*
4. *(all (s:snail b:bird) (mst s b))*
5. *(all (c:caterpillar b:bird) (mst c b))*
6. *(all (g:grain w:wolf) (~ (eats w g)))*
7. *(all (f:fox w:wolf) (~ (eats w f)))*
8. *(all (b:bird c:caterpillar) (eats b c))*
9. *(all (b:bird s:snail) (~ (eats b s)))*
10. *(all (s:snail) (exists (p:plant) (eats s p)))*
11. *(all (c:caterpillar) (exists (p:plant) (eats c p)))*

Our goal is now:
(exists (a1:animal a2:animal) (all (g:grain)(∧ (eats a1 a2)(eats a2 g))))

The reduction in complexity in the formulae resulting from the adoption of a sorted representation can be clearly seen: the first three formulae of the unsorted axiomatisation are now captured by the sort hierarchy. In the other formulae, all expressions containing the unary predicates w, f, b, c, s, g and p have been simplified since these predicates are now incorporated in the sort hierarchy. For example, all propositions of the form:

(all (x)(⇒ (t x) P))

where t is now a sort have been replaced by

(all (x:t) P), eliminating all but one implication.

So the number of formulae has been reduced from 14 to 11. Furthermore, the number of variables appearing in these formulae has been reduced from 32 to 24 and the number of connectives from 42 to 6.

A second way in which we said the efficiency of a natural deduction system could be helped was by the omission of unnecessary inference rules. For the purposes of the Steamroller problem, the required inference rules were selected by constructing a hand-written proof. The inference rules used in this hand-written proof were then included in the mechanical prover. (In expert system domains it is in general much easier to select appropriate inference rules than in a hard logical problem of this nature. Two expert systems have been reimplemented in Socrates and have confirmed this (Corlett 87)).

Below we give a list of the inference rules selected. Objects of the type P or Q are metavariables which can range over valid logical formulae. In our system, inference rules are used in a 'backward', goal-directed manner. On the left hand sides of the inference rules, commas separate a list of formulae which are sufficient to prove the right hand side. Thus IR2 says that if we can deduce P and we can deduce Q then we can deduce $(\land P Q)$. Of course, deducing P, say, may result in a unifying substitution for P to hold. In this case, Q must be deduced in the context of this substitution and furthermore, $(\land P Q)$ is then deduced in the context of the combination of the two substitutions from P and Q.

IR1: $P \vdash P$ Lookup
IR2: $P, Q \vdash (\land P Q)$ Conjunction Introduction
IR3: $P, (\Rightarrow P Q) \vdash Q$ Modus Ponens
IR4: $\sim P, (\lor P Q) \vdash Q$ Disjunction Elimination
IR5: $\sim(\land P Q), P \vdash \sim Q$ Negated-Conjunction Elimination
IR6: $(\Rightarrow P Q), \sim Q \vdash \sim P$ Modus Tollens
IR7: $P, \sim Q \vdash \sim(\Rightarrow P Q)$ Negated-Implication Introduction

4. A natural deduction proof of Schubert's Steamroller

We have now declared a logical language, presented an axiomatisation of the problem at hand and decided on the set of inference rules that can be used in a proof (that is, we have a proof theory). We have therefore defined all the possible inferences the system can make.

A third way to enhance the efficiency of a system written in

Socrates is to provide a proof strategy which controls the application of inference rules and hence determines the course of the proof.

As in many AI problems, the process of finding a proof can be cast as a state space search. In theorem-proving, we are searching a proof tree. The representation used here for proof trees is as follows. Each node in the tree is a list of goals. The root is a list containing a single goal, the formula we are trying to prove. The children of a node N are also lists of goals. Each of these lists is obtained by the application of an appropriate inference rule to one of the goals in the goal list at N, appended to the list of the other goals at N.

The application of an inference rule to a goal involves replacing that goal (which should match the right hand side of the inference rule) by the left hand side of the inference rule. For example, if we have as a goal ~P where P is some well-formed formula, applying IR6 (modus tollens) would mean replacing ~P by (⇒ P Q), ~Q (where Q is a metavariable) in the relevant goal list. IR1 (lookup) is a special inference rule in the sense that if it is successful (that is, if the current goal can be unified with one in the knowledge base), the formula is not replaced but simply deleted from the goal list. So whereas all the other inference rules lengthen the goal list, lookup shortens it.

As we traverse the proof tree, we carry with us a substitution which represents the bindings we have made in progressing from the root node to the current node. If at any point in our traversal of the proof tree, we find an empty goal list, we have completed a proof of the original goal, in the context of the current substitution.

Our proof strategy can thus be viewed as the search strategy we use in traversing the proof tree. In section 5, we describe four search strategies and the effect they have on the time required to solve the problem. First, we show the path that the program takes to the solution (ie the proof). We present the proof as the sequence of nodes (which are of course goal lists) traversed by the program on its path to the solution. The complete proof is given in Appendix 1. We show the first few steps here to demonstrate the method of proof.

As the proof proceeds, the types of variables change, due to the substitutions returned as a result of unifying goals with assertions in the knowledge base. The final substitution at the end of the proof binds a1 to a universally quantified variable of type fox, a2 to a universally quantified variable of type bird and g to a universally quantified variable of type grain.

Thus, substituting this in the original goal, the solution found is:

(all (a1:fox a2:bird g:grain) (∧ (eats a1 a2) (eats a2 g))),

which clearly entails the original goal.

With each goal list, we give the inference rule and formulae from the knowledge base (as identified in section 3 above) used. This shows how the goal list was arrived at from the previous goal list.

We have declared the connectives ∧ and ∨ to be associative and commutative as discussed in Section 2. This means that the following inference rules for ∧ (and equivalent ones for ∨) are included in the unifier:

> (∧ P Q) ⊢ (∧ Q P)
> (∧ (∧ P Q) R) ⊢ (∧ P (∧ Q R)).

We will indicate those steps in the proof where these inference rules have been applied 'automatically' by the unifier.
    Note that objects of the form ?MV007 are metavariables which can stand for any well-formed formula. We start at the root node, the original goal:

1. *(exists (a1:animal a2:animal)(all (g:grain) (∧ (eats a1 a2)*
                                               (eats a2 g))))

2. Conjunction Split

   (exists (a1:animal a2:animal) (eats a1 a2))
   (exists (a2:animal)(all (g:grain) (eats a2 g)))

3. Modus Ponens

   (exists (a1:animal a2:animal) (⇒ ?MV3568 (eats a1 a2)))
   ?MV3568
   (exists (a2:animal) (all (g:grain) (eats a2 g)))

4. Disjunction Introduction

   (exists (a1:animal a2:animal)(∨ ?MV3586 (⇒ ?MV3568 (eats a1 a2))))
   (~ ?MV3586)
   ?MV3568
   (exists (a2:animal) (all (g:grain) (eats a2 g)))

5. Lookup, (1)

   (exists (a1:animal var3624:plant) (~ (eats a1 var3624)))
   (exists (a2:animal a1:animal var3622:plant)
         (∧ (eats a2 var3622) (mst a2 a1)))
   (exists (a2:animal) (all (g:grain) (eats a2 g)))

....

The whole proof consists of 27 such inference steps.

5. Meta-level proof strategies

    We present four different proof strategies which have been used to attempt to solve Schubert's Steamroller. A comparison of the results of using these strategies shows the significant gains in efficiency which can be achieved by the use of meta-level guidance of the proof.
    The first of these strategies is probably the most obvious: to exhaustively search the proof tree in a breadth-first manner. This is

done by maintaining a list of goal lists (ie a list of nodes). At every point in the proof-finding process, the first goal list is taken, expanded appropriately according to the applicable inference rules and the resulting goal list(s) placed at the back of the list of nodes.

The second proof strategy is to modify this breadth-first strategy in a simple way to a best-first strategy. This involves always selecting the shortest goal list (rather than the first) from the current list of nodes and expanding this.

Another way in which the search can be constrained is by pruning branches of the proof tree which have no chance of yielding a solution (cf alpha-beta search (Knuth 1975)). One such class of useless branches can be identified by examination of the inference rules and the axiomatisation.

Given the goal-directed way in which we use inference rules, rules IR3, IR4, IR5 and IR6 are all 'introduction' type inference rules which replace the current goal with formulae containing the current goal rather than dividing the goal into simpler parts (as in IR2 and IR7, 'splitting' inference rules). However, in our axiomatisation the connectives which these introduction rules use ($\wedge$, $\vee$ and $\Rightarrow$) are never nested: that is to say, a conjunction never appears inside another conjunction in any of the formulae in the knowledge base (and similarly for implications and disjunctions). Thus it is pointless to apply an introduction inference rule which introduces a new (compound) formula containing a connective already occurring in the current goal; a lookup cannot possibly succeed and there are no inference rules to split such formulae. (The only splitting inference rules split conjunctions and negated implications: none of the introduction inference rules produce such formulae as new goals).

Whenever a goal is encountered containing a conjunction, disjunction or implication, none of the introduction inference rules are applied to it, thus pruning the proof tree considerably.

	No Pruning	Pruning
Best-first search	24:55; 716	2:06; 204
Breadth-first search	> 970:00; > 3000	10:37; 980

Figure 2. CPU time (*mmm:ss*) and Number of Nodes Visited

Figure 2 shows the number of nodes traversed and cpu time used to find a solution for each of these proof strategies. The times given are for Socrates implemented in Poplog Common Lisp running on a SUN-2/120 workstation.

As can be seen, no solution for the breadth-first, no pruning strategy has yet been found, although one must eventually be found given enough computer resources, since the possible solution space this strategy investigates is a superset of that of the other strategies. It is interesting to note that the best-first, no pruning strategy takes longer than the breadth-first, pruning strategy even though it visits less nodes. This is because the 'quality' of the nodes when pruning is used will in general be better, in the sense that the goal lists will in general contain less complicated formulae which will in general be faster to manipulate.

The times reveal that the use of even relatively simple meta-level guidance of the proof can dramatically reduce the

computational resources required to find a solution in terms of both time
and run-time storage. The importance of the use of meta-level control in
expert systems is widely recognised (Genesereth 1983). In Socrates, the
identification of suitable heuristics is facilitated by the use of a
logic-based scheme and in particular the explicit representation of both
the inference rules to be used for a particular application and of the
logical formulae which these inference rules will manipulate. The use of
a natural deduction prover, wherein logical formulae are not rewritten
into clausal form, also makes it easier to identify effective heuristics.

6. Concluding remarks

        Schubert's Steamroller has been solved in a natural deduction
style theorem prover. We have exploited a number of techniques which we
believe are suitable for logic-based expert systems to improve the
efficiency of the prover. The techniques which have enabled a solution
of this difficult (for automated theorem provers) problem are: the use
of a sorted logic, the need only to incorporate relevant inference rules,
the inclusion of a certain class of inference rules into the unifier and
the use of heuristics to guide the proof. We have shown how each of
these has improved the efficiency of the mechanical proof of Schubert's
Steamroller.
        All the techniques mentioned above are incorporated in the
Socrates toolkit for building expert systems. In this paper, we have
concentrated on the theorem-proving techniques used by Socrates as its
inference mechanism. It is worth stressing that Socrates is not only an
automated theorem prover but also provides a wide range of useful tools
for the construction of expert systems. Furthermore, Socrates' knowledge
representation scheme is not restricted to the sorted first order logic
we have used here. The Socrates system can be configured to use a number
of different logics appropriate to different domains, via the
declarations of logical language, inference rules and proof strategy. A
temporal logic suitable for implementation in Socrates has been devised
(Reichgelt 1987) and our future plans include incorporation of this logic
into Socrates. For further details of the Socrates system, see (Davies
et al 1987) and (Reichgelt and van Harmelen 1986).

Acknowledgements

        The author would like to thank Rob Corlett, Robin Khan and
Han Reichgelt for their helpful comments on an earlier draft of this
paper.

References

Bledsoe, W.W. (1977).
"Non-resolution Theorem Proving".
Artificial Intelligence $\underline{9}$, pp 1 - 35.

Cohn, A. G. (1985).
"On the Solution of Schubert's Steamroller in Many Sorted Logic".
In Proc. 9th IJCAI, pp 1169 - 1174.

Corlett, R.A. (1987).
"The DOCS System in Socrates".
Socrates Project Internal Report, MRC-41,
Marconi Research Centre, Chelmsford, UK.

Davies, N.J., Corlett, R.A., Khan, R. and Brunswick, D. (1987).
"Socrates: a Logic-based Expert Systems Toolkit".
In Proc. 1st Alvey SIGKME Workshop, Reading University. Alvey.

Genesereth, M.R. (1983).
"An Overview of Meta-Level Architecture",
In Proc. AAAI-83, Washington DC, USA.

Hayes, P. (1977).
"In Defence of Logic"
In Proc. IJCAI-77, Cambridge, Mass., USA

Knuth, D.E. and Moore, R.W. (1975).
"An Analysis of Alpha-Beta Pruning",
Artificial Intelligence, 6, No. 4.

Reichgelt, H. (1987).
"Semantics for Reified Temporal Logic",
In Proc. AISB-87, Edinburgh, UK.

Reichgelt, H. and van Harmelen, F. (1986).
"Building expert systems using logic and meta-level interpretation".
DAI Research Paper No. 303, Dept. of Artificial Intelligence,
University of Edinburgh, UK.

Walther, C. (1984).
"A Mechanical Solution of Schubert's Steamroller by Many-Sorted Resolution",
In Proc. 4th AAAI, pp. 330-334, Austin, Texas, USA.

Appendix 1. The Proof.

(exists (a1:animal a2:animal)(all (g:grain) ($\land$ (eats a1 a2) (eats a2 g))))

Conjunction Split
(exists (a1:animal a2:animal) (eats a1 a2))
(exists (a2:animal)(all (g:grain) (eats a2 g)))

Modus Ponens
(exists (a1:animal a2:animal) ($\Rightarrow$?MV3568 (eats a1 a2)))
?MV3568
(exists (a2:animal) (all (g:grain) (eats a2 g)))

Disjunction Introduction
(exists (a1:animal a2:animal)($\lor$?MV3586 ($\Rightarrow$?MV3568 (eats a1 a2))))

```
(~ ?MV3586)
?MV3568
(exists (a2:animal) (all (g:grain) (eats a2 g)))


Lookup, (1)
(exists (a1:animal var3624:plant) (~ (eats a1 var3624)))
(exists (a2:animal a1:animal var3622:plant)
        (∧ (eats a2 var3622) (mst a2 a1)))
(exists (a2:animal) (all (g:grain) (eats a2 g)))


Negated-Conjunction Introduction
(exists (a1:animal var3624:plant) (~ (∧ ?MV3632 (eats a1 var3624))))
?MV3632
(exists (a2:animal a1:animal var3622:plant)
        (∧ (eats a2 var3622) (mst a2 a1)))
(exists (a2:animal) (all (g:grain) (eats a2 g)))


Modus Tollens
(exists (a1:animal var3624:plant)
             (⇒ (∧ ?MV3632 (eats a1 var3624)) ?MV3678))
(~ ?MV3678)
?MV3632
(exists (a2:animal a1:animal var3622:plant)
        (∧ (eats a2 var3622) (mst a2 a1)))
(exists (a2:animal) (all (g:grain) (eats a2 g)))


Disjunction Introduction
(exists (a1:animal var3624:plant)
        (∨ ?MV3706 (⇒ (∧ ?MV3632 (eats a1 var3624)) ?MV3678)))
(~ ?MV3706)
(~ ?MV3678)
?MV3632
(exists (a2:animal a1:animal var3622:plant)
        (∧ (eats a2 var3622) (mst a2 a1)))
(exists (a2:animal) (all (g:grain) (eats a2 g)))


Lookup, (1)
(exists (var3867:animal var3868:plant) (~ (eats var3867 var3868)))
(exists (a1:animal var3867:animal) (~ (eats var3867 a1)))
(exists (a1:animal var3867:animal) (mst a1 var3867))
(exists (a2:animal a1:animal var3622:plant)
        (∧ (eats a2 var3622) (mst a2 a1)))
(exists (a2:animal) (all (g:grain) (eats a2 g)))


Lookup, (6)
(exists (a1:animal var3869:wolf) (~ (eats var3869 a1)))
(exists (a1:animal var3869:wolf) (mst a1 var3869))
(exists (a2:animal a1:animal var3622:plant)
        (∧ (eats a2 var3622) (mst a2 a1)))
(exists (a2:animal) (all (g:grain) (eats a2 g)))


Lookup, (6)
(exists (a1:fox var3869:wolf) (mst a1 var3869))
(exists (a2:animal a1:fox var3622:plant)
```

```
                     (∧ (eats a2 var3622) (mst a2 al)))
(exists (a2:animal) (all (g:grain) (eats a2 g)))


Lookup, (4)
(exists (a2:animal al:fox var3622:plant)
        (∧ (eats a2 var3622) (mst a2 al)))
(exists (a2:animal) (all (g:grain) (eats a2 g)))


Conjunction Split
(exists (a2:animal var3622:plant) (eats a2 var3622))
(exists (a2:animal al:fox) (mst a2 al))
(exists (a2:animal) (all (g:grain) (eats a2 g)))


Disjunction Introduction
(exists (a2:animal var3622:plant) (∨ ?MV3899 (eats a2 var3622)))
(~ ?MV3899)
(exists (a2:animal al:fox)(mst a2 al))
(exists (a2:animal) (all (g:grain) (eats a2 g)))


Lookup, (5)
(exists (a2:animal var3925:plant var3924:animal)
        (~ (⇒ (∧ (eats var3924 var3925)(mst var3924 a2))
              (eats a2 var3924))))
(exists (a2:animal al:fox) (mst a2 al))
(exists (a2:animal) (all (g:grain) (eats a2 g)))


Negated-Implication Split
(exists (a2:animal var3925:plant var3924:animal)
        (∧ (eats var3924 var3925) (mst var3924 a2)))
(exists (a2:animal var3924:animal) (~ (eats a2 var3924)))
(exists (a2:animal al:fox) (mst a2 al))
(exists (a2:animal) (all (g:grain) (eats a2 g)))


Conjunction Split
(exists (var3924:animal var3925:plant)(eats var3924 var3925)))
(exists (a2:animal var3924:animal) (mst var3924 a2))
(exists (a2:animal var3924:animal) (~ (eats a2 var3924)))
(exists (a2:animal al:fox)(mst a2 al))
(exists (a2:animal) (all (g:grain) (eats a2 g)))


Lookup, (11)
(exists (a2:animal var3952:snail) (mst var3952 a2))
(exists (a2:animal var3952:snail) (~ (eats a2 var3952)))
(exists (a2:animal al:fox)(mst a2 al))
(exists (a2:animal) (all (g:grain) (eats a2 g)))


Lookup, (2)
(exists (a2:bird var3952:snail) (~ (eats a2 var3952)))
(exists (a2:bird al:fox)(mst a2 al))
(exists (a2:bird) (all (g:grain) (eats a2 g)))


Lookup, (9)
(exists (a2:bird al:fox)(mst a2 al))
(exists (a2:bird) (all (g:grain) (eats a2 g)))
```

Lookup, (3)
(exists (a2:bird) (all (g:grain) (eats a2 g)))

Disjunction Introduction
(exists (a2:bird) (all (g:grain) (∨ ?MV3997 (eats a2 g))))
(~ ?MV3997)

Lookup, (1), *(∨ P Q) ⊢ (∨ Q P)*
(exists (a2:bird) var3999:plant var3998:animal)
*   (~ (⇒ (∧ (eats var3998 var3999)(mst var3998 a2))*
*   (eats a2 var3998)))))*

Negated-Implication Split
(exists (a2:bird var3999:plant var3998:animal)
*   (∧ (eats var3998 var3999) (mst var3998 a2)))*
(exists (a2:bird var3998:animal) (~ (eats a2 var3998)))

Conjunction Split
(exists (var3998:animal var3999:plant)(eats var3998 var3999))
(exists (a2:bird var3998:animal) (mst var3998 a2))
(exists (a2:bird var3998:animal) (~ (eats a2 var3998)))

Lookup, (10)
(exists (a2:bird var4016:snail) (mst var4016 a2))
(exists (a2:bird var4016:snail) (~ (eats a2 var4016)))

Lookup, (4)
(exists (a2:bird var4016:snail) (~ (eats a2 var4016)))

Lookup, (9)

QED

INFERENCE TOOLS FOR KNOWLEDGE BASED SYSTEMS IN INDUSTRIAL APPLICATION AREAS

J. Bigham & V. H. Khong
Department of Electrical & Electronic Engineering,
Queen Mary College, London E1 4NS

G. I. Williamson & S. G. King
British Telecom, TA 12.2.2,
151 Gower Street, London WC1E 6BA

Abstract

This paper describes some inference tools being developed as part of the Esprit project 387 KRITIC (Knowledge Representation and Inference Techniques in Industrial Control). These tools have been designed to allow flexible input of data. They can cope with dynamic input of information over time and handle cases where input is inconsistent through such things as operator error or changing conditions. This is achieved by constructing a TMS inference network as rule sets or knowledge sources are invoked during the inference process. Inferences are made bidirectionally through the network. Inconsistencies are detected by an associated logic based truth maintenance system and handled by an error analysis system which is under development.

One tool builds directly on a forward and backward chaining rule based system which was constructed and used effectively in an earlier phase of the project. It allows domain knowledge to be partitioned into rulesets and will support dynamic reordering of goals. Another tool expands the ideas of the first by augmenting the control facilities and is a form of blackboard system.

The tools have been applied to the problem of PABX maintenance, and this is described briefly.

1.0 Introduction

This paper describes the main features of a blackboard system currently named BBF and a forward/backward chainer named MIKIC-TMS, both targetted towards industrial applications. They have both developed from a forward/backward chainer called MIKIC.

In industrial applications there is often a considerable amount of documentation to support the operational system. In the diagnosis of faults in a telecommunications switching system, the case study discussed here, this incorporates information on functional dependencies, power dependencies etc. and detailed steps for diagnostic testing and repair. Much of this knowledge is based on design knowledge of the system. Full input/output functional models of components are usually very complex, and commonly only facets of these are required. Such abstractions of the design knowledge can be vital in effective fault identification and maintenance. On the other hand heuristic knowledge can shortcut many deductive steps in a causal chain and are valuable in cases where the process model is not well understood. The tools discussed in this paper are specifically designed for such "hybrid" systems where a mixture of heuristic information and design knowledge is required. The knowledge can be held either in a frame or rule base, whichever is the more appropriate.

It is assumed that the application system, such as the telecommunications exchange, has been represented in some frame system such as is available in KEE (Intellicorp) or CRL (Carnegie Group Inc.). In the KRITIC project an object oriented knowledge representation language called Avalon has been developed, which was designed to provide good support for representing the relationships between components, and this is described elsewhere (Varey 1987). The object oriented representation gives an economical representation of knowledge and exploits the hierarchical organisation found in many man made systems.

The inference mechanisms have also been built in the object oriented paradigm. For example, one of the main features of the forward/backward chainers (MIKIC and MIKIC-TMS) is a rule based environment where rule packages are called similarly to methods of objects. (See section 2.)

It is important to allow the users to have considerable flexibilty in the input of test information and application system status. This also applies to input from sensor data or background tests. This flexibility is provided through the integration of a truth maintenance system with MIKIC. This system is known as MIKIC-TMS and described in section 3.2. MIKIC-TMS provides an integrated inferencing system which retains the basic simplicity and structuring of the MIKIC system, but with the flexibility and the power of the TMS added. When a MIKIC backward chaining rule set is instantiated a TMS propositional network is automatically created. As the MIKIC control fires rules, truth values in the TMS network are updated and their consequences propagated. In operation, truth values may be input to the system at any time, rather than waiting for MIKIC to ask a question. Furthermore truth values may be retracted and also contradictions detected.

In industrial systems the status of the application system such as the exchange, is often continually monitored. This is supported by tests either performed automatically or on request. In different situations the strategies for focussing on and confirming suspected faults may need to change. (For example the strategy for handling fault reports in a suspected crisis situation may well be different than in the usual case.) The blackboard system was developed to provide additional flexibility in the control of inferencing so that it can be more context dependent. In the telephone exchange example the TMS has also been linked to the control of hypotheses at one level of the blackboard. The blackboard system is described in section 3.3.

Section 4 gives a description   of an application of the tools to the maintenance of a PABX. Aspects of this case study are introduced at various points in the paper in order to clarify some of the ideas.

2.0 The basic MIKIC inferencing system

The inference mechanisms to be described in section 3 have been built upon the forward/ backward chaining system called MIKIC, described by Khong (1985), which has been used successfully in the KRITIC project to help in the diagnosis of faults in telecommunications switching systems (Williamson, Butler, Gaussens, King & Khong 1986) and in the power load control of a distribution network (Wittig 1985 &1987).

2.1 The MIKIC system

To understand the reasons for the development of the sytems described a brief description of the strengths of the original MIKIC system is given and then its limitations discussed. The inference mechanisms described in section 3 are designed to eliminate or ameliorate the limitations.

MIKIC is a reasonably straightforward inference mechanism. It includes several important features which made it practical for the two application domains on which it has been tested. These are:

(i)   It allows data-driven and goal directed knowledge to be represented in a simple rule structure.

In diagnosis it is common to use data driven rules to focus attention on particular types of fault and goal directed reasoning to prove the fault type and refine the

definition of the fault.
(ii)   It allows easy integration into other knowledge which has (say) a frame based representation.
In the KRITIC project Avalon is used, and much of the structural and functional information is held in that knowledge base.
Since MIKIC supports the use of message calls within rulesets it can easily access any object oriented knowledge representation system. It allows typed rulesets to be defined. Ruleset variables are instantiated with reference to the frame base.
(iii) It allows partitioning and structuring of the rule base.
This enhances computational efficiency and allows incremental development of the rule base. The inclusion of further fault types, for example, may involve adding rule sets with little or no modification to existing rule sets.
(iv) It allows the user to specify generic rules.
The design philosophy of MIKIC is to make rules and rulesets object oriented. This makes the invocation of rules only possible within the context of an object, or in the context of the class and sub-classes of that object. When the taxonomy of the structure of the system does not lend itself to a specific task, such as controlling the power consumption in a geographical area, the generic rules provide an elegant way of letting a backward chaining process span the different taxonomies. For example, in order to decide whether the current group of consumers should be turned off, it may be necessary to find out the state of power consumption of another group of consumers. This other group may not necessarily be in the same taxonomy. The generic rules allow the user to formulate the goal in such a way that it is proven in the context of another class of objects instead of the current class.

2.2 The limitations of the initial work

It was realised through the work in the application domains that, whilst the rule and the frame knowledge base together provided a powerful capability, there were aspects of knowledge representation and inference which were still not captured. This mainly concerned:-
(i) A need for more flexible control.
MIKIC only provides basic control mechanisms for forward chaining. (Albeit having the advantage of making it easy to formulate the domain application in the MIKIC framework.) The limitation in the control manifests itself in several ways.
(a) There is a need to provide information directly, rather than wait for MIKIC to ask the appropriate questions or take the approriate sensor readings. This required increased flexibility of the input to the inference process.
(b) New facts (e.g. fault reports) are not guaranteed to be reported in exactly the same time order as they are generated and the inference system needed the ability to revise its beliefs dynamically as the information changes. Similarly components which were believed to be working may become faulty, etc..
(c) In MIKIC, during backward chaining the subgoals are explored depth first in the order they appear in the syntax of the rules. However answers to questions may make it desirable to adapt the order in which subgoals are pursued as this not only potentially speeds up the search but makes for greater correspondence to "rational" reasoning.
(d) Whilst the forward control in MIKIC is through the firing of rules, it is still essentially procedural. There was a wish to enhance the control to allow reordering of inference activities, particularly in the forward reasoning. This was to allow new information, such as new fault reports, to be incorporated into the reasoning process and to allow different strategies for inference to be adopted when this is considered important. This has led to the development of a blackboard system.

(ii) Proper recovery when something inconsistent happens.

For example the instruction to the operator to replace a fuse should, with hindsight, have cleared a fault. However the replacement fuse was faulty, and so the diagnostic system continues since it assumes that the fuse was not the fault, until eventually it exhausts all possible faults without identification or perhaps identifies a fault which could well be the wrong fault.

Incorrect or inappropriate actions by operators are not uncommon and should be accommodated by the inference system. This led to the development of the truth maintenance system which supports dependency directed backtracking and motivates the work on error analysis and correction.

(iii) Ability to use default reasoning.

In both domains considered in the KRITIC project there are instances when it is desirable to proceed with deductions based on the assumption that a fact or heuristic rule is appropriate. For example a simple heuristic which may be used in the selection of when a consumer of electricity may or not be turned off, is "if it is currently a high tariff period then do not turn off". If the problem becomes insoluble then some of the assumptions have to be relaxed and alternatives tried. Truth maintenance systems can be used to support this kind of reasoning.

3.0 Additions to the basic inferencing system

This section gives an outline of the tools constructed. Firstly the TMS system is described. This is a stand alone system which can, in principle, be integrated with many different inference mechanisms. Then the integrated TMS forward/backward chainer is described, i.e. MIKIC-TMS, followed by the blackboard system. Each has its own identity but they can be regarded as successive developments. In MIKIC-TMS, reasoning is performed using if .. then rules, an inference network, and information obtained by querying or polling the representation of the system in the frame knowledge base. In the blackboard system knowledge sources are used, which can be procedures or rule sets as used in the forward/backward chainer.

3.1 The Truth Maintenance System (TMS)

This is based on the work of McAllester (1980). This has been categorised by Forbus (1986) as a "logic" based TMS and described as an excellent tool for rapid prototyping. It differs in a number of regards from the justification based system of Doyle (1979) and the assumption based system (ATMS) of de Kleer (1986). Its key characteristics include

(a) the representation of a belief in a proposition as true, false or unknown. (c.f. believed or not believed as used by Doyle and the ATMS)

(b) in built propositional deduction through a form of unit clause resolution.

Propositions are represented by nodes. Relationships between propositions, or nodes, are represented by clauses. For example suppose the propositions A and B are represented by the nodes N1 and N2 respectively, and also suppose that A and B are related by A->B. The proposition A->B, i.e. the truth or falsity of the relation A->B, can be represented by another node N3, say. The following clauses, easily derivable by considering the truth table for ->, would then relate the three nodes to form a simple network:-

$$\neg N3 \lor \neg N1 \lor N2$$
$$N3 \lor N1$$
$$N3 \lor \neg N2$$

When the truth value of a node is asserted the clauses are used to propagate beliefs through the network.

To limit the amount of computation performed only TMS networks which are relevant to the current diagnosis are considered. This comes from the use of only those rulesets or knowledge sources pertinent to the hypotheses. The limited number of interconnections in the the networks constructed also reduces the computational requirements to significantly below that which is theoretically possible in a general network.

Without the use of refutation there are cases where the inference mechanism is incomplete, though still sound. The propositional deduction mechanism is faster because of this. The networks constructed have almost a tree structure with only the terminal nodes allowed to have multiple parents. For such networks incompleteness does not arise.

3.2 MIKIC-TMS

The forward/backward chaining system MIKIC has been integrated with the TMS above to provide a more dynamic inference mechanism. The system is first described, followed by an example to clarify the nature of the network constructed.

3.2.1 An overview

Forward rules are used to suggest hypotheses which have to be confirmed and refined by the backward chaining.

Associated backward rule sets are then translated by the system to construct a corresponding TMS network. This network then serves as a memory of partially computed beliefs and dependencies. Initially all goals, subgoals and terminal leaves are assumed to be unknown. Inferences are made by propagating beliefs through the network. By utilising the network representation the user is allowed to input information both in any order and at any time e.g through a menu. Sensor data can easily be incorporated as it becomes available.

As information is propagated immediately the system automatically bypasses goals which lead to requests for redundant information. If inconsistent information is given the dependency directed backtracking mechanism is invoked to allow consistency to be reinstated. At present the user resolves conflicts by using a restricted menu of clauses whose retraction will resolve the inconsistency. In future this will be improved as part of the work on error analysis.

The user can change his mind, at any time, about the answers he has given, and if this causes an inconsistency, dependency directed backtracking is again invoked. Changing values of sensor data are handled in an analogous manner.

A rule set is commonly generic in that it is used to, say, diagnose faults in modules of a given type. Specific instances of a module may be identical or have variations in structure, such as having different numbers of some types of sub-component. Rule sets, therefore, often incorporate variables. However at the time the rule set is converted the values of the variables are known and so the inference network created is propositional. The network nodes incorporate these values.

3.2.2 An example of a rule network

A typical hypothesis is a statement such as "there is a fault in the concentrating shelf interface". The first steps in the refinement and proving of this hypothesis are described below. The application is discussed further in the case study. The complete network for this hypothesis (a tree in this case) is shown in figure 1. The terminal leaves correspond to askable questions or sensor inputs. For clarity some detail has been omitted from figure 1.

Rules are represented as clauses in disjunctive normal form. For example the rule, if A & B & C then D, could be represented as $\neg A \lor \neg B \lor \neg C \lor D$. It is in fact sometimes convenient to represent the conjunction A&B&C explicitly, in which case other clauses have to be added to express the relationship between A, B and C and A&B&C. To make the representation clear a simplified example from the application domain is given.

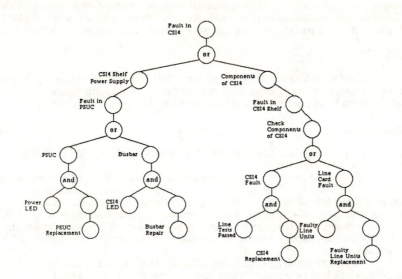

Figure 1 : TMS proposition network for the CSI shelf ruleset

As an illustration a simplified diagnostic example is described. Consider a concentrating shelf interface (CSI) to be made up of only two parts, (i) the CSI-shelf power supply, and (ii) the "other components of the CSI". Two simple rules arise out of this:-

(a) An is-part-of rule:-
    if fault is in the CSI-shelf power supply or the other components of the CSI
    then the fault is in the CSI

(b) A completeness rule:-
    if the fault is in the CSI
  then it is either in the CSI-shelf power supply or in the other components of the CSI.
    Expressing these rules slightly more abstractly, they are

$$\text{if } A \vee B \text{ then } C$$

and

$$\text{if } C \text{ then } A \vee B$$

Relationships between propositions such as A, B and C are not represented as rules in the inference network, but as *clauses* . For example, the first rule is represented by the clause

$$\neg[\text{AorB}] \vee C$$

and the second by

$$[\text{AorB}] \vee \neg C$$

where [AorB] represents the proposition "A or B".

The relationships between A, B and [AorB] are also represented by clauses, namely ¬A v [AorB], ¬B v [AorB], and A v B v ¬[AorB].

The pair of rules is represented in the inference network, therefore, by three nodes representing the belief in A, B and C; one node representing the belief in AorB; and five clauses representing the relationships between the nodes. The network created is illustrated in figure 2.

An important feature of this representation arises from the fact that a clause is used to make inferences in different directions. For example a rule such as if A then B and its contrapositive, if ¬B then ¬A, has the same clause representation ¬A v B. This results in all contrapositive inferences being automatically made. A common example in the diagnosis of switching faults is if an object's controller fails then the object itself must fail. Similarly if an object is known to be working fully then it is reasonable to assume its controller works also.

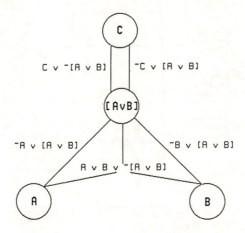

Figure 2 : TMS "OR" network

3.3 The blackboard system BBF

The need for a flexible, general and powerful control mechanism is central to many diagnostic problems. A blackboard based system called BBF has been developed to provide these features. The development of BBF has drawn extensively on reports on blackboard systems in the literature, e.g. (Aiello 1981; Hayes-Roth 1985; Nii 1986a 1986b)

3.3.1 The blackboard system

The blackboard system is intended to provide a general purpose blackboard structure with enough flexibility to allow easy modification for the solution of a wide range of problems. Once again it builds on the tools available, i.e. MIKIC, TMS and MIKIC-TMS. In one sense it could be viewed as replacing most of the forward chaining done in MIKIC. The blackboard system controls the execution of KS's which may be MIKIC rulesets or Lisp functions.

A layered blackboard architecture has been chosen where the levels correspond to abstract steps in the problem solution. Figure 3 shows the levels relevant to the case study. This architecture lends itself well to the object oriented programming style used. This is due to the commonalities in the functions and variables used by the various levels. This will become more apparent when the partitioning of control is described.

The high level inference on the present blackboard is primarily data driven as goals may only be postulated at the top level. The blackboard configuration may change if the application demands.

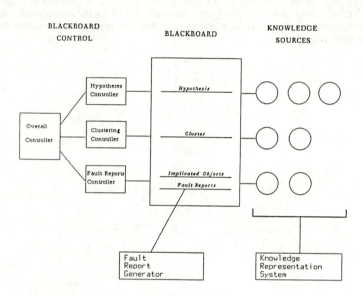

Figure 3 : BBF blackboard architecture

3.3.2 Partitioning of the control

The control is partitioned into controllers for each level and an overall controller. In the current application (detailed in the case study) this corresponds to a hypotheses controller, a cluster controller, and a fault-report controller plus the overall controller.

At each cycle pre-conditions for each of the KSs at a level may be matched to the blackboard contents at that level. If there is a match then a knowledge source activation record (KSAR) is created. A KSAR is analogous to an activation record in a procedure call and contains all the information relevant to running the body of the KS should it be chosen as well as information to allow selection for firing. Once all KSARs are created the list of KSARs at a level are sorted according to the priorities at that level. This sorted list forms the agenda for that level. Each level controller has its own agenda, current list of KSARs, history and list of associated KSs.

The overall controller also has knowledge sources associated with it, but these are mainly to schedule level controllers. It can have an agenda formed by combining results from the level controllers.

The main purpose of the overall controller is to schedule the level controllers. To make this clearer consider two possible strategies which the overall controller could choose to adopt. (i) To only select for firing the "best" KSAR offered by a particular level controller (so no KS's on the other level transitions need even be triggered) or (ii) select the best KSAR's offered by the lowest level, and if there are none the best at the next highest level etc.. (So only the KS at the lowest level need to be tested for triggering in the first instance. If none trigger the KS's at the next level are considered for triggering etc.) This would have the effect of pushing new data into consideration quickly, but has obvious limitations. Each of these strategies could be equivalently described by triggering all KS's and assigning priorities to the KSAR's. For example in the case (i), giving a priority of zero to all KSAR's of the level transitions which are not of interest would have the same effect. However this view is computationally more expensive and so a strategy is viewed partly as sequential procedure which looks for a KSAR to fire. The ordering of the steps in the procedure corresponds to the implied priorities. The aim is to have a good trade off between an ordered search and selection of the "best" from a number of possibilities.

Whatever the selected overall strategy, this has to be devolved into appropriate sub-strategies for the level controllers. For the simple strategy (ii) above then the strategy passed to each level controller could be to pick the best KSAR for firing, based on the (also devolved) individual controller strategy.

Since the controllers described above have many common data structures and procedures they are organised in a taxonomy of controllers. (This is a different hierarchy from the hierarchy of control described above.) The general controller class contains important general purpose variables and methods which are inherited, specialised or overridden by the more particular level. These include methods which define a general purpose control loop to determine the triggerable KSs, sort them according to specified criteria, i.e make the agenda, and execute the chosen KSAR. All these methods are relatively simple but are generally applicable. If a more sophisticated control loop is required (e.g. by a particular level controller) then this can be defined locally to this level. Since the system has been implemented in an object oriented language these features are provided by utilising the built in inheritance features of the language. Additional classes have been defined to provide the basic data structures for KSs and KSARs.

3.3.3 Using the TMS to assist in the control

One of the more novel ways in which this blackboard can be used is through the way some of the KSs implemented in MIKIC rulesets have been integrated with the TMS. The proposition nets used by the TMS are set up as hypotheses rulesets are generated - or invoked. These are effectively identical to the proposition networks corresponding to the backward chaining with separate hypotheses OR'ed or XOR'ed. The control KS of the blackboard is able to construct the proposition nets automatically using MIKIC-TMS capabilities. This allows more flexible handling of the queries in the hypotheses layer of the blackboard.

In the application a small TMS network is created by ORing each of the hypotheses associated with a cluster. The TMS network for the backward chaining KS is created as the KS is executed. This is described more fully in the case study.

4.0 Case Study - Application to the diagnosis of faults in a PABX

The inferencing tools described in the previous sections have been applied to the problem of diagnosing faults in the telecommunications switching domain. This domain will now be used as a case study to further illustrate the concepts previously introduced.

4.1 Domain Background

The particular application chosen is that of fault diagnosis in a PABX. Though this is a relatively small problem when compared to large digital switching systems which may contain more than 10,000 printed circuit boards of several hundred types, the inferencing strategies will be similar. This is because knowledge about these systems can be represented in a highly structured, hierarchical and generic manner. The engineering design methodology for both hardware and software has ensured the hierarchical structure of these systems by use of data abstraction and hiding of detail.

More details of the telecommunications domain can be found in Williamson, Butler, Gaussens, King & Khong (1986). This used the earlier inference system outlined in section 2 of this paper. More recently Williamson, Bigham, Butler & King (1987) describe the application of the more advanced inference systems and knowledge representation systems to the telecommunications domain.

4.2 Case Study

In the diagnosis of faults in the PABX (and this is typical of other switching systems) fault symptoms will be presented to the user by the built in test capabilities of the PABX. When they are presented the general aim is to generate a minimal number of hypotheses, corresponding to possible fault cases, which may then be checked. It is desirable to allow flexible ordering of these hypotheses, both to satisfy the user requirements and to permit adaption mechanisms. In addition it may be necessary to integrate new events into existing diagnostic sequences and to take into account the new information accordingly.

A layered blackboard structure based on BBF has been devised to allow this kind of functionality. The structure of the blackboard can be seen in figure 3.

The chosen structure consists of a *fault report controller*, a *cluster controller* and a *hypotheses controller*. These are the level controllers which are in turn scheduled by an overall controller. Each level controller has a number of knowledge sources associated with it and each of these may access detailed information concerning the configuration of a particular exchange and models of an exchange which may be run in simulation.

Within this overall architecture there are a number of steps:
(i) At level 1: Fault reports from various sources (e.g. diagnostic test and lamp conditions) are translated to their implicated objects, i.e. the object suspected as faulty.
(ii) At level 2: These implicated objects are then clustered - since numbers of symptoms may be related to the same cause.
(iii) At level 3: There are a number of separate hypotheses - possible faults and the information required to check and repair them - are generated for each cluster and executed. In operation data generally percolates up the blackboard until a solution is found.

These steps correspond to the levels of the blackboard (see figure 3) and to key steps in the solution strategy. KS's are allocated to each layer of the blackboard.

Part (iii) above refers to a number of possible hypotheses being generated for a single cluster fault. An example of this is if the cluster fault was a CSI. The following hypotheses, each of which has a backward chaining knowledge source, are created.

CSI-CARDS	Powering	hypothesis 1
	CSI card	hypothesis 2
	Line cards of CSI	hypothesis 3
CSI-LINKS	Signalling/speech	hypothesis 4
	CSI edge connectors	hypothesis 5
	Line unit edge connector	hypothesis 6
LINE-SHELF	Backplane	hypothesis 7
	Piecewise card replacement	hypothesis 8

These hypotheses are "ORed" together by a TMS network. (See figure 4.) This was described briefly in 3.3.3. This will help the system to detect whether a fault has been cleared or not.

The general strategy currently employed is for the overall controller to hand control over to a level controller according to some criterion, such as which level controller has an urgent task to perform. This level controller will then check through its associated knowledge sources determining which is triggerable, thus creating a list of activation records. These are then sorted into the agenda and the top item of this agenda is then executed. The list of activation records is then recomputed and the above cycle repeated as long as the list is not empty. If it is, then the level controller returns control to the overall controller. This strategy is continued until no further actions are possible.

Future work may allow concurrent working of non interacting KSs at the hypothesis level.

The work on this case study is still undergoing development. A demonstrator version is expected in October 87.

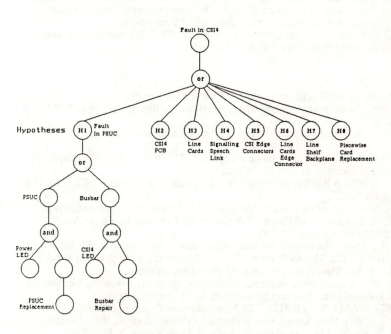

Figure 4 : TMS OR'ed hypothesis tree

5.0 Conclusions

The tools described have been constructed so as to be generally useable in industrial applications. Their design benefited from the experience gained in using a good, but relatively simple inference mechanism earlier in the project. The new inference mechanisms are more responsive to changes over time, can recognise an inconsistency, and allow much greater flexibility of input. The blackboard has in addition the greater flexibility in inference control.

Though a considerable amount of progress has been made there are areas where it is recognised that further work is necessary. One of the most important is the representation of control strategies for inference. Other areas on which it is hoped to make progress are error analysis and the handling of uncertainty in the inference process. The two topics are related. It is hoped to associate likelihoods with default facts and rules, which can be used to guide retraction if inconsistencies arise. Heuristics gained from the analysis of typical error situations will also guide the retraction process.

The tools are being validated and refined as part of the current phase of the KRITIC project.

Acknowledgements and project information

We would like to thank our partners in the Esprit P387 project for their help and many valuable discussions.

The overall objective of the KRITIC project is to make possible the development of KBS for complex industrial application areas. The partners in this project are: Krupp Atlas Elektronik GMBH (West Germany) - the prime contractor; Queen Mary College, British Telecom and Framentec (France).The views expressed here are purely those of the authors and not necessarily those of the P387 Consortium.

This research was partly funded through the CEC. We also acknowledge support and permission to publish from British Telecom.

References

Aiello, N. et al, (1981). AGE reference manual, Stanford University.
de Kleer, J. (1986). An assumption based TMS, Artificial Intelligence 28, pp127-162, North Holland.
Doyle J., (1979). A truth maintenance system, Artificial Intelligence, Vol 12, No. 3, North-Holland
Forbus, D.K., (1986). The qualitative process engine, UIUCDCS -R-86-1288, Dept. of Computer Science, University of Illinois, Urbana
Hayes-Roth, B., (1985). A blackboard architecture for control, Artificial Intelligence, Vol 26 No. 3, North-Holland.
Khong V., (1985). A study of rule-based, frame-based and constraint representation in A.I., Ph. D. Thesis, Department of Electrical & Electronic Engineering, Queen Mary College, Mile End Road, London E1 4NS.
McAllester, D.A., (1980). An outlook on truth maintenance, AI memo No 551, MIT.
Penny Nii H., (1986a). Blackboard Systems: The blackboard model of problem solving and the evolution of blackboard architectures, AI magazine, Summer.
Penny Nii H., (1986b). Blackboard Systems: blackboard application systems, blackboard systems from a knowledge engineering perspective, AI Magazine, August.
Varey, S., (1987), AVALON, in KRITIC 24 Month Review Document (Standard Deliverable 5), available from Krupp Atlas Elektronik GMBH, Bremen, West Germany.
Williamson, G. I., Butler, J.W., Gaussens, E., King, S. G. & Khong, V.H. (1986). Using a KBS in telecommunications, in Proc. of Esprit Technical Week III, Brussels, September 86.
Williamson, G.I., Bigham, J., Butler, J.W., King S.G., (1987). Using a KBS in telecommunications 2, in Proc. of Esprit Technical Week IV, Brussels, September 87
Wittig, T. (1985). The KRITIC project: Esprit supported project in industrial control, UNICOM seminar- Experts Systems for Process Control, 3-5 Dec 85.
Wittig, T., (1987). Power distribution falls under KRITIC's eye, Modern Power Systems, London.

SAYING "I DON'T KNOW" AND CONDITIONAL ANSWERS

Dave Wolstenholme
Department of Computing
Imperial College of Science and Technology
London SW7 2BZ

Abstract

When asked questions by expert systems, users may be unable or unwilling to answer, or may only be able to give an incomplete answer. Methods employed by various expert systems and shells to allow the user to say "I don't know" or to give an incomplete answer are described and discussed. In general, these methods either require explicit consideration by the knowledge engineer of the "unknown" situation or suffer from potential control problems. The approach to the problem taken in a recent version of APES, a PROLOG expert system shell, is described. This is based on an interpreter that suspends if information is unavailable. The conditional answers that may be generated by the system when incomplete information is supplied are also described and compared with fully qualified answers.

1. Introduction

A feature of most expert systems is that they do not have built in to them all the information necessary to provide the advice requested so the user must be asked to supply the information that is missing.

Most expert systems and shells present the user with a problem: when asked a question, the user is expected to give a full answer. Saying "I don't know" or giving an incomplete answer is frequently not an option, even though the user may know that answering this particular question fully, or even at all, is unimportant.

The effect of incomplete information supplied to the expert system depends on the situation. The fact that a user is unable to answer a question does not necessarily mean that there is inadequate information to provide a full solution. For example, if a woman knows that she has a liver disorder but is not sure whether she is suffering from diabetes, the appropriate expert system should still be able to advise her to avoid alcohol as it aggravates both conditions. On the other hand, advice on whether to avoid ice-cream would have to be conditional on whether she was, indeed, diabetic.

Following a brief description of APES, the augmented PROLOG system, we discuss the problem of allowing users to say "I don't know" or to give an incomplete answer to a question. We review previous methods of dealing with the problem and describe the way it is handled in a recent version of APES being developed to run under sigma-PROLOG. This version uses a suspending interpreter that can generate conditional answers. These we compare with fully qualified answers.

2. APES

APES, Augmented Prolog for Expert Systems, was developed by Hammond and Sergot (1984) both as an expert system shell and as a logic program development tool. The two main features that make it suitable for these purposes are:

> a dialogue facility based on Query-the-User (Sergot 1983) under which, by default, if a relationship to be solved is not defined in the program, the system asks the user to confirm the relationship or supply variable bindings that satisfy the relationship. Such a relationship is termed interactive;

> the construction of a trace of the computation, used to supply explanations of solutions found and to provide reasons why questions are being asked.

To demonstrate the syntax of APES, consider the following program which expresses the fact that if a person is a widow and is not aged over 60 then she is entitled to social security benefit of 2500. Initial underscore indicates a variable.

```
gets-social-security-benefit (_person 2500) if
     widow (_person) and
     has-age (_person _years) and
     not greater-than (_years 60)
```

The following demonstrates the way users ask APES to provide solutions to a query and the way that Query-the-User results in questions to the user. The user's input, including responses, is shown **bold**.

find (_amount : gets-social-security-benefit (Jane _amount))

Is it true that widow (Jane) ?
=> **yes**

which (_X : has-age (Jane _X)) ?
=> **42**

Answer ====> 2500

The next query, to confirm a statement, uses this information.

confirm (gets-social-security-benefit (Jane 2500))

Answer ====> Yes, gets-social-security-benefit (Jane 2500)

Apart from **not**, used, as in the above rule, to mean negation as failure, other extensions to pure Horn Clauses are available in APES, including **isall**, described below, which is used in later examples:

    _list isall (_term : | _goals)

i.e. _list is the list of all the solutions to _term found by solving _goals. APES inherits from PROLOG the use of | as its list constructor.

3. Handling incomplete information from the user
3.1 Previous methods

One common way of allowing the user to say "I don't know" is inherited from early expert systems, where **unknown** is offered as an explicit option. For example:

Do you suffer from diabetes ?

    1 yes
    2 no
    3 unknown

Such a system will generally contain rules with ugly conditions, such as

user-suffering-from-diabetes ((status = yes)) and
user-has-heart-trouble ((status = unknown)) and .... etc.

Clearly, the main problem with this approach, apart from the appearance of the rules, is that the user can say "I don't know" only to questions for which the **unknown** status has been explicitly considered at the object level. To do this throughout greatly increases the work of the knowledge engineer.

A slightly different approach, which has the advantage of more elegant rules but still requires explicit consideration of the unknown state, is to have the question of whether or not the answer is known dealt with separately, before the main question.

Do you know whether or not you suffer from diabetes ?
=> **yes**

Do you suffer from diabetes ?
=> **no**

An early approach implemented in Sergot's Query-the-User was to give the user the option of responding with "?" to a yes/no question. Evaluation of the query continued, all such unknown goals being collected and used to offer a conditional answer to the user, for example

Conditional answer ====> should-avoid (Jane ice-cream) if
                               suffers-from (Jane diabetes).

However, this implementation could not handle programs with negation, **isall** or other high-level operators in them, so was of limited value.

Edmonds (1986) proposes a system, NASK, in which the response "do not know" is always available for a yes/no type of question. This reflects the underlying extended PROLOG interpreter of Aida, Tanaka & Moto-oka (1983). In this, the introduction of negative knowledge into the system is permitted and a goal can be considered to have three possible results: **true, false,** or **unknown.**

The above approaches are essentially concerned with answering "I don't know" to a yes/no question. Another situation, common in logic programming systems, is that of supplying incomplete solutions, where the

user is asked to supply an indefinite number of solutions, or variable
bindings, that satisfy an incompletely defined relationship, but only
knows some of them. The approach to this problem taken in earlier
versions of APES was to allow the user to say **enough** after supplying some
solutions, to indicate that the solutions given might be incomplete.
During evaluation of the query that gave rise to the question, the same
question would not be asked again, but further solutions would be
requested, if necessary, during subsequent queries. The program behaviour
during the initial query was, however, unsatisfactory, since it behaved as
if the user had indicated that all solutions had been given. So, for
example, if the user was questioned and replied as follows:

> which (_X : takes-drug (Bill _X)) ?
> => **aspirin**
> => **lomotil**
> => **enough**

the goal **takes-drug (Bill colchicine)** arising during the query would fail.
The user might well have expected this goal to be undecidable.

A more comprehensive approach, applying to yes/no and
solution-supplying questions, was taken by Vasey (1986), who allowed any
relation to be incompletely defined, and therefore undecidable, and
generated qualified answers based on the incomplete definitions. So, for
example, given the rules

> entitled-to-free-entry if not in-work
>
> in-work if self-employed
> in-work if employee

where the user was asked to confirm **self-employed** and **employee** but replied
"I don't know" in each case, then a qualified answer to the query
entitled-to-free-entry would be produced as follows:

> Qualified answer ====> if   not self-employed and not employee
>   then entitled-to-free-entry

In order to provide such qualified answers, all goals in a
conjunction were evaluated even when one of the goals was undecidable. In
real expert systems, however, this can lead to severe practical problems,
since the order in which goals are evaluated is extremely important and
the conventional left-to-right evaluation is often relied upon, by the
programmer, to ensure correct behaviour. The two main problems that would
be encountered in real expert systems are:

variables in an undecidable goal remain unbound

This can lead to control problems when evaluating the remaining goals
of a conjunction. For example, consider the rule

> .... if
> amount-available (_n) and
> LESS (_n 3000)

If **amount-available (_n)** is unknown, then running the next goal,

LESS (_n 36), would lead to a control error in most PROLOG systems.

dialogue generation

Several goals in a conjunction may involve querying the user. The
programmer will often rely on the fact that previous goals attempted
have succeeded, even if these do not generate any variable bindings,
to ensure that questions asked are sensible. So, for example, the
conjunction

        suffers-from-diabetes (_person) and
        duration-of-diabetes (_person _years)

would lead to sensible behaviour if the first goal were decidable (if
yes, then the duration would be asked, if no, the duration would not
be asked). On the other hand, attempting to solve the second goal if
the first one were undecidable would not be sensible: the duration of
the illness would be asked even though the user did not know whether
or not the person was suffering from it.

        Whilst not insuperable, these problems mean that the
programmer would need to supply a great deal more meta-level control
knowledge to the system to guard against them.

3.2 Handling incomplete information using a suspending interpreter

        The approach taken to dealing with incomplete information from
the user in a recent version of APES is general, conceptually simple, free
of the control problems described above and, in contrast to NASK, does not
rely on a three-valued logic-programming language as its basis.
        The main objective is to allow the user to give incomplete
information to any type of question, i.e.

say "I don't know" to a yes/no question;

give an incomplete (or empty) solution set when asked to supply
solutions.

        The knowledge that the information is incomplete should be
used, where appropriate, to return some sort of conditional answer to a
query posed by the user.
        Currently, implementation is through an interpreter. Before
describing the new interpreter, we shall look at the standard APES
interpreter as this provides a basis for comparison.
        The standard APES interpreter, **interpall**, reflects the
underlying PROLOG interpreter. The following definitions are simplified,
and omit the important proof trace arguments for clarity.

```
interpall (())
interpall ((_goal|_rest-goals)) if
     interp (_goal) and
     interpall (_rest-goals)
```

The first **interpall** definition states that an empty goal list
succeeds. The definition of **interp** is complex, so we shall condider only
the cases of interpreting defined relationships, undefined (interactive)
relationships and negation of a conjunction.

```
interp (_goal) if
     defined-predicate (_goal) and
     database-clause (_goal _subgoals) and
     interpall (_subgoals)
interp (_goal) if
     not defined-predicate (_goal) and
     variable-free (_goal) and
     user-confirms (_goal)
interp (_goal) if
     not defined-predicate (_goal) and
     has-variables-in-goal (_goal _vars) and
     user-supplies-var-bindings (_goal _vars)
interp (not _goals) if
     not interpall (_goals)
```

In this interpreter, the result of interpreting a goal may be
success or **failure**, although only **success** is dealt with explicitly, as in
the underlying PROLOG system.

The new interpreter must deal with goals that have three
possible results: **success, failure** or **unknown**. Because the underlying
PROLOG system can deal with only two results, success or failure, the new
interpreter has an additional argument to cope. As before, failure is not
handled explicitly, whilst the other two are indicated by the value of the
argument. Omitting trace and other arguments for simplicity, the new
interpreter, **susinterpall**, is defined as follows:

```
susinterpall (() success)
susinterpall ((_goal|_rest-goals) _result) if
     susinterp (_goal _result1) and
     continue-interpall (_rest-goals _result1 _result)

continue-interpall (_rest-goals unknown unknown)
continue-interpall (_rest-goals success _result) if
     susinterpall (_rest-goals _result)
```

The behaviour of this interpreter is that a call to
susinterpall succeeds with the result argument set to **unknown** whenever the
result of a call to **susinterp** is **unknown**. That is, normal interpretation
is suspended and no remaining goals in a conjunction are attempted - thus
avoiding the control problems described earlier. Of course, if
alternative solutions are sought, the calls to **susinterp** and **susinterpall**
may then result in **success**. That is, a goal may have several results,
which may be a mixture of **success** and **unknown**.

The definition of **susinterp** for defined and interactive goals
is, in simplified form, as follows:

```
susinterp (_goal _result) if
     defined-predicate (_goal) and
     database-clause (_goal _subgoals) and
     susinterpall (_subgoals _result)
```

```
susinterp (_goal success) if
    not defined-predicate (_goal) and
    variable-free (_goal) and
    user-confirms (_goal)
susinterp (_goal unknown) if
    not defined-predicate (_goal) and
    variable-free (_goal) and
    user-does-not-know (_goal)
susinterp (_goal success) if
    not defined-predicate (_goal) and
    has-variables-in-goal (_goal _vars) and
    user-supplies-var-bindings (_goal _vars)
susinterp (_goal unknown) if
    not defined-predicate (_goal) and
    has-variables-in-goal (_goal _vars) and
    user-indicates-solutions-incomplete (_goal _vars)
```

Clearly, in the case of a goal with variables, where the user may supply any number of solutions, the result may at first be **success** as the user supplies one set of variable bindings, but on backtracking for further solutions, the user may indicate that they are incomplete so the result would then be **unknown**.

The interpretation of **not**, i.e. negation as failure (Clark 1978), is based on the assumption that a relation P is false if and only if we do an exhaustive search to find a proof of P, but find that every possible proof fails in finite time. Now, if the search results in an incomplete proof of P, that is, the result is **unknown**, then the search is not exhaustive so the falsehood of P can not be assumed. On the other hand, a proof with the result **success** demonstrates that P is true, i.e. that not P is false. If the search yields only proofs that have an **unknown** result, then the result of not P must itself be **unknown**.

```
susinterp ((not _goals) _result) if
    _set isall (_result1 : susinterpall (_goals _result1)) and
    result-of-negation (_set _result)

result-of-negation (() success)
result-of-negation (_set unknown) if
    not ON (success _set) and
    ON (unknown _set)
```

This program for interpreting negation makes the attempted exhaustive search explicit as it involves finding the set of all the results of interpreting the unnegated goals. The result of the negation is **success** if an empty set is found and **unknown** if the set does not contain a result of **success** but does contain an **unknown** result. The call to **susinterp** fails if the set contains at least one result of **success**.

The following points on this handling of negation should be noted:

in practice, the search for the set of all solutions is cut off when the first result of **success** is found;

if all solutions are sought, and no **success** result is found, the result of negation will be **unknown** for as many times as there are

unknown results in the set, due to the multiple solutions of the **ON**
relation. This is important when you remember that the trace
arguments are not shown, since, in reality, each **unknown** result will
be associated with a different trace argument and hence a different
conditional answer (see below).

3.3 Conditional Answers

The suspending interpreter described above had certain
arguments omitted for clarity. These included the ones containing the
proof trace constructed during evaluation of the query. When the
interpretation suspends, i.e. yields the result **unknown,** the resulting
trace argument contains the partially evaluated proof tree. This is used
to generate a conditional, or partially qualified, answer. To demonstrate
conditional answers, consider the following rules:

```
suitable-driver-for-party (_person) if
     enjoys-parties (_person) and
     should-avoid (_person alcohol)

should-avoid (_person alcohol) if
     suffers-from (_person diabetes)
```

If the query is posed:

confirm (suitable-driver-for-party (Jane))

the following dialogue may occur, resulting in the conditional answer
shown:

```
Is it true that enjoys-parties (Jane) ?
=> yes

Is it true that suffers-from (Jane diabetes) ?
=> I don't know

Conditional answer ====>  if    suffers-from (Jane diabetes)
                          then suitable-driver-for-party (Jane)
```

If the following query is posed:

find (_person : suitable-driver-for-party (_person))

the following dialogue could occur, with resulting solutions as shown.

```
which (_X : enjoys-parties (_X)) ?
=> Tom
=> Jane
=> incomplete answers

Is it true that suffers-from (Tom diabetes) ?
=> yes

Answer ====> Tom
```

```
Is it true that suffers-from (Jane diabetes) ?
=> I don't know

Conditional answer ====> if   suffers-from (Jane diabetes)
                            then suitable-driver-for-party (Jane)

Conditional answer ====> if   suffers-from (_X diabetes)
                            then suitable-driver-for-party (_X)
```

In this case, one real answer to the query is found, Tom, and two conditional answers. The first is specific to Jane, and results from the **I don't know** response, while the second is more general and arises from the **incomplete answers** response. The second is essentially a relevant condensing, or summary, of the program rules.

3.4 The limitations and strengths of conditional answers

The first conditional answer given above is also the fully qualified answer that would result from Vasey's interpreter. However, in general, a conditional, or partially qualified, answer will differ from a qualified answer - the quality of the conditional answer is not as high as that of the qualified answer. This is the price that is paid for the avoidance of control problems. To compare the two, consider the following program

```
a if b and
     not c and
     d
a if h

b

c if e and
     f
c if g

d

e
```

where **f, g,** and **h** are all **unknown** and pose the query

```
confirm (a)
```

Two fully qualified answers would be generated :

```
Qualified answer ====> if   not f and
                          not g
                       then a

Qualified answer ====> if   h
                       then a
```

whilst the suspending interpreter would yield three conditional answers:

```
Conditional answer ====> if   f
                         then c

                         if   not c and
                              d
                         then a
Conditional answer ====> if   g
                         then c

                         if   not c and
                              d
                         then a
Conditional answer ====> if   h
                         then a
```

The main differences are:

a conditional answer is not necessarily a single theorem or rule.
Instead, it is a set of related theorems that should contribute to
the user's understanding of the problem;

a conditional answer does not make full use of available information
because further evaluation of a conjunction is cut off. For example,
the first conditional answer (similarly the second) could be reduced
to

```
                         if   f
                         then c

                         if   not c
                         then a
```

because **d** is given in the program.

    Whilst acknowledging the above shortcomings of conditional
answers, we would claim that this method of generating conditional
answers, and the answers themselves, have certain advantages:

the knowledge engineer, or programmer, does not need to supply any
additional meta-level information to guard against control problems.
If the program runs without control problems when all information is
supplied by the user, it will also run without control problems when
only some, or none, of the information is supplied;

in complex situations, a conditional answer comprising a set of
related theorems can be easier to understand than a single theorem.
In particular, the user can easily see the direct effect any of the
incompletely defined goals might have.

4. Other applications of the suspending interpreter

    One useful application of the suspending interpreter is to run
a program that contains interactive relations in non-interactive mode.

This yields a set of conditional answers, useful for:

a)   posing **how-can** queries, such as "how can **a** be true", above;
b)   informing a user **why** a question is being asked, by re-running the
     original query without interaction and displaying those partially
     qualified answers conditional on the current question;
c)   program testing.

The suspending interpreter is, however, quite general and may be applied
to problems other than interaction with the user.   An application in which
it has already been used for a different purpose is the development of
GLIMPSE (Wolstenholme & O'Brien 1986), a front end to a statistics package
GLIM.   The front end is designed to advise the user what commands to give
the package to find out information about a data set.   The information
found is used when advising further commands as it is explicitly referred
to in the rules on which the advice is based.   When interpreting these
rules, the interpreter suspends if a relationship cannot be evaluated
because the information referred to, necessary to provide the advice, has
not yet been found from the system.   In this case, rather than give a
conditional answer based on the missing information, the interpreter uses
meta-level knowledge to advise the user on the commands to give the system
in order to find it out.

Acknowledgements

The author wishes to thank Peter Hammond both for his
encouragement and advice and for his comments on an earlier draft.

References

Aida, H., Tanaka, H. & Moto-oka T. (1983).   A prolog extension for
handling negative knowledge.   New Generation Computing, $\underline{1}$, pp. 87 - 91.

Clark, K.L. (1978).   Negation as failure. $\underline{\text{In}}$ Logic and Data Bases, eds.
H. Gallaire and J. Minker.   New York: Plenum Press.

Edmonds, E. (1986).   Negative knowledge toward a strategy for asking in
logic programming.   Int. J. Man-Machine Studies, $\underline{24}$, pp. 597 - 600.
Academic Press Inc.

Hammond, P. & Sergot, M. (1984).   APES: Augmented Prolog for Expert
Systems, Reference Manual. Surrey: Logic Based Systems.

Sergot, M. (1982).   A Query-the-User Facility for Logic Programming. $\underline{\text{In}}$
Integrated Interactive Computing Systems (1983), eds. P. Degano and
E. Sandewall.   North-Holland.

Vasey, P. (1986).   Qualified answers and their applications to
programming. $\underline{\text{In}}$ Procs. of 3rd. Int. Conf. on Logic Programming, London,
ed. E. Shapiro. Springer-Verlag.

Wolstenholme, D.E. & O'Brien, C.M. (1986). GLIMPSE - A statistical
adventure. $\underline{\text{In}}$ Procs. IJCAI 1987, Milan.

THE INTEGRATED USER

Robin Muir
Systems Research Specialist
Rolls-Royce plc
P.O. Box 3
Filton
Bristol

Abstract

        Artificial Intelligence (AI) technology will
impact on industrial processes only through the people who
operate those industrial processes.
        The methods of interaction available to todays
user limit the effectiveness and novelty of the
application systems which can be developed.
        To make fuller use of knowledge in application
systems, a closer and more diverse relationship between
user and system is needed. To integrate the user properly,
the user should be able to interact with the application
system by the sense appropriate to the information being
conveyed.
        Closer interaction, with an understanding of the
users intentions, will not be achieved without the use of
AI techniques.
        Viewing the future however imperfectly, this
paper proposes and describes a general purpose, integrated
interface to capitalise on various current AI research
topics.

1. Introduction

        When invited to provide a paper discussing the
impact of AI technology on industry, the author considered
that AI technology will impact on industrial processes
only through the people who operate those industrial
processes. Further consideration led to the realisation
that, in general, application systems implement
communications in industrial processes, either to human
beings or between human beings, conveying information
about the current state of the industrial processes. This
realisation then led to an examination of the
communications faculties used by human beings, in an
industrial context, to establish where AI technology can
improve applications by supporting those communications
faculties.

2. Industrial context

        The conventional computing industry as we know
it today has developed over the past 40 years. During that

time the primary thrust of development has been to
increase the power and complexity of the computer itself.
The user is limited to the methods of communication
available through the interface device provided (usually a
Cathode Ray Tube (CRT) and keyboard), rather than being
free to choose his own methods of communication, depending
upon the subject and context of his work.

Human beings communicate in a variety of ways,
which, in combination, provide a rich spectrum of
communicative ability. Reducing user-to-system
communication to the commonly supplied interface provides
a very pallid emulation of human faculties and constrains
our opportunities to develop more effective and more novel
application systems.

Although human beings are trained, from birth,
to use spoken natural language as their primary means of
communication, in providing communications between user
and system, developers are forced to substitute and
specialise.

In constructing user dialogue, which would be
conducted more naturally in speech, the developer
substitutes the use of a CRT and keyboard which are
physically connected to the computer. The developer
translates the dialogue into the framework and limitations
of the physical devices. Constraints stem from this
substitution. The most common general purpose CRT imposes
80 character X 24 line format for screen design, within
which all user dialogue must be made. This results,
generally, in contrived, form filling screens with
everything included, whether relevant or not. Furthermore,
human speech is relatively fast, certainly much faster
than the speed with which most systems users can provide
keyboard input. Using a keyboard effectively (even with
two fingers) requires practice, and, where significant
input is required, the keyboard limits the potential speed
of the dialogue and the potential effectiveness of the
users application. In addition, the keyboard imposes
physical ties on the user, primarily of location. However,
not only does the user need at least one hand free but, in
some cases, he needs both hands and multiple fingers on
each hand in order to use the keyboard.

Specialisation occurs in the developers use of
different keys or combinations of keys for controlling
what are essentially common functions in application
systems. In effect, the human users are forced to learn a
new mini language for each new system, ignoring the fact
that the users already have a common language for
communication ie. their own natural language.

For some areas of industry, a typical user
reaction to the above situation is shown in Figure 1.

The complement of speech in verbal communication
is speech recognition. The authors experience of
communications in industry is that virtually every major
communication document is supplemented verbally by

Figure 1

I'm not a ****** typist, I can't use that!

presentations or explanations. This leads the author to
believe, quite pragmatically, that humans understand the
spoken word better than the equivalent text. The
constraint of using printed output on a CRT screen (or
printer) limits the understanding and interpretation of
the results of our application systems.
        The above points are related to the
effectiveness of the applications. However, the absence of
other facilities, which humans have and use instinctively,
limit the novelty of the ways in which applications can be
provided.
        The visual element of human communication is
frequently observed when one party in a conversation draws
a diagram or shows an example. A visual representation of
the subject matter provides a very succinct way of
communicating meaning or understanding. Although visual
communication can be provided in application systems by
providing graphical or pictorial representations of the
output, communication with the user is limited to being
one way. In general, the user cannot, in return, show the
system a visual representation of his desired goal.
        The audio element of communication (other than
speech recognition) is observed in the recognition of
sounds relevant to the current context of the human
listener. A simple example is provided by the sound of the
wind through obstructions. The level and quality of sound
provides the human listener with an instant approximation
of the wind strength. In industry, the operation of plant
and equipment causes characteristic sound patterns to be
produced. The human listener uses these patterns to
confirm his belief in normal operation or to detect
abnormal operation. While application systems do, on
occasions, provide sonic output (eg. identifying errors),
again the process is one way. The user has no facility to
ask his systems to listen to the object in question for
advice or interpretation on the sound pattern which it
produces.

In addition, human communications involve touch, smell and taste to convey information, although more rarely. The author is not aware of any application systems which are capable of supporting any of these ways of communicating, even unidirectionaly.

The above examination leads the author to the conclusion that the user is the least integrated element of his own application systems. The user interface lacks the versatility of human faculties and, in that lack, imposes limitations on physical location, effectiveness of operation and novelty of application. Indeed, it can be said that we design human systems to satisfy computers instead of designing computer systems to satisfy human beings.

3. Objectives

There are three objectives for a general purpose, integrated interface capable of overcoming the above limitations and providing the user with a closer and more effective interaction.

First of all, it must be a multi function (ie. multi sensory), interface. Many real world problems depend on knowledge from different sources; and, by inference, from different senses.

Secondly, to achieve a closer and more effective interaction between user and application, the interface must be intelligent and must be able to understand the users intentions, in the context of his work.

The third objective for the interface is that it be portable and, by implication, light weight and compact.

To provide the physical capablities and the understanding necessary in the interface, AI techniques, which are currently being researched, will be essential.

4. Interface Functions

A great deal of human activity is carried out with the aid of sensory knowledge. Thus, the functions of the interface are based upon the human senses, including the faculty of speech.

            ie.   speech
                   sight
                   sound
                   touch
                   smell
                   taste

Each faculty will be examined to consider the contribution it can make to an integrated interface.

4.1 Speech

The major means of communication between human beings is by speech; more accurately, it is by spoken natural language. From a systems users viewpoint, the desire to use natural language (as opposed to short hand codes or artificial languages) is strong. However, to convey natural language by mechanical means such as a keyboard, is extremely long winded. Hence, an interface intended to be closely supportive of a users requirements (ie. modelling a users faculties) must provide both speech recognition and generation (speech I/O) coupled with natural language processing.

A good argument for using speech I/O in an interface is found by looking at the stilted and constrained interfaces which exist in todays systems. Where an interactive dialogue is used, the system waits for a response or input from its user. The use of speech I/O would improve the speed of communication between user and system (perhaps by a factor of 10).

However, on its own, improving the speed of communication ignores the opportunity to do something better. In order to provide a closer relationship between the user and his applications and to enhance the (knowledge based) systems efficiency, the interface must "understand" the users intentions. This could be achieved by the use of user models (Sparck Jones) to distinguish between user states and to control system behaviour in the context of the current task.

As an interface, natural language provides convenience and flexibility, facets which are related to its expressive power. But, more importantly, natural language is argued to be the only rich enough source of information for user models.

To support this requirement, the interface will enable the user to verbally communicate with his applications using a speech I/O facility, supported by a natural language processing capability.

Research which is relevant to supporting this function is in progress in natural language research (Alvey IKBS 019), speech input (Alvey LD 006) and speech I/O (Alvey MMI/SP 054) among others.

4.2 Sight

Sight or vision also plays a big part in human interaction with the real world.

In a user interface, what would we require from a vision facility?

Two user requirements emerge immediately.

First of all, the user will want to see what the system is trying to portray to him. this may take the form of graphs or diagrams or stored pictures in addition to succinct textual output. Therefore, we need a facility on

which the computers information can be shown. Ideally,
this will be a head up display too avoid restricting the
user to the location of a CRT device.

Secondly, the user will want to show to the
application system, objects at which he himself is
looking. The application will have the ability to
recognise the objects and to provide the user with advice
or interpretation about these objects.

Relevant supporting research is being carried
out into thin film electroluminescent flat panel displays
(Alvey MMI/DIS 066), user programmable image processing
(Alvey MMI/IP 093) and real time vision systems (Alvey
MMI/IP 137), among other projects.

4.3   Sound

Sound adds a further significant element to the
human interaction with the real world.

The perception of sound or, more usually, a
sound pattern, can be used in two ways.

First of all, it can be used to detect the
presence or absence of a sound (pattern). The presence or
absence of a sound (pattern) is evidence of a physical
event which has happened or is about to happen.

Secondly, the perception of sound can be used to
recognise a characteristic sound signature (pattern) from
which minor deviations may or may not be acceptable. Where
minor deviations from the sound (pattern) are acceptable,
the recognition of the sound (pattern) is evidence of a
physical process being carried out. The ability to detect
minor deviations from a characteristic sound (pattern)
provides the capability of using the deviations themselves
as evidence of a departure from some physical norm.

The user of systems which require sound
(pattern) detection or recognition will want his
applications to hear the sound to which he himself is
listening.

While further research and development will be
required to implement this requirement, techniques which
underpin it already exist. The sonar devices in naval
vessels are purported to be capable of detection and
identification of the sound patterns produced by other
vessels. Proprietary software to perform knowledge based
vibration analysis can already be purchased on the open
market.

4.4   Touch

The sense of touch provides the fourth function
of the user interface.

By this means, human beings are able to detect
and assess physical objects qualitatively, without
supporting metrics. Many tasks are carried out by using
qualitative assessments of physical attributes such as

sharpness, smoothness, flatness, hardness, firmness, texture, surface finish, etc.
     The provision of a tactile sensor in the user interface will enable the users applications to qualitatively evaluate the attributes of the object with which the user is working.
     Research which could support this function has been undertaken, for example, in the context of machine learning (Michie).

4.5 Smell and Taste

     The senses of smell and taste will be dealt with together for two reasons.
     The senses of smell and taste are based on chemical processes rather than physical processes. In addition, these two senses work in a complimentary way. Smell is enhanced by the sense of taste and taste is enhanced by the sense of smell.
     There will be a number of applications which require olefactory or taste sensors and the majority of those will be found in the drug, cosmetic and food and drink industries.
     A knowledge based system has been developed for chemical structure elucidation from mass spectral data (Buchanan and Feigenbaum) which could underpin further work on this requirement. However, the author is not aware of current research in this area.
     Never the less, for a number of industries, the requirement will remain that olefactory and taste inputs be part of a future integrated user interface.

4.6 External Communications

     A function which has not hitherto been mentioned is that of communications. To satisfy the requirement of having a truly portable device, the interface will need two-way communication, without physical connection, with application systems which are resident in remote computers. This function will enable the user to have access to his application systems wherever he is, subject to the coverage of the communications link; ie. the device goes with the user to his current place of work.
     Research work which underpins this need is in progress into mobile information systems (Alvey LD 002).

5. Sensory Priorities

     The two senses of speech and vision are essential to the interface.
     The core of the interface is speech I/O with supporting natural language processing. The normal way in which human beings intercommunicate is by speech and that speech is expressed in natural language. Therefore it

would seem quite natural and logical that a computer
interface be based around speech and natural language
facilities.

However, a significant proportion of
communication is done visually. Passive use of vision
occurs where a small group of people wish to communicate
remotely in distance or time with a wider audience. In the
every day world, road signs, traffic lights, advertising
posters and television are obvious examples. However, in
industrial situations, much of the visual communication is
carried out interactively, using representations such as
drawings, diagrams or pictures. This interactive facility
is essential in the interface.

Hearing and touch are highly desirable, either
as primary sources of information or as confirmation of
information partially established by speech or vision.

The senses of taste and smell are least
necessary for general purpose communications. However,
they are desirable in the interface. In particular, if a
way can be found to provide sensors and to store
olefactory and taste templates for comparison and
reference, the application of knowledge based systems in
industries such as food and drink, pharmaceutical,
chemical and perfumery would be greatly extended.

Although not a sense, the external
communications function is also an essential.

6. The Physical Device

A physical interface device which provides a set
of functions such as have been described, should provide
the functions where the most significant group of the
sense organs already are, ie. on the head.

Bearing in mind the third objective for the
interface, such a device could be based on a development
of the simple spectacles and would have a configuration as
shown in Figure 2 and as suggested below -

bridge unit   - To provide a separate speech input
                 channel, the bridge unit will carry a light
                 weight boom microphone.
                 - For visual input to the computer, the
                 bridge will carry cameras to provide
                 binocular vision from the same viewpoint as
                 the users eyes.
                 - The bridge will also carry twin
                 microphones to provide sonic detection with
                 directional capability.
                 - In addition, the bridge unit will carry
                 necessary processor boards.

lens   - For visual output from the computer, the
                 lens position would be used for a head up
                 display.

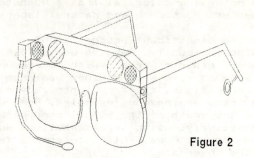

Figure 2

arms	— For speech output from the computer, the arms would support hearing aid devices, positioned beside the users ears.
plug in cord	— interchangeable tactile sensors
frame	— The frame will serve as an aerial for the radio link to access external computers.

It is difficult to recommend how to mount smell and taste sensors without knowing the form or the method of operation of them. However, it is likely that plug in devices would be most convenient.

In the event that the bridge cannot carry the necessary processor boards, the head set will be connected to a pocket size or belt mounted processor in an enclosure approximately the size of a portable Compact Disc player. Advantage would be taken from this arrangement by the provision of local storage capacity using an optical WMRM laser disc.

7. Conclusion

Users can view technological research and development very cynically. Advancing technological frontiers prompts the familiar phrase "technology looking for a place to happen". There is a need for an "application pull" for technology expressed as a user requirement.

The preceding sections of this paper have described a user requirement for a general purpose, integrated interface through which the user will have a closer and more diverse relationship with his application systems. Such an interface will be implemented only by using AI technology, and, as has been pointed out, research is already in progress on many relevant strands of the technology. However, we must generate the will to pull the various strands together, although, at the same time, we must not underestimate the size and complexity of the problems which have yet to be solved, before such a device can be produced.

8. References

Alvey IKBS 019, Automatic Natural Language Research, In Alvey Programme Annual Report, 1986, Poster Supplement, IEE.
Alvey LD 002, Mobile Information Systems, In Alvey Programme Annual Report, 1986, Poster Supplement, IEE.

Alvey LD 006, Speech Input Wordprocessor & Workstation, In Alvey Programme Annual Report, 1986, Poster Supplement, IEE.

Alvey MMI/DIS 066, Thin Film Electroluminescent Flat Panel Display Technology, In Alvey Programme Annual Report, 1986, Poster Supplement, IEE.

Alvey MMI/IP 093, Techniques for User-Programmable Image Processing, In Alvey Programme Annual Report, 1986, Poster Supplement, IEE.

Alvey MMI/IP 137, Real Time 2.5D Vision Systems,, In Alvey Programme Annual Report, 1986, Poster Supplement, IEE.

Alvey MMI/SP 054, Speech I/O: An Implementation for Chinese, In Alvey Programme Annual Report, 1986, Poster Supplement, IEE.

Buchanan B. and Feigenbaum E. DENDRAL and META-DENDRAL: Their Applications Dimension In Artificial Intelligence 11, 5-24 (1978).

Michie D. Memory Mechanisms and Machine Learning In On Machine Intelligence, Ellis Horwood Ltd, 1986, ISBN 0-7458-0084.

Sparck Jones K. Natural Language Interfaces for Expert Systems: An Introductory Note In Research and Development in Expert Systems 1984, Ed. M.A.Bramer, Cambridge University Press.

9. Disclaimer

The opinions expressed in this paper are the authors own and are not necessarily supported by Rolls-Royce plc.

A FORMAL EVALUATION OF KNOWLEDGE ELICITATION TECHNIQUES FOR
EXPERT SYSTEMS: DOMAIN 1 (*)

A M Burton, N R Shadbolt, A P Hedgecock and G Rugg
Department of Psychology, University of Nottingham, Nottingham
NG7 2RD

Abstract

Four knowledge elicitation techniques are compared in an
experimental study. The techniques are interview, protocol analysis,
laddered grid and card sorting. Knowledge bases were elicited from 32
experts, each being subject to two techniques. Protocol analysis is seen
to take longer, and yield less information, than comparable techniques.
Laddered grid and card sorting, despite being contrived and unusual
techniques, are shown to be as efficient as more traditional techniques.
Data are presented relating experts' individual characteristics
(personality and cognitive style) to the efficacy of each technique. The
possibility of matching experts to knowledge elicitation techniques is
discussed.

1. Introduction

A major stumbling block in the development of Expert Systems
is the process of getting knowledge from a human expert (Hayes-Roth et al,
1983). The problem of knowledge elicitation (KE) is an applied problem in
Cognitive Science embodying as it does issues of human memory and
artificial systems of knowledge representation. In this paper we present
an experimental study of the efficacy of various established techniques.

The literature on KE is disappointing for those wishing to
build an Expert System. Most studies of the effectiveness of various KE
techniques fall into two categories: (i) those which report a case study;
and (ii) those which attempt to match KE techniques with types of
knowledge on theoretical grounds. The first type of study (e.g. Smith and
Baker, 1983) is unsatisfactory because one may not generalise the results.
The efficacy of the various techniques will very probably vary across
domains and even across individual experts. Moreover, the recommendations
that emerge, such as "don't forget to record your interview", leave one
with the feeling that there ought to be more to say. The second type of
study (e.g. Gammack and Young, 1985) tends to be uncompelling. Certainly
the mapping of KE techniques onto domains often seems plausible, but then
alternative mappings seem equally plausible. For instance, it is all very
well to recommend a procedural technique when tapping procedural
knowledge, but how is a novice meant to decide what is procedural and
what declarative for a given knowledge domain?

This distinction, between procedural and declarative knowledge
has been used a great deal in KE work. Varieties of the distinction can
be traced through the work of a number of philosophers and psychologists
(Ryle 1949; Anderson 1983). The essence of the distinction can be

(*) This work was carried out as part of an ALVEY award to the authors
(IKBS 134). We would like to thank Prof. Baker, Dept. of Geology, University of Nottingham, and his colleagues for their kind help in preparing
the stimulus materials for this study.

captured in the difference between knowing how (procedural knowledge) and knowing that (declarative knowledge). Different techniques in KE are seen as differentially tapping procedural and declarative knowledge.

Our dissatisfaction with the KE literature led us to undertake a study evaluating KE techniques. We have reduced this study to a laboratory experiment. Of course this may incur scaling problems, but this risk seems worthwhile considering the gain we make by being able to generalise results from a multi-expert study.

2. The Techniques

The four techniques we have chosen to evaluate in this study are:

1. Formal Interview: this is the standard common sense KE technique. The interview is formal in that its structure is closely specified. The format used in this study involves the expert providing an overview of the task, followed by the elicitor seeking verification of particular assertions in a recursive manner. The elicitor is only allowed to use certain probes, and the whole process is directed at eliciting rules, rather than vague recommendations etc. This is allied to Grover's (1983) 'forward scenario simulation'. During the interview hypothetical problems arise, and are solved by the expert. The formal interview primarily elicits procedural knowledge.
2. Protocol Analysis: in this technique one observes the expert actually solving problems in the domain of interest. The expert is encouraged to verbalise decisions taken on the way to a solution. Rules are induced in a post hoc manner from the surface behaviour of the expert. Protocol Analysis primarily elicits procedural knowledge.
3. Goal Decomposition (laddered grid): in this technique the problem space is represented as a hierarchy of goals - terminating in solutions to the problem. The elicitor makes a random entry into the space and moves around it with prepared probes to explore up, down and across the hierarchy. The space is built up with pencil and paper in front of the subject. As an example, imagine the domain is the classification of animals - one may enter the domain with the target "dog", and use such probes as "what examples are there of dogs?" in order to move down the hierarchy. There are other versions of goal decomposition (Grover 1983), but the laddered grid provides a suitable example of the generic technique here, because it is easy to hold constant for many KE sessions. A laddered grid primarily elicits declarative knowledge.
4. Multi-dimensional analysis (card sort): this technique provides a qualitative multi-dimensional mapping of the elements in the problem domain. This is achieved by repeated sorts of a deck of cards, marked with the domain elements. On each sort, the expert is required to label the overall scale (factor) and the individual piles (levels), Rules are then extracted through classification matches. The card sort primarily elicits declarative knowledge.(*)

These techniques are not designed to be used alone (Welbank 1983). Clearly, as we have suggested, different techniques will favour

(*) Burton and Shadbolt (in press) give a full account of the techniques.

different kinds of knowledge, both within and between domains.

In this study we have examined plausible combinations of two techniques. In fact we have chosen combinations of a procedural with a declarative technique. This allows us to examine not only the efficacy of individual techniques, but also their efficacies in combination.

We have also restricted ourselves to elicitation directed toward a single target representation - production rules. Expert systems can embody a range of representational formalisms, and production systems are a very popular device (Waterman 1985). It is important to point out that Expert Systems can also be built round structured objects such as semantic nets or frames. The results presented here may not transfer to these alternative representations. We have chosen production rules for three reasons. They are the most commonly used representation. Production rules have a simple and regular structure, this has the added advantage that it is easier to take measures of the quality of the knowledge bases built out of productions. Finally, a purely pragmatic reason, choosing one target representation kept the size of our experimental design under control.

3. The Domain

The domain for this study is the identification of igneous rocks. In choosing a domain for which there are many experts and for which an experimental study is possible, we need to restrict it in such a way that the study is feasible, but the domain remains non-trivial. In consultation with an expert Geologist (see acknowledgement at the start of this paper) we constructed a set of 16 igneous rocks which are not trivially discriminable, but which form a homogeneous set. The students used as subjects have learned these rocks early in their University careers and subsequently used, and built upon, these discriminations. For the benefit of anyone reading this article with a knowledge of igneous rocks, the set of rocks used was: Adamellite, Granite, Granodiorite, Kentallenite, Diorite-Tonalite, Nepheline-Syenite, Gabbro, Peridotite, Dunite-Periodotite, Dolerite, Microgranite, Dacite, Rhyolite, Trachyte, Andesite and Basalt. These rocks can be discriminated on the basis of such characteristics as colour, and the crystal shape, cleavage, hardness and optical interference colours of their constituent minerals.

4. Method

Subjects

Subjects were 32 undergraduate Geology students. The students were all volunteers from the 2nd or 3rd year of study, and so had all used the skills necessary in this task repeatedly (see above). We therefore assert that these subjects function as models for genuine experts. Subjects were paid a small sum (£4) for their participation.

Design

Each subject took part in elicitation sessions for two KE techniques. Subjects were randomly assigned to one of four groups: interview and laddered grid; interview and card sort; protocol analysis and laddered grid; protocol analysis and card sort. This means that we can compare the four groups against each other (8 subjects per group) but can also compare the two procedural techniques and the two declarative techniques (16 subjects per group in each comparison). Order of testing in the four groups was counterbalanced so that order could be analysed as a factor.

Dependent measures in this type of study are not easy to establish - what constitutes the efficacy of a technique? Different knowledge engineers will have different constraints on the system development. For this reason we took a variety of measures here, with the notion that engineers can decide for themselves upon the relative importance of the various factors. Dependent measures taken were: time taken for the elicitation session; time taken to code the transcripts of the session into a set of rules; number of rules elicited; number of clauses constituting the elicited rules; completeness of rule set. The final three measures need some explanation.

The total number of rules is simply the number of rules elicited, whether 'correct' or not. As rules can have multiple LHSs, the number of rules is not a good indicator of how much information is encapsulated in the rule set. For example, a typical rule in this domain has the following form:

```
IF grain size        IS coarse
AND p_clase feldspar IS absent
AND colour           IS melanocratic
AND content          IS mainly olivine
THEN rock            IS peridotite
```

Therefore we have taken the 'number of clauses' measure; this is simply a count of the LHS elements of all the elicited rules. So, a rule of the form: IF A and B and C and D then E, counts as having four clauses. In addition to quantity, we need a measure of quality of our elicited rule bases. In order to measure this, a senior expert Geologist was recruited to construct a 'gold standard' rule set. The 'completeness of rule set' measure is a comparison of elicited rule sets with this gold standard. That is, how much of the information encapsulated in the gold standard, is encapsulated in the elicited rule base.

In addition to these measures, each subject was given two psychometric tests - personality and cognitive style. It may be that individual experts' characteristics make them more or less amenable to the different KE techniques. The personality test constituted the Introvert-Extravert questions from the Eysenck Personality Inventory, or EPI. The cognitive style measure is a psychological differentiation between field-dependent and field-independent subjects (see Witkin and Oltman 1967). It has been known for some time that people have different 'styles' for thinking. Field-dependent people have a tendency to see problems as a whole, and rely on the context of a given problem. On the other hand field-independent subjects can extract the important parts of a problem from the prevailing context. This dimension is sometimes called the global-articulated dimension and has been used to predict a number of other interesting variables - for instance the styles are differentially prevalent in different professional occupations. This measure was made on the Embedded Figures Test, or EFT (Witkin, Oltman, Raskin and Karp 1971).

Procedure

Each subject was asked to attend two elicitation sessions.

Subjects were told the nature of the study, and the set of rocks which we were interested in was explained. Subjects were also briefed on the nature of the target representation. They were shown a production rule from another domain in order that they understood the nature of the rules we were seeking.

The procedure for the formal interview was as described above. For the protocol analysis sessions, subjects were given a randomly-chosen subset of the rocks. A sample of each of the rocks was available, and subjects were asked to make their classification, verbalising wherever possible. A microscope, prepared slides for each of the samples, and other laboratory equipment was available to them.

The card sort was performed with a deck of cards, each bearing the name of one of the rocks in the domain. The laddered grid technique required only a large sheet of paper and a pencil to draw out the domain.

All sessions were recorded, as asides often form useful snippets for knowledge engineers. Any information gathered from one of these asides was counted as coming from the techniques being used when it was made. This is a defensible line, as we remain agnostic about whether the techniques work in the simple way they are assumed to work.

5. Results

With regards the overall efficacy of the techniques, two sets of analyses are appropriate, one comparing the four groups, and one comparing individual techniques. This is because the analysis by group represents the combined DVs, and not just the mean of each technique. So, in the combined analysis, completeness of rule set (for example) reflects the completeness of the rule set gained from a combination of both techniques. There is overlap between the techniques, and so the analysis by individual technique provides a different measure - completeness from a single technique.

Table 1 shows the results of the analysis of the four different groups. For none of the five measures is there a significant effect of KE combination. Although there are some interesting trends, there is just too small a number of subjects to pick up any but the largest of effects here. The 'number of rules' measure is omitted here for reasons that will be apparent in Table 3. Notably, the card sort technique reveals very few rules in the first instance, simply a categorical analysis reflecting the number of sorts. This is not really very interesting, and has no bearing on the amount of information present.

	Interview & Ladd. Grid	Interview & Card Sort	Prot. An. & Ladd. Grid	Prot. An. & Card Sort
Elic. Time (min)	51	44	61	57
Trans Time (min)	109	97	129	129
Total Time (min)	160	140	191	185
Total Clauses	170	130	166	143
Completeness (%)	34	39	30	33

Table 1: Mean DV scores on the four combinations of techniques (n=8/gp)

Table 2 shows the results of the analysis of the procedural techniques. The two significant results here are total time $(F(1,30)=4.2, p<0.05)$ and completeness of rule set $(F(1,30)=39.3, p<0.05)$; protocol analysis taking longer and giving less information than the interview.

	Interview	Protocol Analysis	
Elic. Time (min)	24.4	30.6	
Trans Time (min)	56.4	79.7	
Total Time (min)	80.8	110.3	$(p<0.05)$
Number of Rules	54.9	45.1	
Total Clauses	94.4	75.8	
Completeness (%)	27.9	7.9	$(p<0.05)$

Table 2: Mean DV scores for the procedural techniques (n=16/gp)

Table 3 shows the results of the analysis of the declarative techniques. The two significant results here are number of rules $(F(1,30)=46.4, p<0.05)$ and number of clauses $(F(1,30)=10.7, p<0.05)$. The number of rules elicited from each technique is uninteresting for the reasons given above. However, it is interesting to note that even though the card sort provides fewer clauses, it still produces the same coverage of the gold standard rule set as the laddered grid.

	Laddered Grid	Card Sort	
Elic. Time (min)	28.5	22.7	
Trans Time (min)	51.3	44.8	
Total Time (min)	79.8	67.0	
Number of Rules	73.9	14.9	$(p<0.05)$
Total Clauses	101.4	63.4	$(p<0.05)$
Completeness (%)	28.1	30.0	

Table 3: Mean DV scores for the declarative techniques (n=16/gp)

We now consider the data from the psychometric measures. Table 4 shows the correlation coefficients relating scores on the EPI to the various dependent measures. This is interesting in that the measure only seems to covary with success in the interview technique. In brief, introverts take longer to complete the interview, but provide more rules and clauses. We shall come back to this in the discussion section.

Table 5 shows the correlation coefficients relating scores on

	Interview	Protocol Analysis	Card Sort	Laddered Grid
Elic. Time	-.73**	.21	.02	-.53*
Trans Time	-.59*	.06	.20	-.25
Total Time	-.65**	.11	.14	-.36
Number of Rules	-.73**	.43	.12	-.07
Total Clauses	-.71**	.15	-.15	-.17
Completeness (%)	-.43	-.05	-.01	.30

* $p < 0.05$;   ** $p < 0.01$

Table 4: Correlation coeffs for the EPI with each DV, across the techniques (Introvert = low; Extravert = high; n = 16)

the EFT to the various dependent measures. Once again, a fairly consistent pattern emerges. Cognitive style only covaries with measures for the protocol analysis and laddered grid techniques. In the case of the laddered grid, field-dependent (global) subjects provide transcripts which are harder to convert into rules than do their field-independent (articulated) colleagues. In the case of the protocol analysis, global subjects provide more rules and clauses than their articulated colleagues, though this does not have a bearing on completeness of rule set.

	Interview	Protocol Analysis	Card Sort	Laddered Grid
Elic. Time	.27	.46	.29	.48
Trans Time	.26	.31	-.17	.62*
Total Time	.27	.39	.01	.63**
Number of Rules	.39	.72**	-.01	.32
Total Clauses	.33	.66**	.13	.26
Completeness (%)	.43	-.48	-.49	-.02

* $p < 0.05$;   ** $p < 0.01$

Table 5: Correlation coeffs for the EFT with each DV across the techniques (articulated = low; global = high; n = 16)

We now consider the proportion of coverage given by the various techniques. It seems somewhat surprising from tables 1, 2 and 3 that so little of the gold standard is covered by each of the subjects. In fact almost all the rules of the gold standard are covered by the union of all the subjects, but the different techniques do not seem to access the same proportion. Table 6 shows a breakdown of the proportion of gold standard rule set by technique. We can see that once again protocol analysis comes out worse than the other techniques.

Technique	Amount covered (%)
Interview	79.5
Protocol Analysis	56.8
Laddered Grid	85.2
Card Sort	81.8
All (union)	91

Table 6: Proportion of Gold Standard rule set covered by union of subjects

Finally, we note that in none of the appropriate comparisons did order have an effect. That is to say, no technique fared better or worse according to whether it was administered first or second. This result holds for all dependent measures.

6. Discussion

One of the most interesting aspects of these results is the poor showing of protocol analysis. Not only does protocol analysis take longer to perform and analyse than the comparable technique (table 2), but it also seems to retrieve a substantially smaller amount of the necessary information than the other techniques (table 6). Of course, our method of applying protocol analysis may be at fault - only a random subset of the rocks was given to each subject. This was done in order to make the time spent in each elicitation session roughly comparable. However, if we should have given more rocks, we can say that protocol analysis is insufferably slow, if we gave about the right number of rocks, we can say that it doesn't provide us with much information. Either way, protocol analysis comes out quite poorly.

The data from the psychometric measures is particularly interesting. Of course when one is looking at a large set of correlation coefficients, some are bound to come out significant as the type I error rate is going to be quite high. For this reason we have illustrated the level of significance for each of these correlations (tables 4 & 5). The pattern of significance is very consistent in these results. It is perhaps not surprising that introverts take longer on the interview than do extraverts (table 4). However, it seems surprising that they should produce more rules and clauses than the extraverts in order to convey the same amount of information. A possible reason for the effect of personality is that the interview is the only exclusively face-to-face technique. In all other techniques there is an external focus of attention for elicitor or expert, i.e. cards, diagrams or rocks. The cognitive style results are also interesting. It seems that global individuals have some difficulty with the laddered grid. This technique assumes a potentially spatial organisation for the domain. Our global subjects may not conceptualise the domain in a spatial way (as they would find it hard to disambiguate information). This is reflected in the fact that these subjects provide transcripts which are harder to convert into rules. A similar explanation might account for the fact that global individuals produce

more rules and clauses on the protocol analysis than do articulated
subjects. If this domain is best conceptualised in 'spatial' terms,
perhaps the global subjects find it difficult to conceptualise the problem
as they do it, and hence make more of a meal of it (these subjects also show
a (non-significant) trend towards providing a smaller amount of the domain
knowledge than their articulated colleagues).

What can we say about the process of knowledge elicitation
from these results? Firstly there are clear differences between these
techniques in this domain. Whether this will be the case for other
domains will be the focus of future studies. It may be the case that
protocol analysis fares so poorly in this domain because of the
declarative nature of the knowledge. To test this hypothesis we are
currently repeating the study with another, similar, classification domain
and with two further domains richer in procedural knowledge. Secondly,
there are clear differences in the efficacy of the techniques across
experts. This is an issue which must be faced by future work on KE
techniques - it's no good recommending a technique without being sure
about who it will work for. With regard to this, it is worth pointing out
that some of the psychometric effects are very large. For instance,
personality accounts for over 50% of the variance in elicitation time for
the interview technique.

We are now forced to ask whether the different techniques used
here are actually tapping different subsets of the necessary knowledge.
The results from table 6 show that most of the appropriate knowledge is
tapped by each of the techniques. Study of the different rule sets shows
that there is no clear dissociation between the knowledge which each of
the techniques taps. This leads us to suspect that the techniques do not
divide neatly into procedural and declarative as was previously suggested.

A more general finding to emerge from this and early pilot
studies (Schweickert et al, in press) concerns an expert's own estimation
of the worth of a technique. The impression people gain about the value
of an elicitation session bears little relation to the objective information obtained from an analysis of the session. In particular, techniques
which force the expert's knowledge into an unfamiliar format, such as card
sorts or laddered grids, are much more useful than experts think.

We are also aware of the limitations of our study. One
important restriction is that we have considered only a 'single-pass'
elicitation. It is widely accepted that one does not build an Expert
System in a simple linear manner; first eliciting the knowledge, and then
implementing it. After a first pass elicitation, the practice is to
implement a rough and ready version of the Expert System. A knowledge
engineer then compares the behaviour of the system with that of the
expert. It is usual to carry out a second pass elicitation in which the
expert is interviewed in front of the prototype system. This stage often
reveals a great deal of extra information, as well as allowing fine tuning
of the system.

In fact Expert Systems are usually subject to many stages of
refinement - and we refer to this as multi-phase elicitation. Part of our
research can be seen as an attempt to pin down more efficient KE
techniques in order to reduce the number of passes necessary in development. One direction for future research is to instate a form of
structured second phase elicitation as another type of technique. It
would then be possible to investigate how much information, and of what
sort, is obtained to supplement the first pass knowledge elicitation.

7. References

Anderson, J.R. (1983). The Architecture of Cognition. Cambridge, Mass.: Harvard University Press.

Burton, A.M. and Shadbolt, N.R. (In press). Knowledge Engineering. In Expert Systems for Users, eds. N. Williams and P. Holt, McGraw-Hill. Also available as TR 87-2-1, Department of Psychology, University of Nottingham

Gammack, J.G. and Young, R.M. (1985). Psychological Techniques for Eliciting Expert Knowledge. In Research and Development in Expert Systems, ed. M.A. Bramer, Cambridge: Cambridge University Press.

Grover, M.D. (1983). A Pragmatic Knowledge Acquisition Methodology. Proceedings of the 8th IJCAI.

Hayes-Roth, F., Waterman, D.A. and Lenat, D.B. (1983). Building Expert Systems. Reading, Mass.: Addison-Wesley.

Ryle, G. (1949). The Concept of Mind. Hutchinson.

Schweickert, R., Burton, A.M., Taylor, N., Corlett, E.N., Shadbolt, N.R., and Hedgecock, A (In press). Comparing Knowledge Elicitation Techniques: A Case Study. Artificial Intelligence Review.

Smith, R.G. and Baker, J.D. (1983). The Dipmeter Advisory System: A Case Study in Commercial Expert System Development. Proceedings of the 8th IJCAI.

Waterman, D.A. (1985). A Guide to Expert Systems. Reading, Mass.: Addison-Wesley.

Welbank, M.A. (1983). A Review of Knowledge Acquisition Techniques for Expert Systems. British Telecom Research, Martlesham Heath.

Witkin, H.A. and Oltman, P.K. (1967). Cognitive Style. International Journal of Neurology, 6, pp. 119-137.

Witkin, H.A., Oltman, P.K., Raskin, E. and Karp, S.A. (1971). A Manual for the Embedded Figures Test. Palo Alto: Consulting Psychologists Press.

GOALS FOR EXPERT SYSTEMS RESEARCH: AN ANALYSIS OF TASKS AND DOMAINS

Alison L Kidd and William P Sharpe
Hewlett Packard Laboratories, Filton Road, Stoke Gifford, Bristol, BS12 6QZ.

Abstract

This paper considers two issues: a theory of co-operative problem solving between user and system and a framework for analysing tasks and domains. We argue that these are the two critical factors underlying the successful transfer of expert systems from laboratory to application domain.

1. Introduction

The first generation of expert systems have powerfully demonstrated the application of Artificial Intelligence (AI) techniques to solve a variety of domain specific problems within a research environment. Success here has been measured in terms of the technical performance of these programs, for example in comparison with a human expert in the field. In theory, the potential impact of these techniques in commercial and industrial applications is enormous. In practice, their transfer to successful and widespread use in day to day applications has so far been severely and disappointingly limited.

In this paper, we take the view that to make this applications transfer a success is primarily a scientific problem for AI rather than a commercial one. The current generation of expert systems have been experiments, focussed on achieving impressive levels of computational performance on particular problem solving tasks in isolated domains. However these experiments have often not been well grounded in theory and as such they form an inadequate and unreliable basis for the successful design of expert systems for commercial applications. A similar view is shared by numerous other authors, eg. Nilsson, 1980; Reiter, 1986; McDermott, 1986. In this paper, we identify two important aspects of this problem: what are the problem solving tasks which expert systems *need* to solve; and which domains *can* they solve those problems in?

1.1 What tasks?

The emphasis in expert systems research has been on isolating a single problem solving task within some narrow domain and attempting to simulate this. Despite the fact that the goal is usually to provide an automated consultant for a human carrying out that same task, few people have addressed the central question: '*what problems does a system need to solve in order to be an effective consultant on a particular task?*' The consequence, in our experience, is that many systems are able to solve powerfully a pre-specified problem within a target domain but fail repeatedly to help the user formulate and solve *his* particular problem in that domain (Pollack et al, 1982; Coombs & Alty; Kidd, 1985).

1.2 Which domains?

The current generation of expert systems experiments have been carried out in an extremely diverse set of domains, for example, mathematics, medicine, geology, manufacturing, programming, finance and law. In each case, the success of the system is directly determined by the appropriate representation and application of specific knowledge from that domain to solve an isolated problem. Despite the vast amount of data now available as a result of these experiments, we are still unable either to explain the 'why' or how' of successful systems or to predict for which other domains and tasks the current techniques will work. This is because no theory of domains or tasks currently exists. With the exception of Clancey (1986), little effort has even been made towards developing such a theory by analysing and comparing the task and domain data available. The emphasis has rather been on collating a set of surface level, ad-hoc heuristics for selecting appropriate domains (eg. Prerau, 1985). Not only are these vague but, because they lack any theoretical framework, they are also weak in predictive power and cannot be formally tested.

In this paper, we suggest a dual approach for tackling these two issues. In the next section, we discuss what problems expert systems need to solve if they are to be effective domain consultants and show the need to develop a theory of co-operative problem solving between two active agents: the user and the system. In the second section, we discuss an approach to analysing and describing domains and tasks as a framework for predicting the feasibility of applying expert systems techniques today.

2. What tasks? - Developing a theory of co-operative problem solving

2.1 Results of empirical studies

Despite their problem solving capabilities, many expert systems have failed to be useful consultants in practical applications for two major reasons:

(i) The systems do not necessarily solve the exact problem which the user actually wants or needs help in solving (Kidd, 1985). For example, current diagnostic systems perform classification problem solving to answer the questions: *'What is the fault?'* or *'What is the remedy?'*. Empirical studies have shown that users, engaged in a range of diagnostic-type tasks, rarely ask experts either of these questions. More often, to help them solve their problem, they want answers to questions such as: *'Why did fault X happen?'*, *'Will remedy Y cure it?'* or *'Can I test W without affecting the level of Z?'* (Kidd, 1985). Data from other sources (eg. Pollack et al, 1982) imply that similar types of questions occur in a wide range of task domains, not just diagnostic.

(ii) The systems do not allow the user an active role in the problem solving process. The user is therefore unable to harness the system's problem solving capability to his particular problem requirements. Again, empirical studies have shown that, in consulting with experts, the user needs to be able to:

* Set out his own constraints on an acceptable solution, eg. *'It must be quick'* or *'I can't take the back panel off because I haven't got the tools'*.

* Put forward his own plans, solutions or explanations for evaluation, eg. *'Will swapping that component clear it for good?'* or *'Did it fail to work because of the sequence I used?'*

* Reject or request alternatives to solutions proposed by the expert, eg. *'I've already tried that and it didn't work'* or *'Are there any cheaper options?'*

(Kidd, 1985; see also Pollack et al, 1982 for similar results in other domains.)

        If an expert system does not take the above knowledge into account in its reasoning, then it will be severely limited in its ability to produce solutions which are optimal for the situation or acceptable to the user.

2.2 Developing a theory of co-operative problem solving

        Rather than developing one-off solutions for particular aspects of co-operative system behaviour (eg. co-operative responses to database queries), we believe that the aim should be to develop a *theory* for the design of co-operative problem solving systems. This should comprise two levels (cf. Marr, 1977; Newell, 1982):

* The set of tasks which a co-operative problem solving system needs to compute.

* The different types of knowledge required and how this knowledge must be used to perform these tasks.

        Our theory is not yet well developed. On the basis of the currently available empirical data from naturally occuring consultations (Kidd, 1985; Pollack et al, 1982; Coombs & Alty, 1984), we have formulated an initial description of the task requirements of a co-operative problem solving system, as follows:-

Question answering - A useful system must be able to answer a range of questions about a problem solving task. Our next step is (a) to analyse what questions are associated with what problem solving tasks and (b) to classify these questions in terms of their knowledge requirements.

Co-operative problem formulation - The user's problem (in the world) has to be formulated into the terms of the system's domain model and what that model can solve for him. Humans find this a very difficult part of solving any problem (Mitroff and Featheringham, 1974). A negotiation process between system and user is required to ensure the formulation captures the significant aspects of the user's problem. Our next step is to analyse the negotiation process involved in formulating common user problems in different domains.

Co-operative generation of alternative solutions - If a user's question, eg. 'Will X achieve Y?' fails, then the system needs to provide

alternative solutions which are useful to the user, eg. 'No, but W will';
'No, but X will achieve V', 'No, not unless Z becomes true' (cf
co-operative database query work, eg. Kaplan, 1982; Motro, 1986).
Similarly, if the answer is 'yes', the system should be able, when
appropriate, to provide responses such as: 'Yes, but so will W', 'Yes,
but it will also cause A' or 'Yes, as long as Z is true'. Our next step
is to analyse what knowledge is required to control the search for these
alternative solutions eg. knowledge of the user's problem, purposes,
solution constraints as well as knowledge of the domain model and the
search tree.

Co-operative explanation - The system requires an explanation capability
which at least includes:-
- the ability to debug significant user misconceptions.
- the ability to describe the relationship between alternative
  solutions and user purposes, constraints and situation specific
  factors.
- the ability to provide brief justification of the proposed solution.

     Our next step is to analyse (i) what knowledge constitutes the
object of the explanation (eg.. a fact, a rule, the domain model or the
reasoning trace) and (ii) what knowledge of the user, the domain and the
current context are the necessary requirements for generating these
explanations.
     We believe that even a limited implementation of the
co-operative task requirements listed would significantly enhance the
utility of a wide variety of systems. In the second section of this
paper, we propose the development of a related theory of domains and
tasks which should enable us to identify those applications for which it
is computationally feasible to provide these co-operative abilities.

3. Which applications - a framework for analysing tasks and domains

     Our aim is to provide a framework for analysing both domains
of knowledge and tasks to be performed with that knowledge. The resulting
classification should relate in a useful way to existing and next
generation techniques of knowledge based programming. This would serve
both to guide implementors in the choice of feasible applications today,
and focus research onto the required techniques for usefully extending
this set of feasible task and domain applications.
     Firstly, since we are concerned with knowledge based systems,
our framework must allow us to determine whether a machine representation
of a domain corresponds in a precisely stated way to human knowledge of
that domain. We therefore have three components to specify: domain
knowledge, machine representations of that knowledge, and mappings
between the two. Secondly we have to be able to describe tasks. In our
view, a task is performed by the user and the machine working together:
the user manipulating his knowledge, the machine manipulating its
representation, and mappings between the two being established. A task
specification is therefore a set of specifications for those
manipulations and mappings. In the language of logic, if domain knowledge
is expressed in a theory, then tasks will be expressed in metatheories
because they are about manipulations of the theory.

3.1 Developing a framework for task/domain analysis

In our view, knowledge representation is concerned with the question: *if a theory exists for a particular area of human knowledge, can we represent it within a computer without loss of information and in such a way that we can manipulate it as the human does?* The importance of this statement is that it allows us to distinguish representation problems which belong to AI, from those which belong to some other science. In other words, for any subject area of interest, it is an empirical question whether or not the human race has yet discovered and formalised that knowledge. If no such language exists then a study of machine representations is not well founded; there is a scientific knowledge representation problem to be solved first. Although AI may provide tools to help in the process (see Stefik & Conway, 1982), it is not primarily the job of AI researchers to discover theories of medicine, management, geology etc. Rather, it is the job of the domain experts.

Expert system developers should therefore recognise that if a chosen application domain lacks a coherent underlying theory, then developing a machine representation of that domain involves solving a double problem, ie. a scientific as well as an AI problem. Also, unless they solve the scientific problem satisfactorily, their AI solution is likely to be ad-hoc and ill-founded. For example, recent attempts to build expert advisors for inherently ill formulated software systems would seem to fall into this category.

For most tasks (ie. human problem solving competence within some domain), no languages or theories have yet been developed. We believe that, in this case, formalising tasks for machine representation *is* a cognitive science problem and therefore does have to be solved by AI researchers. For example, the preceding section of this paper addressed the need to develop a theory of co-operative problem solving to enable us to build useful consultant systems.

The framework of logic provides us with a way of discussing the state of human knowledge in a particular domain. For example, in the domain of mathematics, a problem may be stated as:

A metatheoretic specification of a computation to be performed with respect to:-

Problem specific assertions + Axioms of mathematical theory

stated in *A formal logic.*

(See Reiter, 1986 for more discussion of task specification considered as metatheoretic concepts). The point we wish to make here is that *all* domain problem solving comprises these components: logic, theory, problem statements, and metatheoretic computational specification; and that domains differ in the degree to which any of these components are explicit, agreed, stable and formal. For example, many parts of medicine are formulated in reasonably well described theories, but not in an explicit logic. Legal reasoning is an interesting case as a large amount of what goes on in a court of law seems to consist in arguing about the way in which a particular explicit theory (legislation and precedents) accounts for a particular set of problem statements (human behaviour).

Many authors have now begun to analyse the weaknesses of expert systems that are built purely from heuristic problem solving rules (eg. Clancey,1983), finding that the systems are weak because they have

no explicit theory (Clancey uses the term *support knowledge*). We argue
that without such an explicit theory, we cannot even begin to specify the
tasks. This means that heuristic problem solvers in domains with no
mature theory must always remain highly task specific, fragile and of
limited usefulness.

In relation to analysing tasks, we note two points. firstly,
we have already remarked that to specify a task we must specify the
transformations in both the machine and user knowledge. We can now
realise that tasks will become progressively more difficult to specify
(and hence implement) as these transformations involve more of the
components, ie. computation, problem statement, theory and logic. For
example, in a mathematical advisor, transformations may only be necessary
at the problem statement level; whereas in a tutoring system, the system
has to reason about the user's domain theory. Secondly, we must beware of
naive analysis of the knowledge in a domain. For example, the knowledge
of electrical circuits required for fault diagnosis is of two types:
knowledge of correctly behaving components, which is quite well
formulated; and knowledge of faulty components, which is very poorly
formulated. Adequate explanation of a diagnosis may depend on
communicating the theory of faulty behaviour, a tutoring problem, so will
be doubly difficult if the theory of faults is ill formulated.

4. Conclusions

We believe that the move from successful development of expert
systems in the laboratory to successful applications in the field is
primarily a scientific problem for AI rather than a commercial one. In
this paper, we have concentrated on two aspects of this problem: what
problems an expert system needs to be able to solve and in what
application domains can these currently be solved.

We advocate a move away from one-off solutions towards the
development of a theory of co-operative problem solving which describes
the component tasks which the system has to compute and the knowledge
which is required to compute these.

We also propose an initial framework for domain and task
analysis. The important features of this framework are:-

(1) Recognising the separation of AI knowledge representation problems
    from scientific knowledge representation problems (or 'do not test
    the depth of the water with both feet at once!').

(2) Classifying domains by the degree to which the logic and
    theories of the domain are explicit, formal, stable, and agreed.

(3) Describing tasks as metatheoretic manipulations of knowledge within
    both user and machine.

Development of classifications along these lines will, we believe, be
more sound and fruitful than the current methods of classification by
secondary properties.

We argue that the dual approach described in this paper should
firstly enable expert systems researchers to focus their efforts more
efficiently on which important problems need solving first. Secondly,
they should provide them with an appropriate vocabulary for describing
the results of their experiments. And thirdly, they should enable

practitioners in the commercial world to know which techniques do what and be able to select reliably where they can currently apply them.

References

Clancey, W.J. (1983). The epistemology of a rule-based expert system: a framework for explanation. Artificial Intelligence, 20, no.3, 215-251.

Clancey, W.J. (1986). Qualitative student models. Annual Review of Computer Science, 1, 381-450.

Coombs, M. & Alty, J. (1984). Expert systems: an alternative paradigm. Int. Jnal. Man-Machine Stud., 20, 21-43.

Kaplan, S.J. (1982). Co-operative responses from a portable natural language query system. Artificial Intelligence, 19, 165-187.

Kidd, A.L. (1985). What do users ask? - Some thoughts on diagnostic advice. In Expert Systems '85, ed. M. Merry. Cambridge: Cambridge University Press.

Marr, D. (1977). Artificial intelligence - a personal view. Artificial Intelligence, 9, 37-48.

McDermott, J. (1986). Making expert systems explicit, In Information Processing '86, ed. H.J. Kugler, pp. 539-544. Elsevier Science Publishers.

Mitroff, I.I. & Featheringham, T.R. (1974). On systemic problem solving and the error of the third kind. Behavioural Science, 19, 383-393.

Motro, A. (1986). Query generalization: a method for interpreting null answers. In Expert Database Systems, ed. L. Kerschberg, pp. 597-615.

Newell, A. (1982). The knowledge level, Artificial Intelligence, 18, 87-127.

Nilsson, N.J. (1980) The interplay between experimental and theoretical methods in artificial intelligence. Cognition and Brain Theory, 4, no. 1, 69-74.

Pollack, M.E., Hirschberg, J. & Webber, B. (1982). User participation in the reasoning processes of expert systems. Proc. AAAI '82,358-361.

Prerau, D.S. (1985). Selection of an appropriate domain for an expert system. The AI Magazine, Summer, 26-30.

Reiter, R. (1986). Foundations for knowledge-based systems, In Information Processing '86, ed. H.J. Kugler, pp. 663-668. Elsevier Science Publishers.

Stefik, M. & Conway, L. (1982). Towards the principled engineering of knowledge, The AI Magazine, Summer, 4-16.

EXPERT SYSTEMS AND EXPERT OPINION

R.A.Young
Philosophy Department,
University of Dundee

Abstract

In designing a diagnostic or advisory expert system it is desirable to specify
the institutional rules governing its use, for example concerning who is
responsible if its advice has disastrous results. The capacity to make
inferences with regard to these rules may be built into the system itself.
Speech Act Theory and the Theory of Communicative Action are theories
that can be applied to these aspects of expert system design. Society
provides rules to govern communication between a human expert and his/her
audience. These rules vary greatly from one institutional context to another.
Despite this variation there are central principles of rational human
communication that are relevant throughout institutional contexts. A
distinction needs to be made between the role a human can undertake and
the role an expert system can undertake, if only because the human being
has world knowledge and general communicative competence, whilst any
expert system designed in the near future will in contrast have severe
limitations. But after making this distinction one can still apply central
principles drawn from human communication to expert system design.

1. Introduction: The Theory of Speech Acts

This paper is concerned with expert systems which offer expert
opinions. Not all expert systems are of this kind - for example real-time
systems designed to control industrial plant need not be of this kind - but in
general diagnostic and advisory systems are concerned with offering expert
opinions. The first component in the strategy of the paper is to analyse
what it is for a human to offer an expert opinion in order to identify the
requirements that expert systems need to meet if they are to do anything
comparable with this. The second component is to ask in what ways the
human model is relevant. This is a question that can be raised at different
levels of sophistication and therefore it is a question which I raise throughout
the paper. The theory that I shall be applying in this paper is commonly
known as the theory of speech acts. But it is important to realize that it
applies to linguistic acts in general, not just to the spoken word. Modern
speech act theory has developed from the work of J.L.Austin (Austin 1962),
who was a linguistic philosopher at Oxford. Speech act theory is concerned
with the procedures by which a speaker, or more generally a language-user,
invokes conventions, rules, principles, legal statutes etc. which lay down
requirements on the speaker, on the audience, and on the context. For the
sake of brevity I shall use the term "rule" to cover conventions, principles,
statutes etc.

Some of these rules lay down requirements on how the speaker,
the audience and the context are to be, if the rules are to be satisfactorily
invoked. Other rules lay down requirements on how the speaker, the
audience, and sometimes other specified people, are to behave, if the rules

are to be satisfactorily invoked and followed. In the case of offering an expert opinion it is obviously required that the speaker be an expert - it would be fraudulent for a non-expert to purport to offer an expert opinion and in some cases the rules will require that an "expert" be a qualified member of a professional body e.g. a doctor, chartered accountant etc. Rules governing behaviour may govern non-linguistic behaviour, e.g. rules that the expert is to pay compensation if the opinion has been negligently formed and has proved costly to a client. Rules may also govern linguistic behaviour e.g. the doctor is to give such explanations as are necessary for the the welfare of the patient. Corresponding to requirements on one or more of the parties to a speech act other people may have entitlements. For example, if one person is required to pay compensation then another is entitled to receive it. Before we begin to consider the speech acts involved in presenting an expert opinion let us remind ourselves of the variety of speech acts involved in our social intercourse: a judge delivering a verdict or a sentence, a friend making a promise, an acquaintance answering a question, a witness making a statement, a counsellor offering advice, a passerby warning a householder of a fire. From this short list (out of a vast variety of speech acts) it will be apparent that in some cases the speech act is an element in a highly formalized institution with precise rules, whilst in others, e.g. a friend making a promise, the rules are less precise and it is more contestable what the rules are. For example does the promisee have to accept a promise in order for it to be binding on the promisor? An important question for us is the question of whether we should seek to develop formalised institutional rules for the use of expert systems or not.

I shall argue that a great variety of speech acts fall under the heading of "offering an expert opinion". In the case of some of these acts, e.g. the act of a surveyor issuing a professional survey of a house to a client, the expert is legally guaranteeing the opinion - rules of law are being invoked which specify that the expert is to pay compensation if the expert has been negligent in forming this opinion. In other questions there is no question of compensation. This is an important distinction and different conceptions of "opinion" go with it:

2. A Distinction between two kinds of Speech Act

1. To offer an expert opinion is to issue a statement which purports to be authoritative and for which the issuing authority can be held responsible by the recipient e.g. the example just given of a surveyor issuing a professional survey of a house to a prospective purchaser.

2. To offer an expert opinion is to issue a statement which purports to be informed and which the expert is advocating as the answer to some question, but which it is the responsibility of the recipient to evaluate (e.g. a panellist making a considered statement about his/her field at a conference like this one).

I shall argue that in our institutions it is standardly required that the expert will make his/her opinion intelligible to his/her audience and so provision is made in the rules for further dialogue with clients. As a model for expert systems building (1) is problematic. An expert system is not at present regarded as a legal person (unlike a company which is) and therefore it cannot have assets with which to compensate people, moreover, at least in the present state of knowledge engineering, it is questionable whether any legal person associated with an expert system would be wise to undertake to compensate for loss ensuing from an opinion offered by their system. The most cogent reason for this is not that the expert system may prove technically unreliable in its advice. The most cogent reason is that *human experts have a responsibility to take reasonable steps to make the opinions that they offer intelligible to their clients and can be held liable for failing to do this. They are expected to make use of their world knowledge in order to ensure that any relevant ignorance on the part of clients is overcome.* At present we cannot build expert systems that can provide for all the idiosyncracies of clients with which human experts cope.

(2) is to be preferred as a model for expert system building, but if we take (2) as the model then the expert, in offering an opinion as an expert opinion, is advocating the opinion and implying that the opinion is to be evaluated positively by the recipient. Where the audience consists of fellow experts, who share precisely the same expertise, the audience may not need much help in evaluating the opinion. But when the audience consists of laymen or of people who are relatively inexpert in a particular field then the audience, or its representatives, may need to be able to question the expert about his/her opinion in order to evaluate it and the audience may also need help from other experts. Thus, in adopting (2) as the model, we have not completely removed the need for the expert system to provide explanations, if it is to compare with a human expert. Different institutions have different ways of meeting these requirements and these lead to different rules, conventions, or principles for posing questions to the expert. When the expert offers an opinion in a court of law he/she makes different commitments as regards question answering from the commitments that are made in a scientific meeting. These differences in commitment mean that the speech act of offering an expert opinion varies from one institution another. When an expert offers an opinion in a court of law it is thought proper for counsel to call character and integrity into question and to suggest that there may be hidden motives for what is said. Such challenges are not usually thought to be in order in scientific assemblies, where it is thought appropriate for questioners to concentrate on the rigour of the expert's theorizing, the repeatability of experiments etc.

3. Question Classification

In most institutions human experts are expected to cope with a large range of questions. In comparison with this the range of questions with which a typical expert system deals is quite slight: typically it deals with "how" and "why" questions which are interpreted in a very restricted way. In Expert Systems86 S.Hughes (Hughes 1986) presented a very interesting paper on categories of question. It seems to me that her approach was incomplete because (a) it did not concern itself with questioning as a speech act that is to say it did not concern itself with the contextual rules that govern questioning as an activity and (b) it (as a consequence, I think) presented a rather restricted range of questions. She presented a categorization of questions into thirteen categories. An example of a question which does not fit readily into her categories is the question,

What is the difference between Measles and German Measles?

She did, in her paper, have a category of comparison and categories of definition and of slot-filling. But she regarded comparison questions as being equivalent to questions of the form:

>Which has more of attribute X, entity A or entity B?

and definitional questions and slot-filling were considered to be intraconceptual rather than interconceptual, that is they were not considered to be comparative. It may be argued that my "measles" question is ambiguous and that therefore it is not a valid counterexample to Sheila Hughes's categories. It is indeed ambiguous and thus an appropriate response to it, if it were posed in general conversation, would be:

>With respect to what? Do you mean with respect to causal mechanism, symptoms, cure, rigorous medical classification of diseases, or what?

And then a more precise version of the question would be formulated. Probably the more precise version would still not fit neatly into S. Hughes's categories. But it is not my intention to carp at her scheme of categories. Rather I want to suggest that in dealing with such questions context is important. It is usually context that settles the meaning of the question without any need for explicit disambiguation. In the doctor's surgery the doctor is advising on the patient's health (and on the health of any foetus or family members) and what the patient needs to know about are symptoms and prognosis of cure rather than technical details. Thus the question will be interpreted as a request for clarification of the significance of the doctor's diagnosis for the health of the patient et al. (a polite request which is entitled to an answer). This is the kind of speech act in which the patient is thought to be entitled to engage. The patient is not thought to be entitled to take up the doctor's time with requests for technical medical education. Of course in a medical school the students would be expected to pose questions concerning causal mechanism and rigorous medical classification. The main point of my argument here is to stress the way in which we need to think of questions in terms of context, and indeed in terms of a speech act analysis of context. S.Hughes does recognize the need to take context into account when she proposes that a script-based approach, and not just a rule-based approach, is necessary if expert systems are to support a genuine co-operative dialogue with the user. Explanations are not just to be based upon the rules that the system follows in generating its expert opinion. The speech acts approach suggests that a second tier of rules can be identified concerning, amongst other things, the way in which the expert system is to answer questions about the opinions that it offers, how it is to explain its own institutional role, how it is to differentiate between different levels of expertise in its users etc. Can speech act theory provide any general guidelines for the identification of such rules? Or is the identification of these rules a matter for detailed systems analysis which varies so much from case to case that no general guidelines can be given?

4. Institutionally Bound and Unbound Speech Acts

It will help us to answer this question if we recognize a distinction that J.Habermas (Habermas 1979) makes between institutionally bound speech acts and institutionally unbound speech acts. An institutionally bound speech act is one whose rules are the rules of a specific institution, whereas an institutionally unbound speech act is one which depends upon no rules other than the general principles for rational communication. An example of an institutionally bound speech act would be a general practitioner's diagnostic opinion given in Britain. An institutionally unbound speech act would be an opinion delivered in general conversation with no specific institutions defining what it is to give an opinion. Institutionally unbound speech acts rely on the use of the general communicative competence of human beings and their willingness to try to communicate relevant knowledge where this is necessary to ensure genuine communication. Only a system with full natural language capacities and world knowledge comparable to that of a human being could be expected to cope with institutionally unbound speech acts. We cannot expect to build such systems in the foreseeable future. T. Johnston of Ovum Consultants has suggested (Johnston 1986) that the most we can reasonably expect from natural language processing is systems using a restricted, and perhaps artificially contrived, subset of a natural language as a company language. Turning back to institutionally bound speech acts, a general truth about these is that they themselves tend to rely upon institutionally unbound speech acts which are used in cases where the rules of the institution turn out to be ambiguous, or badly designed, or where outsiders or newcomers interact with the institution (e.g. a newcomer to British medicine having a consultation with a doctor). How are we to deal with this factor in expert systems design, given that expert systems themselves cannot be expected to cope with institutionally unbound speech acts? A possible way of dealing with the problem is to create institutional contexts in which it is clear that an expert system is only required to answer certain well-defined questions and it is the role of well identified back-up personnel to cope with further questions. If we are to deal with the problem in this way then we must regard the design of an appropriate institutional context as a key element in expert systems design and ideally the expert system itself should be designed to convey sufficient understanding of this context to the user.

Even if we adopt this approach we should still pay attention to the theory of institutionally unbound speech acts which for Habermas is a component in a general theory of communicative action. We should pay attention to it because it provides a key component of the context within which specific institutions are created and modified. According to the theory of communicative action general principles of rational communication provide us with the rules for institutionally unbound speech acts. According to the theory anyone engaged in a genuine and pure attempt to communicate is committed to making his/her attempt to communicate, his/her speech act,

1. intelligible

2. true

3. sincere

4. appropriate to its context.

and to gaining the agreement of the audience that the speech act meets these requirements.

A communicator is committed to explaining how a speech act fulfils these requirements, by, amongst other things, explaining why the act was performed as it was. A complicating factor in human communication is that the so-called "communicators" are often following competitive strategies which are furthered by flouting these principles of pure communication. Thus a person purports to tell the truth, but in fact lies in order to gain advantage. In this case we get strategically distorted communication. It is important to recognize another factor which modifies the application of these principles in some cases. Consider a doctor who is asked to provide a diagnosis and prognosis to a terminally ill person. Doctors often lie in such cases and they defend their action as professionally and ethically correct on the grounds that it is their role to say what will further the well-being of the patient. This is recognized practise in many medical institutions and may even be recognized by patients who do not feel entitled to press their questions. We can interpret this as manifesting a tension between the second principle of pure communication (truth) and the fourth (appropriateness to context); perhaps it also manifests an ambiguity in the third principle (sincerity). Despite the fact that institutions depart from the principles of pure communication in their rules and/or illustrate tensions in the principles, these principles nevertheless contribute an important component to the general theory of institutionally bound speech acts. We can use them in expert systems design even if we depart from them because of constraints on expert systems or the objectives of particular institutions. Let us then consider the application of these principles to the offering of an expert opinion by an expert system. We can consider the principles as laying down that the system, or alternatively its designers, or the institution in which it is embedded, be committed:

1. *to intelligibility of the opinion and to gaining the agreement of users, and of experts that evaluate it, that the opinion is intelligible.* If we envisage this objective as something that we are to build into the system itself, then we need to build into the system "knowledge" of the semantics of the opinion it presents, and "knowledge" of how to identify and correct errors in understanding on the part of users. This means going well beyond the strings of text that many expert systems are designed to provide when asked for definitions of key terms. It could involve, where appropriate, the ability on the part of the system to give a knowledge-based account of the relationship between its key terms and a graphical illustration of the disease or fault that it diagnoses, or the advice that it gives. It could also involve an ability to respond to syntactically diverse natural language questions about its diagnosis or advice. It could involve an ability to model the users errors in understanding in order to guide explanation. If designers are less ambitious than this, and envisage it as up to themselves to provide clear canned explanations and up to the institution which uses the system to provide the backup to make it intelligible to individual users, it is nevertheless appropriate to distinguish between novice users and others, and also it is appropriate to give a clear indication of what the system cannot explain, and of where further explanation can be found.

2. *to the truth of the opinion and to gaining the agreement of users and experts that the opinion is true* It is important here that the system be designed to make clear that its conclusion is probabilistic, if it is, and also to make clear any caveats as to lack of data etc. But we also need to consider cases, like that of a doctor advising a terminally ill patient where rules of specific institutions may require departure from this principle. One can envisage this sort of case arising even in the case of fault diagnosis in a computer network. The designers of an expert system might think it inappropriate for the system to

advise a novice user of the details of a fault, since there might
be a danger of the user creating problems by an over-ambitious
attempt to fix the fault, and the system could be designed to
conceal its opinion from the novice and to reserve it for an
expert. A case where a strong argument might be mounted for
this approach would be where a breakdown in security had
occurred, or might occur if an explanation were given to the
wrong category of user. Systems could also be designed to
mislead for less ethical reasons. This possibility deserves ethical
and legal study.

3. *to sincerity and to gaining the agreement of users and experts
   that the opinion is sincere* It might be thought that sincerity is
   a property of the human designers of systems rather than of
   systems themselves, but we have just seen that there could be
   cases where a system reached an opinion upon the basis of its
   domain rules, but was designed to censor its opinion when
   interacting with a certain category of user because undesirable
   consequences would ensue. In the case of a doctor concealment
   of a diagnosis may be regarded as sincere in the sense that the
   doctor is sincerely pursuing the objectives of his/her profession,
   which are publicly known and accepted. Presumably at least
   this kind of sincerity should be built into expert systems, and
   therefore it is preferable if they can give some account of their
   objectives. There is another sense in which the question of
   sincerity arises for expert systems. If one is sincere as to the
   truth of what one is saying then one tries not to say that
   something is true when one has the information that it is false.
   It is common for an expert system to have "information", in the
   form of canned text, which is inaccessible to its inference engine.
   This makes it possible, no matter how efficient its inference
   engine, for a system to produce opinions which are inconsistent
   with the account that it offers of itself. It will then appear
   unreliable, or even insincere, to its human user.

4. *to appropriateness to context and to gaining the agreement of
   users and experts that the opinion is appropriate* This covers
   appropriateness in terms of the objectives built into the system,
   and objectives of experts, designers and users, both institutional
   and personal. It also covers appropriateness in terms of the
   rules of institutions, ethics, the law etc. In many professions (for
   example civil engineering) there are complex professional
   standards that are layed down by institutions such as professional
   institutes, Parliament, the E.E.C., which may well conflict with
   each other. Not only does the opinion that an expert system
   offers need to be appropriate in some sense to each relevant
   institution and to the user, but it may need to mediate between
   different standards and objectives, if it is to offer anything useful
   to the user. It must be remembered that explanations as well as
   diagnostic opinions and advice need to be appropriate in this
   sense. This factor of appropriateness suggests that expert
   systems that offer expert opinions ought to have built into them
   some "knowledge" of relevant objectives, and institutional rules
   and should be able to make inferences concerning the

appropriateness of their opinions and explanations in the light of these objectives and rules.

This discussion of what is required of an expert system may at some points seem idealistic. This is not entirely surprising since it is a feature of speech act theory that it concerns itself not only with rules that lay down the minimal requirements for a speech act to take place, but it also concerns itself with rules that specify what is required if the speech act is to have its optimal context and outcome. The principle of intelligibility has its expression in rules that lay down what is minimally necessary for communication to take place, but it also finds its expression in rules that specify what is necessary for optimal communication to occur. In the case of an institutionally bound speech act there are rules for the optimal running of the institution as well as rules that lay down the minimal requirements for participation in it. A minimal rule of promise-making is that one does not say anything of the form "I promise to do X but I will not do X". A minimal rule for giving an expert opinion is that one does not say anything of the form "It is my expert opinion that X, but I do not believe it myself". Standard rules for optimal running of these institutions are that the promisor knows he/she will keep the promise and that the expert knows his/her opinion to be true. Perhaps the best that we can hope for from expert systems is that, like human communicators, they will approximate to their ideal specification sufficiently often to make interaction with them worthwhile.

5. Conclusion

In conclusion I propose the following recommendations:

- Developers of Diagnostic and Advisory Expert Systems should identify clear institutional rules to regulate a System's interaction with its users.

- Speech Act Theory should be recognised as an aid in this aspect of Systems Analysis.

- It is best to avoid the model in which the System is regarded as offering "opinions" in the way that a professional, e.g. a doctor, offers opinions in a professional consultation, since this involves potential dangers for the user and corresponding heavy legal liabilities, arising not only from technical error, but also from misunderstanding of the opinion by a user.

- It should be clear where the human responsibility lies in evaluating "opinions" offered by the System.

- It should be clear that a user can call upon advice from specified people as a backup to the System and to interpret the output of the system.

- Where it is feasible, the System should itself have a capacity to make inferences concerning its institutional context, and to make use of these inferences in formulating its opinions and explanations.

- Principles of rational human communication, qualified for particular cases, may be used as a basis for identifying the necessary institutional rules.

Acknowledgements

I would like to thank my referees S.Hughes and M. Cooper for their comments on an earlier draft of this paper. Thanks is also due to the following people at the University of Dundee: J.D.Bastow, E.Broumley, D.Kinane and R.White, and to Portia File at the Dundee College of Technology.

References

Austin,J.L. (1962). How to do things with words. Oxford: Oxford University Press
Habermas,J. tr.McCarthy. (1979). Communication and the Evolution of Society. London: Heinnemann
Habermas,J. tr.McCarthy. (1984). A Theory of Communicative Action. Vol.1. London: Heinnemann
Hughes,S. (1986). Question Classification. In Research and Development in Expert Systems III, ed.M.A.Bramer, pp.123-131. Cambridge: Cambridge University Press
Johnston,T. (1986). Natural Language Computing: The Commercial Applications. Knowledge Engineering Review,Vol. 1 No. 3, 11-23.
Searle,J.R. (1969). Speech Acts. Cambridge: Cambridge University Press

QUESTION AND ANSWER TYPES

G. Nigel Gilbert

Alvey DHSS Demonstrator
Department of Sociology
University of Surrey
Guildford GU2 5XH

Abstract

A number of classifications of the kinds of question which users could ask a rule-based system have been proposed, but because of the often ambiguous meaning of questions, a more useful approach is to classify the answers the questions expect. This paper proposes a classification of answer types derived from a categorisation of knowledge in which each answer type draws on a specified form of knowledge. The link between the classifications of knowledge and answer types means that computational strategies for generating answers can be specified. The answer types are exemplified by questions drawn from a study of the information sought by a sample of claimants and potential claimants of welfare benefits. It is shown that providing facilities to allow users to ask questions to obtain all the various types of answer would greatly enhance the flexibility and utility of rule-based systems.

1. Introduction

Most conventional advisory expert systems are designed to answer only one or two types of question. For example, the classic MYCIN system (Shortliffe, 1976) will answer the questions: does the patient have a disease, what disease does he or she have and what is the recommended treatment. To a limited extent, it will also tell the user how a conclusion was deduced, an answer to a 'why' question or justification. Later work, especially that by Swartout (1983), Clancey (1983) and Hasling, Clancey and Rennels (1983), has explored answering other kinds of question, such as those which require knowledge of the reasons for MYCIN's rules. This paper continues the theme, suggesting ways in which one can go beyond conventional systems in supporting a wider range of questions

The need to understand how to provide users with more powerful opportunities for asking questions arose in the design of a demonstration expert system, the 'Advice System', aimed at helping those who want information and advice about UK welfare benefits. There are a large number of these benefits, many of them means tested, the eligibility and amount awarded depending on the claimant's circumstances. Specific information on eligibility in an easily understandable form is hard for claimants to obtain and this lack of information tends to discourage applications.

A few experimental systems have been developed to provide information on eligibility (Hammond, 1983; Ticher, 1986), but these aim only to calculate the benefits the user is likely to be eligible for and the amount likely to be received. A study of potential users of these systems, involving lengthy interviews with a stratified sample of low income households (Dawson, Buckland and Gilbert, 1987, see also Epstein, 1984) clearly showed that, while assessments of eligibility would be useful and welcomed by the respondents, they also needed advice on a much wider range of issues, including information on procedural matters, such as where and when to claim, the effect of claiming one benefit on the amount received in other benefits, the rules determining the award of benefit, and so on. It seems that users would find an advice system more helpful if they were able to pose a variety of kinds of question to get advice on these matters. However, in order to design such a system, a clear conception of the range of questions which it should be designed to support is needed.

This paper begins by briefly reviewing previous attempts to develop a classification of questions. It is suggested that it is a mistake to attempt to classify the questions themselves because their syntactic form can be misleading; what is required is a classification of types of answer. Such a classification is proposed, based on data about what users might want to ask about state welfare benefits and on a consideration of possible approaches to a knowledge base. In the last half of the paper, the answer types are described in more detail and some procedures which might be used to extract answers of the various types from a knowledge base are described. Although the examples are drawn mainly from social security, the classification and the procedures proposed are not specific to this context and should be applicable equally to advisory systems in quite different domains.

2. Question Types

A first step in devising a system which will answer a range of questions is to get an idea of what different types of question there are. There have been a number of attempts to categorise questions into types, especially by those concerned with the retrieval of information from databases and with answering questions about texts (typically, news reports or fairy stories). One of the pioneers was Lehnert (1977) who developed a question answering system for news reports and identified 13 categories of question.

Hughes (1986) reviewed these categories. She made a number of changes to the categories and noted that the classification could be arranged better as a hierarchy by dividing them into those with a temporal aspect and those without. The temporal categories could in turn be divided into result-seeking (causal consequent, goal orientation and procedural) and cause-seeking (enablement, expectational and causal antecedent). The atemporal categories could be divided into inter-conceptual (the comparison category) and intra-conceptual (the verification, definition, concept completion, instrumental, quantification and feature specification categories).

Graesser and Murachver (1985) suggest seven question types, called Why, How, Enable, Cons (ie what is the consequence of), When, Where and Sig (ie what is the significance of). These are cross-classified with three 'statement categories', Action, Event and State, giving 21 categories in all. An Action is a behaviour by an animate actor which is directed toward a goal. An Event is a change of state in the physical or social worlds or in the mind of an animate being, while a State is an ongoing characteristic of an entity or a relationship between entities.

Graesser observes that questions may be considered functions of the form:

QType(QConcept, Knowledge)

where QType is the question type (eg What, Who, Why...), QConcept is what the question is 'about', classified into the three statement categories (Action, Event and State), and Knowledge is the knowledge base to be used to answer the question. QConcept is sometimes also called the question's 'presupposition', because it states a fact which is presupposed by the questionner. Application of the appropriate QType function to the given QConcept in the context of the given knowledge base results in an answer to the question. Graesser suggests 'symbolic procedures' for discovering answers from a semantic network for each of the 21 different combinations of QType and QConcept.

3. The Difficulties of Classifying Questions

Despite the development of these increasingly sophisticated classifications, when one attempts to classify 'real' questions, such as those which potential users say that they would like to ask, the boundaries between the categories turn out to be remarkably unclear. One reason for this is that very different questions can be asked using superficially similar question forms. Conversely, what appears to be the 'same' question can be asked in many syntactically different ways. A further difficulty stems from the effect of the pragmatic force of a question. What people say when they ask questions is not necessarily what they are heard to mean. These are clearly serious difficulties for a system which is prepared to accept natural language input and which aims to interact with the user in a human-like way. But, while important, they tend to mask the more tractable problem of how one can most usefully classify what the user really wants to know, that is, how one can classify the answers to questions. Attempts to classify questions risk confounding the problem of semantic and pragmatic interpretation with the problem of developing classifications and methods of answering questions once their meanings have been determined

It therefore seems more profitable to consider, not a typology of kinds of question words (the Graesser approach) nor a rather slippery classification of question types such as Lehnert and Hughes suggest, but a classification of types of answer. Such a classification of answers is the topic of the next section.

4. A Classification of Knowledge and a Classification of Answers

A number of distinctions between types of knowledge have been made in the literature. Differentiating knowledge and 'meta knowledge' has long been commonplace. Strategic control knowledge has also often been separated from domain knowledge. A contrast between deep and surface knowledge is sometimes made. However, these various distinctions need to be brought together and systematised. One way to do this is to classify knowledge along two dimensions, one concerned with the type of the knowledge (eg control knowledge vs causal knowledge) and the other, its level (eg domain level vs meta-level). We distinguish four types of knowledge: Taxonomic, Formal, Contingent and Control knowledge. Taxonomic knowledge concerns the entities which make up the domain, their attributes and their taxonomic ('class') structure; Formal knowledge consists of analytic relations between entities, ie relations of a definitional or formal kind; Contingent knowledge is synthetic, for example, causal or temporal; and Control knowledge is knowledge concerned with the operation of the system itself, including the way it performs inference.

Cross-cutting these four types of knowledge are three levels: the Theory level, the Domain level and the Case level. The Case level comprises knowledge which is specific to the particular problem or case which the system is being applied to. In a medical system, it can include, for example, details of the patient and the history of the session so far. The Domain level consists of knowledge which is specific to a problem area (the symptoms and treatment for a medical condition, the characteristics of alternative investments, or whatever). The Theory level contains knowledge which is abstract and general: at this level is located knowledge about meta-procedures for determining the creation and linkages between entities, general principles of inference, causal models and theories and control strategies.

The twelve cells resulting from cross-tabulating the four types and three levels are shown in Table 1, with examples of the knowledge which can be placed in each cell.

	Taxonomic	Formal	Contingent	Control
Theory	MetaClass	Principle	Causal model	Strategy
Domain	Class	Formal Rule	Causal rule	Inference mechanism
Case	Instance	Deduced conclusion	Representation of an event or an action	Proof

Table 1 A cross-classification of levels and types of knowledge

Some of the advantages of distinguishing all these types of knowledge explicitly in an expert system have been described by Clancey (1983) and Swartout (1983). For example, Swartout divides the knowledge of an expert system into a 'domain model', which contains the domain level knowledge, and 'domain principles', which include the theory level knowledge of the system. He argues that useful explanations can only be generated by systems which have access to an explicit representation of their theory level knowledge. Clancey proposes that control strategy needs to be represented abstractly, that is at the theory level, rather than implicitly in the ordering of clauses in domain rules.

A primary benefit of the clear classification of knowledge is that there can be a correspondence between the categories of knowledge and categories of answer. Each knowledge category serves as the basis for one or more types of answer. Thus, Table 2 mirrors Table 1, but the body of the table contains the answer types which draw on the knowledge in the corresponding cells of Table 1.

	Taxonomic	Formal	Contingent	Control
Theory	Existence	Warrant	Process	Strategy
Domain	Generalisation Exemplification Identification	Definition Relevance	Implication	Capability
Case	Instantiation	Classification Prescription Sensitivity	Procedure Antecedence	Justification Rationale

Table 2 Answer types related to their knowledge sources

Answers relying on Case level knowledge can only be constructed during a consultation and will depend on the particular circumstances of the user and the history of the interaction. The Domain answers can be given without knowledge of any particular circumstances - they are 'generic' answers which depend only on formal relationships between entities and attributes, on procedures and causal connections and on the scope of the knowledge built into the system. Theory level answers give reasons for the domain level knowledge, answering 'Why' questions of various kinds. Each of the answer types in the Table 2 is defined and exemplified in the next section.

5. The Answer Types

Case Level answer types

Instantiation: whether an instance of a class is present in the case under consideration, for example, who constitutes the claimant's assessment unit for the purposes of benefit regulations.

In a frame-based system, a strategy to obtain such answers would examine the instances which have been created by the system as it makes inferences using domain rules.

Classification: whether a proposition is true of some entity, for example, whether the user is entitled to a benefit.

Classification answers are one of the traditional kinds of response generated by expert systems and conventional strategies, typically backward chaining on the domain level rules, will serve to obtain them.

Prescription: advice about the expected attributes of an entity, for example, the amount that would be received if the user claimed Child Benefit.

In a medical expert system, the prescription is the advice offered after diagnosis (ie classification) has taken place. The procedures used for classification and prescription are similar, backward chaining at the case level, but classification is concerned only with set membership, while prescription offers advice depending upon the classification the system has made.

Sensitivity: advice about the degree to which circumstances would have to change to produce a specified outcome, for example, how much the user's rent would have to rise before he or she would start being eligible for Housing Benefit.

This type of answer can be obtained using case level knowledge with the domain rules, but require driving the rules 'backwards'. This can be achieved by writing the domain rules as constraints (cf Sussman and Steele, 1980).

Procedure: the actions required to achieve a goal , for example, the procedure which should be followed to claim a benefit.

The procedures cited in the answer are deduced from a domain specific set of rules about the preconditions and consequences of actions and states, using a planner which can reason about the actions required to move from the initial state to the desired goal.

Antecedence: the events or states which have led up to or caused a given state, for example, the reasons why benefit was stopped.

One way to generate Antecedence answers is to locate all possible causes of the specified event, find the causes of all these causes and so on, thus generating an expanding tree. To be useful this tree needs to be pruned to focus on those events in which the user is interested. It is not possible to do this *a priori*: either the question will have stated or the questioner will need to be asked to specify which of all the known causal chains should be pursued.

Justification: the deductions which lead to a conclusion, for example, the deductions which justified the conclusion that a particular claimant was eligible for a benefit.

The justification may be derived from the proof trace, the record of the rules used to deduce a conclusion. However, the full trace is likely to be too long and too detailed for most purposes. Several operations need to be carried out before the trace is displayed The trace should be pruned of records of low-level procedures, such as arithmetic primitives, and of justifications for facts which the user already knows. As Weiner (1980) suggests, the trace should also be pruned of inferences which the user may be assumed to have already made. Intermediate deductions can also be pruned if the user can be expected to be able to replicate them without difficulty (this eliminates 'obvious' inferences). In this way, the pruning can be taken to the point where only one statement from the proof trace remains This then becomes 'the' reason or justification for the conclusion The selection of which steps to retain depends on the intention of the question, ie the pragmatics, as well as on the questioner's prior knowledge.

Rationale: the reason why a particular question is being asked by the system, for example, the reason why the system needs to know how many children the claimant has.

    The rationale is provided by the goal which is currently being solved. If this goal is a sub-goal of a higher goal which in turn is a sub-goal of a still higher goal and so on, these goals can be maintained in a stack which the user can ascend to get more and more general rationales for the system's questions (Sergot, 1983). Much the same considerations about pruning the proof trace to provide a justification apply to pruning the goal stack.

Domain level answer types

Generalisation: an explanation of an entity as being a kind or type of some other entity, for example, Widow's Allowance being a kind of contributory benefit.

    Generalisation answers may be obtained by looking up through a taxonomic hierarchy.

Exemplification: an explanation of an entity by providing examples of it, for example, that Widow's Allowance, Unemployment Benefit and Sickness Benefit are kinds of contributory benefit.

    Exemplification answers are obtained by looking down the taxonomic hierarchy. The procedure may either trace down the taxonomic tree to find the leaves and report only these (for example, the names of every benefit), or it may move down only one level to immediately below the entity enquired about.

Identification: the entity which has some specified characteristics, for example, the benefit for lone fathers is One Parent Benefit.

    For this answer type, the entity is identified by means of its attributes. The procedure involves searching through the knowledge base for entities with the given set of attributes and reporting either the first or all of those found.

Definition: an explanation of the meaning of a term or condition by citing rules which define it, for example, the meaning of the term 'dependent' in terms of the criteria used to determine dependency.

    A definition is provided by quoting a domain rule or rules. Other terms referenced in the rule may in turn need to be defined by citing the rules which define them.

Relevance: whether and how a characteristic could affect an outcome, for example, whether water rates have any bearing on the amount of Supplementary Benefit awarded.

    In contrast to the sensitivity type, which will report whether in given circumstances a factor is relevant to a specified outcome, this answer type is concerned with whether the factor could ever be involved. Provision of an answer of the relevance type requires inspection of the tree which shows the interdependencies between the conclusions of rules and the variables which are included in their premises.

Implication: the consequences of an action, for example, what happens if one reports a change of circumstances to the DHSS.

This type of answer reports what would change as a result of a (possibly hypothetical) action. It is thus concerned with predicting causal effects at the domain level, that is, without specific reference to the facts of any particular situation. The answer given is therefore bound to be a general one, formed by citing the causal relationships which apply in the domain. These relationships are those which the planner uses to generate Procedure answers and which represent the causal chains used for Antecedence answers.

Capability: the scope of the system, for example, what questions the system is able to answer.

The capability answer type provides explanations about the system itself and the way it works and therefore requires that the inference engine and the way it is controlled be available for inspection and reasoning by the answering mechanism.
Theory level answer types

Existence: the reasons for the existence of or the form of an entity, for example, the reason for the existence of a benefit targeted at lone parents.

The knowledge required to provide existence answers is the knowledge which is used at the time a system is designed to decide the entities to be represented and their attributes. It is rarely made explicit, either by system designers or in the sources of the knowledge being represented. In the case of welfare benefits, which are governed by acts and regulations that have accumulated in a largely unsystematic way over a period of thirty or more years, it is hard to derive general principles which do not have numerous exceptions. In other fields, those subject to natural laws and where theoretical understanding is deeper, there may be more knowledge available at this level.

Warrant: the reasons which explain the form of a rule, for example, the reason why Widow's Allowance is paid for only 26 weeks.

The warrant answer type provides the reasons 'behind' a rule. For example, for knowledge bases concerned with physical processes, the laws of physics may constitute a warrant, while in a medical domain, warrants are likely to draw on knowledge of biological structure and function.

Process: an explanation of the causal sequence or process which generates activities or outcomes, for example, the process involved in paying benefit to a claimant.

Answers about process explain the causal model underlying the domain. They may need to include information about time sequencing, the effect of triggering events, the inhibiting and encouraging effect of prior states and so on. These answers aim to show not what would happen (the topic of implication answers), but why it should happen. They therefore require knowledge of the structure and function of the entities in the domain, their causal inter-relationships and some general principles about causality, such as that causes cannot follow effects.

Strategy: the reason for the system asking a question or series of questions, for example, the reason why the system asks general questions before asking ones about more specific issues.
        This type of answer concerns the control strategies which the system uses. As an example, Clancey (1983) offers the following example of a control strategy (which he calls a 'metarule'):
        METARULE073
        IF there is a datum that can be requested that is a characterising feature of the recent finding that is currently being considered,
        THEN find out about the datum.

He further distinguishes between abstract and concrete explanations of strategy. In the classification of Table 2, a concrete explanation would be a capability answer, while an abstract explanation would be a strategy answer. As with other answer types drawing on theory level knowledge, once the difficulties of obtaining and representing the knowledge have been overcome, extracting the answer for the user is relatively straightforward.

Hypothetical answer types

        There are two further answer types which were identified in the data from the study of potential users, but which do not figure in Table 2 because they are built from and depend on the others. A hypothetical answer is one which is true under some given assumption. A comparative answer is one which compares the consequences of two alternative situations. One can construct hypothetical and comparative answers by compounding answers from most of the other types.

Hypothesis: the likely result if a hypothetical or possible state of affairs were to come about, for example, the effect on benefits if the claimant were to get married.
        A difficulty with generating answers of this type is dealing correctly with the frame problem - what else should be assumed to be different in the hypothetical state in addition to what is specified in the question. Projections into the hypothetical future are hazardous, and the questionner needs to be aware of the grounds on which the advice was computed.

Comparison: a statement of the differences between the answers provided from two similar queries, for example, the impact on one's net income of remaining unemployed and claiming Income Support, as compared with taking on a part-time job and not claiming Income Support.
        This type of answer involves the comparison of two states, often with an implied evaluation of them to see which is the better The comparison may either be between two projected states (eg

Would I be better off if I claimed X or Y?) or between the present state and a projected state (eg Would I be better off if I claimed X [compared with not claiming X]?) and will usually depend on classifications or prescriptions to obtain facts about the states to be compared. The comparison procedure involves evaluating the goal in each state in turn and reporting the two results, together with the differences in the proof traces from each evaluation. These differences will show why the two results differ.

6. Conclusion

The classification of answer types was derived from the classification of knowledge with, broadly speaking, each kind of knowledge providing a different type of answer. However, five of the cells in Table 2 are occupied by more than one answer type. This is because the answer types located together in one cell offer different perspectives on their knowledge. The Generalisation and Exemplification answer types look respectively up and down a subsumption (a-kind-of) hierarchy. The Identification type locates an entity within this hierarchy. The Definition and Relevance types examine rules, in the first case providing the body of the rule given the head, and in the second, finding the heads whose bodies mention the factor enquired about. The Classification and Prescription types are closely associated, the former providing a 'yes/no' answer and the latter a qualitative or quantitative answer. The Sensitivity type shows for a specific case what the value of a factor would have to be to yield a given conclusion. The Procedure and Antecedence types look respectively forwards to show how a goal could be achieved and backwards to show how a state or event occurred. The Justification type shows the deductions which have been used to arrive at a conclusion: either the final result or at an intermediate stage. The Rationale provides the reasons why a particular question is being asked on the way to deducing a conclusion.

Table 2 also shows how limited conventional systems are in the types of answer they can provide. Most advisory expert systems are capable of giving Classification and Prescription answers and many offer some variety of Justification and Rationale answers in response to How and Why questions. However, the existence of the remaining answer types has not been widely recognised. If knowledge-based systems are to provide the flexibility and expressive power which users, especially naive users, often expect of computer systems, we need to build facilities to allow users to ask for all the types of answer included in the table. To do this, we need a conceptually clear way of classifying answers and relating them to the knowledge in the system. This paper has begun to suggest that, by relating the answer types to a classification of knowledge, this may be achieved.

Acknowledgements

This work has been carried out as part of the DHSS Demonstrator Project supported by the Alvey Directorate of the UK Department of Trade and Industry and the Science and Engineering

Research Council. The project collaborators are ICL, Logica, Imperial
College, London, and the Universities of Surrey and Lancaster. Thanks
to my colleagues for comments, especially Betsy Cordingley and Paul
Luff at Surrey, and Alison Kidd of Hewlett Packard, Bristol and
members of the Alvey KBS Explanation SIG. The views expressed are
those of the author and may not necessarily be shared by other
collaborators.

References

Clancey, W. J. (1983) 'The advantages of abstract control knowledge in
expert system design', Stan-CS-83-995, Stanford University.

Dawson, P., Buckland, S. and Gilbert, G.N. (1987) 'Expert systems and
the public provision of welfare benefit advice', Alvey DHSS
Demonstrator Project Research Report 21, University of Surrey.

Epstein, J. (1984) New technology, new entitlement?, London:
Research Institute for Consumer Affairs.

Graesser, A. C. and Murachver, T. (1985) 'Symbolic procedures of
question answering', Chapter 2 in A.C. Graesser and J.B. Black, The
psychology of questions, Hillsdale, New Jersey: Lawrence Erlbaum.

Hammond, P. (1983) 'Representation of DHSS regulations as a logic
program', Expert Systems '83, Cambridge: Cambridge University Press.

Hasling, D. W., Clancey W. J. and Rennels, G. (1983) 'Strategic
explanations for a diagnostic consultation system', International J. of
Man-Machine Studies, 20, 3-19.

Hughes, S. (1986) 'Question classification in rule-based systems', Expert
Systems '86, Cambridge: Cambridge University Press.

Lehnert, W. G. (1977) 'Human and computational question-answering',
Cognitive Science, 1, 47-73.

Sergot, M. (1983) 'A query-the-user facility for logic programming', in
P. Degano and E. Sandwell (eds), Integrated Interactive Computer
Systems, North-Holland.

Shortliffe, E.H. (1976) Computer based medical consultations: MYCIN,
New York: Elsevier.

Sussman, G. J. and Steele, G. L. (1980) 'Constraints - a language for
expressing almost hierarchical descriptions', AI Journal, 14, pp 1 -39.

Swartout, W. R., (1977) 'A digitalis therapy advisor with explanations',
Proc 5th IJCAI, pp 819-826.

Swartout, W. R., (1983) 'XPLAIN: a system for creating and explaining
expert consulting programs', Artificial Intelligence, 21, 285-325.

Ticher, P. (1986) Welfare Benefit programs, Computer Factsheets,
London: Community Information Project.

Weiner, J. L. (1980) 'BLAH, a system which explains its reasoning',
Artificial Intelligence, 15, pp 19- 48.

AN INTELLIGENT MAINTENANCE SYSTEM

C M Brode
Plessey Research and Technology, Roke Manor, Romsey, Hants.
M K Hook
((Vanilla-Flavor-Company)), 2-4 Southgate St, Winchester, Hants.*
G M Parker
The Networking Centre, Focus 31, Mark Road, Hemel Hempstead, Herts.*

Abstract

This paper describes the development of an Intelligent Maintenance System (IMS) for diagnosing multiple fault reports from a System X Exchange. The architecture used in this project is generally applicable to any maintenance task but is particularly suited to diagnosis of faults in large, complex systems where a primarily rule-based approach is impractical. The approach described is also suited to situations where rules are scarce but design information is available eg in new systems. This architecture is based on the use of deep modelling techniques to provide the basic diagnosis. Rules may be used to increase the diagnosis capability. Where uncertainty exists between a number of diagnoses, multiple worlds are spawned with a method of assessing the merit of each hypothesis. The origins and handling of uncertainty is discussed in some detail. A number of practical lessons that have been learned are described here including the need to consider the user environment from the outset to ensure acceptance of the product.

* This work was carried out whilst these authors were at Plessey Research and Technology.

1. Introduction

This paper describes the development of an Intelligent Maintenance System (IMS) for correlating multiple fault reports from System X telephone exchanges in order to assist complex fault diagnosis. The work was carried out by a team drawn from Plessey Research at Roke Manor and Plessey Major Systems Ltd over the period 1986-1987, following on from an initial Alvey study in this area (British Telecom 1984-1986).

Prerequisite to the development of IMS was the elaboration of a general architecture for fault diagnosis in large complex systems. Central to this architecture is the use of deep modelling techniques together with a mechanism for handling uncertainty, which permits selection between multiple conflicting hypotheses.

To ensure the acceptance of a system such as IMS it was necessary to consider a number of factors which impact upon the development cycle. In particular integration of the system into the end user organisation, associated human factors need and target hardware/software requirements.

2. Background

2.1 Aim

        The aim of the project was to produce an expert system which
could improve the efficiency of maintenance personnel in identifying
faulty components so that the down-time of exchanges was reduced. In
order to limit the problem, but still prove the viability of an IKBS
approach, it was decided that IMS should model a single large subsystem.
The Digital Switching Subsystem (DSS) was chosen as it provided a single
large complex subsystem which could be easily related to many existing
fault reports and for which there was easy access to experts and
documentation. DSS provides the capability of switching up to 2,048
channels within a System X exchange.

2.2 System X

        System X consists of a number of subsystems which can be
either hardware, software, or combined hardware and software. Each
subsystem is responsible for detecting inconsistencies in its own
operation, identifying them with a particular element (resource) within
that subsystem, and passing these as fault reports to the Maintenance
Control Subsystem (MCS). During operation a single fault may sometimes
result in a number of fault reports as functionally related components
detect inconsistencies due to the failed component. The MCS then acts on
these fault reports and outputs them along with the action taken (see
figure 1). The action taken by the MCS is usually to remove the resource
from service. Each resource is made up of nought or more Slide In Units
(SIUs), cables and data. The maintenance engineer isolates the fault to
a particular element by following procedures for fault tracing laid down
in the Operations and Maintenance Manual. It can take some time for a
novice maintenance engineer to go through these diagnostic tests if a
large number of fault reports occur. However, an experienced maintenance
engineer will be able to analyse a fault report set, pick out the most
'important' faults and so significantly reduce the time it takes to
identify the source of the problem. The process of reducing a set of
faults to a smaller subset of 'root' faults is referred to as fault
correlation; this is the main function of the IMS expert system.

2.3 The Maintenance Task

        Maintenance has been a productive area for expert system
applications in the past, and telephone exchanges have been the subject
of a number of expert systems. In particular, the work by the GTE
Laboratories on COMPASS (Goyal 1985) and NEMESYS (Macleish 1986) shows
the commercial application of expert systems to exchange maintenance.
Both these systems have been developed to maintain well-established
systems for which there is a good deal of maintenance experience. A
major problem faced during the development of IMS was how to design an
effective expert system given that there are relatively few experienced
maintenance engineers available for consultation, due to the relatively
recent introduction of System X to service. The shortage of empirical

knowledge and indeed the sheer size of System X with its combination of possibilities for multiple fault occurrence precluded the possibility of using explicit rules for all eventualities. This fact, together with the existence of detailed design documentation encouraged the adaption of a causal reasoning approach based upon an underlying deep model of System X supplemented whenever possible by engineers heuristics or 'rules of thumb'. Despite the shortage of actual maintenance experience there is nonetheless, still a wealth of experience within the design and commissioning teams.

```
++++0482516          0552  86-09-10  0753
      SOFTWARE FAULT REPORT                86-09-10  0753-07

PROCESS: CBC0 (H'03D) MODULE:    3 FAULT:    49
EXTERNAL MESSAGE LOST          NO ACTION                    H'000
H'0011 H'800B H'0000 H'0000
H'1404 H'A009 H'5FFF H'1223 H'0000 H'0062
H'0000 H'0400 H'8541 H'2840 H'0497 H'1223
H'0080 H'0202 H'0000 H'0000 H'2000 H'0000


AAAA0482516          0553  86-09-10  0753
      EQUIPMENT FAULT REPORT               86-09-10  0753-11

NUMBER:  0276  PRIORITY: 2  CLASS: 06  SYMPTOM: H'03
RESOURCE: DCMP CCR  0- 0                 ( 0)  STATE: EQ
AUTO-RTS: NO    INHIBITS SET: OOS
      FM CODE:  000    RM CODE:  0      0  0
TIME OF CLEAR: 00-00-00  0000-00


AAAA0482516          0554  86-09-10  0753
      EQUIPMENT FAULT REPORT               86-09-10  0753-13

NUMBER:  0277  PRIORITY: 2  CLASS: 06  SYMPTOM: H'03
RESOURCE: DCMP CCR  0- 1                 ( 0)  STATE: EQ
AUTO-RTS: NO    INHIBITS SET: OOS
      FM CODE:  000    RM CODE:  0      0  0
TIME OF CLEAR: 00-00-00  0000-00


AAAA0482516          0555  86-09-10  0753
      EQUIPMENT FAULT REPORT               86-09-10  0753-15

NUMBER:  0278  PRIORITY: 2  CLASS: 06  SYMPTOM: H'03
RESOURCE: DCMP CCR  0- 2                 ( 0)  STATE: EQ
AUTO-RTS: NO    INHIBITS SET: OOS
      FM CODE:  000    RM CODE:  0      0  0
TIME OF CLEAR: 00-00-00  0000-00
```

Figure 1: Sample Output from the MCS

3. IMS Development

3.1 System X Models

The underlying System X design can be interpreted by engineers in a number of different ways depending on their viewpoint. These interpretations can be treated as separate models.

IMS currently employs three different models for the DSS subsystem. These are the Adjacency Model, the Power Supply Model, and the Functional Model. All the models support fault correlation. The Adjacency Model represents System X in terms of the physical location of the SIUs relating to the resources. This will identify faults that are related to their physical locations (eg hot spots, flooding) to be identified. The Power Supply Model represents System X in terms of the interconnection of power supplies and resources. This means that faults reported by a number of resources with a common noisy or intermittent power supply will be identified as being caused by that power supply.

The third model, and probably the most powerful one, is the Functional Model. This model represents System X in terms of the fault propagation paths within the exchange in a similar way to a data flow diagram. Faults are classified into a number of types (eg Speech, Clock or Alarm faults) and each resource has directional links connecting it to other resources. These links are of the same types as the faults thus indicating that a fault of a certain type may propagate from one resource to others along links of the same type. One strength of this model lies in the fact that a great deal of very useful information can be represented in a concise and understandable form. It must be noted however that IMS uses only underlying description to support all these different models. The models are different uses of that common description.

3.2   Knowledge Acquisition

Knowledge Harvesting for IMS presented a number of issues which influenced the whole approach to the problem. These were:

i)   There is not enough experience of System X to enable an entirely heuristically-based approach. There is, however, a great deal of design documentation.

ii)   Maintenance experience is mainly limited at present to the design and commissioning teams who are very busy.

For these reasons the architecture of IMS is based upon an underlying deep model and uses only available heuristics to speed up the processing time. These factors affected the knowledge harvesting in that:

i)   The majority of the information was derived from documentation.

ii)   The use of the expert's time had to be optimised.

Knowledge harvesting personnel with communications experience were selected. They familiarised themselves with the System X documentation and from this developed the deep models which IMS would use. The expert could then be approached with a working prototype IMS. During such sessions he would assess the performance of the various models and suggest improvements. These improvements were then incorporated into the model. The loop was repeated until a satisfactory model was developed.

4.   End User Aspects

4.1   Organisational Issues

The introduction of a system such as IMS into an end user organisation has considerable implications for that organisation. It became clear during discussions with potential users of IMS (ie current System X installations and also commissioning engineers) that the introduction of such technology was not a matter of simply installing new kit. The use of an IMS-like system inevitably alters the maintenance task, hopefully reducing the downtime of the maintained system and thereby leaving the engineer with less routine work to perform. This may in turn lead to a reduction in the number of engineers required. Changes in the number of staff and their job descriptions will also alter the role of managerial staff in the end user organisation. Clearly these factors must offset the cost of any extra hardware/software required for adoption of the system. The increasing availability of low cost/high performance systems clearly is of importance to the cost/benefit equation surrounding the adoption of knowledge based technology.

4.2 Human Factors Needs

Underlying the IMS project is the idea that a set of tools should be provided to assist the maintenance engineer, rather than trying to replace him. IMS is the first step in developing a range of tools and facilities which will provide the System X maintenance engineer with a 'Maintenance Support Environment' designed to allow him to work as efficiently as possible. As with any system which must interact with humans, the quality of the Man-Machine Interface (MMI) plays an important part in the acceptability of the software tool. The present MMI (see figure 2) provides the engineer with a suitable display of the fault reports received. The engineer is already familiar with the format of the fault reports. In addition there is a set of tools to allow the engineer to invoke the IMS fault correlation functionality and to employ the more complex set of functions for interacting with IMS. This approach encourages user acceptance of IMS by allowing him to determine how much he may change his current working practices to use the new tools available.

4.3 Hardware/Software Constraints

The selection of an appropriate target machine for a system such as IMS places constraints on the design and development stages. Within this section these constraints are discussed in the context of IMS.

The development of IMS was initiated on an LMI Lambda Lisp machine (providing a rich environment for fast prototyping) and then moved onto a Sun 3/160M workstation, since the target was required by PMSL to be a Unix machine. The Sun workstation runs UNIX4.2BSD and the SUN Common Lisp derivative of Lucid Common Lisp.

From the outset, all coding was performed in Common Lisp (Steele 1984) in order that the system could be ported between the machines. The need to port onto a Unix run time system precluded the use of any non-Common Lisp constructs, (such as the Zetalisp Flavors system), for representing the various system objects (worlds, knowledge systems and fault hypotheses). Accordingly all objects within IMS are represented as Common Lisp Structures, with the exception of 'resources' which for reasons of efficiency are implemented in terms of property lists. In so far as porting was concerned, the lack of a common windowing system was found to be a significant obstacle.

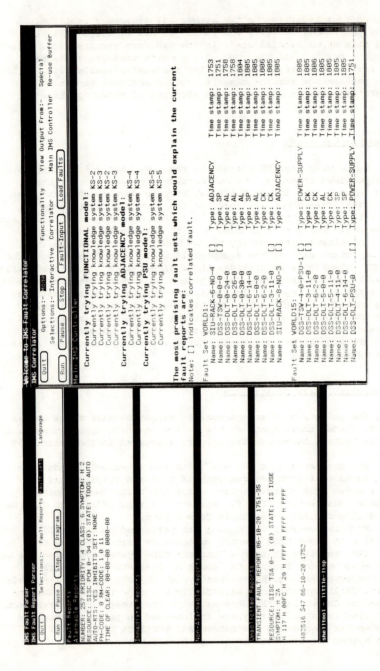

Figure 2: The Current Man Machine Interface

5. The Architecture of IMS

5.1 The Deep Model

IMS makes use of an explicit representation of System X in order to identify the most likely minimum set of root faults, which could explain the observed, generally larger, set of fault reports.

Central to the functionality of IMS is an object oriented representation of the components of a System X exchange. The granularity of representation is at resource level, corresponding to the level of information which System X emits as fault reports. Each resource (line terminal, multiplexer etc) descriptor has instance variables referring to its number, location, type, links, status, power supplies and component SIUs or boards.

5.2 Use of Temporal Information

Each fault report has associated with it a time stamp. This information is used in IMS to indicate when a fault can be considered 'stale' and hence will not be correlatable with more recent fault reports. It has been found empirically that faults occurring more than fifteen minutes apart are not correlatable. Accordingly IMS uses a 15 minute moving window and discards faults outside this timeframe. IMS does not simply use abutting 15 minutes slices, but rather takes a rolling slice, collecting a 15 minute sample every minute or so, the actual interval according to the number of faults in the sample and hence upon the time taken to complete a correlation cycle.

5.3 Reasoning in IMS

Reasoning over the resource description is controlled by a number of knowledge systems (KSs). These knowledge systems communicate via a common blackboard as in the Hearsay II architecure (Lesser 1977). The system differs from that model however, in that there are a number of blackboards, each blackboard being associated with a different hypothetical world. During the course of reasoning, worlds may be spawned in order that mutually inconsistent hypothesis sets can be developed in parallel. The knowledge systems consist of Common Lisp structures containing (aside from housekeeping information) either a set of production rules or a method (a block of procedural code). Invocation of a given knowledge system results in either, the repeated selection and firing of rules until nothing further happens, or else the activation of the method. The models employed by IMS are comprised of one or more knowledge systems.

In operation the world system is cleared and fault reports from a rolling fifteen minute time slice are posted as hypothetical fault structures onto the blackboard of a new root world. After determining the subsystem(s) from which the reports originated, IMS selects the subsystem dependent models available, together with any subsystem indepedent models and invokes them repeatedly in a round robin fashion. Each model corresponds to at least one knowledge system which in turn may contain either a number of rules or else a method. Selection

of which KS to try next is fixed at present but future development of
IMS may require the adoption of a more complex architecture using
meta-level control knowledge, to determine when knowledge systems should
be invoked.

During the operation of a particular KS, hypotheses on the
blackboard of the current world are inspected, and those which the KS is
competent to consider are identified. Each KS contains rewrite rules
which allow IMS to replace a number of related hypotheses by a single
new one. Before actually performing a rewrite, IMS determines the
relative merit of the postulated hypothesis and compares it with the
summed merit of the various faults about to be rewritten. If the
improvement in merit is above a certain threshold, IMS proceeds to
assert the new hypothesis into the current world. It removes the old
explained hypotheses, and appends them to the parent field of the new
hypothesis. The merit of the new hypothesis is also attached to it and
the change in merit added to a world-merit field associated with the
current world. If the merit change is below a second threshold, the
proposed rewrite is rejected. If it falls into the grey region between
the two, a new world is spawned and the new hypothesis asserted in the
daughter only.

New worlds will also be spawned if several mutually
inconsistent explanations of approximately equal merit (within 20% of
each other) can be proposed.

A world is frozen if all models are applied to it and none can
cause any change. The current world is always taken to be that unfrozen
world which has the greatest summed merit.

6. Uncertainty in IMS

6.1 Origin of Uncertainty

Any model of a complex system is necessarily a generalisation
of the behaviour of that system. As a result any inferences based on
such models must themselves be generalisations and hence the subject of
uncertainty.

Model based uncertainty can be ameliorated to some extent by
the provision of heuristic rules which can simplify interpretation of
repeatedly occuring faults.

6.2 Representation

Hypotheses within IMS differ in merit. The merit of a
particular hypothesis depends upon three factors:
* the number of fault reports explained (n)
* the number of non-reporting System X resources which ought
  to be reporting if the hypothetical fault is correct (i)
* the total link distance from the hypothetical fault to all
  its parent faults (l)
Within IMS each hypothesis has a triplet associated with it.
This triplet consists of fields corresponding to the 3 factors above
(n, i, l). Merit triplets allow IMS to differentiate between competing
hypotheses.

A particular hypothesis can be said to be 'good' if it:

    i)explains a number of reports,
    ii)does not implicate too many non reporting nodes, and
    iii)does not require the propagation of faults over a
    considerable distance

Some samples of 'good' and 'poor' hypotheses are shown in figure
3.

By storing the fields separately in the merit triplet, one
can relatively easily combine hypothesis values. The first two fields
are simply added, the third (link distance), is more complicated to
compute
and requires consideration of the shape of the history tree hanging from
the parents field of each hypothesis.

The comparison of hypotheses by the direct comparison of
triplets was found to be messy and was replaced by the strategy of
initially mapping triplets onto a merit value by an ad hoc algorithm
based on set theory.

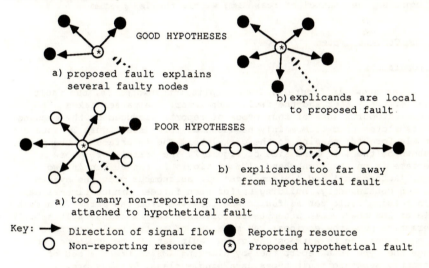

GOOD HYPOTHESES

a) proposed fault explains
several faulty nodes

b) explicands are local
to proposed fault

POOR HYPOTHESES

b) explicands too far away
from hypothetical fault

a) too many non-reporting nodes
attached to hypothetical fault

Key: → Direction of signal flow   ● Reporting resource
     ○ Non-reporting resource   ⊛ Proposed hypothetical fault

Figure 3: Examples of Good and Bad Hypotheses

It is worth noting from a development point of view that
handling uncertainty is generally difficult. One can very easily end up
with numbers of a dubious nature either because of uncertain inputs,
less than rigorous operations, or a combination of the two.

If the initial certainty values are of questionable validity
then the subsequent use of statistically rigorous algorithms for
combining uncertainties, such as the Bayes' or Dempster-Shafer theorems,
lends a spurious degree of support to the results they produce. It is
often very difficult in 'real world' situations to ensure that certainty
factors have a legitimate foundation and moreover only undergo
legitimate operations. In the case of IMS the certainty factors are
empirically reasonable and appear to be good for sorting hypotheses of

dissimilar merit. Their ability to discriminate finely is, however, questionable. Accordingly in IMS the view was taken that any hypotheses (or worlds) whose merits are within 20% of one another, should be taken to be of functionally equivalent merit. There being no justification for selecting between mutually inconsistent hypotheses or worlds of such similar merits on the basis of merit value alone. Note therefore that IMS cannot generally be expected to produce a single unequivocal solution.

6.4 Multiple Worlds Ameliorate Uncertainty

The adoption of a multiple worlds architecture in IMS simplifies the use of such loose certainty comparisons. Rather than 'arbitrarily' selecting one hypothesis and thereby running the risk of subsequently having to backtrack and try an alternative, one can take a strategy of least commitment and assess the alternatives in parallel, hoping that subsequent processing will discriminate with better validity between the alternatives. The use of a multiple worlds strategy greatly simplifies and improves the control of reasoning within the IMS system.

7. The Current System

7.1 Operation

As shown in figure 2, IMS is split into two parts, the fault parser or translator and the fault correlator. The parser takes alarmable reports (one of four types of report) produced by the exchange and translates them from mainly hexadecimal form (see figure 1) into a suitable form for passing to the correlator. The interface to the parser is shown on the left hand side of figure 2. The correlator (whose interface is on the right hand side of figure 2) can be run in two modes, 'autonomous' and 'interactive'. In autonomous mode the system will run continuously, building up for each fifteen minute time-slice, an increasing fault set as faults are received from the parser. In each cycle of IMS the system attempts to correlate the existing fault set. In interactive mode the engineer can make use of system tools together with his own expertise to work on any given fault set. For example he can change the type in a report thereby allowing IMS to treat a set of apparently separate fault types as a single class. Various browsing tools are also provided allowing the enginer to inspect the knowledge base and reasoning processes employed by IMS if he should wish to do so. In the long term it is highly desirable that this interface be simplified and extended to allow the average engineer to extend the knowledge base and modify the reasoning processes on the fly. This requires further study.

7.2 Results

A prototype version of IMS, as described above has been built which, given a fault set of twenty reports, will produce a minimum set of correlations in less than forty seconds. The knowledge base occupies approximately three megabytes of memory. The speed of response of the system is largely dependent on the number of faults, the size of the network being of rather less importance.

8. Future Developments

8.1 Completion of System X Modelling

To date only the Digital Switching Subsystem (representing roughly half of a typical trunk exchange) and its associated models have been completed. Future development will focus initially on modelling the main processing subsystem before moving on to complete all modelling. This will necessitate the modelling of inter-subsystem fault propogations.

8.2 Modelling Control

At present the control of the application of individual knowledge systems follows a simple round robin scheduler. A more complex meta-level control strategy, basing the selection of KS on aspects of the fault set, may yield a solution more quickly.

8.3 Learning

In certain instances, wherein a fault set has taken a long time to be correlated, or an incorrect solution was generated, it would be appropriate for IMS to 'learn' by storing the observed fault set and its associated current correlations for future reference.
Clearly there is little point in IMS learning every fault set; such learning should be constrained and if possible generalised.

9. Conclusions

This paper has described the development of a knowledge-based system to aid in diagnosing fault reports from a System X telephone exchange.
As a result of this work an architecture was developed which addressed the problems imposed by large complex systems and is generally applicable to maintenance of these systems. The architecture made use of deep modelling techniques combined with a mechanism for handling uncertainty which allows selection between multiple conflicting hypotheses. This architecture is not rule-based, which can be inadequate for complex systems, instead it uses deep models of the system to provide fault correlation. Any rules which are available may be used to improve the speed and accuracy of the correlation.
A number of practical lessons have been described in this paper, the most significant being to consider fron the outset the integration of the system into its environment. This is the only way to ensure acceptance of the final product.

References

1. British Telecom Research Laboratories, Information Technology
   Research Centre University of Bristol, & Plessey Major Systems
   Ltd.(1984-1986). An Intelligent Maintenance System for
   Telecommunications Networks. Alvey Project IKBS/042 Report.

2. Goyal, S.K. Prerau, D.S. Lemmon, A.V. Gunderson, A.S. & Reinke,
   R.E. (1985). COMPASS: an expert system for telephone switch
   maintenance. Expert Systems, 2, no. 3, pp 112 - 126.

3. Macleish, K.J. Thiedke, S. & Vonnergrund, D. (1986). Expert
   Systems in Central Office Switch Maintenance. IEE Communications
   Magazine, 24, no. 9, pp 26 - 33

4. Steele, G.L. (1984). Common Lisp - the Language. Digital Press.

5. Lesser, V.R. & Erman, L.D. (1977). A Retrospective view of the
   Hearsay-II Arcitecture. Fifth International Conference on
   Artificial Intelligence. Cambridge, Mass. 2, pp 790 - 800

Helping Inexperienced Users to Construct Simulation Programs: An Overview of the ECO Project

Dave Robertson †, Alan Bundy †, Mike Uschold †, Bob Muetzelfeldt ‡

†Department of Artificial Intelligence, University of Edinburgh.
‡Department of Forestry and Natural Resources, University of Edinburgh.

Abstract

We provide an overview of the development of ECO, a program which enables ecologists with minimal mathematical or computing skills to build simulation models. The first version of this system used a System Dynamics formalism to represent users' models and relied on simple interface techniques. Subsequent trials revealed that the formalism was insufficiently expressive to represent the sophisticated models which users sometimes required. The system was also over–reliant upon users to drive dialogue during model construction and provided insufficient guidance for inexperienced users. We discuss techniques for solving these problems. Finally, we note the key contributions of this research in the context of related work.

1 Introduction

Ecological researchers are becoming increasingly reliant upon mathematical models as a means of concisely representing their understanding of ecological systems. Having constructed a model of a given system, it is possible to test the validity of the representation using computer simulation and analysis of results. Models which are deemed valid may be used to predict the behaviour of their corresponding real world system when subjected to a specific set of conditions. This capability is particularly necessary in the assessment of environmental impact of resource management decisions.

Ideally, it should be possible for any ecologist to fit his/her description of an ecological system into a modelling framework which allows it to be easily accessed and analysed by other researchers. Currently, this is not possible for the following reasons :

1. Many ecologists do not have the mathematical or programming skills needed to construct ecological models.

2. There has been little standardisation of modelling approaches. Individual modellers tend to write large, one–off, representations using their favourite modelling language and/or mathematical framework. These models are extremely difficult to analyse unless one is familiar with the formalisms involved. Model defects are thus liable to pass unnoticed by the ecological community.

3. Model parameters and relationships are scattered through a wide range of literature and are expressed in different formalisms (*e.g.* mathematical formulae ; Fortran subroutines). Therefore, a large amount of effort is wasted in defining model components which have already been used elsewhere.

Ecologists need to be free to concentrate on investigating the dynamics of the systems which interest them, rather than wasting time learning esoteric programming techniques or deciphering obscure mathematical formalisms. They require an *Intelligent Front End* [Bundy 84], which will help them convert their ecological ideas into a simulation model. An Intelligent Front End is a kind of expert system which builds a formal description of a user's problem through a user–oriented dialogue. This task specification is then used to generate suitably coded instructions for the target computer package. Our research aim was to provide an ecological modelling system which could be used by ecologists with minimal mathematical or programming skills. In order to address the problems (listed above) of our target user group, we considered that the following features were required in the system:

- **A task specification formalism** which is capable of representing a wide range of ecological simulation models. This helps provide a standard representation for different models, tackling problem 2 in the list above.

- **A front end** which would interact with the user in terms familiar to him/her, converting the user's ecological statements into a mathematical formalism capable of translation into source code for a simulation model. The purpose of this dialogue control mechanism is to help overcome the technology barrier of problem 1 by making it easier for users formally to describe the program they require.

- **An automatic checker** of the consistency and ecological sense of the model. This also addresses problem 1 by preventing all syntactic and some semantic errors during the interactive specification phase.

- **A data base and browsing mechanism** for storing and accessing ecological data and relationships. By providing this repository of information, users should find it easier to isolate model structures appropriate to their application (alleviating problem 3).

- **A back end interpreter** to run the completed model and display the results.

The current ECO system, although prototypical, largely achieves these original requirements for a subset of ecological modelling. However, it also exhibits a number of deficiencies which we are attempting to remedy in our current research.

This paper contains a summary of the programs which we have constructed in order to provide the facilities listed above. We begin by describing our first prototype system and its relationship to our original objectives. We highlight some important inadequacies in the basic system and provide a short discussion of our attempts to alleviate these problems. We then summarise the benefits of this project – its contribution to artificial intelligence and ecological research.

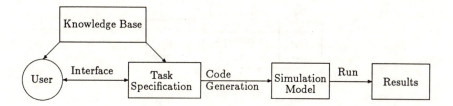

Figure 1: The original ECO system

2   Description of the First ECO System

ECO, ([Uschold et al 86], [Muetzelfeldt et al 85]) is a computer program – written in Prolog – for constructing ecological models. A diagram illustrating the general architecture of the system appears in figure 1. It relies upon a System Dynamics formalism [Forrester 61] to express model structure. This formalism can be manipulated by users, via an interface package, to produce a task specification for the model they require. A knowledge base of ecological relationships is used by the system to perform some simple checks for ecological consistency in the developing task specification. When complete (as determined by the syntactical structure of the formalism), the task specification is automatically converted into a target language (*e.g.* Fortran) and the simulation may then be executed. Recently, we have added the ability to run simulations directly in Prolog, our chosen implementation language, using a special purpose interpreter. This bypasses the code generation phase but does not effect the core of our research – the interface between user and formal task specification. We now consider the main components of the system, in relation to our original objectives from section 1.

2.1   The Task Specification Formalism

ECO can be used to build a special class of models, called System Dynamics models. This methodology encompasses the technique of compartment modelling, commonly used in ecology to model the flow of materials such as energy, nutrients, and pollutants. System Dynamics modelling makes use of a concise schematic representation which helps the ecologist think about the model without mathematical formulae. This representation was adapted and expanded to produce a task specification formalism which helps to bridge the gap between the user's view of the problem in ecological terms and the final Fortran simulation program. Each model is represented by an instance of this formalism which is built up while the user is interacting with the system. Figure 2 shows a diagrammatical representation of this formalism for a very simple model in which wolves are preying upon sheep. Predation is represented as a flow of some material (*e.g.* sheep biomass) from compartment *sheep* to compartment *wolf*, with the rate of flow as a function of the current values for *sheep* and *wolf* compartments and a *coefficient*. The initial values for *sheep* and *wolf* are set to 100 and 10 respectively.

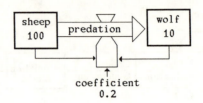

Figure 2: A System Dynamics Model

2.2   Interacting with the User

At the most general level, the ecologist user describes a model in terms of objects (such as trees, sheep, wolves) and relationships between these objects (such as predation, photosynthesis, etc). Equations and parameters defining these objects and relationships can be selected by the user, with automatic connection of appropriate structures in the underlying task specification. The user is free to decide how to approach the task of model construction. For example, submodels can be constructed separately and linked together later or, alternatively, the user can specify all the objects and relationships at the general level before finally attaching equations and parameters.

In order that ecologists should readily accept the system, it is crucially important to have a friendly means of interaction. Initially, users were required to input ecological statements in stylised English. For example, if a user inputs the statement "`wolves eat sheep`", this would be converted into a *predation* flow from a *sheep* to a *wolf* compartment (see figure 2). This allows the user to decide how the model will be constructed but requires that the user remember the syntax of each command. As a means of providing more guidance for users, an alternative menu based interaction system was implemented and, recently, computer graphics techniques are being tested as a more convenient way of eliciting input and displaying the developing model. This removes the necessity for remembering command syntax but provides no help with decisions about strategies for building the model (*e.g.* Should a sheep population be represented as a single entity or as separate individuals). Incorporating this sort of advice into the system will be tackled in future research. Currently, the user must make strategic decisions which are only checked for mathematical and simple ecological consistency by the system.

2.3   Consistency Checking

As the user is building the specification for his/her model, it is continually checked for internal consistency. Two separate types of consistency checking are performed. First, there is a syntactic or mathematical consistency associated with the formalism (*e.g.* destructive circularity should not occur in the task specification, a parameter must have an initial value). Since these consistency rules are few in number and clearly defined, we can ensure that ECO never produces a model which cannot be run – the user is guaranteed to get something that works. Secondly, there is semantic consistency checking which helps maintain ecological sense in the specification. Ideally, we should like to guarantee that a final model will be ecologically sound and, furthermore, will accurately and appropriately describe the behaviour of the ecological system to meet the original goals of the user. This is well outside the capabilities of our current implementation but we do provide limited semantic checking capabilities. For example, if the user says that "sheep eat wolves" he/she is warned that this relationship may be the wrong way round. If the system does not recognise a particular object, it will make default assumptions on the basis of the context in which it appears. Thus if the user says "foo eats sheep", the system assumes that "foo" is a carnivore. All future uses of the object "foo" must be consistent with it being a carnivore. However, this rudimentary form of semantic checking is not always desirable, since a user may want to test non–standard ecological theories which are not recognised as valid by the system. A more comprehensive attempt to define specific objects and relationships in terms of general ecological principles is described briefly in section 3.1. This should facilitate improved checking and explanation capabilities.

2.4   Storing and Accessing Ecological Data

During the model building phase, the user has access to a base of ecological knowledge and data. Its primary function is to provide the user with the building blocks necessary for creating the model. This includes such things as ecological objects which may be contained in the models (*e.g.* animals, trees etc), taxonomic information relating classes of objects when possible (*e.g.* primates are mammals), mathematical relationships (with associated contexts indicating their appropriateness), and processes (*e.g.* grazing and evaporation) each with the appropriate types of objects which may participate (*e.g.* only animals may graze). Note that this knowledge is used to perform semantic consistency checking as described above.

Ecologists need the capability to store data from field observations or laboratory studies and retrieve them in a flexible, efficient manner. Often, these observations are made in different contexts and ecologists want to store and retrieve information according to the circumstances in which it was first recorded. For example, an observation may be made that "A tree in plot 5 of the Glentrool plantation was 5 metres high in summer 1976". Another observation may state that "The rate of photosynthesis of Sitka spruce is 10 mgC kg^{-1} day^{-1} in bright sunlight". We have utilised relationships between items in different observations to provide a structure for browsing through observational records, progressively refining the user's description of the observation he/she wants to find. Ecologists who have used the system find the browsing mechanism easy to understand and operate. For a more detailed description of the ECO browser see [Robertson et al 85].

2.5   Running the Completed Model

Completed models can be passed to a code generation subsystem which translates the task specification into Fortran source code. Due to the constrained nature of our formalism for expressing models, this process was relatively straightforward. The user can then compile this code, run it and revise the task specification if the program does not behave as expected. Currently, the onus is on the user to decide whether revisions to his/her task specification are necessary. Ideally, there would be a much closer association between the system for eliciting the model specification and the subsystem for running the model so that feedback on program execution can be related to the specification. As a first step towards integrating these systems a Prolog program for running simulations has been developed. This allows test simulations to be executed directly from the task specification (no intermediate translation phase) and provides for the possibility of automatically passing back information from the simulation to influence subsequent model refinement. Because our research effort is directed primarily at formally representing user's models rather than analysis of program execution, we have yet to concentrate on these more sophisticated execution issues.

3   Improving the Original ECO System

The system described in section 2 can construct a particular type of simulation model easily and efficiently, provided that the user knows what he/she wants to do. We tested this version of the system on undergraduate students of ecology and on various visitors to the department. These trials revealed several shortcomings of the original system. The most important of these are that the task specification formalism is insufficiently expressive; the system is too reliant upon the user to drive dialogue during model construction and the modelling guidance provided by the system is insufficient for naive users. We then diverted our attention to exploring ways to combat these difficult problems. Our current progress in each area is summarised below:

3.1   Extending the Task Specification Formalism

Although the System Dynamics formalism was useful for constructing a wide range of simulation models, it could not easily be adapted to represent certain more complex computational structures (*e.g.* models with age class subdivisions or models in which structural components were created and destroyed, perhaps representing births and deaths).

3.1.1   The Submodels Modelling System

A separate program (the Submodels system [Muetzelfeldt et al 87]) was developed to achieve a more flexible way of representing model structure. In this system, users are provided with a library of "base" models, each of which requires a fixed set of input data; generates a fixed set of output data; and performs some procedure in order to obtain output from input. Users may arrange base models hierarchically to represent subunits of the ecological system which they want to describe. Communication between models is achieved by connecting data–flow links between appropriate inputs and outputs. This method allows arbitrarily complex computational procedures to be

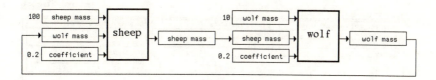

Figure 3: A Submodels Model

incorporated into the model but, like the System Dynamics formalism, places a heavy burden of responsibility on users, who must directly express their models in terms of the computation involved. Figure 3 shows a display, using Submodels symbols, of the System Dynamics model from figure 2.

3.1.2   Use of Typed Logic

Ideally, users should be able to state, in ecological terminology, the problem which their model has to solve and the system should help them convert this description into a computable solution. This raises the problem of how to represent formally these, often qualitative, "high level" statements of modelling problems and how to link these statements to a computable program.

We have performed initial experiments with a formalism in which common ecological statements are represented using a typed logic. Some examples of typical ecological statements expressed in the logic are:

"All wolves prey upon all sheep at all times."
$\forall W \in wolf \ \forall S \in sheep \ \forall T \in time \ predation(W, S, T)$

"If animal A preys upon animal B at any instant in time, there will be some probability distribution determining whether A kills B at that time"
$\forall A, B \in animal \ \forall T \in time \ \exists P \in probability\_distribution$
$\quad predation(A, B, T) \rightarrow probability(\lambda T \ kill(A, B, T)) = P$

The procedural structure of the simulation is supplied by introducing fragments of simulation code (schemata), similar to those used in the Submodels system, each being active only under certain conditions of the user's description of the ecological system. This approach to program construction provides greater representational power along with increased ability to represent ecological statements in a form close to that employed by users. It also provides a foundation for future work on dialogue and guidance. A more detailed discussion of these issues appears in [Robertson et al 87a].

3.2   Flexible Dialogue Control

Many computer systems (ECO included) tend to force users into a rigidly structured dialogue, designed to suit some "average" user. In the original ECO system, the dialogue was primarily user driven, with the system responding to the user's commands.

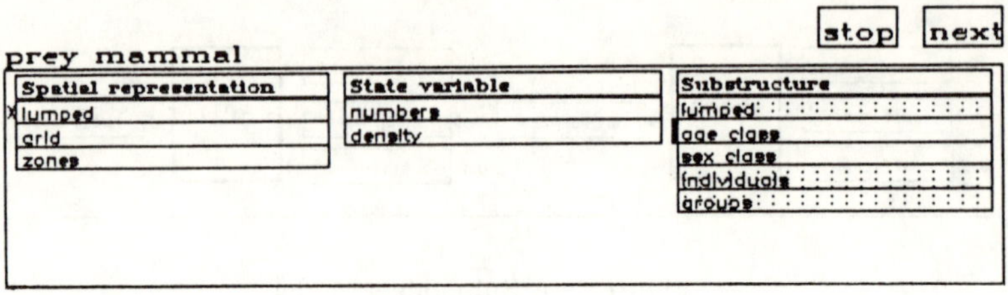

Figure 4: Menu System – Sample Display

As a means of exploring the other extreme of the range of possible dialogue mechanisms we have constructed several simple systems in which the computer plays a strongly active role in guiding the design. Principal among these is a system in which important characteristics of users' models are represented using frame–like structures, possessing attributes which users must instantiate to suit their required model. The system determines the sequence in which these frames are presented to users and suggests values for attributes. The users' role is simply to accept or reject the information offered by the system. A sample of the display produced by this system appears in figure 4. The user has been shown sets of options for three attributes of a prey mammal and has chosen an *age_class* substructure. In response to this choice, the system has excluded the options *lumped*, *individuals* and *groups* because they could not apply at the same time as *age_class*. However, *sex_class* option remains available, since mammals may have both age and sex classes simultaneously. The user may also select options from the *state_variable* or *spatial_representation* attributes. When all the required options have been selected, clicking the "next" button prompts the system to generate a new set of menus for related attributes.

In reality, different types of user require different balances between system and user initiative during model construction. Expert users want freedom to define task specification structure as they see fit. Novice users want to be guided through the model construction process until they become accustomed to the system. A flexible dialogue system is required, which allows users to take the initiative if they want to but continually provides advice as to what it thinks would be a useful move at any time. This suggested to us a dialogue architecture which utilises graphics displays and multiple windowing facilities to simultaneously display different possibilities for interaction. Among the options available to the user would be :

- A graphical display of the model which the user could manipulate by hand (direct user initiative). This approach is similar to that used in the existing ECO program.

- A window in which users may, of their own volition, provide information about model structures and their goals for the current model. This has been implemented, based on a mechanism for selecting and editing typed logic statements, rendered into English text [Robertson et al 87a]. The left–hand window in figure 5 shows a sample display in which the user has, using a browsing system, selected a sentence (number 218) from the system's knowledge base. This sentence is represented internally as:

$$\forall A, B \in animal \ \forall T \in time \ predation(A, B, T)$$

but has been rendered into stylised English to make the logic more understandable to ecologists. The user has edited this sentence by restricting the type of A to *wolf* and B to *sheep*, forming the expression:

$$\forall A \in wolf \ \forall B \in sheep \ \forall T \in time \ predation(A, B, T)$$

which has then been added to the problem description.

- A suggestion box of system advice about model construction. These suggestions are generated by the system, allowing an entire model to be constructed simply by following the system's advice. This part of the system has been only partially implemented (see section 3.3). A display from our current prototype appears in the right–hand window of figure 5. Here the system has used the expression added by the user (see above) in conjunction with the following rule from its knowledge base:

$$\forall A, B \in animal \ \forall T \in time \ \exists P \in probability\_distribution$$
$$predation(A, B, T) \rightarrow probability(\lambda T \ kill(A, B, T)) = P$$

to generate a suggested sentence, rendered into stylised English by the system but represented internally as:

$$\forall A \in wolf \ \forall B \in sheep \ \forall T \in time \ \exists P \in probability\_distribution$$
$$probability(\lambda T \ kill(A, B, T)) = P$$

By referring to the appropriate identification number, the user may get the system to implement this advice.

This architecture would allow smooth and flexible changes of initiative during the session. It also avoids the perennial problem of ordering the sequence suggestions because the user is allowed to choose which to accept at any time. Further discussion of dialogue issues may be found in [Robertson et al 87b].

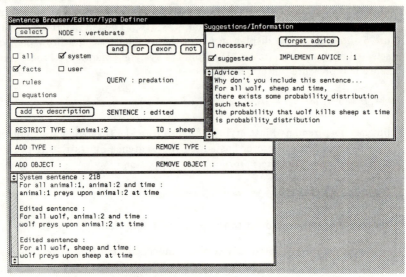

Figure 5: Mixed Initiative System – Sample Display

3.3   Guiding the Design of Specifications

Even when presented with a friendly dialogue system, many users have difficulty in constructing program specifications. This is because they have only a vague notion of what should be included in their model and how to represent it (a problem common to all non–trivial specification systems). For example, the user may be unable to decide whether to represent a sheep population as a single entity or as a number of individual objects and, if the latter option is chosen, he/she may not know the appropriate structures to insert into the task specification. Novice modellers do not know how to idealise the objects in models so that they are consistent with the overall objectives of the model. Without this information, they may construct inelegant specifications or, worse, may leave out crucial structures. The system must be able to advise users about the best structures for representing objects in the model, based on an analysis of existing model structure and a knowledge of the user's goals for the finished program. We have investigated possible methods of providing this form of guidance and hope to provide a working implementation, utilising a typed logic problem description (see section 3.1).

At the start of a session, advice may be provided by asking users to specify their modelling objectives or to provide some of the principal high level components of their model – for example, the fact that wolves prey on sheep. From this general description, the system may be able to select a modelling framework – a predator–prey schema, perhaps – and display this to the user as a suggested structure. If the structure is acceptable, it may be further elaborated, using additional schemata if necessary. For instance, a respiration subschema might be added to the predator (wolf) component of the predator–prey schema. This feature should fit cleanly into the dialogue architecture mentioned above, allowing the user to obtain guidance in converting his/her initial vague ideas into a final formal specification and making sure that important parts of the specification are included. The resulting system would be an expert modelling consultant rather than merely a convenient tool. A discussion of the guidance requirements in ECO can be found in [Uschold 86].

4 Related Work

The ECO system synthesises Fortran programs from specifications in ecological terminology provided by the user. As a program synthesis system it occupies an important niche on the power/generality spectrum between general-purpose synthesis systems like NuPRL, [Constable et al 86], and the special-purpose, application generators [Horowitz et al 85]. ECO is restricted to the synthesis of a particular class of programs, but this is a much wider class than application generators can typically deal with. It exploits this restriction by synthesising more complex programs than those that can be dealt with by general-purpose systems.

An exciting aspect of our recent work using typed logic for specifying ecological problems, is that it is upwards compatible with the techniques used by the general-purpose synthesis systems. This gives the hope of a smooth transition between weak general-purpose synthesis systems and more powerful special-purpose systems employing domain specific knowledge. Our long range goal is to develop mechanisms for incorporating such domain specific knowledge in a general-purpose framework: to extract specifications from users, to guide the synthesis process and to interpret the results of the program.

ECO is an example of an intelligent front end package (*i.e.* a system which acts as an intermediary between a user and a complex program, making it easier for the user to use the program correctly). Previous work in our group concerning intelligent front ends has included the Mecho system, [Bundy et al 79], which built sets of equations for describing a mechanics problem stated in English, and the ASA system, [O'Keefe 82], which built instructions for a statistics package to analyse the results of a psychological experiment. These three systems have a strong family resemblance to the extent that we have suggested the possibility of a general intelligent front end framework or 'shell' to simplify the generation of similar systems, [Bundy 84].

5 Conclusion

The development of the ECO system can be divided into two phases. Our initial work relied upon a simple System Dynamics formalism which represented users' ecological models in a mathematical framework. Users were assumed to be capable of constructing *solutions* to their ecological problems by directly manipulating System Dynamics constructs. Our justification for this assumption was that ecologists were familiar with System Dynamics and that a large number of ecological problems could be easily represented in this formalism. However, tests of the initial system revealed that the number of users who fitted into this classification was smaller than we had anticipated. Users sometimes required more complex models than could be represented using System Dynamics. They also wanted to describe their modelling *problem*, using terminology with which they were familiar, and receive guidance in converting this into a computable solution. This requirement provided the impetus for the second phase of development, which continues today. We have constructed prototype systems which allow users to describe their modelling problem using ecological statements – represented in a typed logic. Typed logic permits a much wider range of problems and solutions to be represented than was possible using System Dynamics. These statements can be used to isolate fragments of simulation code (represented in a formalism similar to that used in the Submodels system) which, together, constitute a computable simulation model. We are also designing guidance mechanisms, based on a "suggestion box" system. This will allow the system to take control of dialogue at a user's request, thus elevating ECO from the role of a passive assistant to that of an active participant in the modelling process.

Acknowledgements

This work was funded by SERC/Alvey grants GR/C/06226 and GR/D/44294. We are grateful to members of the Mathematical Reasoning Group in the Department of Artificial Intelligence at Edinburgh University for their practical advice and support during the course of this project.

References

[Bundy 84]   A. Bundy. Intelligent front ends. In J. Fox, editor, *State of the Art Report on Expert Systems*, pages 15–24, Pergamon Infotech, 1984. also in proceedings of British Computer Society Specialist Group on Expert Systems 1984 and available from Edinburgh as DAI Research Paper 227.

[Bundy et al 79]   A. Bundy, L. Byrd, G. Luger, C. Mellish, R. Milne, and M. Palmer. Solving mechanics problems using meta-level inference. In B.G. Buchanan, editor, *Proceedings of IJCAI-79*, pages 1017–1027, International Joint Conference on Artificial Intelligence, 1979. Reprinted in 'Expert Systems in the microelectronic age' ed. Michie, D., Edinburgh University Press, 1979. Also available from Edinburgh as DAI Research Paper No. 112.

[Constable et al 86]   R.L. Constable, Allen, Bromley, Cleaveland, Cremer, Harper, Howe, Knoblock, Mendler, Panangaden, Sasaki, and Smith. *Implementing Mathematics with the Nuprl Proof Development System*. Prentice Hall, 1986.

[Forrester 61]   J. W. Forrester. *Industrial Dynamics*. MIT Press, 1961.

[Horowitz et al 85]   E. Horowitz, A. Kemper, and Narasimhan. A survey of application generators. *IEEE Software*, January:40 – 54, 1985.

[Muetzelfeldt et al 85] R. Muetzelfeldt, M. Uschold, Bundy A., N. Harding, and Robertson D. An intelligent front end for ecological modelling. In *Working Conference on Artificial Intelligence in Simulation*, Flanders Technology International, University of Ghent, Belgium, 1985.

[Muetzelfeldt et al 87] R. Muetzelfeldt, D. Robertson, M. Uschold, and A. Bundy. Computer–aided construction of ecological simulation models. In *International Symposium on AI, Expert Systems and Languages in Modelling and Simulation*, Elsevier Science Publishers, Barcelona, Spain, 1987.

[O'Keefe 82]   R. O'Keefe. *Automated Statistical Analysis*. Working Paper 104, Dept. of Artificial Intelligence, Edinburgh, 1982.

[Robertson et al 85] D. Robertson, R. Muetzelfeldt, D. Plummer, M. Uschold, and A Bundy. The Eco browser. In *Expert Systems 85*, pages 143–156, British Computer Society Specialist Group on Expert Systems, Coventry, England, 1985.

[Robertson et al 87a] D. Robertson, A. Bundy, M. Uschold, and R. Muetzelfeldt. *Synthesis of Simulation Models from High Level Specifications*. Research Paper RP-313, DAI, 1987.

[Robertson et al 87b] D. Robertson, M. Uschold, A. Bundy, and R. Muetzelfeldt. Dialogue in Eco: a system for building ecological simulation models. *in preparation*, 1987.

[Uschold 86]   M. Uschold. *Computer–Aided Design of Program Specifications in the domain of Ecological Modelling*. Technical Report DP-35, DAI, 1986.

[Uschold et al 86]   M. Uschold, N. Harding, R. Muetzelfeldt, and A. Bundy. An intelligent front end for ecological modelling. In T. O'Shea, editor, *Advances in Artificial Intelligence*, Elsevier Science Publishers, 1986. Also in Proceedings of ECAI-84, and available from Edinburgh University as Research Paper 223.

THE POTENTIAL OF EXPERT SYSTEMS FOR DEVELOPMENT CONTROL
IN BRITISH TOWN PLANNING

Michael Leary and Agustin Rodriguez-Bachiller
Town Planning Department, Oxford Polytechnic, Oxford OX3

ABSTRACT

This paper outlines the approach taken and presents some
early findings from a research project which aims to examine the
potential of expert systems in British Development Control (*) - a
domain with a combination of a strong legal basis and a high degree of
discretion. Drawbacks of current models of knowledge engineering are
discussed in conjunction with an empirical analysis of expertise,
which seeks to extend those models. An examination of the structure of
the knowledge and expertise in development control provides insights
into the suitability and limitations of current expert system tools.
Conclusions are drawn which point in the direction of more appropriate
methodologies for building expert systems in areas of professional
competence which draw on multi-level knowledge and expertise.

1. Introduction

This paper is a progress report more than an account of
finished research. In it we will discuss methodological and
substantive issues arising from our research into the potential of
expert systems for Development Control. There has been some
preliminary discussion of how expert systems might be applied in land
use planning, but little progress as yet (Cullen 1986; Leary 1986;
Ortolano and Perman 1987). Development Control has been chosen as a
first domain within land use planning, on the one hand because it is
relatively well structured (due to its basis in legislation) and, on
the other, because local authorities have been granted a large amount
of discretion when making decisions, in order that development of land
is flexible enough to take account of local needs, resources and
priorities. This paper follows the structure of the research project,
dealing first with methodological issues to be clarified in order to
proceed, and then moving on to discuss the specific domain of
application, for which a first prototype system will be designed.

2. Methodological Issues: Expert Systems and Knowledge Acquisition

It is becoming widely accepted that some of the greatest
problems of expert systems (their lack of real 'intelligence' and the
poor quality of the explanations they provide) can be traced back to

(*)Financed by the Economic and Social Research Council, reference
   D 00 23 2254. The authors wish to thank South Oxfordshire District
   Council for their cooperation in this project, and also Tony
   Priest, Oxford Polytechnic, for useful comments on a previous draft
   of this paper.

methodological problems concerning the nature of the knowledge incorporated into the system, its acquisition (Grover 1983), and the nature and role of experts (Hawkins 1983; Chandrasekaran and Mittal 1984; Bloomfield 1986) and expertise (Davis 1982; Kolodner 1984).

Many of the problems encountered in connection with these issues derive from the particular model of what knowledge is and how its acquisition works, that is implicit in most of the expert system applications: expert systems have been developed according to what we call the pure-consultancy model, based on a rather peculiar self-image that the knowledge engineer has of his relationship with the expert: 1)the Knowledge Engineer knows nothing about the substantive domain 2)the Expert knows everything about it. In this context, knowledge elicitation has a logic to it that can be represented in a simple diagram (Figure 1).

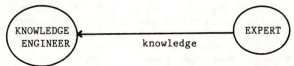

Figure 1. The Pure-Consultancy Model of Knowledge Engineering

However, this simplistic model soon creates problems that require some refinement. The evidence suggests that the expert passes on a simplified version of his knowledge (what in the terminology has become known as 'shallow' knowledge), which has become in his mind tacit knowledge (Polanyi 1967). This often consists of a set of impressionistic rules-of-thumb of how to do certain things, but not why (what is often called deep knowledge). Therefore, in our view, the pure-consultancy model has to be modified to reflect this filtering effect (Figure 2).

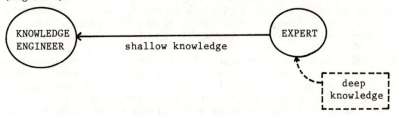

Figure 2. The Filtering of Real Expertise

Because of this difference between real expertise and the knowledge that is passed on by the expert (what we will call the 'deep-shallow dichotomy'), the deep-knowledge basis for the rules contained in expert systems is usually implicit. Because of this, problems of explanation constantly arise in expert systems (Hughes 1987). Instead of genuine explanation, what is provided is a description of the step-by-step inferential sequence, but not the 'real why'. Problems of knowledge acquisition for expert systems can be said to relate to the difficulty of accessing deep knowledge. Because of this, the need increasingly arises for a more explicit reference in expert systems to causal models of knowledge (Chandrasekaran and Mittal 1984; Steels 1987).

To solve the problem we have to investigate the reason for the apparent gap between deep and shallow knowledge. Firstly, discussions of 'shallow' knowledge, and even the term itself, seem to convey a derogatory view of this type of expertise which is unjustified (see section 2.1). Secondly, there seems to be no inherent reason for such a gap: as soon as we start looking into the history of science or the knowledge in any domain, it becomes apparent that there is no such thing as a level of absolute knowledge which is the causal model for all other levels. We are more attracted to the idea of a continuous scale of <u>deeper</u> and <u>shallower</u> knowledge: for each level of knowledge, there is always another that can be said to represent deeper knowledge. The depth of knowledge becomes a purely relative concept between a particular level of enquiry and another level that provides causal explanations sufficient for that enquirer.

To solve the deep-shallow gap, it has been suggested (Gaines 1986) that the domain expert should become the expert system designer ("doing away with the knowledge engineer"), but this will not always solve the problem, precisely because many experts are no longer conscious of the causal model that underlies their operational knowledge. Another solution is to introduce into the expert-system design process a stage of domain-learning (Grover 1983). Learning can probably make a crucial difference to the deep-shallow gap precisely because it is about the 'whys'.

2.1.The Nature of Expertise

If there is no reason for the deep-shallow dichotomy which is inherent in the knowledge itself, to find better clues as to its source we have to look closer at the nature of the expertise in which deep knowledge is supposed to be embedded. Central to this line of thinking is the realisation that the expert himself often "doesn't know how much he knows" (Schon 1983), he has lost track of the reasoning that lies behind some of his knowledge. It could be argued that expertise involves an element of what could be called 'forgotten reasoning', by which step-by-step logical connections are remembered as one-step jumps from the premise to the conclusion. Also, Hawkins (1983) identifies in the expert the ability to: learn, understand, propagate effects, handle conflicts, justify and explain results; Davis (1982) describes expertise as involving a more ambitious list of behaviours: solving a problem, explaining the result, learning, re-structuring knowledge, breaking rules, determining relevance, and degrading gracefully when approaching the boundary of the expertise. Clancey (1983) stresses the importance of strategic knowledge, to provide the guiding principles for 'surface' knowledge.

To expand this line of inquiry, we carried out a survey, asking a group of experts in their own field (six colleagues in our own academic environment and one practising professional) about the nature of expertise and the attributes that defined experts. After eliminating repetitions and overlaps, we reduced these attributes to the short-list shown below, in order of frequency (the first seven clearly dominated over the others):

1) Judging significance: to be able to tell the important from the unimportant, to "tell the wood from the trees"
2) Understanding: to have insight into what is really going on, to be aware of causal connections
3) Detailed knowledge: having a lot of domain knowledge, being able to see a lot of detail in a situation
4) Broad strategy: having the skill to interrogate a situation, to "know what the position is" with respect to the objective, to be able "to see a whole methodology"
5) Patterns of responses developed from experience over a long time
6) Being able to see a structure in a situation
7) Balancing conflicts, seeing ways out of dilemmas
8) Knowing the limits of knowledge
9) Innovation and lateral thinking, seeing opportunities for new ideas
10) Critical ability and seeing variables where others see "received" monolithic knowledge

Some of these attributes have already been mentiones by other authors, such as the role of experience (Kolodner 1984), or the lists by Hawkins and Davis mentioned before. Ours does not pretend to be an exhaustive survey but, considering the amount of repetition in the answers, it became possible towards the end of the survey to detect some kind of consensus about what represents a core of expertise. This was not just an amorphous set of elements, but a pattern was emerging and the attributes listed above could be grouped into three categories.

First, the emphasis on sheer volume and detail of knowledge of the subject (atribute 3), this is what would normally be perceived by the lay-public as the only component of expertise. On the other hand, what seems to emerge from our survey is that, although being a necessary component of expertise, this element is not sufficient.

Secondly, a group of these attributes refer to processes of simplification that the expert carries out in order to be able to handle complexity, variety, and sheer volume of information. They refer to being able to judge what is most important in a situation, to being able to abstract patterns from the maze of detail, to seeing short-cuts through that maze, to broad strategies of action (this is not unrelated to the "strategic knowledge" of Clancey 1983).

Thirdly, there is a group of attributes that refer to more explanatory processes of a different kind (it might be said, of the opposite kind). Instead of simplifying reality for operational reasons, they look deeper into it, digging underneath the surface, being able to recognise more detail than is apparent to the non-expert, seeing causal relationships implicit in the situation, even looking beyond the frontiers of accepted wisdom.

In Figure 3 we have re-grouped the attributes listed above according to these three categories, using a graph-analogy to represent a problem-situation, and expressing the second and third groups of attributes as dynamic variations of the purely descriptive graph.

Detail
A lot of domain knowledge

DESCRIPTION/DETAIL

Judging significance
Short cuts from experience
Seeing patterns and structure
Interrogating reality with a strategy
Balancing conflicts/dilemmas
Patterns of responses to situations

SIMPLIFICATION/ABSTRACTION

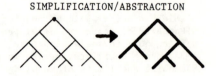

Seeing variables where others see constants
Understanding, recognising causality
Knowing the limits of knowledge
Seeking new knowledge
Innovation and lateral thinking

EXPLANATION/EXPLORATION

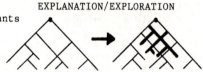

Figure 3. Patterns of Expertise

Having identified these three components of expertise, when we put them together in a dynamic model, a more convincing picture of how expertise works emerges. The three elements (description, simplification, explanation) can be seen as constituting three mechanisms with three different levels of complexity, called upon by the expert in a cummulative way, depending on the difficulty of the situation (Figure 4).

1)First, description and detail
2)Second, patterns and short cuts
3)If these fail, expand with
   deeper level of explanation

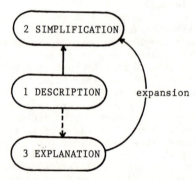

Figure 4. A Dynamic Model of Expertise

1) At the lowest level of difficulty, expertise needs only to manifest itself as detailed knowledge.
2) As the difficulty increases, a simplification strategy of patterns and short-cuts needs to be used to manage complexity. This is the most common level at which expertise manifests itself, and many professional experts only very rarely need to go beyond this level;

this is the 'shallow' knowledge that becomes transmitted to the knowledge engineer.

3) If the simplification strategy fails, it needs to be expanded with a deeper level of explanation (going back to first principles, Chandrasekaran and Mittal 1984), finding out more, even extending the frontiers of knowledge.

Over time, the 'budding expert' builds up in his carrer a lot of descriptive and causal knowledge (types one and three in our model), which he gradually transforms into simplified patterns (type two) to improve its efficiency, so that he only needs to go back to the other (more cumbersome) types of knowledge when faced with difficult cases.

Most discussions of deep and shallow knowledge seem to rest on the implicit view that deep is better than shallow. We feel this is a misunderstanding that should be dispelled: shallow knowledge is not 'deteriorated' knowledge, on the contrary, it is a more condensed, practical and efficient form of knowledge, developed over many years by the expert in order to increase his own effectiveness. Shallow and deep knowledge do not represent 'corrupt' and 'pure' knowledge respectively, they are simply two types of knowledge which are suited to different (routine and non-routine) problems.

2.2. Deep Knowledge and Expert System Consultation

Usually, the knowledge-base of an expert system of the diagnostic type is represented at only one level, which can be characterised by a form of graph that will direct the inference according to the inputs from the dialogue during consultation by the user. As it has been repeatedly argued here, the standard methodology is flawed because it assumes that knowledge about 'how to' is sufficient, and rules-of-thumb obtained from the expert are all that are needed to apply the system. It assumes that only one mechanism is in operation. An implication of the argument developed here is that several different levels of representation are needed (it could be said, two or more graphs of different grain): one to represent the actual inference used to solve the problem in practice, and others to represent the underlying logical structure of the domain, used only when the first mechanisms fail, and for explanation purposes. Paradoxically, the standard methodology does not encounter this problem because the graph used, representing the shallow knowledge, is the same as the graph tracing the inference-sequence in a consultation session.

But if we differentiate between deep and shallow knowledge within the expert system itself, the inference-graph can be seen as only a sub-set of a deeper graph, and two distinct stages appear as logical steps in the development of the knowledge base. Firstly, the formalisation of the deeper-model graph into logical rules and, second, the specification of the particular sub-graph which the expert actually uses to short-cut through the more general network. It is this second sub-graph that provides the basis for the dialogue with a user, and we can call it the dialogue-graph.

2.3. Knowledge and Time

We can now look briefly at the question of time and its
relationship with expertise. On the one hand, considering first the
case of 'unconscious' expertise, where the expert "doesn't know how
much he knows", we can see shallow knowledge as a kind of forgotten
deep knowledge, and the effect of the passage of time on knowledge can
be summarised by the equation DEEP KNOWLEDGE + TIME = SHALLOW
KNOWLEDGE (which shows the process of what we could call 'knowledge
obsolescence').

Of course, time in this equation is not just the ticking
of the clock, but the experience that accompanies it, helping build up
the patterns and short-cuts that make up shallow knowledge. Our survey
showed, and it has been stressed by others (Kolodner 1984), that time
is an essential factor in the accumulation of expertise through
experience consisting of cases built up over time, necessary to
accumulate sufficient numbers of successes and failures to be able to
discern the reasons for them. This would correspond to our second type
of expertise identified above, which we called abstraction-
simplification.

In such a context, to maintain the usefulness of an expert
system, it becomes crucial to be able to renew the source of
knowledge, and this suggests a second set of useful methodological
implications: the need to introduce into expert system design the
question of updating the expertise. The extreme case of this could be
the suggestion (Riesbeck 1984) that the initial knowledge-base of an
expert system should contain relatively non-expert rules, real
expertise building up as the system learns for itself; this could have
the advantage of being able to use the system's non-expert knowledge
to communicate with non-expert users.

We have argued above that the underlying deep model
(therefore the one that needs updating) is a step-by-step logical
model through which the shallow knowledge identifies short-cuts.
Therefore, the issue of updating the expertise becomes that of
updating the step-by-step model, and not just adding another rule-of-
thumb, another short-cut. Updating of three kinds is needed:

1) Incremental additions to the rule-base of knowledge derived from
   the experts, as conditions change and new facts become known, to
   replicate the way their expertise was acquired. This raises the
   technical problem of how to fit these incremental additions into
   the structure of the expert system. From another perspective, it
   raises the design issue of how to design a knowledge-base structure
   to which new rules can be added incrementally without destroying
   its original architecture.

2) Incremental additions to the data-base, adding the experience
   derived from each use of the expert system itself. A system must be
   able to remember its own past performance, learning from both its
   successes and its failures (Kolodner 1984). This suggests the need
   for the expert system to be designed so that its evaluations feed
   into external data-bases which are in turn used as sources of
   evidence in subsequent runs. This highlights the need for a two-way
   link with external data-bases.

3) Reorganisation of the knowledge as a result of 1) and 2), a necessary aspect of the updating of a knowledge-base, as already suggested (Riesbeck 1984, Kolodner 1984).

Let us now consider the domain of our area of application, and the possible implications of the methodological discussion so far.

3. Substantive Issues: Advisory Systems in Development Control

Development Control is a major Local Government function involving every district and county council in the determination of about 350,000 planning applications each year. To avoid administrative overload, a host of minor operations and changes of use (permitted development) do not require planning permission, because it is automatically granted, subject to precise conditions, by a piece of subordinate legislation, the General Development Order. The concept of administrative discretion is fundamental to the operation of the system. It allows officers and elected members to regard any plan for their area as just another material consideration to be taken into account when deciding an application for development. From the outside it may appear that decisions in this field are purely technical ones of the kind "if you are in accordance with the rules, then permission is granted". Reality is more complex than this, because officers and committees have discretion to interpret plans in the light of current priorities and perceptions about the future. This adds a layer of complexity and uncertainty to what at first glance is a rigid rule-based system, and makes the idea of investigating the possible role of expert systems in this process quite appealing.

3.1. An Empirical Model for the Study of Development Control

An interview survey was carried out to establish how practitioners control development, the kind of expertise they use, and how they perceive their own problem-solving activities. From this series of interviews, a model of Development Control emerged (Figure 5): Under the blanket-term Development Control, we found several almost self-contained modular tasks (of the kind identified by Breuker and Wielinga 1983 asindicating potential for the use of expert system technology) which vary enormously in the extent to which they use different types of expertise of the kind discussed earlier:

1) Permitted development decisions are guided by the General Development Order with relatively little scope for interpretation or discretion. It is experience and the detailed knowledge of a complex set of legal regulations that are required here.

2) Filling-in planning applications (by the applicant) has become a cumbersome task because one application form is used by virtually all local authorities for all types and scales of development, from house extensions to city centre redevelopments. This has resulted

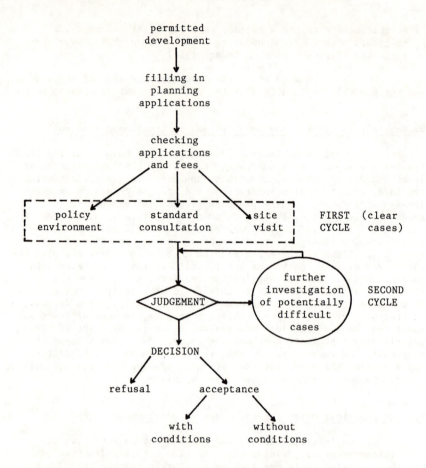

Figure 5. A Modularised Diagram of Development Control

in lengthy and complex guidance notes for applicants which are often almost incomprehensible, and agents are often employed to deal with the job of putting in the application. The rules are all there, it is simply a matter of length and complexity.

3) Checking applications and calculating the fees to be paid present similar problems: different kinds of development require certain information to be included, for example the number of parking spaces is required for an office block proposal but not for an application to build a single house. Checking is mainly about attention to detail. The fee structure is also complex and subject to frequent revision.

4) Standard consultation procedures establish that certain individuals and agencies have the right to be consulted on any development that

affects them. Although the list varies for different types of development (neighbours, other local authorities, water and highway authorities), there are rules on who has the right to be consulted in each case.

5) Policy environment investigation needs to be carried out to assess which central government, county or district policies are applicable to each development proposal, in the form of government circulars, county the district plans, which may be in different stages of preparation or approval, therefore of more or less importance.

6) Site visits are an essential feature of the control process, and they represent probably the most open-ended of the tasks involved at this routine level of Development Control, introducing different knowledge into the process in the form of assessment of environmental impacts and neighbour effects.

It is at this point that the expert makes a judgement on whether a case can be decided or not: difficult cases need a new iterative process (see Figure 6), involving more consultation, negotiation and requests for more information, until a decision can be made.

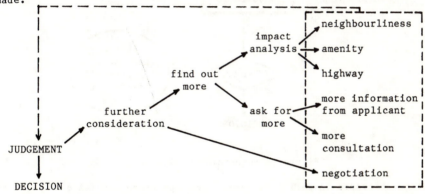

Figure 6. A Strategy for Difficult Cases

This higher-level process is in fact composed of another set of identifiable tasks which can be seen as relatively self-contained, modular, and requiring their own specific mix of expertise. This level has not been examined yet in the same degree of detail, but our initial findings indicate that this is where expertise of types two and three (in our typology) becomes more relevant.

3.2. Structured Knowledge in Development Control

What the above discussion hints at is the varying degree to which different activities in Development Control use public and structured knowledge as opposed to private and less structured knowledge (Figure 7). Without fear of excessive simplification, we can say at this stage in the research that all the tasks enclosed in heavy

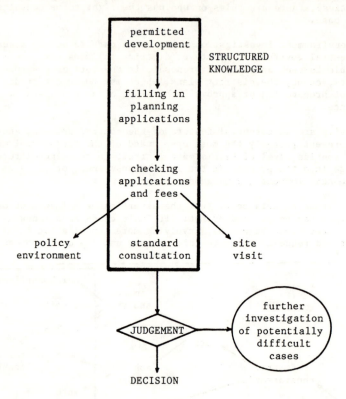

Figure 7. Structured Knowledge

outline are based on well structured knowledge where expertise consists mainly in applying well defined (although often complex and voluminous) procedures in a pre-defined manner. The application of judgement and type-three expertise to guide further information gathering, investigation and analysis, seems appropriate mostly for the second stage, and is only necessary for the minority of potentially difficult cases.

There is a general belief amongst practitioners in Development Control that this kind of level-three expertise is unstructured and based on intuition and 'gut reaction'. However, our initial findings seem to indicate that even this type of expertise reveals itself to be structured and able to be articulated to a much greater extent than the experts – and even ourselves – thought possible. Subsequent stages of the research will be able to provide more thorough tests of this hypothesis.

4. Conclusions

We have outlined in this paper an empirical analysis of the nature of expertise, stressing the importance of time and learning, and suggesting the existence of 3 types of such expertise (description-detail, simplification-abstraction, explanation-exploration) which can be combined into a dynamic model where different types of expertise expand the capabilities of previous ones when they fail. This has obvious implications with respect to the kind of tools that may be required to handle so-called second-generation expert systems, in terms of multi-level knowledge-bases and their incremental updating.

The modular structure that we have identified in our domain of application and the highly structured knowledge on which we have found some of those modules to be based, suggest some implications (that maybe can be generalised to other domains) for the approach needed to extract the full potential expert systems have without getting into unnecessary sophistication. A 'first-generation' approach using current tools and shells is perfectly sufficient for a first-level of problem-solving (covering in our domain over two thirds of cases) which uses type-one and type-two expertise. It is only a minority of difficult cases that require type-three expertise for which second-generation approaches will be needed.

REFERENCES

Bloomfield, B.P. (1986). Capturing Expertise by Rule Induction. The Knowledge Engineering Review, 1, no.4

Breukner, J.A. and Wielinga, B.J. (1983). Analysis Techniques for Knowledge Based Systems. Part 2 : Methods for Knowledge Acquisition. Report 1.2 ESPRIT Project 12, University of Amsterdam (mimeographed)

Chandrasekaran, B. and Mittal, S. (1984). Deep Versus Compiled Knowledge Approaches to Diagnostic Problem-Solving. In Developments in Expert Systems, ed. M.J. Coombs. London: Academic Press Inc.

Clancey, W.J. (1983). The Epistemology of a Rule-Based Expert System - A Framework for Explanation. Artificial Intelligence, 20, 215-51

Cullen, I. (1986). Expert Systems in Planning Analysis. Town Planning Review, 57, n.3

Davis, R. (1982). Expert Systems: Where Are We? And Where Do We Go From Here? The AI Magazine (spring), pp 3-22

Gaines, B. (1986). State of the Art Report from the AAAI Workshop on Knowledge Acquisition. Fringes ES'86 Workshop. BCS Expert Systems 1986 Conference

Grover, M.D. (1983.) A Pragmatic Knowledge Acquisition Methodology. Paper presented at the 8th ICJAI 436-438

Hawkins, D. (1983). An Analysis of Expert Thinking. International Journal of Man-Machine Studies, 8, 1-47

Hughes, S. (1987). Question Classification in Rule-based Systems. In Research and Development in Expert Systems III, ed. M.A. Bramer. Cambridge: Cambridge University Press

Kolodner, J. (1984). Towards an Understanding of the Role of Experience in the Evolution from Novice to Expert. In Developments in Expert Systems, ed. M.J. Coombs. London: Academic Press Inc.

Leary, M. (1986). Expert Systems : What Potential for Planning. The Planner (December)

Ortolano, L. and Perman, C.D. (1987). A Planner's Introduction to Expert Systems. Journal of the American Planners Association (Winter), 98-103

Polanyi, M. (1967). The Tacit Dimension. New York: Anchor Books

Riesbeck, C.K. (1984). Knowledge reorganization and reasoning style. In Developments in Expert Systems, ed. M.J. Coombs. Academic Press Inc., London

Schon, D. (1983). The Reflective Practitioner. New York: Basic Books

Steels, L. (1987). Second Generation Expert Systems. In Research and Development in Expert Systems III, ed. M.A. Bramer. Cambridge: Cambridge University Press

Structuring Meta Knowledge - A Knowledge Representation System for Cooperative Systems

A.L. Rector

Department of Computer Science
University of Manchester
Manchester M13 9PL
061-273-7121 ext 5417/5550
JANET: rector@uk.ac.man.cs.ux

Abstract

This paper describes the structured portion of a medical knowledge representation system designed to support browsing, mixed initiative advice and multi-level explanations. The system deals consistently with multiple inheritance and treats relational statements as first class objects which are themselves organised into an inheritance network. It has a general mechanism for defining and controlling the 'prototypes' of relations which provides a powerful mechanism for dealing with special cases and a means of tailoring the system to individual users. The paper outlines a formal definition for operations on prototypes and discusses the general role of inheritance systems in medical knowledge representation.

1   Introduction

This paper describes the structured portion of a medical knowledge representation system designed to support browsing, mixed initiative advice, and multi-level explanations, the IMMEDIATE* Representation Language (IRL). The system has been built in the course of developing cooperative decision support and information systems for general practitioners. Although various inheritance networks and frame-like formalisms are popular for medical applications, there are few principled accounts of their functions in medical systems. This paper analyses the function of the inheritance networks in medical systems which motivate the IMMEDIATE system and describes the special facilities for representing meta knowledge within the same structured framework as is used to describe the primary objects of the system.

Structured knowledge serves three functions in the IMMEDIATE Representation Language:

- Extension of the Knowledge Representation -

  - To deal with defaults, exceptions and common sense reasoning;
  - To provide a systematic means of linking surface knowledge with underlying causal representations for meta level explanations;
  - To manage special cases and terminologies through the use of 'prototypes' such as 'fracture of femur' or 'ear infection which occurs in children';

```
predicate calculus:              Inheritance Network:

All birds fly.                   Most birds except Penguins
                                 and ostriches fly.

for_all X (bird X ==> flies X)      bird: can_fly=true
                                      /      \
                         penguin: can_fly=false  \
                                                   \
                                    ostrich: can_fly=false
```

Figure 1: Comparison of Inheritance Networks and Predicate Calculus

- Control of the search space in paradigms such as 'heuristic classification' and 'cooperative search'.

- Support for knowledge engineering tools and partial validation of the knowledge base

The focus of this paper is the the use of inheritance networks in the knowledge representation itself, but it will touch on the features in IRL which assist in controlling the search space and knowledge engineering. Further details may be found in [Rector 1987].

2   Taxonomies, Defaults and Intensional Knowledge

Consider the statements 'All birds fly' and 'Most birds except penguins and ostriches fly'. Figure 1 gives a translation of these statements into predicate calculus and a inheritance network notation based on the IMMEDIATE Representation Language.

The predicate calculus has straightforward translations for what can be said *always* to be true while the inheritance network has straightforward translations for what can be said *usually* to be true. The predicate calculus is *extensional*, that is the truth or falsity of any statement depends solely on the sets of objects which satisfy each predicate. By contrast, systems of common sense or default reasoning are examples of *intensional* systems; they express what is typically understood or intended to be true. Most medical statements are intensional statements about what is typically true, for example: ' 'most cancers except basal cell carcinomas of the skin metastasize' or 'most gram positive bacteria except staphylococci are sensitive to penicillin'.

Investigation of the relation between default reasoning and formal logic has revealed the key role played by inheritance networks. Touretzky [1986] has formalised inheritance networks and proposed a well defined semantics. In previous work the author has used a similar semantics to provide criteria for inheritance of binary as well as unary relations, to provide computationally efficient means of detecting ambiguities, and to extend the concept of inheritance from the primary objects in the system to the attribute links which connect them [Rector 1986; 1987].

A formal system default theories based on the predicate calculus was developed by Reiter [1980], but the only computationally tractable subset which he could then identify was too weak to be useful [Etherington & Reiter, 1983]. It has recently been shown that

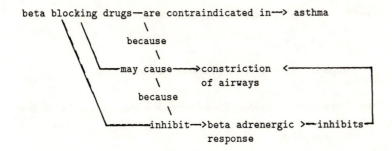

Figure 2: Structured Meta Knowledge for Explanations. Because links allow users to explore several levels of explanation. At the surface level is a statement that beta blockers should not be used in asthma. Its explanation at the next level is because beta blockers cause airway constriction, which in turn can be explained at the next level by the fact that they inhibit the beta adrenergic response which normally prevents airway constriction.

unambiguous inheritance networks can be mapped directly onto a powerful subset of logical default theories, and it appears that this mapping defines the most powerful computationally tractable subset of such theories [Froidveaux 1986; Etherington 1987].

3   Structured Meta-Knowledge, Contexts and Levels of Explanation

Statements about other statements, or meta knowledge, are necessary in order to express contexts and describe the underlying reasoning. An example is shown in figure 2. Statements can be set into an inheritance network derived from the inheritance network of the primary objects as shown in figure 3.

The *because* links provide the basis for multiple levels of explanation and reasoning. It is not intended at this stage that higher level statements be derivable from the deeper statements to which they are connected by *because* links. In most of medical practice the theory is insufficient to make this possible. Rather the *because* links serve as 'rationalisations' which doctors can explore using the browsing system. Used alone, the surface level knowledge of the system often makes for unsatisfying explanations such as: "Do not use beta blockers because rule 23 says that beta blockers should not be used in asthma". Explanations of the form "Don't ... because you shouldn't ..." are helpful if the user merely needs to be reminded of a known fact. They can be irritating if the fact is unfamiliar and give users no help in evaluating unexpected advice or deciding whether or not to accept it.

In future work it is intended to explore the use of *because* links by the reasoning system to test the plausibility of the surface statements and to direct the reasoning by relating surface facts to underlying goals. A major aim of our work towards cooperative systems is to make the reasoning process more sensitive to the current goals and context.

```
beta_blocker           beta blockers are contraindicated by asthma
     .                               .
  is_a                          is a
     .                               .
atenolol          atenolol is mildly contraindicated by asthma
```

Figure 3: Inheritance Network of Statements. The inheritance of statements is derived from the primary objects.

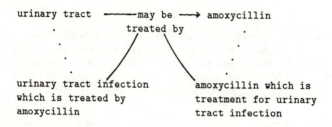

Figure 4: Prototypes defined by an Attribute Link. Each attribute link defines two prototypes. Doted lines indicate *is_a* links. Arcs represent *prototype_of* links.

4   Analytic and terminologic knowledge

Another important function of structured meta knowledge is the representation of terminologies and prototypes. New medical terms are often constructed by adding a new anatomic or etiologic descriptor to an existing term, e.g. 'pneumocystis pneumonia' or 'dislocation of shoulder'. 'Pneumocystis pneumonia' is said to be the 'prototypes' for the attribution 'pneumocystis causes pneumonia'. The fact that 'pneumocystis pneumonia is a kind of pneumonia' or is an example of what Brachman [1983] calls 'terminological knowledge'. The distinction between terminological and factual statements is similar to the philosophical distinction between analytic and synthetic knowledge but relates to the representation of the statements in the system rather than to their epistemological status.

IRL uses prototypes as a general mechanism for managing terminological knowledge. They provide a means of dealing with special cases and indicating which combinations of factors must be considered explicitly. Each attribute link between two nodes generates two prototypes. For example, consider the statement in figure 4 'urinary tract infection may be treated by amoxycillin'. Details of drug treatment depend not just on the drug, but on the disease and patient being treated. 'Amoxycillin *which is* used for urinary tract infection' contains the specific information on dosages and method of treatment of urinary tract infections by amoxycillin; 'urinary tract infection *which is* treated by amoxycillin' describes the characteristics of a urinary tract infection suitable for such treatment.

The dosage of drugs is also modified by other factors; for example the dosage for children is normally less than for adults. An attribute 'special case' is used to link a disease or drug with the condition which must be applied, as shown in the example in figure 5.

Prototypes may be combined as shown in figure 5. Since prototypes themselves inherit

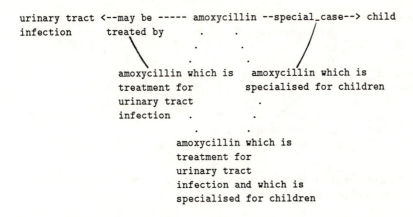

Figure 5: Combination of Prototypes. The criteria list for the combined prototype is the union of the criteria lists for its parents.

the special case links, combining prototypes could lead to an infinite cascade of subtly different objects:

amoxycillin which is treatment for urinary tract infection which is in children

amoxycillin which is for children which is treatment of urinary tract infection

amoxycillin which is for children which is for treatment of urinary tract infection which is in children

. . .

To avoid this cascade IRL provides that any attribute-object pair may occur only once in a criteria list. There is therefore a maximally specialised case for any set of criteria, and all of the special cases form a lattice with uniquely defined maximal and minimal nodes.

5   Possibility Attributes and Actuality Attributes

Up to this point, prototypes have been presented as referring simply to attribute links. More generally, prorotypes relate to the *possibility* of an attribute link being present.

All attributes in IRL come in pairs - a *possibility* attribute and an *actuality* attribute. For example, 'may be treated by' in figure 5 is a *possibility* attribute and the corresponding *actuality* attribute is 'treated by'. The *possibility* of an event may be qualified by a frequency or strength of association; the *actuality* of the event is qualified by a probability tat it actually occured. For example, 'urinary tract occurs *frequently* in children' but 'john *probably* has a urinary tract infection'. Both possibilities and actualities are inherited. For example in figure 5 in addition to the information that amoxycillin is a *possible* treatment for urinary tract infection, we might add the information that it was by default the *actual* treatment.

Possibility links perform many of the functions of type declarations and restrictions in other representation systems. However, possibility links are first class objects in the system

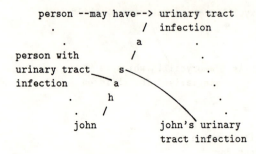

```
person --may have--> urinary tract
       .          /    infection
       .         a          .
person with     /           .
urinary tract___s           .
infection        a          .
     .          h           .
     .         /            .
        john        john's urinary
                    tract infection
```

Figure 6: Structure of 'John has a urinary tract infection'. *John* is an instance of the prototype *person with urinary tract infection.*

and do not increase the computational complexity of the system as do restriction schemes [Brachman & Levesque 1984].

6   Observations and extensional attributions

All of the attribute links discussed to this point have been 'intensional', that is they have been general statements about what was true by definition or default. The prototype of an intensional attribute link may be thought of as the subset of the objects which satisfy the general principle represented. Observations of particular objects in the world are *extensional* they mean that a particular object is an instance of the extension of the corresponding attribute. For example consider figure 6. Because 'john' is an instance rather than a category, the statement 'john has a urinary tract infection' is equivalent to: 'john is a person with urinary tract infection'.

The second prototype is the instance of urinary tract infection which affects john. The statement that 'john's urinary tract infection is treated with amoxycillin' would then be represented as in figure 7.

john, john's urinary tract infection, and *amoxycillin for john's urinary tract infection* are all instances. Each extensional use of an attribute links an instance with a category and creates a further instance. Only *actuality attributes* may be used be used extensionally in this way. *Possibility attributes* are only used intensionally.

This representation gives an explicit meaning to each of the linguistic usages for making statements about objects, e.g. 'John has a urinary tract infection', 'John's urinary tract infection is severe', 'The dose of amoxycillin for John's urinary tract infection is 500mg', etc.

7   General Quantified Assertions - Statements which do not have structured representations in IRL

Consider the statement 'if two drugs have the same effect then they interact'. This translates straightforwardly into the predicate calculus as

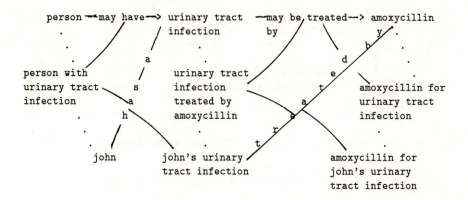

Figure 7: john's urinary tract infection treated by amoxycillin. The *has_a* link between *john* and *urinary tract infection* generates the new prototype instance *john's urinary tract infection*. The *treated_by* link between *john's urinary tract infection* and *amoxycillin* generates the new prototype instance *amoxycillin for john's urinary tract infection*.

```
for_all Drug1, Drug2
        (there_exists Effect such_that
                Drug1 causes Effect and
                Drug2 causes Effect)
                        ==> Drug1 interacts_with Drug2.
```

There is no straightforward way of translating this statement into the representation based on taxonomies and attributes described here. In general, this is true of any statements involving more than one universally variable quantified or any existentially quantified variables. General assertional knowledge of this type occurs in at least two different contexts in knowledge bases: in statements such as that above which are about the domain in question, and in control statements which indicate how the domain knowledge should be interpreted and presented. General assertions outside the structured framework also tend to occur in many systems during their construction as an ad hoc way of capturing knowledge for which the formal structure is not yet clear.

It might well be possible to extend the representation presented following ideas such as those of Attardi [1986] or Sowa [1984] to provide a general representation with the full power of the predicate calculus. However, the primary appeal of the current system is that the structures described can be described compactly by a few axioms, can be efficiently verified to be unambiguous, and can perform a useful subset of inferences much faster than a general theorem prover. It is probably better, therefore, to use the structured knowledge as an efficient skeleton on which to hang general assertional knowledge than to sacrifice the virtues of the structured knowledge in a quest for generality. Treating structured knowledge as sortal information in a many sorted logic might be a promising approach to a more thorough integration of structured and assertional knowledge.

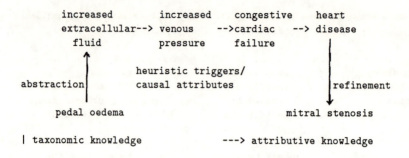

Figure 8: Causal Process Classification

8   Heuristic Classification

Taxonomies are ubiquitous in the medical literature and play important roles in medical teaching and reasoning. Any medical knowledge representation system must support these traditional uses of classification in medical problem solving. In a recent paper in which he analyses most of the major medical expert systems, Clancey [1985] claims that 'causal process classification' is the predominate method used in medical diagnostic systems. Figure 8 illustrates the basic pattern. Observed patient data are 'abstracted' up a classification system until they form an understandable unit which triggers consideration of a class of diseases. The diagnosis is then refined from the original category to a specific diagnosis. This process reduces the search space from the unmanageably many associations between individual symptoms and individual diseases to a workable set of general principles.

The inheritance network is used to summarise the total range of possible causes and therefore reduce the search space. A number of other systems which do not conform completely to the causal process model such as INTERNIST/CADUCEUS [Pople 1982] and our own work on cooperative search [Rector 1985] also use the structure of the inheritance network to control the search strategy.

The heart of Clancey's claim is that there are two distinct types of knowledge used in the classification process: taxonomic knowledge which connects instances to subclasses and subclasses to classes, and attributive knowledge which links manifestations and causes across taxonomies. In the previous examples, *is_a* shown as dotted lines are *taxonomic* statements; attribute links shown as solid lines are *attributive* statements. (Clancey uses the terms 'hierarchical' and 'non-hierarchical'.) A review of the psychological literature on medical decision making [Patel & Groen 1986; Brooke, Rector & Sheldon 1983; Gale and Marsden 1985] provides additional confirming evidence.

Much of the formal work on inheritance systems eliminates the distinction between attributes and objects, at least for purposes of analysis [Fahlman et al, 1981, Touretzky 1986; Etherington 1987; Attardi 1986]. Clancey's claim is a strong argument for retaining the distinction in practical systems.

9   A Medical Knowledge Representation System: Implementation and Discussion

The structured representation described is not a complete inference system. Rather the structure is intended to provide a skeleton to support the knowledge engineer in organising the mass of facts into general principles and special cases. The notion of a cannonical form for a prototype prevents an infinite propagation of prototypes and a proliferation of similar but distinct entities. Prototypes provide a cleaner solution to the problems addressed by the system of 'links' and 'usages' previously described by the author [Rector 1986, 1987]. Only those cases which are referred to by other objects and which would otherwise be ambiguous in some way need be dealt with explicitly. Once a special case is identified, the system guarantees that the knowledge engineer will be prompted to consider it when dealing with each specialisation of the original concept.

The structure provides a consistent and well defined semantics for default reasoning within a multiple inheritance network and supports the distinction between taxonomic and attributive statements needed by paradigms such as heuristic classification and cooperative search. This structure supports our goals in developing cooperative systems in several important ways:

- The structure provides and open representation in which control and contextual statements can be represented so as to be accessible to the system itself. Some degree of 'understanding' of its own goals and activities is essential to effective cooperation with users.

- The representation makes possible a range of modes of explanation including indications of causal mechanisms and descriptions of the general principles embodied in the current example.

- The system of prototypes provides a means of managing large numbers of special cases coherently. This has two consequences:

    - The information presented to users can be filterd so that only that applying to the current case is shown.

    - Special case prototypes of any object can be maintained for individual users and groups of users. This is expected to allow the system to be tailored to an arbitrary number of individual users simultaneously without disturbing the basic structure. In effect, most of the 'user model' is distributed throughout the system in the form of special case prototypes. Special case prototypes are also used to define the system of views on which the user interface is based.

IRL is written in PROLOG and reflects PROLOG's relational approach to data management. The knowledge representation system maps directly onto flat relational structures. One result is that it is relatively easy to map the instances in IRL onto the tuples of standard medical data bases to provide a smooth integration of the knowledge base and existing or future data bases.

A second result of the relational approach is that an object is simply an opaque handle identifying a node in the network. The only overhead in creating a new object is the space for the entries in the *is_a* network linking that object to its parents and children. In this respect IRL differs from SMALLTALK and many LISP based knowledge representation systems in which creating an object entails significant allocation of storage. Even so, creating all potential prototypes would impose an intollerable overhead. An explicit entry for a prototype is only created when a statement is made concerning that prototype or when an ambiguity would otherwise occur. The prototype network in the drug information knowledge base is quite sparse and the total space required much less than might be imagined. Whether or not this will be true in other domains remains to be seen. The overall structure is closely related to the Qualified Binary Relational Model of Jiang [1986] and Jiang and Lavington [1985], and has been heavily influenced by their work.

The representation scheme described has developed out of work on medical record and browsing systems [Rector 1986, 1987], and the original IMMEDIATE Representation Language remains the basis of the current applications developments. It is in use as the basis of systems for medical records, drug information, and specifying medical treatment protocols. As a further test of its overall capacity and robustness the fact base from the Oxford System of Medicine project [Fox et al, 1987] was loaded into the system. This experiment demonstrated the robustness of the basic design, its capacity for detecting errors, and the importance of multiple inheritance. In this independently created knowledge base approximately 15% of nodes have multiple parents, and multiple classification affects between 25% and 30% of the total nodes in the network.

Two new implementations are planned. One is an implementation of as much of the system as possible in PROPS2 [Frost & Fox 1986]. The PROPS2 implementation will provide a clean prototype of the basic axiomatisation, but will be limited by the PROPS2 parsing scheme and computational overheads. The second is a complete redevelopment in PROLOG of the IRL system starting from a revised specification based an axiomatisation along the lines outlined in this paper and including many performance and user interface enhancements.

10   References

Attardi G, Corradini A, Diomedi S and Simi S (1986). 'Taxonomic reasoning'. *in* Proceedings of ECAI-86 pp 234-245.

Brachman RJ (1983). What IS-A is and Isn't: an analysis of taxonomic links in semantic networks. Computer 16:30-36.

Brachman RJ and Levesque HJ (1984). The tractability of subsumption in frame-based description languages. *in* Proc AAAI-84 pp 34-37.

Clancey WJ (1985). Heuristic Classification. Artificial Intelligence 27 289-350.

Gale J and Marsden p (1985). Diagnosis: process not product. in MG Sheldon JB Brooke and AL Rector (eds) Decision Making in General Practice. pp 59-91. London: MacMillan Press Ltd.

Etherington DW (1987). Formalizing nonmonotonic reasoning systems. Artificial Intelligence 31 41-85.

Etherington DW and Reiter R (1983). On inheritance hierarchies with exceptions. *in* Proceedings of AAAI-83 pp 104-108.

Fahlman SE, Touretzky DS & van Roggen W (1981). Cancellation in a Parallel Semantic Network. *in* Proceedings of IJCAI-81. pp 257-263. Los Altos, California: William Kaufman.

Fox J, Glowinski A & O'Neil M (1987). The Oxford System of Medicine: Towards an electronic information system for general practice. To be presented at the Second European Conference on Artificial Intelligence in Medicine, August, 1987, Marseille.

Froidevaux C (1986). Taxonomic default theory. *in* Proceedings of ECAI-86, The 7th European Conference on Artificial Intelligence. pp 123-129.

Frost D & Fox F (1986) PROPS II reference manual. Internal report, Research Computer Group, Imperial Cancer Research Fund, Lincoln's Inn Fields, London WC1.

Jiang YJ (1986). A Qualified Binary Relational Model of Information. Unpublished PhD thesis, Department of Computer Science, University of Manchester.

Jiang YJ and Lavington SH. (1985) The qualified binary relationship model of information.*in* Proceedings of the fourth British National Conference on Databases, Keele, July 1985

Patel VL and Groen GJ (1986). Knowledge based solution strategies in medical reasoning. Cognitive Science *10* 91-116.

Pople HE (1982). Heuristic methods for imposing structure on ill-structured problems. *in* P Szolovits (ed) Artificial Intelligence in Medicine AAAS Symposium 51. Boulder Colorado: Westview Press Inc.

Rector, AL (1987). Defaults, exceptions and ambiguity in a medical knowledge representation system. Medical Informatics *11* 296-306.

Rector, AL (1986). Defaults, exceptions and ambiguity in a medical knowledge representation system. in Proceedings of ECAI-86, The 7th European Conference on Artificial Intelligence vol II pp 177-182.

Rector, AL (1985). The knowledge based medical record - IMMEDIATE-I - a basis for clinical decision support in general practice. in Proceedings of the International Conference on Artificial Intelligence in Medicine, Pavia, Italy, September 1985. pp 37-49. Amersterdam: North Holland Press.

Reiter R (1980). A logic for default reasoning. Artificial Intelligence *13* 81-132.

Touretzky DS (1986). The Mathematics of Inheritance Systems. Research Notes in Artificial Intelligence. London: Pitman, London & Los Altos, California: Morgan Kaufmann Publishers, Inc.

* IMMEDIATE stands for Intelligent Medical Information Advice Treatment and Education

TRESLOG: TRANSLATING FROM SPANISH TO CLAUSAL
FORM PROPOSITIONS.

Guillermo Morales Luna and Silvia Guardati de Cairó.
Sección de Computación. CINVESTAV-IPN.
P.O.Box 14-740, 07000 México, D.F.

ABSTRACT

The design of the translator TRESLOG is shown. TRESLOG
converts Spanish sentences into Clausal Logic formulae. The
translator consists of an editor to specify the grammar for
the accepted sentences, a parser to match the given sentences
with their defined grammar and an output unit that puts the
received information as a clausal logic formula and as a
PROLOG statement. In TRESLOG any term is represented as an
object list, any clause as a pair of term lists and any
proposition as a clause list. Hence LISP is a natural
environment for TRESLOG. In principle, the system is able to
deal with any first order formula, via skolemization.
However, the inference procedure is applied just in Horn
clauses.

1. Introduction.

In this paper we present a processor of Natural
Language, particularly a processor of Spanish, that uses
PROLOG as an inference machine becoming thus a manipulator of
logical databases. We think our system as an interface for a
future expert system shell.
The methods presented here relate Logic Programming
(Kowalski 1981) with the Processing of Spanish (Dahl 1981).
TRESLOG (TRaductor del ESpañol a LOGica clausular) is an
interpreter for Spanish sentences which converts them into
clauses. The information given in Spanish is stored in a
relational database, and later it is converted to a PROLOG
program. The translator consists of a grammar editor, a
syntactic analyzer and an output unit. The grammar editor
allows an user to specify, in a Backus Normal Form, a context
free grammar for the Spanish sentences to be accepted. This
restricts the level of analysis for Spanish sentences, thus
the editor includes some *macros* , which are context sensitive
rules that act locally in the analysis of a phrase, to check
the number and the gender between articles, nouns and verbal
forms . The accepted sentences assert instances of a
relation. The syntactic analyzer matches a given sentence
with the corresponding declarative grammar, it recognizes its
keywords and forms the clause representation of the asserted
proposition. Essentially, the Predicate Calculus is the
transformation basis. The main characteristics of our
approach is the list representation of clauses, very close to
Wang's algorithm for Propositional Calculus. A further

development of our treatment may consist of a deductive procedure for non-Horn clauses.

The implementation of TRESLOG has been done mainly in LISP.

2. Clausal Logic.

2.1. An *universe* of *discurse* is a structure U = (Obj , Obj_Typ , Rel , Rel_Typ , Ar) where Obj is a non-empty set of *objects*, Obj_Typ is a partition of Obj whose elements are called *object types*, Rel is a non-empty set of *relations*, Rel_Typ is a partition of Rel whose elements are called *relation types* and
Ar = (A , B):Rel_Typ $\longrightarrow \mathbb{N}$ × (Obj_Typ)$^+$is an *arity function* such that $\forall$ $\mathcal{T}$ $\in$ Rel_Typ: long $B(\mathcal{T})$ = $A(\mathcal{T})$.

For any a $\in$ Obj and any t $\in$ Obj_Typ we will write a:t whenever a $\in$ t , and by an abuse of notation, we will write $a_1 \ldots a_n$:$t_1 \ldots t_n$ whenever $\forall$ i = 1,...,n : a_i:t_i . Also, for relations, we will write R:$\mathcal{T}$ if R $\in$ $\mathcal{T}$. Thus for any relation type $\mathcal{T}$ $\in$ Rel_Typ, $A(\mathcal{T})$ will be the number of arguments in any R:$\mathcal{T}$, and $B(\mathcal{T})$ will be the type of its argument list.

2.2. An *atomic proposition* is a term $R(a_1, \ldots, a_n)$ where R $\in$ Rel and $a_1, \ldots, a_n$ $\in$ Obj are such that
$\forall$ $\mathcal{T}$ $\in$ Rel_Typ : R : $\mathcal{T}$ $\Rightarrow$ n = $A(\mathcal{T})$ & $a_1 \ldots a_n$: $B(\mathcal{T})$.

An atomic proposition is in this way a list of symbols in Obj $\cup$ Rel.

Let Prop be the set of *propositions*. Then ϕ $\in$ Prop if either ϕ is an atomic proposition or ϕ = *false* or ϕ = $\Rightarrow \psi \xi$ where ψ and ξ are propositions. We use a prefix notation for connectives just for a non-ambiguous interpretation of propositions. As usual $\neg$ ϕ, $\vee$ ϕ ψ and $\wedge$ ϕ ψ stand for abreviations of $\Rightarrow \neg \phi$ *false* , $\Rightarrow \neg \phi$ ψ and $\neg$ $\vee$ $\neg \phi$ $\neg \psi$ respectively. With the usual semantics in Propositional Calculus, any proposition has equivalent disjunctive and conjunctive normal forms.

2.3. Let P be the set of lists consisting of atomic propositions and let λ be the empty word.

A *clause* is a pair (**a** , **b**) $\in$ P^2 and is interpreted as *the conjunction of the components in* **a** *implies the disjunction of the components in* **b** . Let Clause be the set of clauses. Any list of clauses will be interpreted as the conjunction of their components. Any proposition ϕ $\in$ Prop will be represented as a list of clauses $\mathcal{R}(\phi)$ $\in$ Clause$^+$ as follows:

    1. $\forall$ ϕ $\in$ Atom_Prop: $\mathcal{R}(\phi)$ = [$(\lambda \phi)$]
                                   $\mathcal{R}(\neg \phi)$ = [$(\phi \lambda)$]
    2. $\mathcal{R}(false)$ = [$(\lambda \lambda)$]
    3. $\forall$ ϕ , ψ $\in$ Prop: if $\mathcal{R}(\phi)$ = [(a_1, b_1) ... (a_n, b_n)]
                 and $\mathcal{R}(\psi)$ = [(c_1, d_1) ... (c_m, d_m)]

then

$$\mathcal{R}(\rightarrow \phi\,\psi\,) = [\ (b\ c_j, a\ d_j)\ |\ (I \subset \llbracket 1,n \rrbracket,\ a \in \prod_{k \notin I} a_k,\ b \in \prod_{i \in I} b_i)\ \&$$
$$j \in \llbracket 1,m \rrbracket\ ]$$

Now observe that whenever $c \subset a$ and $d \subset b$ (regarding the inclusions as set inclusions) then (c , d) $\rightarrow$ (a , b) . Thus the list [(c,d)(a,b)] may be substituted by the list consisting just of (c , d), since by Modus Ponens (a , b) can then be deduced. Also any two clauses consisting of permutations of both the same antecedent and the same consequent may be substituted just by one clause. At any application of the connective $\rightarrow$ it is important to reduce in this way the obtained clause.

It can be seen that if $\mathcal{R}(\ \phi\ ) = [\ (a_1, b_1)\ \ldots\ (a_n, b_n)\ ]$ and $\mathcal{R}(\ \psi\ ) = [\ (c_1, d_1)\ \ldots\ (c_m, d_m)\ ]$ then

$$\mathcal{R}(\ \neg\,\phi\ ) = [\ (\ b\ ,\ a\ )\ |\ (\ I \subset \llbracket 1,n \rrbracket\ ,\ a \in \prod_{k \notin I} a_k\ ,\ b \in \prod_{i \in I} b_i\ ]$$

$$\mathcal{R}(\ \wedge\,\phi\,\psi\ ) = \mathcal{R}(\ \phi\ )\ \mathcal{R}(\ \psi\ ) \qquad\qquad \text{and}$$
$$\mathcal{R}(\ \vee\,\phi\,\psi\ ) = [\ (\ a_i c_j\ ,\ b_i d_j\ )\ |\ i \in \llbracket 1,n \rrbracket\ \&\ j \in \llbracket 1,m \rrbracket\ ]\ .$$

EXAMPLE: Let $\phi(a,b,c,d) = \rightarrow \wedge ab\ \neg \vee cd$ ($= a \wedge b \rightarrow \neg(c \vee d)$)

We have $\mathcal{R}(\ a\ ) = [(\ \lambda\ a\ )]$, $\mathcal{R}(\ b\ ) = [(\ \lambda\ b\ )]$,
          $\mathcal{R}(\ c\ ) = [(\ \lambda\ c\ )]$, $\mathcal{R}(\ d\ ) = [(\ \lambda\ d\ )]$,
then $\mathcal{R}(\ \wedge ab) = [(\ \lambda\ a\ )\ (\ \lambda\ b\ )\ ]$, $\mathcal{R}(\ \vee cd) = [(\ \lambda\ cd\ )]$
and $\mathcal{R}(\neg \wedge ab) = [(\ ab\ \lambda\ )]$, $\mathcal{R}(\neg \vee cd) = [(c\ \lambda)\ (d\ \lambda)]$
hence $\mathcal{R}(\ \phi\ ) = [(\ abc\ \lambda\ )\ (\ abd\ \lambda\ )]$ ▓

3. Treslog design.

3.1. A *declarative grammar* G is a context free grammar G = (C , V , S , R) where C is a non-empty set of *grammatical categories*, V is a *vocabulary*, $_*S_* \in \varsigma$ is an *initial* grammatical category and $R \subset C \times (\ (C\ )\ \cup V\ )$ is a set of *grammatical rules*.
Any rule r = (c , L) $\in$ R will also be written as
c ::= $l_1 | \ldots | l_k$ whenever $L = l_1 \ldots l_k$. L is said to be the *antecedent* in the rule r and c is said to be the *consequent* of r. It is also required that $\forall\ c \in C$ the following two conditions be satisfied:
  i. $\exists!\ L \in (\ C_*^*\ )^*$: (c,L) $\in$ R, in this case let L = Comp(c)
  ii. $\exists!\ L \in V$: (c,L) $\in$ R, in this case let L = Set(c).
A category c_0 is a *component* of a category $c \in C$ if either c_0 appears in a list appearing in Comp(c) or there is a sequence $c_1, \ldots, c_k$ in C such that c_{i-1} is a component of c_i i = 1 , $\ldots$, k , and $c_k = c$. A category c $\in$ C is said to be *simple* if Set(c) $\neq \lambda$. Finally let us call *phrases* the elements of V^*. In order to characterize the *accepted language* of a declarative grammar we define

simultaneously by induction two functions RC: $C \times V^* \longrightarrow V^*$
and RL: $C^* \times V^* \longrightarrow V^*$. Let

$$RC(c , Y) = \begin{cases} cdr\ Y & if\ car\ Y \in Set(\ c\ ) & (*) \\ RL(\ l_{i_0}\ ,\ Y\ ) & if\ Comp(c) = l_1 \ldots l_k\ and \\ & i_0 = min\{\ i\ |\ RL(l_i, Y)\ is\ defined\ \} \\ undefined & otherwise \end{cases}$$

and let

$$RL(\ l\ ,\ Y\ ) = \begin{cases} RC(\ car\ l\ ,\ Y\ ) & if\ cdr\ l = \lambda \\ RL(\ cdr\ l\ ,\ RC(\ car\ l\ ,\ Y\ )\ ) & if\ cdr\ l \ne \lambda \end{cases}$$

    If $Y \in V^*$ is such that RC(c , Y) = λ we say that the phrase Y *belongs* to the category c and we write Y:c . The accepted language of a grammar consists of the phrases belonging to the initial category.

    A program that evaluates both functions RC and RL is a parser for the declarative grammar G.

3.2. For any relation type $\mathcal{T} \in$ Rel_Typ a declarative grammar $G = G(\ \mathcal{T}\ )$ shall be built. Initially we associate to $\mathcal{T}$ a *signature vector* Sgn($\mathcal{T}$) = (n t_0 t_1 ... t_n) where n = A($\mathcal{T}$) is the number of arguments in each $\mathcal{T}$-relation, t_0 is a simple grammatical category which gives the name of a $\mathcal{T}$-relation and $t_1 \ldots t_n$ = B($\mathcal{T}$) is the type of the argumant list of any $\mathcal{T}$-relation. Each object type t_i is given as a simple grammatical category. In Spanish, as in English, the name of a relation not necesarily appears at the beginning of a phrase asserting an instance in the relation. So, it is required to specify an index i = Pos($\mathcal{T}$), $0 \le i \le n$, that indicates the position, relative to the other arguments, where the relation name appears in the phrase.

    We generate as a first rule in G($\mathcal{T}$)

$$Ins\_\mathcal{T}\ ::=\ A_1\ \ldots\ A_i\ Name\_Rel\ A_{i+1}\ \ldots\ A_n$$

To each category A_j ; j = 1,...,n ; and Name_Rel, the user shall define corresponding grammatical rules in such a way that t_j is a component of A_j , j=1,...,n , and t_0 is a component of Name_Rel.

    During the syntactic analysis of a given phrase Y, asserting an instance of a $\mathcal{T}$-relation, we shall recognize its keywords and form the list $\mathcal{R}$(Y) : AP that represents the atomic proposition asserted by Y. Given a phrase Y we realize its syntactic analysis by evluating both functions RC and RL with adequate arguments depending on Y. During this

process we form a vector $M(j)$, $j = 0, \ldots, n$ consisting
of the key words of Y, each simple category t_j gives a   key
word. Then we let:

$$\mathcal{R}(Y)(j) = \begin{cases} M(i) & \text{if} \quad j = 0 \\ M(j-1) & \text{if} \quad 1 \leq j \leq i \\ M(j) & \text{if} \quad i+1 \leq j \leq n \end{cases}.$$

The connectives used to compose atomic propositions to
obtain more general propositions are *conjunctives*,
disjunctives, *negatives* and *implicatives*. In this list they
appear ordered by their *precedence* in decreasing order.
Connectives with higher precedence are assumed to act   first,
and when the precedence are equal, the connectives   appearing
more to the left act first. Conjunctives, disjunctives and
negatives have two modes: *implicit* and *explicit*. Implicatives
appear just in their explicit mode. In the implicit mode, the
connectives may appear between objects and relations,
determining several instances. In their explicit mode, the
connectives appear just between propositions.The set of
phrases that assert a proposition by using connectives in
their implicit mode will consist of the phrases that belong
to the category DC_$\mathcal{T}$ where

```
DC_𝒯      ::= T_1 ... T_i T_0 T_{i+1} ... T_n
T_j       ::= S_j      |      S_j  Imp_Con  T_j    j=0,1,...,n
S_j       ::= A_j      |      A_j  Comma    S_j    j= 1,...,n
S_0       ::= Name_Rel | Name_Rel Comma     S_0
Imp_Con ::= I_Con  |  I_Dis
I_Con   ::= y | e | también(Spanish conjunctive propositions)
I_Dis   ::= o | u        (Spanish disjunctive propositions)
Comma   ::= ,
```

In order to recognize the   propositions asserted by a
phrase Y:DC_$\mathcal{T}$ we use three stacks: Curr_Typ, Cm and DL.   In
Curr_Typ we put the argument list type of any $\mathcal{T}$-relation. The
first element in Curr_Typ gives the current argument type. In
Cm, which is a list of type (Obj + Rel)   we shall store each
keyword appearing before a Comma. The   first   implicit
connective to scan will provide the value for the commas.   DL
is a list of type $((Obj + Rel)^+)^+$ and will be   interpreted
as its elements connected dy disjunctions. Each list CL in DL
consists of symbols Obj + Rel and is interpreted as its
elements connected by conjunctions.

EXAMPLE: Consider the phrase: *fobos y deimos o io y
europa son satélites e hijos de júpiter o marte* (Phobos and
Deimos or Io and Europe are satellites and sons of   Jupiter
and Mars).

The relations are Satelite,Hijo : $\mathcal{T}$, where $\mathcal{T}$ is a
relation type such that Ar($\mathcal{T}$) = (2 , (Name Name)) ,
Sgn($\mathcal{T}$) = (2 Name_Rel Name Name)   and   Pos($\mathcal{T}$) = 1.
The correspoding declarative grammar G is the following:

```
DC_𝒯          ::= T₁  T₀  T₂
T₀            ::= S₀ | S₀  Imp_Con  T₀
T₁            ::= S₁ | S₁  Imp_Con  T₁
T₂            ::= S₁ | S₁  Imp_Con  T₂
S₀            ::= Nr    | Nr    Comma  S₀
S₁            ::= Name  | Name  Comma  S₁
Imp_Con       ::= I_Con | I_Disj
I_Con         ::= y | e | también
I_Disj        ::= o | u
Comma         ::= ,
Nr            ::= Verb  Name_Rel | Name_Rel
Verb          ::= es | son
Name_Rel      ::= satélites | hijos
Name          ::= fobos | deimos | io | europa | júpiter | marte
```

It can be seen that the given phrase Y belongs to $DC\_\mathcal{T}$. The result of the above procedure is

DL_1 = ((*fobos deimos*) (*io europa*))

DL_2 = ((*satélites hijos*))

DL_3 = ((*júpiter*) (*marte*)) .▓

Up to this point we may construct the list of clauses representing the proposition asserted by a given phrase.

Suppose that for a phrase $Y:DC\_\mathcal{T}$ the keywords lists

$$DL_j = (CL_{kj})_{k=1,\ldots,k_j} \text{ , with } CL_{kj} = (a_{lkj})_{l=1,\ldots,l_{kj}}$$

are already formed.

Let us introduce some notation for index manipulation. Let $ID = [\![1,k_1]\!] \times \ldots \times [\![1,k_{n+1}]\!]$, let $\sigma: [\![1,K]\!] \longrightarrow ID$ where $K=k_1 \cdots k_{n+1}$ be an enumeration of ID and, for $j=1,\ldots,n+1$ let $\pi_j: ID \longrightarrow [\![1,k_j]\!]$ be the projection $\pi_j(\mathbf{x}) = x_j$. Then we can enumerate $\mathbb{DL} = DL_1 \times \ldots \times DL_{n+1}$ as

$$\mathbb{DL} = (\mathbb{CL}_{\sigma(k)})_{k=1,\ldots,K} \text{ where for each } k \leq K :$$

$$\mathbb{CL}_{\sigma(k)} = (CL_{\pi_1(\sigma(k)),1} , \cdots , CL_{\pi_{n+1}(\sigma(k)),n+1})$$

Now, for each $k = 1,\ldots,K$, let $l_j(k) = long\ CL_{\pi_j(\sigma(k)),j}$ with $j=1,\ldots,n+1$.

Let $IC_k = \prod_{j=1}^{n+1} [\![1,l_j(k)]\!]$ and let $\tau_k: [\![1,L_k]\!] \longrightarrow IC_k$, where $L_k = l_1(k) \cdots l_{n+1}(k)$, be an enumeration of IC_k . For each $j = 1 , \ldots , n + 1$ let $\rho_{jk}: IC_k \longrightarrow [\![1,l_j(k)]\!]$ be the projection $\rho_{jk}(\mathbf{x}) = x_j$.

Then we can enumerate $\mathbb{PCL}_{\sigma(k)} = \prod_{j=1}^{n+1} CL_{\pi_j(k)}$, the cartesian product of the elements of $\mathbb{CL}_{\sigma(k)}$, as

$$\mathbb{PCL}_{\sigma(k)} = (\ ^{\mathbb{0}}\tau_k(1))_{1=1,\ldots,L_k} \quad \text{where for each } 1 \le L_k$$

$$^{\mathbb{0}}\tau_k(1) = (\ ^{a}\rho_{jk}(\tau_k(1)), \ \pi_j(\sigma(k)) \ , \ j\ )_{j=1,\ldots,n+1}$$

Note that when we write the $(i+1)$-th element of $^{\mathbb{0}}\tau_k(1)$ at its beginning, we get the representation of an atomic proposition. Remember that any $\mathbb{CL}_{\sigma(k)}$ specifies the conjunction of atomic propositions. This conjunction may be represented by the list of clauses $[(\ \lambda\ (\ ^{\mathbb{0}}\tau_k(1)\ )\ )]_{1=1,\ldots,L_k}$ On the other side $\mathbb{DL}$ specifies the disjunction of such conjunctions. Hence, according to the transformation seen in 2.3., we have that the proposition asserted by Y is represented by the list of clauses

$$\mathcal{R}(Y) = [\ (\ \lambda\ (\ ^{\mathbb{0}}\tau_1(1_1)\ \cdots\ ^{\mathbb{0}}\tau_K(1_K)\ )\ )]_{(1_1,\ldots,1_K)\in}\ \prod_{k=1}^{K}\ [1,L_K]$$

EXAMPLE: From the last example we have

$DL_1 = (\ CL_{11}\ CL_{12}\ ) = (\ (\textit{fobos deimos})(\textit{io europa})\ )$ k = 2

$DL_2 = (\ CL_{21}\ )\qquad = (\ (\textit{satélites hijos})\ )$ thus k = 1

$DL_3 = (\ CL_{31}\ CL_{32}\ ) = (\ (\textit{júpiter})\ (\textit{marte})\ )$ k = 2

With the same notation as before, we have K=2.1.2=4 and

$$\sigma: \quad \begin{array}{l} 1 \longmapsto (\ 1\ 1\ 1\ ) \\ 2 \longmapsto (\ 1\ 1\ 2\ ) \\ 3 \longmapsto (\ 2\ 1\ 1\ ) \\ 4 \longmapsto (\ 2\ 1\ 2\ ) \end{array}$$

Then for any k = 1,2,3,4 we have

$1_1(1) = \text{long } C_{11} = 2$ $\qquad$ $1_1(2) = \text{long } C_{11} = 2$

$1_2(1) = \text{long } C_{21} = 2$ $\qquad$ $1_2(2) = \text{long } C_{21} = 2$

$1_3(1) = \text{long } C_{31} = 1$ $\qquad$ $1_3(2) = \text{long } C_{32} = 1$

$1_1(3) = \text{long } C_{12} = 2$ $\qquad$ $1_1(4) = \text{long } C_{12} = 2$

$1_2(3) = \text{long } C21 = 2$ $\qquad$ $1_2(4) = \text{long } C_{21} = 2$

$1_3(3) = \text{long } C_{31} = 1$ $\qquad$ $1_3(4) = \text{long } C_{32} = 1$

Then $L_1= 4$ $L_2= 4$ $L_3= 4$ $L_4= 4$.

The corresponding atomic propositions are:

$^{\mathbb{0}}\tau_1(1) = (f\ s\ j)$ $\qquad$ $^{\mathbb{0}}\tau_2(1) = (f\ s\ m)$

$^{\mathbb{0}}\tau_1(2) = (f\ h\ j)$ $\qquad$ $^{\mathbb{0}}\tau_2(2) = (f\ h\ m)$

$^{\mathbb{0}}\tau_1(3) = (d\ s\ j)$ $\qquad$ $^{\mathbb{0}}\tau_2(3) = (d\ s\ m)$

$^{\mathbb{0}}\tau_1(4) = (d\ h\ j)$ $\qquad$ $^{\mathbb{0}}\tau_2(4) = (d\ h\ m)$

$$^0\tau_3(1) = (i\ s\ j) \qquad\qquad\qquad ^0\tau_4(1) = (i\ s\ m)$$

$$^0\tau_3(2) = (i\ h\ j) \qquad\qquad\qquad ^0\tau_4(2) = (i\ h\ m)$$

$$^0\tau_3(3) = (e\ s\ j) \qquad\qquad\qquad ^0\tau_4(3) = (e\ s\ m)$$

$$^0\tau_3(4) = (e\ h\ j) \qquad\qquad\qquad ^0\tau_4(4) = (e\ h\ m)$$

(the keywords are abreviated by their initial letters).

Hence the asserted proposition is equivalent to the list of $256 = 4^4$ clauses :

$$(\lambda\ (^0\tau_1(p)\quad ^0\tau_2(q)\quad ^0\tau_3(r)\quad ^0\tau_4(s)))\qquad p,q,r,s = 1,2,3,4.$$

Note that, since $Pos(\mathcal{T}) = 1$, the name of the relation in each atomic proposition appears at the $Pos(\mathcal{T}) + 1 = 2$ position.

If we would say: *fobos o deimos o io y europa son satelites e hijos de jupiter o marte*
(Phobos or Deimos or Io and Europe are satellites and sons of Jupiter or Mars)

then $(k_1, k_2, k_3) = (3, 1, 2)$, σ:

1	$\longmapsto$	(1 1 1)
2	$\longmapsto$	(1 1 2)
3	$\longmapsto$	(2 1 1)
4	$\longmapsto$	(2 1 2)
5	$\longmapsto$	(3 1 1)
6	$\longmapsto$	(3 1 2)

$$(1_j(k)) = \begin{bmatrix} 1 & 1 & 1 & 1 & 2 & 2 \\ 2 & 2 & 2 & 2 & 2 & 2 \\ 1 & 1 & 1 & 1 & 1 & 1 \end{bmatrix} ,\ L_k = (2\ 2\ 2\ 2\ 4\ 4)\qquad and$$

$$^0\delta_k(1) = \begin{bmatrix} f\ s\ j & f\ s\ m & d\ s\ j & d\ s\ m & i\ s\ j & i\ s\ m \\ f\ h\ j & f\ h\ m & d\ h\ j & d\ h\ m & i\ h\ j & i\ h\ m \\ & & & & e\ s\ j & e\ s\ m \\ & & & & e\ h\ j & e\ h\ m \end{bmatrix}$$

Hence the modified proposition is equivalent to the list of $2^4.4^2 = 256$ clauses :

$$(\lambda\ (^0\tau_1(p)\quad ^0\tau_2(q)\quad ^0\tau_3(r)\quad ^0\tau_4(s)\quad ^0\tau_5(u)\quad ^0\tau_6(v)\ ))with$$

$p,q,r,s = 1,2$; $u,v = 1,2,3,4$

3.3.   Concerning the negated assertions, firstly we allow an atomic form of negation by preceding a relation name with the negative particle "no".

In order to recognize such atomic negations we slightly modify the rule for DC_$\mathcal{T}$ already introduced. Actually, let

DC_$\mathcal{T}$ ::= T_1 . . . $T_i\ U_0\ T_{i+1}$ . . . T_n with

U_0 ::= T_0 | NP . T_0 ,

NP ::= "no"

and everything as before.

Then we proceed in the same manner as in 3.2 with the only exception that whenever a relation name appears negated we mark as negated all its corresponding atomic propositions. Finally we transform the resulting clause list by substituting each clause of the form
$(\lambda \ (\Box_1 \ . \ . \ . \ \Box_r \overset{*}{\Box}_{r+1} \ . \ . \ \Box_n \ ) \ )$, where the $\overset{*}{\Box}_j$'s
are the negated atomic propositions, by the equivalent clause:
$(\ (\Box_1 \ . \ . \ . \ \Box_r) \ .(\Box_{r+1} \ . \ . \ .\Box_n) \ )$.

3.4.   Now let us introduce a grammatical rule in order to accept phrases asserting a composed propositions by the use of connectives in their explicit mode. Let
Prop_$\mathcal{T}$ ::= DC_$\mathcal{T}$ |
                    | Prop_$\mathcal{T}$. E_Conj . Prop_$\mathcal{T}$ |
                    | Prop_$\mathcal{T}$. I_Disj . Prop_$\mathcal{T}$ |
                    | Neg . Prop_$\mathcal{T}$ |
                    | Pre_Imp . Prop_$\mathcal{T}$. Imp . Prop_$\mathcal{T}$
E_Conj ::= " Y " | " E "
E_Disj ::= " O " | " U "
Neg   ::= " NO_ES_CIERTO_QUE " | " NO_OCURRE_QUE "
           ("It's not true that"| "It does not happen that")
Pre_Imp::= " SI " | " DADO_QUE "
           ("If" | "Given")
Imp   ::= " ENTONCES " | " TENDREMOS_QUE "
           ("Then" | "We have that")

Note that we have written the constant words in capital letters. This is for explicitly distinguish their declared connectives explicit mode.

During the syntactic analysis of a phrase Y: Prop_$\mathcal{T}$ we construct the clause list that represents the asserted propositions by Y in a rather usual way by means of two stacks: Rep and Oper. In Rep we put the partial propositions already represented and in Oper we store the connectives to be applied.

3.5.   In order to deal with quantifiers we should consider variables.

Let $\mathcal{T} \in$ Rel_Typ be a given relation type.
Let sgn $\mathcal{T}$ = (n t_0 t_1 . . . t_n) and i= Pos ($\mathcal{T}$). To any object type t_j , j=1,. . ., n , the user should add a set of *variables*, with the understanding that each such variable will run over Set(t_j). We distinguish the variables and the elements of a type by requiring the variables first letter to be a capital letter. The quantifiers we use are of two categories: *universal* and *existential*. They are the following:
UQ ::= *las* | *los* | *cada* | *todo* | *cualquier* | *cualesquier* |
       cualesquiera | *todos-los* | *todas-las* | *ningun*| *ninguna*
EQ ::= *un* | *uno* | *una* | *unos* | *unas* | *algun* | *alguno*| *alguna*|
       algunos | *algunas* | *varios* | *varias* | *pocos* | *muchos* |
       una-cierta-cantidad-de.

Firstly, let us describe the phrases asserting a quantified atomic proposition. Let us introduce the following rules:

```
QI_𝒯 ::= QT₁ . . . QTᵢ . T₀ . QTᵢ₊₁ . . . QTₙ
QTⱼ ::= Aⱼ | UQ . Aⱼ | EQ . Aⱼ          j = 1,. . . ,n
QP_𝒯 ::= Q₁ . . . Qₙ . Prop_𝒯
Qⱼ ::= λ | PUQ . U Q . tⱼ | PEQ . E Q . tⱼ . Sep
PUQ::= para
PEQ::= hay | existe | existen
Sep::= tal-que | tales-que | de-manera-que
```

The categories that are not defined here, have already been defined.

During the syntactic analysis of a phrase Y :QI_𝒯 + QP_𝒯 we construct a quantitication vector Qvect = $(q_1 . . . q_n)$ such that q_j: UQ + EQ + {λ} is the quantifier appeared in the j-th argument.   Hence Y asserts a proposition $(q_1 \ var_1)...(q_n \ var_n)$ $\varphi(var_1,...,var_n)$,   which   can   be represented by the clause list representing $\varphi(var_1,...,var_n)$ together with an specification for the quantifier. Thus, to any phrase Y:QI_𝒯 + QP_𝒯 we associate a *variable dependencies* (vd) vector Var_Dep indexed by the variables appearing in Y, such that

$$Var\_Dep(var_j) = \begin{cases} var_j & \text{if } var_j \text{ appears universally quantified} \\ (var_{j_1}...var_{j_k}) & \text{if } var_j \text{ can be written as a Skolem function of } var_{j_1},...,var_{j_k} \text{ and} \\ Free & \text{if } var_j \text{ appears as a free variable} \end{cases}$$

Var_Dep is easily obtained from Qvect by marking   the existentially quantified variables. Namely, let us apply the following procedure:

Let I = λ and Var_Dep(j) = λ   ∀j = 1,...,n
For j=1,...,n proceed by the next cases:

q_j : UQ   : put var_j into I and let Var_Dep(var_j) =var_j

q_j : EQ   : let Var_Dep(var_j)=I and after this, let I=λ.

q_j : λ   : let Var_Dep(var_j) = *Free*.

EXAMPLE: Let us consider the phrase Y:
cada Satélite es hijo de un Planeta
(Each satellite is son of a planet)
Then the asserted formula by Y is represented by the clause list 𝓡 (Y) = [(h S P)]   and its vector   of variables dependency is Var_Dep = (S S).

3.6.   Now, in order to recognize any first order formula, let us introduce the grammatical rule:
Form_𝒯 ::= QI_𝒯 | QP_𝒯 |

```
| Form_𝒯 . E_Conj . Form_𝒯 |
| Form_𝒯 . E_Disj . Form_𝒯 |
| Neg . Form_𝒯 |
| Pre_Imp . Form_𝒯 . Imp . Form_𝒯 |
| Q_j . Form_𝒯 |            j = 1,. . .,n
```

The representation of a formula asserted by a phrase Y : Form_𝒯 is done with regard to the connectives and new quantifier precedence and their order of appearance, essentially in the same manner as in 3.4. The main characteristics of the formula representation procedure is the manipulation of vd_vectors.

Suppose that for two given phrases Y, Z we have already built their clause representations $\mathcal{R}(Y)$ and $\mathcal{R}(Z)$ with their respective vd_vectors Var_Dep$_Y$ and Var_Dep$_Z$.

Rename if necesary, the bounded variables appearing in $\mathcal{R}(Z)$ in order to have distinct bounded variables in both $\mathcal{R}(Y)$ and $\mathcal{R}(Z)$. Then act on $\mathcal{R}(Y)$ and $\mathcal{R}(Z)$ according to the actual connective as in 3.4.

If the connective is a conjunction or a disjunction the new vd_vector is the concatenation of both Var_Dep$_Y$ and Var_Dep$_Z$.

In the case of a negation,say of $\mathcal{R}(Y)$,the new vd_vector is :

$$\text{Var\_Dep}_{\neg Y}(var) = \begin{cases} var & \text{if Var\_Dep}(var) \neq var \\ \text{the former block of} & \\ \text{existentially quantified} & \text{otherwise} \\ \text{variables in Y before } var. & \end{cases}$$

In the case of an implication Y ⇒ Z, act as ¬Y ∨ Z.
In the case of a new quantifier, on Var_nq, just let:

$$\text{Var\_Dep (var\_nq)} = \begin{cases} var\_nq & \text{if the quantifier is universal} \\ \lambda & \text{if the quantifier is existential} \end{cases}$$

Thus any first order formula is represented as a clause list with a corresponding vd_vector.

3.7.   Let us notice that all transformation we have used are provable in the Predicate Calculus. Particularly each quantified formula is equivalent to a Prenex Form. Actually with our procedures, we get the prenex form of a formula whose quantifiers are specified by the vd_vector and whose scope is given in a conjunctive normal form by $\mathcal{R}$. Nevertheless the transformations used may fail to be correct in our natural language understanding.

Example: Consider the phrase Y:
"Si los Planetas son atraídos por el sol entonces los Satélites son atraídos por el sol."
(If the planets are attracted by the Sun then the satellites are attracted by the Sun.)

The asserted formula can be written as the first order

formula: $(\forall\ P\ :\ at(P,Sol)\ )\ \Rightarrow\ (\forall\ S\ :\ at(S,Sol)\ )$
which is provably equivalent to either
1. $\exists\ P\ \ \forall\ S\ \ (\ at(P,Sol)\ \Rightarrow\ at(S,Sol)\ )$ or
2. $\forall\ S\ \ \exists\ P\ \ (\ at(P,Sol)\ \Rightarrow\ at(S,Sol)\ )$
    Our procedure represents Y as in 1. The representation
is:
$\mathcal{R}(1)$ = [(((at P Sol)) ((at S Sol)))], Var_Dep = $(_\lambda^P\ {}_S^S)$

    Formula 2. would be represented as:
$\mathcal{R}(2)$ = [(((at P Sol)) ((at S Sol)))], Var_Dep = $(_S^S\ {}_S^P)$

    The equivalent formulae may be rephrased as
1. *Hay un planeta tal que para todo satélite, si el planeta
es atraído por el sol entonces el satélite es atraído por el
sol.*
2. *Para todo satélite hay un planeta tal que si el planeta es
atraído por el sol entonces el satélite es atraído por el
sol.*
    Each of them has a different meaning!.
3.8.   Finally let us note that any phrase Y:Form_$\mathcal{T}$ such
that the corresponding vd_vector Var_Dep has some variables
declared as *Free*, may be considered as a *query* asking to
instantiate the free variables in order to make $\mathcal{R}(\ Y\ )$ true.

4. Concluding remarks.

    TRESLOG is a quite general translator, able to handle
Predicate Calculus. Its deductive procedures, justified in
the Predicate Calculus, may not be correct in our intuitive
accepted Spanish understanding. The discrepancies are mainly
due to the fact that implication does not have a "causality"
notion as it has in Spanish. We do not allow the use of
function symbols but this is not a serious restriction since
any function may as well be represented by a relation. The
representation of a formula may ocupy a great amount   of
space, this is a limitation of our system. We actually are
looking for a more economical formulae representation.
    The implementation has been done mainly in LISP. Up to
now, we have an editor that builts grammars $G(\mathcal{T})$ according to
user's specifications. The formulae representation procedure
is completed to section 3.5 in the presentation of TRESLOG
design.

References.

Dahl(1981):" Translating Spanish into logic through logic   ".
Amer. Jour. of Comp. Linguis. (7) Nr. 3 , pp 149 - 164.

Kowalski(1981):"Logic for Problem Solving". North Holland.

DISCIPLE: AN EXPERT AND LEARNING SYSTEM

Gheorghe Tecuci[1], Yves Kodratoff[2], Zani Bodnaru[3], Thierry Brunet[2]
[1]ICSIT-TCI, 71316, Bd. Miciurin 8-10, Bucharest 1, ROMANIA.
[2]LRI, Bât. 490, UA 410 du CNRS & Université de Paris-Sud, 91405 Orsay, FRANCE.
[3]IEIB, Str. Baicului, Bucharest 2, ROMANIA

Abstract

In this paper we present DISCIPLE, an integrated expert and learning system for weak theory domains. The problem solving mechanisms of DISCIPLE combine problem reduction, problem solving by constraints, and problem solving by analogy. The learning mechanisms of DISCIPLE combine explanation-based learning, learning by analogy, and empirical learning. DISCIPLE and its user are in constant interaction, both proposing solutions and explanations to the other. From each problem solving step contributed by the user, DISCIPLE is trying to learn a general rule so that, when faced with problems similar to the current one, to be able to give a solution similar to the solution given by the user. The examples given in this paper illustrate the use of DISCIPLE to the design of technologies for the manufacturing of loudspeakers.

1. Introduction

Recent Machine Learning achievements (Mitchell, Carbonell & Michalski, 1985; Langley, 1987) have given expert systems the ability to acquire knowledge automatically. Our system DISCIPLE is part of this effort. DISCIPLE is an interactive expert and learning system for weak theory domains. It directly assimilates new knowledge by observing, analyzing and questioning about the problem solving steps contributed by its user through his normal use of the system. The user formulates the problem to solve and DISCIPLE starts solving this problem by showing the user all the problem solving steps. The user may accept or reject them. Therefore, during the course of its functioning as an Expert System, DISCIPLE may encounter two situations.

The current problem-solving step (which we shall also call the *partial solution*) may be accepted by the user. In this case, the current state of the knowledge base is judged as satisfactory, and no learning will take place.

Alternatively, DISCIPLE may be unable to propose any partial solution (or the solution it proposes may be rejected by the user). Then, the user is compelled to give his own solution. Once this solution is given, a learning process will take place. DISCIPLE will try to learn a general rule so that, when faced with problems *similar* with the current one (which it has just failed to solve), it will become able to propose a solution *similar* to the solution given by the user to the current problem.

In this paper we shall present the way DISCIPLE solves problems and learns by using examples from the technology design domain. More precisely, we shall consider the problem of designing (and learning) manufacturing techniques for loudspeakers, defined as follows:
- given the specifications of a loudspeaker
- design (and learn) the actions needed to manufacture the loudspeaker.

The design of technologies is viewed here as a successive decomposition of complex operations into simpler ones, and better defining these simpler operations by choosing tools, materials or verifiers, which are in turn successively refined. To design a technology, DISCIPLE needs some knowledge about the components of the loudspeakers, about the technological solutions for manufacturing of loudspeakers, about the tools, materials and verifiers one can use to manufacture loudspeakers. All this knowledge constitutes the domain theory. It is characterized as *weak* since it is both constructed in an ad hoc way and incomplete.

2. Knowledge representation

One of our prime concerns was to design a knowledge representation and organization in which the main operations involved in learning (that is generalizations and particularizations) can be easily performed. It has its roots in (Sridharan & Bresina, 1983; Tecuci, 1984; Kodratoff, 1985).

The basic elements of DISCIPLE's knowledge base are the *concepts*. A concept may represent a set of objects or a set of actions. For example, 'adhesive' represents the set of adhesive objects while 'dry' represents the set of drying actions. A *concept definition* describes a *necessary and sufficient condition* for an instance to be an example of the concept. In DISCIPLE, this condition is always expressed as a conjunction of predicates. For example, the expression

(x ISA adhesive) & (x TYPE fluid) & (x GLUES glass)

defines the fluid adhesives that may glue glass, while the expression

(d ISA dry) & (d OBJECT h) & (d TOOL f) & (h ISA hair) & (f ISA fan)

defines the actions of drying hair with a fan.

In general, an object concept is defined as belonging to a super-concept and having additional properties (Minsky, 1975). The value of a property may be a constant or another concept. Also, an action concept is defined by specifying some of its cases (the agent performing the action, the object on which the action is performed, the instrument used etc.), as well as the descriptions of these cases (which are always object descriptions). DISCIPLE's interface exploits these features giving a quite natural appearance to the concept definitions:

(adhesive x (TYPE fluid)	DRY OBJECT (hair h)
(GLUES glass))	TOOL (fan f)

However, in this paper we shall represent the concepts as predicate calculus expressions.

The elementary operations performed on concepts consist in checking if a concept is more general than another one, generalizing a concept, and specializing a concept. These operations are defined in the following.

A concept is said to be *more general than* another one if the set of instances of the first concept includes the set of instances of the second one. This extensional definition is made computable by using the notion of substitution, as defined in the following (Kodratoff & Ganascia, 1986).

A *substitution* has the form $'\sigma = (x1 \leftarrow f1, \ldots, xn \leftarrow fn)'$, where each xi $(i=1,\ldots,n)$ is a variable or a concept and each fi $(i=1,\ldots,n)$ is a term or a concept. If xi is a variable then fi is a term, and if xi is a concept then fi is a less general concept.

Let us consider two conjunctive formulas:

$$A = A1 \ \& \ A2 \ \& \ldots \& \ An \qquad B = B1 \ \& \ B2 \ \& \ldots \& \ Bm$$

where Ai $(i=1,\ldots,n)$ and Bj $(j=1,\ldots,m)$ are literals.

A is more general than B if and only if there exist A', B', and σ such that:

$$A' = A, \qquad A' = A1' \ \& \ A2' \ \& \ldots \& \ Ap'$$
$$B' = B, \qquad B' = B1' \ \& \ B2' \ \& \ldots \& \ Bq'$$
$$\sigma = (\sigma1, \sigma2, \ldots, \sigma p) \quad \forall \ i, \ 1 \le i \le p, \ \exists \ j, \ 1 \le j \le q \ \text{such that} \ \sigma io Ai' = Bj'$$

Otherwise stated, one uses theorems to transform the formulas A and B, so as to make each literal from A' more general than a corresponding literal from B'.

Let A = (u ISA adhesive) & (u GLUES v) & (u GLUES w)

B = (x ISA adhesive) & (x GLUES y) & (x TYPE fluid)

B' = (x ISA adhesive) & (x GLUES y) & (x GLUES y) & (x TYPE fluid)

B = B' (because of the idempotence property of &)

σ = (u←x, v←y, w←y)

σoA = (x ISA adhesive) & (x GLUES y) & (x GLUES y) that is σoA is part of B

Then A is more general than B.

To generalize the concepts, DISCIPLE uses *syntactic rules of generalizations* as, for instance, turning constants into variables, climbing the generalization hierarchies, dropping conditions, or applying theorems (Michalski, 1983; Kodratoff & Ganascia, 1986). Used in the reverse order, these rules will *specialize* the concepts.

The concepts from DISCIPLE's knowledge base are organized into generalization hierarchies. The following, for instance, is a hierarchy of object concepts:

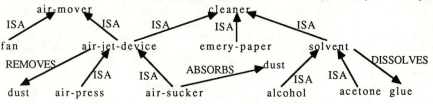

Figure 1. A hierarchy of object concepts.

3. Problem solving mechanisms in DISCIPLE

The problem solving mechanisms of DISCIPLE are based on techniques of problem reduction (Nilsson, 1971), formulation, propagation, and evaluation of constraints (Stefik, 1981), and problem solving by analogy (Carbonell, 1986). All these techniques are reduced to particularizations and generalizations of concepts, and are integrated into an unitary problem reduction method.

The problem reduction method may be formulated as follows:

<u>Given</u> the description of an initial problem, a set of reduction rules for transforming problems into sub-problems, and a set of primitive problems (that is problems with known or immediate solutions).

<u>Determine</u> a set of primitive problems that solve the initial problem.

In DISCIPLE, a reduction rule has the following form:

    IF *condition*

        $K(x1, \ldots , xn, \ldots)$

    THEN *solve the problem*

        $P(x1, \ldots , xn)$

    by solving the following sub-problems

        $C(P1(x1, \ldots , xn, \ldots), P2(x1, \ldots , xn, \ldots), \ldots ,Pm(x1, \ldots , xn, \ldots))$

This rule indicates the decomposition of the problem P into a set of sub-problems P1, P2, ... , Pm. Therefore, we shall further call such a rule a *decomposition rule*. C is a combinator which indicates the way of combining the solutions of the problems P1, P2, ... , Pm so that to obtain the solution to the problem P. K is a conjunction of predicates that has to be true in order for the rule to be applicable. One should notice that K, P1, ... , Pm may contain variables not present in P. These variables are supposed to be existentially quantified.

The rule form given here is general in that it does not represent the decomposition of a specific problem, but the decomposition of an entire set of problems. This set contains any problem which is less general than P and satisfies K. It is defined as follows:

{Pa | there exists a substitution σ such that 'σoP=Pa' and 'σoK=TRUE'}

Let 'Pa' be the problem to solve and σ a substitution such that '$\sigma \circ P = Pa$' and '$\sigma \circ K = TRUE$'. Then, the above rule indicates the following decomposition of the problem 'Pa': 'C($\sigma \circ P1$, $\sigma \circ P2$, ... , $\sigma \circ Pm$)'.

Let us consider a decomposition rule indicating a way to perform the attachment of two objects:

IF *condition*
    (x ISA object) & (y ISA object) & (x PARTIALLY-MATCHES y) &
    (z ISA adhesive) & (z GLUES x) & (z GLUES y) & (z TYPE fluid)
THEN *solve the problem*
    ATTACH x ON y
by solving the sequence of sub-problems
    APPLY z ON x
    PRESS x ON y

This rule states that if we have the problem of attaching the objects 'x' and 'y' and if these objects are characterized by the fact that 'x' partially matches 'y' (i.e. part of the surface of 'x' fits part of the surface of 'y') and there exists a fluid adhesive 'z' that glues both 'x' and 'y', then we may achieve the attachment of 'x' and 'y' by first applying 'z' on 'x' and further pressing 'x' on 'y'. The combinator of this rule indicates that the actions APPLY and PRESS should be performed sequentially. This corresponds to the present status of DISCIPLE. In general one may define a partial ordering on the sub-problems.

Let us now consider the following problem to solve:
    ATTACH membrane ON chassis
In order to solve this problem one must first find a substitution σ such that
    $\sigma \circ$(ATTACH x ON y) = ATTACH membrane ON chassis
This substitution is σ = (x $\leftarrow$ membrane, y $\leftarrow$ chassis)

Next, one has to verify that $\sigma \circ$(condition) = TRUE in the current situation:
    (membrane ISA object) & (chassis ISA object) &
    (membrane PARTIALLY-MATCHES chassis) & (z ISA adhesive) &
    (z GLUES membrane) & (z GLUES chassis) & (z TYPE fluid)
where it is implicitly meant that the variable z is existentially quantified.

If the above expression is true in the current situation then one can solve the problem 'ATTACH membrane ON chassis' by solving the sequence of sub-problems
    APPLY z ON membrane
    PRESS membrane ON chassis
where: (z ISA adhesive) & (z GLUES membrane) & (z GLUES chassis) & (z TYPE fluid)

Notice that the choice of an appropriate adhesive is a problem to be addressed latter.

DISCIPLE is designed to solve problems which are initially imprecisely formulated but become better and better formulated as the problem solving process advances. To this purpose it *formulates, propagates, and evaluates constraints.*

Constraint formulation is the process of imposing constraints on the problems to solve. One way of formulating constraints in DISCIPLE is to apply specialization rules having the following form:

IF *condition*
    K(x1, ... , xn, ...)
THEN *solve the problem*
    P(x1, ... , xn)
by solving the more specialized problem
    P1(x1, ... , xn, ...)

This rule states that if the condition K is satisfied then the problem P may be constrained to the problem P1.

Constraining a problem means providing a more precise specification to it. If P represents an action, then a specialization rule may constrain the action to use a certain instrument:

> IF *condition*
>> (x ISA object) & (y ISA object) & (z ISA press) &
>> (z CAPACITY c) & (x DIMENSION d1) & (y DIMENSION d2) &
>> (c GREATER-THAN d1) & (c GREATER-THAN d2)
> THEN *solve the problem*
>> FIX x ON y
> *by solving the more specialized problem*
>> FIX x ON y WITH z

Another way of formulating constraints in DISCIPLE is to specialize a problem by replacing an object from its description with a less general one, taken from one of the object hierarchies.

Constraint propagation is the process of transmitting the constraints from one sub-problem to another sub-problem. This is the way the sub-problems communicate between themselves.

Constraint satisfaction is the process of determining values for variables, values satisfying the constraints imposed on the variables. In DISCIPLE, the constraints describe the features which are needed for the objects specified in the problems to be solved. Constraint satisfaction is a decision process of the type *buy or build* (Stefik, 1981). First of all, DISCIPLE looks in its knowledge base for an available object that satisfies the constraints. If no object is found then DISCIPLE will try to design the object. Thus, the design of the object becomes a new problem to solve.

Problem solving by analogy in DISCIPLE is a consequence of using incompletely learned rules, as will be presented in section 4.

In a given situation, more than one rule may be applicable and the system has to choose which one to fire. This is the so called *conflict resolution problem*. The conflict resolution problem is solved in DISCIPLE by using *meta-rules* of the form:

> *To solve the problem* P
> *optimizing the criterion* OC
> *consider the applicable rules in the following order*
>> R1, R2, . . . , Rn

This meta-rule defines an order on the rules that may reduce the problem P in that R1 is expected to give the best result and Rn the worst.

4. Learning mechanisms in DISCIPLE

The learning problem addressed by DISCIPLE may be formulated as follows:

Given *a weak domain theory* (the domain theory consists of all system knowledge about the application domain. It is characterized as weak since it is both incomplete and constructed in an ad hoc way: it incorporates defaults, omits details, abstracts away from a complete account of the constraints which may be relevant to the reasoning task to which it is applied), *a problem to be solved,* and *a partial solution to the problem* (a decomposition or a specialization of the problem).

Determine *a general rule* (according to this rule, problems similar to the current problem will receive solutions similar to the one given by the user to the current problem).

Let us consider the situation when DISCIPLE encountered for the first time the problem of attaching two components of a loudspeaker:

> ATTACH ring ON chassis-membrane-assembly

Let us further suppose that the user indicated the following solution

APPLY mowicoll ON ring
PRESS ring ON chassis-membrane-assembly
Note that APPLY and PRESS may be actions previously unknown to the system and, in such a case, it knows nothing about them except they are means of ATTACHing.

Now DISCIPLE knows a solution of the current problem which it will further consider as an example of a general rule to be learned:

Example 1
In order to solve the problem
ATTACH ring ON chassis-membrane-assembly
solve the sequence of sub-problems
APPLY mowicoll ON ring
PRESS ring ON chassis-membrane-assembly

DISCIPLE uses the following generalization method: it *supposes* that the above example faithfully represents the structure of the general rule to be learned. Therefore, the rule DISCIPLE will try to learn has the following form:

IF
x, y, and z satisfy <constraints>
THEN *solve the problem*
ATTACH x ON y
by solving the sequence of sub-problems
APPLY z ON x
PRESS x ON y

That is, rule learning is reduced to learning the concepts 'x', 'y', and 'z' such that the attachment of 'x' and 'y' may be performed as a sequence of APPLY and PRESS.

The learning method of DISCIPLE involves a combination of Explanation-Based, Analogy-Based, and Empirical Learning algorithms:

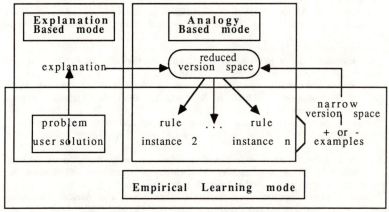

Figure 2. The learning method of DISCIPLE.

First DISCIPLE finds a shallow explanation of user's solution. Then it formulates a reduced version space for the rule to be learned. Each rule in this space covers only instances which are analogous with the user's example. DISCIPLE carefully generates analogous instances to be characterized as positive examples or as negative examples by the user. These are used to further narrow the version space.

In greater detail the learning method is the following one:

Explanation-Based Mode:

1. Find an explanation of user's solution (Example 1) and call it Explanation 1.

Analogy-Based Mode:

2. Over-generalize Example 1, simply by turning all the objects into variables, and call it General Rule 1.

3. Take Explanation 1 as a lower bound for the applicability condition of General Rule 1, and call it Almost Sufficient Condition.

4. Over-generalize Explanation 1 (Almost Sufficient Condition) to the most general expression that may still be accepted as an explanation of General Rule 1.

5. Take the over-generalized explanation as an upper bound for the applicability condition of General Rule 1. Call it Almost Necessary Condition.

The Almost Necessary Condition, the Almost Sufficient Condition and the General Rule 1 define a reduced version space for the rule to be learned.

6. Look in the knowledge base for objects satisfying the Almost Necessary Condition. Call Explanation i the properties of these objects that were used to prove that they satisfy the Almost Necessary Condition.

7. Use the objects found in step 6 to generate an instance of General Rule 1. Call it Instance i. It is analogous with Example 1.

8. Propose Instance i to the user and ask him to characterize it as a valid or an invalid reduction. If Instance i is rejected by the user then go to step 9. Otherwise go to step 14.

Explanation-Based Mode:

9. Take Instance i as a near miss (negative example) of the rule to be learned.

10. Find an explanation of why Instance i was rejected by the user and call it Failure-Explanation i.

Empirical Learning Mode:

11. Specialize the Almost Necessary Condition *as little as possible*, so that not to cover Failure-Explanation i.

12. Specialize the Almost Sufficient Condition *as little as possible*, so that not to cover Failure-Explanation i and to be less general than the Almost Necessary Condition.

13. Go to step 6.

14. Take Instance i as a new positive example of the rule to be learned and Explanation i as a true explanation of Instance i.

15. Look for a maximally specific common generalization of Almost Sufficient Condition and Explanation i, which is less general than the Almost Necessary Condition. Several cases may occur:

- if such a generalization exists and is not identical with the Almost Necessary Condition, then take it as the new Almost Sufficient Condition and go to step 6;

- if such a generalization exists and is identical with the Almost Necessary Condition, then take it as a necessary and sufficient condition of General Rule 1 and show them to the user as the learned rule and stop;

- if such a generalization does not exist then show the Almost Necessary Condition, the Almost Sufficient Condition and the General Rule 1 to the user as the learned rule and stop.

A detailed justification of this learning method is given in (Kodratoff & Tecuci, 87). Here we only illustrate the way DISCIPLE learned the rule for ATTACHing two objects.

In its first step, DISCIPLE enters the *Explanation Based Mode* and tries to find an explanation (within its domain theory) of the validity of user's example (Example 1). But the domain theory contains only shallow and/or incomplete knowledge concerning this example, knowledge consisting here in some of the properties and the relations of the referred objects, as well as some rules for inferring new properties and relations. An essential hypothesis in DISCIPLE is that the explanation is expressible in terms of the relations between the objects from the example ('ring', 'chassis-membrane-assembly', and 'mowicoll') rather than in terms of the features of these objects. Therefore, DISCIPLE will look in its knowledge base for the links and for the paths (i.e. sequences of links) connecting 'ring', 'chassis-membrane-assembly' and 'mowicoll', and will propose the found connections as pieces of explanations of the example. It is the user's task to validate them as explanations (in the dialog below, the user's answers are underlined):

> *Do the following justify your solution*
> ring PART-OF loudspeaker &
> chassis-membrane-assembly PART-OF loudspeaker ? <u>no</u>
> mowicoll GLUES ring ? <u>yes</u>
> mowicoll GLUES chassis-membrane-assembly ? <u>yes</u>

All the pieces of explanation marked by a user's <u>yes</u> form the explanation of the example rule.

<u>Explanation 1</u>

$$\text{mowicoll} \underset{\text{GLUES}}{\overset{\text{GLUES}}{\rightrightarrows}} \begin{array}{l} \text{ring} \\ \text{chassis-membrane-assembly} \end{array}$$

Notice that this explanation may be incomplete. This is due partly to the incompleteness of the domain theory and partly to the heuristic used to find explanations (DISCIPLE looks only for the relations between objects, ignoring their properties). However, the found explanation shows some important features of the objects, features justifying the user's solution.

In its second step, DISCIPLE enters the *Analogy-Based Mode*. The analogy relies on the observation that similar causes tend to have similar effects and on the fact that, in DISCIPLE, the explanation of a problem solving operation may be regarded as a cause for performing the operation. Therefore, if the network of relations between other objects (for instance 'centering-device', 'chassis-assembly', and 'neoprene') is similar with Explanation 1, then DISCIPLE may deduce, by analogy with Example 1, a new decomposition (see figure 3).

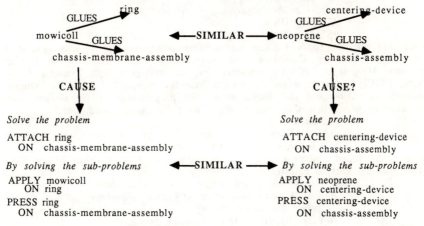

Figure 3. The analogy paradigm in DISCIPLE.

First of all DISCIPLE over-generalizes Example 1 by turning all the objects into variables, thus obtaining :

General Rule 1:

solve the problem
ATTACH x ON y
by solving the sequence of sub-problems
APPLY z ON y
PRESS x ON y

Next Explanation 1 is rewritten as an (Almost) Sufficient Condition for the application of General Rule 1:

(Almost) Sufficient Condition:
(x ISA ring) & (y ISA chassis-membrane-assembly)&
(z ISA mowicoll) & (z GLUES x) & (z GLUES y)

Notice that the above expression is in fact a true sufficient condition because it reduces General Rule 1 to Example 1 which is known to be true. Nevertheless, as soon as this expression will be generalized to cover new explanations it may no longer be considered a sufficient condition because the explanations may be incomplete.

Further, Explanation 1 is generalized to the most general expression that may still be accepted by the user as an explanation of General Rule 1. This over-generalization is taken as an upper bound for the applicability condition of General Rule 1:

Almost Necessary Condition:
(z GLUES x) & (z GLUES y)

We have called this over-generalization an *Almost Necessary Condition* because it is supposed to cover most of the cases of applicability of General Rule 1.

The Almost Necessary Condition, the Almost Sufficient Condition and the General Rule 1 define a reduced *version space* (Mitchell, 78) for the rule to be learned:

IF

G: *(Almost Necessary Condition)*
(z GLUES x) & (z GLUES y)
S: *(Almost Sufficient Condition)*
(x ISA ring) & (y ISA chassis-membrane-assembly)&
(z ISA mowicoll) & (z GLUES x) & (z GLUES y)

THEN *solve the problem*
ATTACH x ON y
by solving the sequence of sub-problems
APPLY z ON y
PRESS x ON y

Each rule in this space has an applicability condition that is less general than the Almost Necessary Condition and more general than the Almost Sufficient Condition. Also, it covers only instances that are analogous with Example 1.

Next, DISCIPLE looks in the knowledge base for objects satisfying the Almost Necessary Condition and call Explanation-i the properties of these objects that were used to prove that they satisfy the Almost Necessary Condition:

Explanation i:
(x ISA centering-device) & (y ISA chassis-assembly)&
(z ISA neoprene) & (z GLUES x) & (z GLUES y)

It uses the found objects to generate an instance of General Rule 1 (see figure 3) and asks the user to validate it:

May I solve the problem
ATTACH centering-device ON chassis-assembly
by solving the sub-problems
APPLY neoprene ON centering-device
PRESS centering-device ON chassis-assembly ?

Let us suppose that the user accepts this decomposition. In this case DISCIPLE computes a maximally specific common generalization of the Almost Sufficient Condition and Explanation i:

(z ISA adhesive) & (z GLUES x) & (z GLUES y)

This generalization is taken as the new Almost Sufficient Condition. Notice that this is always more specific than the Almost Necessary Condition because both the Almost Sufficient Condition and Explanation i are less general than the Almost Necessary Condition.

Coming back to step 6, DISCIPLE looks for other objects satisfying the Almost Necessary Condition and generates another instance of General Rule 1:

May I solve the problem
ATTACH centering-device ON chassis-assembly
by solving the sub-problems
APPLY scotch ON centering-device
PRESS centering-device ON chassis-assembly *?*

Let us suppose that the user rejects this decomposition. In this case DISCIPLE looks for the explanation of the near-miss because this explanation points to important object features which were not contained in Explanation 1. The explanation is that 'scotch' is not fluid (therefore, it might not be applied on a curved surface):

Failure explanation i: NOT (scotch TYPE fluid)

The negation of this explanation is used to specialize both bounds of the version space:

IF
G: (Almost Necessary Condition)
(z GLUES x) & (z GLUES y) & (z TYPE fluid)
S: (Almost Sufficient Condition)
(z ISA adhesive) & (z GLUES x) & (z GLUES y) & (z TYPE fluid)
THEN *solve the problem*
ATTACH x ON y
by solving the sequence of sub-problems
APPLY z ON x
PRESS x ON y

Positive examples generalize the upper bound of the version space while negative examples specialize both bounds. The termination condition is reached when the Almost Sufficient Condition becomes identical with the Almost Necessary Condition or when any generalization of the Almost Sufficient Condition is more general then the Almost Necessary Condition. In this case, the Almost Necessary Condition, the Almost Sufficient Condition and the General Rule 1 represent the learned rule.

5. Discussion and conclusions

DISCIPLE is an expert and learning system for weak theory domains. It integrates different problem solving and learning mechanisms.

In its present state, however, DISCIPLE is still much nearer to a simple Expert System Shell for building practical Expert Systems than to a really clever 'knowledge extractor'. Its means of extracting knowledge are still rather stereotyped and too inefficient. They are perfectly fitted for interaction with an everyday user who has a good, but not deep knowledge of his field. Nevertheless, the very fact that DISCIPLE has been built using Machine Learning techniques, will enable its learning modules to be improved separately and continuously, thus reaching a level of sophistication in the learning processes that may require the best experts in the field to answer its questions. This feature is far from negative since one must first build a Knowledge Base which is not too far from the desired one, and that contains most of the trivial information. Such a Knowledge Base is the indispensable starting point for building a really intelligent one, containing subtle concepts and able to do deep reasoning having to be acquired from a good human expert.

There are several weaknesses of the present version of DISCIPLE, that are currently being worked on. First of all, the method of finding an explanation is not powerful enough. Other sources of knowledge are needed, as well as meta-rules for finding far off explanations. Secondly, the empirical learning method has to be improved. Presently it is a highly controlled variant of the Version Space method (Mitchell, 78), where the sets S and G are restricted to contain one single element only.

There are also several lessons we have learned from this initial design of DISCIPLE. One is that coping with the complexity of real world applications requires using whatever learning techniques are available. Another is that full formalization of weak theories are harmful in the short time. Finally, we have found out that over-generalization is not only harmless but also useful and necessary, when interacting with a user.

DISCIPLE has been implemented in LE_LISP and we are running it on VAX-750, APPOLO, and MACINTOSH computers. It was also translated into COMMON-LISP for SUN stations and EXPLORER LISP-Machines. The following illustrates the interface of DISCIPLE on EXPLORER:

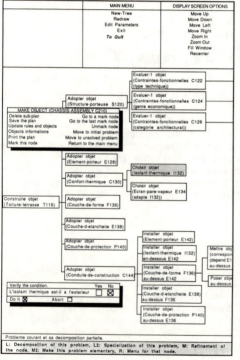

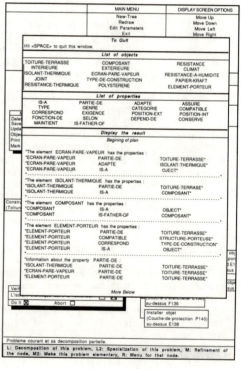

The performance of DISCIPLE in the technology design domain is very encouraging (Kodratoff & Tecuci, 1987). Presently, the Knowledge Base for the design of loudspeakers contains several hundreds of rules and objects. Work is in progress to apply DISCIPLE to Architecture and Air-traffic Control.

A more thorough presentation of DISCIPLE will be given in (Tecuci, 1988).

Acknowledgments

This work has been sponsored by PRC-GRECO 'Intelligence Artificielle' and the Romanian CNST. The paper has been written while one of the authors (Gheorghe Tecuci) was at LRI, on leave from his institute. His expenses have been taken in charge through an agreement between the French CNRS and the Romanian Academy of Sciences. We wish to express our gratitude to both these institutions.

References

Carbonell, J. G. (1986). Derivational analogy: a theory of reconstructive problem solving and expertise acquisition. In R. S. Michalski, J. G. Carbonell, T. M. Mitchell (Eds.), Machine learning: An artificial intelligence approach (Vol. 2). Los Altos, CA: Morgan Kaufmann.

Kodratoff, Y. (1985). Une théorie et une méthodologie de l'apprentissage symbolique. Actes COGNITIVA 85 (pp. 639-651). Paris.

Kodratoff Y., & Ganascia J-G. (1986). Improving the generalization step in learning. In R. S. Michalski, J. G. Carbonell, T. M. Mitchell (Eds.), Machine learning: An artificial intelligence approach (Vol. 2). Los Altos, CA: Morgan Kaufmann.

Kodratoff, Y., & Tecuci, G. (1987). Techniques of design and DISCIPLE learning apprentice. International Journal of Expert Systems, 1, 39-66.

Kodratoff, Y., & Tecuci, G. (1987). DISCIPLE: An integrated expert and learning system for weak theory domains. LRI Research Report, Orsay.

Langley, P. (1987). Proceedings of the Fourth International Workshop on MACHINE LEARNING. Irvine, CA: Morgan Kaufmann.

Michalski, R. S. (1983). A theory and a methodology of inductive learning. Artificial Intelligence, 20, 111-161.

Minsky, M. L. (1975). A framework for representing knowledge. In P. H. Winston (Ed.), The psychology of computer vision. New-York: McGraw-Hill.

Mitchell T. M. (1978). Version spaces: An approach to concept learning. Doctoral dissertation, Department of Electrical Engineering, Stanford University, Stanford, CA.

Mitchell, T. M., Carbonell, J. G., & Michalski, R. S. (1985). Machine learning: A guide to current research. Kluwer Academic Publishers.

Nilsson N. (1971). Problem solving methods in artificial intelligence. McGraw-Hill.

Quillian M. R. (1968). Semantic memory. In Minsky M. (Ed.) Semantic information processing. Cambridge, Mass: MIT Press.

Sridharan, N., & Bresina ,J. (1983). A mechanism for the management of partial and indefinite descriptions (Technical Report CBM-TR-134), Rutgers Univ.

Stefik M. (1980). Planning with constraints (MOLGEN: Part 1). Artificial Intelligence, 14, 111-139.

Tecuci, G. (1984). Learning hierarchical descriptions from examples. Computers and Artificial Intelligence, 3, 211-222.

Tecuci, G. (1988). DISCIPLE: Integrated learning for weak theory domains, Doctoral dissertation, Université de Paris-Sud, forthcoming.

THE ARIES CLUB — EXPERIENCE OF
EXPERT SYSTEMS IN INSURANCE & INVESTMENT

Anthony Butler
Colonial Mutual Life, 24 Ludgate Hill, London EC4
&
Gary Chamberlin
City University Business School, Northampton Square, London EC1

Abstract

The Aries Club was one of nine Alvey community clubs set up in the IKBS sector to promote the awareness of expert systems in industry. During the period 1985-87, the Club successfully developed two new prototype systems in the field of insurance. The first prototype was for fire insurance underwriting, and the second for selection of equities for the investment portfolio. The paper gives a view of the project as a whole, including the two systems, their implementation and characteristics in action. It discusses the main directions taken by the Club, its usefulness as a vehicle for awareness and learning, and the conclusions to be drawn from its experience.

1. OVERVIEW OF THE ARIES PROJECT

Stages of the Work

ARIES stands for "Alvey Research in Insurance Expert Systems". The Club came into being in Spring 1985 as a collaboration between a dozen insurance companies and the computer systems company Logica. Two insurance applications were chosen — the underwriting of commercial fire risks, and equity selection for the life office portfolio — and a budget of £250,000 was set. Half of the funds were to come from the Government via the Alvey Programme, and the other half from the Club Members. Membership of the Club expanded from the initial dozen companies, eventually to reach 30 in all. The 30 included some 18 insurance companies, 1 broker, 4 consultancies and 7 academic and professional bodies.

After the formation of a Steering Committee, and the agreement of Club rules and guidelines, project work itself began in September 1985. The plan was set out in 5 main stages as follows, and the work ran for a duration of 21 months:

1. Preliminary Analysis & Project Planning
2. Hardware & Software Selection

    3. Fire Risks System
    4. Equity Selection System
    5. Porting of Systems to Delivery Environment

Stage 1 was to do the preliminary knowledge elicitation, sketch out the domains in question and produce functional and design plans for the intended systems. It was completed in the first two months, and gave a basis for the equipment decision in Stage 2. The decision, which remained a controversial one in the Club, was to use Intellicorp's Kee on a Sperry Explorer machine. The chief advantage was that the Club was able to make use of a top-grade tool, optimising the productivity of the Logica team, and giving members knowledge of an expensive system that few would be likely to purchase individually. At the same time, the decision pushed the Club to address the crucial question of porting an expert system between development and delivery machines. This was tackled later, with considerable success, in Stage 5.

Stage 3, development of the Fire Risks system, occupied roughly the first half of 1986, and went ahead smoothly. The domain proved a tractable one, and divided easily into a set of logical subsections. A paper model of the experts' reasoning was produced, which proved not only a good tool for logical analysis but also an admirable means of communication between knowledge engineers, experts, users and system implementers. The system was demonstrated to Club Members in mid-1986, and was well received. The experts who had helped build it were pleased with its performance, and even preferred a few of its decisions to their own.

The Equity Selection system followed as Stage 4, with the main work done in the latter half of 1986. As expected, the domain was considerably more difficult to analyse. But with hard work on the part of experts and knowledge engineers, a very workable structure emerged. This contained two parts, a statistical analysis and a judgmental analysis, which complemented each other in an interesting way. Together, they gave rise to an expert system of some subtlety, whose most important feature was the responsive and co-operative character it showed in assisting the expert's concentration. The system was demonstrated in early 1987, and received with much enthusiasm.

The final stage of the work, Stage 5, was the porting exercise. The Club selected two PC shells, namely Crystal and Leonardo, and succeeded in translating both of the Kee/ Explorer systems to the PC in a surprisingly short time. The secret was to reject the Kee code itself, and to base the work on the paper model. The Kee/ Explorer version was of chief assistance in showing the implementer what the final system was intended to look like on the machine. The porting was soon completed, and Club Members received copies for use in their own offices. They provided not only good demonstration tools, but also ready-made models for further development and experimentation. When the project wound up in June 1987, its aims in terms of system development had been more than achieved.

Awareness & Learning

A main purpose of the Alvey community clubs is to promote expert systems awareness in industry. The Aries Club took pains to promote such awareness and learning during the project's currency. The aim was for a continuing flow of information, which was achieved by a number of means:

- Issued project documentation was far more detailed than in a normal DP project, every main Stage Report containing a detailed critique of the work done.

- Special open days were held for the Club Members, with large screen demonstrations of the prototype systems, and management overview by Logica and the Club's Technical Co-ordinators.

- Technical Workshops were run by the Logica project team, at which full exposition of the development and operation of the Equity Selection system was given.

- Steering Committee minutes included full reports on decisions taken and technical issues raised at each stage of the project.

In addition, the Club established Technical Working Parties in three relevant areas: a) Hardware & Software, b) Standards & Methodology, and c) Knowledge Acquisition & Formalisation. The Working Parties had the express aim of involving the general membership in the learning process. They met regularly for discussion and seminars, and to quiz Logica on recent developments in the project.

Selection of Application Areas

Criteria for the selection of expert system applications are undoubtedly important. Those use by Aries were largely as follows:

- The area should be representative of a mainstream company activity.

- It should be sufficiently complex to be convincing, but not so complex as to defy analysis in the project time available.

- It should contain aspects of qualitative reasoning, which it can with advantage mix with the more usual algorithmic methods.

- It must be capable of proper testing and validation.

- The identification of both experts and users must be possible, and the eventual functioning and level of use of the system must be clearly definable.

Selection of Software & Hardware

Once the initial knowledge elicitation had been done in Stage 1 of the project, there were some good pointers to software and hardware needs. A frame-based representation was appropriate, and both forward and backward chaining were required. Algorithmic processing would also be needed, and a good man-machine interface was essential.

A detailed evaluation of the available tools and equipment followed, and a final decision was made in favour of Kee software running on the TI Explorer as marketed by Sperry (now the Unisys Corporation). The decision was clinched by the very favourable conditions offered by Sperry. In fact, the needs of the Fire Risk system might have been satisfied by lower level tools, but the Kee/ Explorer combination was seen as highly desirable for tackling the Equity Selection project. The latter posed considerably more difficult problems of knowledge representation and inferencing.

KEE Software Environment

The Kee system is a complex and sophisticated environment for developing knowledge based systems. Although achieving full mastery of the tool would be a long-term operation — scope for an expert system version of the technical manual? — initial familiarisation for the project team proved straightforward. Some of the features from the Club's experience are as follows:

- Kee's power and flexibility allow elaborate software to be developed at almost frightening speeds. At times it seemed useful to have two people in front of the screen to help control the power!

- Rigorous documentation of the system architecture was very necessary, particularly to identify the place and function of each subroutine as built.

- In spite of the power of Kee, a surprising amount of Lisp coding was required. But Lisp could very readily be brought in to provide such facilities as "How?", "Help" and "What If?"

- Again in spite of the power, the system was slow to run. Aries found that a minimum configuration of 8Mb of main memory with 2 hard discs was essential.

- The size of the Kee system makes loading painfully slow, and the Explorer was normally left switched on during the project.

- On the positive side, input defaults helped speed the data entry process, and Kee's frame-based processing avoided much explicit calculation of intermediate results.

The Paper Model

The role of intermediate representations in Expert Systems has been much discussed. They can be described as structured diagrams which represent the expert's decision-making process. Both Aries systems use the idea in a very practical way, but under the friendlier name of "paper model". The Club was led into this practice almost by acci-dent. At the time when machine implementation of the Fire Risks system was due to begin, there was a delay in delivery of the Explorer. The project team adaptably used the time to develop a much more complete representation of the knowledge on paper, using box-and-arrow diagrams with the associated rule-sets, decision tables and so on.

This paper model gave greatly increased confidence to both experts and project team. It proved possible to dry-run the paper model using test cases from the experts, and to compare the model's decision with the experts' own. Fair to good agreement was obtained. Then improvements in the paper model as a result of the exercise made the agreement excellent.

The paper model also greatly improved communications with two other key groups — the users and the system implementers. Involvement of the users was thought *essential* from quite early on in the project. Everything that happened later on confirmed the importance of this view. Users for Fire Risks were senior branch office staff who, although experienced, would normally pass the more difficult cases to Head Office. The paper model was found to be readily understandable by them, and so acted as a rapid check and feedback mechanism.

Use of Prototyping

It was decided to use a prototyping approach from the beginning, but this was always combined with a strong sense of project discipline. Given the element of discipline, the Club came to view prototyping not as inimical to normal DP procedures, but as providing an added dimension of power and flexibility. Indeed on the Equity Selection project, the existence of prototypes was vital in keeping the lead expert's interest. For both systems, effectively the first prototype was the paper model itself. Then for Fire Risks, two Kee/ Explorer prototypes were successively produced. The first was in skeletal form, to verify the proposed system architecture, while the second fleshed out the skeleton. The development of Equity Selection went through more stages, owing to the added complexity of the domain. One major wrong turning was taken, but the prototyping approach helped make this apparent before too much time was lost.

Conclusion on the Club Endeavour

Did Aries Club members find their participation worthwhile? A survey conducted at the close of the project indicated that 90% or more of them did. The members agreed that Aries gave useful experience in expert systems at very little cost and risk to themselves. One big point was that the value obtained from the project was closely related to the amount of interest and effort put in by the member concerned. In particular, the Aries experts themselves found the exercise useful, revealing and enjoyable.

2. FIRE RISKS UNDERWRITING SYSTEM

Purpose of the System

The purpose of the system is essentially to make scarce underwriting expertise more widely available throughout the company. The main placing for the system would thus be in branch offices, as a tool to assist the less experienced underwriters. Its advantages in operation would be:

- To reduce the number of cases referred to Head Office.
- To ensure better control and consistency of branch office underwriting.
- To train new underwriting staff.

Knowledge Elicitation

The system's knowledge was derived from three experienced underwriters, each hailing from a different company. One of the experts took the lead, with the other two in supporting roles. Agreement between them on the nature and structure of the knowledge was very good indeed. Structured interviewing techniques were used in the elicitation, with the following features:

- All interviews were recorded, but not transcribed. They were followed immediately by a debriefing. The recordings were mainly used for cross-checking questions of fact.

- Two interviewers were generally present, with one in the lead role and one supporter. This was found to aid the flow of discussion.

- Anecdotes recounted by the experts played a vital role in uncovering areas of expertise not elicited by direct questioning.

- Examples and case studies used in the interviews were taken from real-life experience selected by the experts.

The basis of the work consisted of in-depth interviews with the lead expert. This was followed up by conferencing with two or more of the experts present at the same time, in order to provide a check. The conferencing worked well, because the experts had good underlying agreement and high mutual regard. (By contrast, in the Equity Selection case, one of the experts disagreed strongly with the approach of the others).

Early on in the interviews, it was found that Fire Risk assessment as a whole was too broad to handle within the scope of the project. To ensure adequate depth, the system was therefore limited to a single industry, the Clothing Trade. It was thought to be reasonably representative of the domain, rating at difficulty level 7 on an industry scale from 0 to 10. An operational underwriting system would of course need to encompass the other major industries. As it happens, the form of the Aries system is such that extension to other industries would be relatively straightforward.

General Description

The system proceeds by asking questions about six major factor areas, namely:

- Physical Construction of the Building(s)
- Heating Systems
- Trade Processes
- Management & Housekeeping
- Location (including Neighbouring Premises)
- Fire Protection Features

The answers to the questions will come from the underwriter's interpretation of a detailed survey report on the risk in question. The factor areas are pursued to different depths depending on the responses made, so the dialogue has a degree of intelligence and friendliness.

To give an example of the procedure, the Management & Housekeeping area takes account of 14 subfactors in all. Of these, some are deemed highly important, such as trade waste or smoking regulations, while others like stock control are of medium or low importance only. The response for each factor is coded on a 5-point scale:

Very Good	Good	Minor Adversity	Important Adversity	Fundamental Adversity

Reasoning then proceeds on such grounds, say, that a highly important factor coded as Fundamental Adversity will imply that the risk be rejected. Alternatively, several medium factors showing Good to Very Good will imply a modest discount to the premium rate, and so on. After considering each of the major areas in turn, the system gives as its output:

    a) A decision on whether to accept the risk.
    b) If it is acceptable, then a suggested premium rate.

The answers are found after combining the six major factor areas in a top-level analysis. The suggested premium rate comes from applying various discounts and loadings to a given base. The system, however, has no means of determining what the base should be — it must be input as a standard rate derived from the office's past experience, or perhaps from reference to industry data.

System Testing

Nine test cases were prepared, with each of the three experts testing all nine cases, giving 27 tests in all. The test data were surveyors' reports on given risks. From these, each expert assessed the correct system input values and gave his estimate for the final risk rating. The inputs and outputs were used first to test the paper model, and later on the machine implementation. To assist with the latter, a test harness was set up. This allowed entry to the system of a file of user responses together with their expected results, thus automating the process. Running the harness on a new release of the system enabled rule addition and other changes to be quickly tested. In the final form of the system, reasonable agreement was obtained in approximately 70% of the cases.

Features of the System

• An extensive explanation facility is provided so the user can review the system's reasons for a given recommendation.

• There is a "What If?" facility, so that the user can test the effect of changing the answer for particular factors.

• The conceptual version of the system (the Paper Model), has a top-level analysis, 6 major factor areas and c.100 subfactors.

• The system's first implementation, in Kee and Lisp on the Explorer machine, has c.200 rules operating on c.600 Kee objects.

- The ported version is written in Crystal on an IBM PC. In this form, the system has c.800 rules.

Evaluation of Fire Risks System

- The system is of relatively low complexity in AI terms. Acquiring, representing, applying, maintaining and modifying the knowledge was fairly straightforward.

- Sophisticated techniques were not needed — Uncertainty / Complex search/ Hypothesis formulation/ Meta-knowledge and so on do not appear in the system.

- The system does encapsulate useful and valid expertise on the assessment of Fire Risks in the clothing trade. In this sense, it readily qualifies as an expert system.

- Extension of the system beyond the Clothing Industry would not be difficult, involving mainly the adaptation of the Trade Processes module.

- Of the order of 30 major industries would need to be incorporated in this way to convert the Aries prototype into a fully operational system.

- The port of the system on to Crystal has shown that it can be delivered with the main functionality intact on an IBM PC.

3. EQUITY SELECTION INVESTMENT ADVISOR

A Two-Part System

The Aries Equity Selection system has two distinct parts. The first is based on a statistical analysis of the company in question, and is mainly retrospective. The second is a judgmental analysis, and is mainly prospective. Buy or no buy decisions emerge from the latter, while the statistical part provides a firm ground on which the key opinions can be based. The emphasis of the system is thus *co-operation* — co-operation between the two parts of the analysis, and co-operation between the user & the machine.

On the user level, the Equity Selection system contrasts vividly with Fire Risks. The latter's purpose is to make expertise more widely available in the company, and it is pitched for the less experienced underwriter. But Equity Selection is for the highly skilled fund manager or senior investment analyst. Its purpose is to aid concentration and so enable the daily decisions to be improved. It would not be suitable for the investment novice other than as a training aid.

Statistical Analysis

The statistical part of the system takes in standard data, say in Extel card form, in order to calculate the relevant financial ratios. In a fully operational system, use would be made of one or more of the online data services nowadays available. Aries, however, decided it should not expend resources in this direction. As a result, the Aries system does not implement the link, but uses instead a selection of data from a static file.

The hybrid nature of the system makes itself felt already at this stage. In fact, the statistical analysis requires also the input of qualitative information, provided by the user from Extel and other data in his possession. For example, questions might relate to the geographical spread of the business, or its seasonality, or to discontinuities in the share price caused say by a rights issue. (A fully fledged expert system would tackle many of these points automatically, but again the Aries resources were not sufficient for the Club to make the attempt).

Once the data, both numerical and qualitative, have been input, the statistical analysis uses normal forward chaining to reach its conclusions. These are expressed in such form as:

- P/E ratio is very high
- Credit control is erratic
- Share price performance is strong
- Gearing is moderately high

The conclusions are very flexible in the way they are expressed, being built up from a large number of atomic words and phrases. These atoms are held in a Kee knowledge base, to which pointers are set during the reasoning process. As a result, the text can be regrouped and displayed *at any time* it is needed. This feature becomes of great significance during the second, or judgmental, part of the analysis.

Judgmental Analysis

The second part of the system is an in-depth analysis of the company in question. The system puts up a series of query displays to the user to obtain his responses on the key factors in share selection. These are:

- Industry & Company Prospects
- Management & Ownership
- Financial Situation
- Professional Opinions in the City

Each key factor (apart from Financial Situation) has its analysis structured in two or three levels of questions. At the top level, the question is very blunt, eg:

"Do you consider the management: Very Good/ Very Bad/ Neither?"

A reply in one of the first two categories will settle the matter, but the third requires questioning at the next lower level. Thus, opinions will be sought concerning, say, the financial competence of the management, its dynamism, and its durability in office. Here again, firm answers will bring about a conclusion, but if there is doubt the questioning may continue to a further level of detail. The levels, in fact, do not go very deep in the Aries system. It is expected that each company taking up the model will customise it by implementing such further levels as accord with its own way of thinking in investment.

The crucial feature of the system comes into operation during the judgmental phase. As the questions are asked, so the information *particularly relevant to each* from the statistical analysis is displayed in a bulletin panel on the computer screen. The constructed text described above comes into its own here. In addition, there is a permanent display at the top of the screen of the main results from the earlier work. The final element to be mentioned is the projected financial situation, which pinpoints the company's cash flow as estimated over the next five years. In this way, the system fulfils its aim of bringing the totality of relevant information into sharp focus.

Once the main areas have been analysed, the system will come to a possible recommendation to buy the given share (or not) on four possible grounds:

- Growth
- Recovery
- Income
- Discount to Assets

The main method used is to weight the market P/E ratio of the share according to the user's opinions, and to compare this moderated value with the actual P/E. If the result is favourable, then a Buy recommendation will be given, with the reason. But if none of the four grounds is satisfied, the answer is "No Buy".

The system provides a full explanation facility so the user can quickly trace the steps by which the recommendation was reached. In addition, it gives a price range within which the result holds — effectively saying:

"Buy provided the price is less than X", or
"Do not buy if the price is more than Y".

The "What If?" Facility

Both parts of the system allow the user to do a sensitivity analysis by means of the "What If?" facility. Thus, having been through the question session (either for statistical or judgmental analysis), various of the opinions entered can be changed, and the results recalculated. For example, if there are rumours of a probe by the DTI, or new evidence emerges of the company's book of bad debts, then certain of the entries will be liable to change. Not least will be the professional opinions in the City, which always need to be taken into account. The analyst will have to examine such doubtful areas, which the system easily enables him to do. The "What If?" facility can also be effected on the share price value.

The User Interface

One principle in constructing the system has been to provide a clear and easily manipulable interface. This requirement is vital for the investment setting, where time and timing is of the essence. The Kee/ Explorer combination provides an excellent tool in this respect, with its powerful windowing system. Data input is mainly controlled via a mouse (although numerical data must be provided on-line, or from a conventional file). A good example of the flexibility is in using the "What If?" option. A complete screen of all the judgments entered is displayed, and the user can instantly move to any one of these to amend it. He can then view the revised conclusions, but still revert to the original conclusions on demand.

It is the user interface that is the major casualty on making the port to the PC version of the system. The shell Leonardo was used for the purpose, and was found very adequate for the main analytical aspects of the system. But the PC itself, and the main software currently available for it, cannot compete with the fully functional WIMP style of Kee & Lisp on the Explorer.

Technical Features of System

- The system is frame-based, with some use of multi-valued slots. It makes great use of the Kee Active Images and Active Values (Demons).

- The statistical analysis uses forward chaining in its reasoning. The judgmental analysis uses explicit resolution control, and includes backward chaining in its strategies.

- Producing the best interface required considerable use of Lisp in addition to Kee. About 30% of the final system is written in Lisp.

- No internal use is made of uncertainty, in terms of probability, certainty factors or fuzzy logic. Uncertainty is essentially handled through the user's responses to questions in the main dialogue.

- The system has been parameterised where possible, to help provide for its customisation by individual companies.

- The system is complex in its structure, taking account of some 150 factors in all.

Evaluation of Equity Selection System

The system can be criticised in that it contains relatively little algorithmic computation. Its cash flow forecasting is fairly crude, and it does little in the way of financial modelling. Again, although the interface is good, there is no facility for graphical display of data, eg: a graph of earnings over time, or of price relative to the FT indices. Such features will undoubtedly be a part of the complete equity investment system, when it finally arrives.

In the meantime, what the Aries system has successfully done is to model one widely accepted approach to making everyday investment decisions. In action, the system is an impressive demonstrator, as those who have seen it will avow. It captures much of the tenor and flavour of the equity manager's work. Its potential for scanning shares at a faster rate and more consistently than at present possible is enormous. The major lack is the on-line link to Extel information and other financial data-bases, but it can only be a matter of time before that link is commercially implemented. So although the complete equity investment system is still some way off in the future, the Aries system, or something very akin to it, will be an essential component.

4. CONCLUSIONS

The Club's experience shows that expert systems are still very much a leading edge activity. Though many shells and other products are flowing on to the market, developing genuinely useful systems is an activity most often requiring substantial skill and non-trivial investment. The exceptions which stand out are those such as simple tutoring systems or the automation of procedure manuals, which can often be implemented quickly on a good PC shell.

On the hardware and software side, the evaluations carried out during the project show that although shells have definite limitations, some very good ones are now available. They have, however, only very recently begun to offer the strength and facilities which are required for a mature development. On the Kee/ Explorer system, the power is undoubtedly impressive, especially with regard to the man-machine interface and the internal reasoning.

In conclusion, can expert systems be relevant to decision-making in the insurance and investment sphere? The Aries Club's experience has shown that they can. The technology is there for representing knowledge to the expert level, and for delivering it in working form on the selected hardware. But a number of problems still remain, not the least of which are:

1. Integrating the expert systems component with existing DP systems
2. Gaining user acceptance for the resulting products.
3. Quantifying the cost-benefit advantages.

Hard work will be needed to overcome these difficulties but there is little doubt they will be tackled in earnest in the foreseeable future.

On the demand side, pressures to achieve successful expert system implementations in the financial sector are enormous. The modern drive for communications has resulted in one worldwide financial market place. The skills required to operate in that marketplace are scarce, and any means for their amplification must clearly be seized upon. There may be only one chance to get the next deal right, but the prize for successful action will be greatly increased profitability. Properly implemented expert systems will give the company new leverage on a worldwide scale.

Discussion among Aries Club members has shown there to be many fruitful areas for expert systems in insurance. Thus, assessing risks is a substantial part, but only a part, of an integrated system for ratemaking, underwriting, administration and claims. Possession of such a fully integrated system would give the insurer a large competitive advantage. Other areas suggested are: the training of sales staff, and their support via a personal financial planning package; dealing with complex legislation, particularly in the pensions area; and the whole field of investment, including both fundamental and technical analysis, and portfolio planning itself at the top level.

STRUCTURED TECHNIQUES FOR THE DEVELOPMENT OF EXPERT
SYSTEMS

Mark Thomas
Ernst & Whinney Management Consultants
Becket House
1 Lambeth Palace Road
London SE1 7EU

Abstract:

   Expert systems provide a cost-effective approach to
solving certain types of business problem. A planned and controlled
approach to developing these systems is needed.
   Differences between Expert Systems and traditional DP
systems, both in architecture and use, imply that the traditional
system development cycle is inappropriate for Expert Systems. A
modified development cycle, involving a semi-formal specification,
but based on fast prototyping is described.
   The cycle has four stages:
°   Investigation;
°   Prototyping;
°   Development; and
°   Delivery.
   The deliverables from each phase are outlined and a
distinction is drawn between those for which existing techniques
(possibly modified) are appropriate, and those for which new techniques have been developed. This paper does not describe the
techniques themselves.

1 Introduction

     Over the last two or three years, Expert Systems have
been chosen increasingly frequently as a means of solving a particular class of business problem in which scarce expertise in a
well-defined domain is repeatedly demanded.
     The problem of how best to approach the development of
Expert Systems is one which still faces many organisations, and is
the subject of this paper.
     The newness of the technology of Expert Systems and the
differences in architecture between Expert Systems and traditional
Data Processing systems have led to a wide variation in approaches
to the development of Expert Systems. Typical approaches have
been to ignore Expert Systems, to build systems in an unstructured
way using iterative prototyping, to attempt to apply conventional
DP system development techniques to Expert Systems, to develop
structured techniques for Expert System development.

This paper describes a methodology for the Expert System
development cycle used by Ernst & Whinney, which falls into the fourth
category. The methodology described here is one of a series of inter-
related methodologies as illustrated below.

Figure 1: Interrelationships of the Methodologies

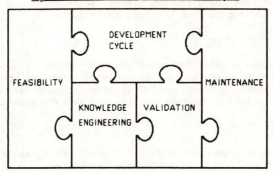

The methodologies illustrated are:
° Feasibility: assessing the technical and business feasibility of constructing an Expert system;
° Development Cycle: (the subject of this paper) structuring
  the development project;
° Knowledge Engineering: the techniques used in analysing
  and designing Expert Systems;
° Validation: the testing of systems;
° Maintenance: controlling change and ensuring that the
  system remains up to date.
The scope of this paper is to describe the structure of
the development cycle, from the point at which an initial assessment
of feasibility has been made through to the stage of implementation
of the system. Although references are made to techniques for
knowledge engineering and validation, these topics are not discussed
in detail.
   The methodology is most appropriate to development of
systems where the domain of application is well-understood and the
reasoning used is deterministic and monotonic - that is to say,
 the forming of certain and unalterable conclusions is possible.
Domains satisfying these criteria have been identified in fields
as diverse as Telecommunications, Pensions, Economic Investment
Appraisal, Banking and Taxation, and the methodology used in
constructing them.
   In practice, the methodology has been found to provide
significant advantages over an unstructured approach including
the following: first, that it ensures that the system is well-
documented in case of any discontinuity in the progress, structure
or staffing of the project;

second, that it assists in the decomposition of the domain into
appropriate sub-domains; and third, that many of the diagrams
produced are readily understood by the expert and thus enable the
expert to verify that knowledge has been accurately engineered.

Significant areas in which the method remains un-
developed are in the process of knowledge acquisition, which is
not described, and rule induction and probabilistic reasoning for
which analytical techniques have not been defined.

2 Characteristics of expert systems

There are several important characteristics of Expert
Systems which are not shared by most traditional batch and on-line
DP systems; these have implications for a successful approach to
development. The principal characteristics are described below.

2.1   Architecture

The architecture of an Expert System, particularly a
shell-based system, might typically be as given below:

Figure 2: Architecture of an Expert System

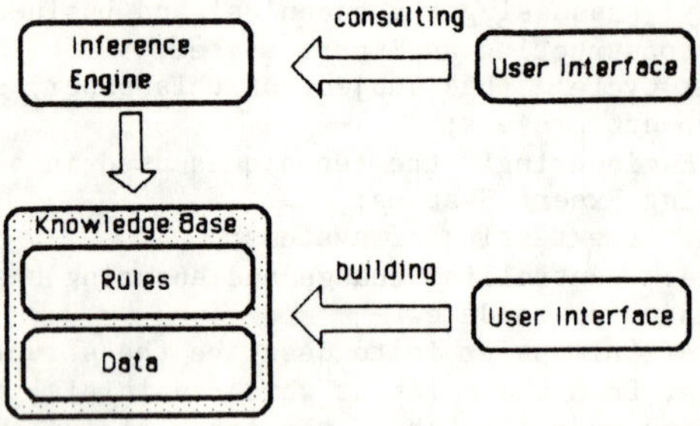

The expert system will typically consist of a knowledge
base, an inference engine and two user interfaces.

The knowledge base is application dependent, it contains
knowledge in the form of logical rules and data, and objects on
which the rules operate; it also contains facts, questions, default
values and other constructs needed in the system.

The inference engine is usually application independent;
this component of the system processes the rules and makes deductions
from them.

The two user interfaces are application independent;
one is the system building interface for construction and maintenance
of the knowledge, it allows the user to enter rules, facts, questions,
defaults etc to the knowledge base; the other is the consultation

interface, which allows the user to ask questions of the system, to answer questions posed and to request explanation of conclusions reached or questions posed by the system.

The application independent components, the inference engine and user interfaces, are often marketed as 'shells' into which the knowledge for a particular domain can be inserted. The implications of this architecture are that development productivity is potentially very high.

2.2   User Interface

A unique characteristic of Expert Systems is that they are 'transparent': that is, their reasoning is visible to the user. During a consultation, the user can ask the system for explanations of the reason it asks a given question or the reasoning it uses to arrive at its conclusions.

This facility may make it far easier for a user to understand the internal workings of an Expert System than a DP system.

2.3   Specification

In an Expert System, where specification of function implies logical specification of the system, to specify fully the functions of the system requires almost the same amount of work as actually constructing the system.

2.4   Sizing

The principal difference between the sizing of an Expert System and that of a traditional DP system is that, for the latter, the main determinants of size are data storage and transaction volumes, while for the former the main determinant is the complexity and breadth of the knowledge base.

2.5   Development and delivery

In Expert Systems development, the shell or other tool used for delivery of the final system may not be the tool which is best for development of the system.

2.6   Validation

The testing of Expert Systems is a difficult area. The aims of testing are to ensure the consistency, completeness and validity of the knowledge base and to check for standard software bugs.

The complexity of the logic may have the effect that the time to test an Expert System exhaustively rises exponentially with the number of factors it considers in producing its results. This means that, in practice, a large system cannot be tested exhaustively.

The types of problem to which Expert Systems are applied
are very different from those suited to solution by traditional DP
techniques, which often have a single verifiable solution, for
example, finding the total commission earned by an individual
during a particular month. Expert Systems, on the contrary, often
reason with uncertain or incomplete information and produce results
which are 'probably correct'.
        In stark contrast to many other computer systems, there-
fore, Expert Systems cannot be fully tested and if they could,
would not necessarily be expected to produce a 100% success rate.
For an Expert System the goal is different: to be cost-effective
they need not be perfect; like human experts, they should be treated
with caution until they have proved themselves.

2.7   Implications of the Expert Systems characteristics

        The difficulty of sizing and specifying Expert Systems
means that the traditional approach of going through a full specification process for the entire system before starting to construct
it is inappropriate. The logical specification is best supplemented
by a first-cut physical model, or prototype.
        The productivity and user-friendliness of the systems
also suggest that a fast prototyping approach might be a suitable
approach to development.
        The distinction between the environment in which the
system is developed and that in which it runs and the difficulty
of validating Expert Systems both indicate the importance of a
formal or semi-formal specification of the systems: one in order
to be sure that the system is portable, the other in order to
provide a statement of requirements against which to test the
system.

3 Expert systems development cycle

        This consideration of the characteristics of Expert
Systems leads to a systems development cycle based on prototyping
and formal specification and split into four stages:
   °   the investigation phase;
   °   the prototyping phase;
   °   the development phase; and
   °   the delivery phase.
        The first three phases involve the use of formal
specification techniques.

3.1   Phase 1: The Investigation Phase

        The purpose of this phase is to define the final
system's objectives and the scope of the work to be done and to
begin to understand the domain of interest.

The major tasks of this phase are to define the scope
and objectives of the final system, define success criteria for
the system, segment the problem to be solved, make a tentative
selection of the development tool, identify the source of the
expertise, identify users who can assist with development and
finally, to familiarise the knowledge engineers with the domain.

Defining the scope and objectives of the final system
requires consideration of business objectives to be met, the domain
and its boundaries, the expert, the users contexts from which the
problem will be addressed, interfaces with other systems and the
use of results. It also provides a suitable point to re-assess
feasibility.

Although the basis for defining success criteria for
the system is subjective, the criteria themselves must be objectively
measurable, eg. gives correct advice 80% of time; produces savings
of 20% in staff time; ensures consistency of decisions or preserves
expertise.

Segmenting the problem(s) involves segmenting the
domain, defining the interaction between segments and identifying
the most promising kernel.

It is necessary, at this stage, to make a tentative
selection of development tool. As noted above, the tool best
suited to development may not be the same as that used for delivery.

Identifying the source(s) of the expertise is a step
which is crucial to the success of the project: a substantial
involvement from an expert may be needed.

It is similarly important to identify users who will
assist with the development and to familiarise the knowledge
engineers (ie. those who elicit and structure the knowledge for
the system) with the background to the domain.

With these tasks completed, it should be clear whether
or not the system is feasible and how it should be tested, and
work can begin on the prototype phase.

Techniques have been developed which are modifications
of a standard systems analysis technique, data-flow diagrams, for
definition of domain and boundaries, segmentation of domain,
definition of the intended integration of the system with existing
systems and defining the context in which the system will be used.

New techniques, based on the use of Knowledge Base Maps,
a technique for representing the structure of knowledge in a way
which is independent of the tool used to implement the system,
have been developed to record the high level structure of the
system.

The deliverables from this phase will be:
° statement of requirements;
° high-level system model;
° statement of system success criteria.

In many cases, a further deliverable, the sampler, may usefully be produced. The sampler is a mini-prototype taking approximately 1 day's work and dealing with one small element of the domain.

3.2   Phase 2:   The Prototype Phase

This phase has two distinct parts: the design of the knowledge base and the construction of the prototype. Prototyping will thus involve carrying out knowledge engineering for kernel, constructing tool-independent 'paper model' defining rules and data and finally constructing the prototype. Techniques have been developed which are modifications of existing systems analysis techniques for defining the structure of the data or objects considered by the system. New techniques, again based on the use of Knowledge Base Maps, are used for defining the content of the knowledge base in a tool independent way.

The value of the prototype should be that it communi-cates to the users and to senior management the likely scope and value of the final system, that it communicates quickly to the expert how successful the knowledge base so far constructed could be and that it enables an accurate assessment of the scale of the project to be made. For these reasons, a prototype should be produced fairly quickly and formally reviewed.

The purpose of the review is to establish what will be the scale of the final system, whether the tool/language chosen has enough expressive power and suitable modes of inference and whether it can cope with a system of the size proposed. Both experts and users need to be heavily involved during the con-struction and review of the prototype.

The deliverables from this phase are a 'paper model' of the prototype system, a prototype, a review of the prototype and a project plan and budget.

3.3   Phase 3:   The Development Phase

The main purpose of the development phase is to produce a completed system segment. The main task in this phase will be to consider the review and enhance and extend the prototype and its paper model, as necessary. During this stage, and for the remainder of the development, traditional project management techniques can be employed.

The environment for the final system should now be selected this may be the same as the development tool; if it is not, then the paper model should ensure that there are minimal problems in transporting the prototype.

The next stage of work is to refine the prototype to produce a final system. This may involve amending and enhancing the logic and the knowledge, improving the user interface, building interfaces with other systems, or improving performance.

When the system has been refined to the stage where it is acceptable to the expert, it must then be formally tested. The criteria for testing are derived from the system objectives and success criteria already identified. Problems and techniques of testing are not discussed here.

Having tested the system segment and found that it has met the success criteria, the development team will release it into the user environment.

The techniques used in this phase are essentially the same as those used in the prototype phase. Techniques for validation are the subject of a separate methodology.

The products of this phase are a detailed test plan, test results and a tested system segment.

3.4   Phase 4:   The Delivery Phase

As stated earlier, the system, even when it has been released, will probably not be perfect. For this reason, it must initially be treated with caution (analogous to the 'probationary period' of a human expert newly recruited into the organisation): its decisions should be independently verified until it has proved itself in practice.

During this period, the performance of the system will continue to be monitored in a formal way to enable the production of an accurate statement of the success of the system as measured against criteria originally defined and a wish list for enhancements.

During the delivery phase, certain tasks must be undertaken in preparation for future enhancements or modifications. These include: monitoring of bugs and wish list and production of a source list, or inventory, showing the sources for all rules and the frequency with which they change.

4   Summary

This paper has described a methodology which, while recognising the unique characteristics of Expert Systems, follows traditional DP practice where possible.

The diagram below illustrates the main deliverables from each phase.

Figure 3:   Deliverables by Phase

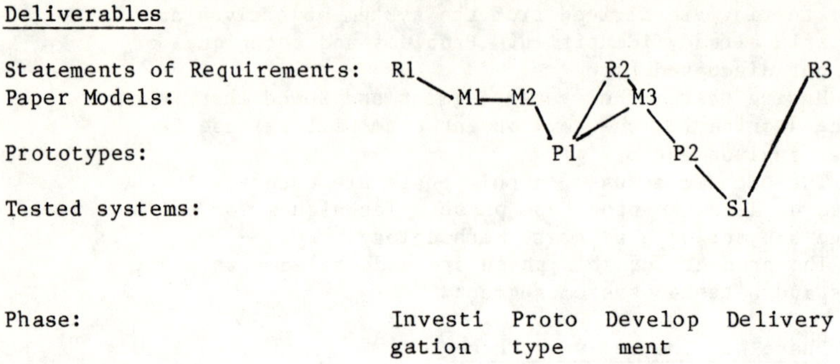

Deliverables

Statements of Requirements: R1   R2   R3
Paper Models: M1—M2   M3

Prototypes: P1   P2

Tested systems: S1

Phase: Investi Proto Develop Delivery
                                gation   type   ment

        The content of the deliverables from each phase has
been described, and mention made of the techniques used for their
production. By the early use of prototyping techniques, an accurate
method of sizing the system has been demonstrated, and a controlled
development facilitated. An approach to documentation which aids
both design and maintenance has been indicated though the techniques
to be used have not been described in detail.

RESCU REVISITED
A Review of a Practical Real-Time Expert System

Dr R Leitch
Intelligent Automation Laboratory
Department of Electrical and Electronic Engineering
Heriot-Watt University
Edinburgh
EH1   2HT

M R W Dulieu
Systems Designers Scientific
Pembroke House
Pembroke Broadway
Camberley
Surrey
GU15   3XD

Abstract

This paper sets out to relate some of the theoretical
requirements for industrial real-time Knowledge Based Systems (KBS) to
a practical development, the Alvey RESCU system. It outlines the
fundamental aspects of KBS technology relevant to real-time systems
and discusses how a number of these were handled within RESCU. An
overview of other prototype systems is presented and comparisons made
between their approaches and that of RESCU. The paper concludes with
a discussion of some of the lessons learned during the project and
makes suggestions for further work.

Introduction

RESCU has been widely recognised as one of the more successful
Alvey community club projects. The club consisted of twenty three
industrial partners, three universities and a systems contractor,
pioneered the formation of community clubs and has been in existence
for two years. It has resulted in the implementation of a working
real time system on a real life industrial plant, and represents one
of the most advanced practical demonstrations of real time KBS to
date. The application, the quality control of a chemical process, is
one which is not susceptible to conventional, algorithmic, process
control methods. It therefore requires experienced and highly skilled
operators to carry out the quality function. The functional objective
of the project, to mimic the performance of these operators, produced
a set of requirements that could not be adequately met by existing
KBSs. It was decided, therefore, to design and implement a Knowledge
Representation Language (KRL) with the specific attributes required
for continuous reasoning under time constraints. This KRL provides a
comprehensive set of primitives and represents one of the very few
KRLs specifically developed for real-time applications. The current
application at ICI has validated most of the functionality of the KRL
and indicated some additional desirable features. This paper relates
the RESCU KRL to theoretical requirements and compares the approach to
other prototype systems.

Requirements on Real-Time Knowledge Based Systems

In the context of industrial operations a real-time system must interact with a dynamic process. Systems must therefore be able to operate continuously, must be reactive to changing external factors and must operate under time constraints which will vary according to the process being monitored. The fundamental need is, therefore, for a continuous reasoning KBS able to operate within a given set of time limits. Systems of this type present problems to the KBS developer which are particular to continuous systems. Whilst little theoretical work is being done, developers tending to produce ad hoc solutions, some aspects can be identified. These cover the requirements to cater for dynamism, temporal memory, uncertainty and limited resources in terms of computer power and available processing times.

Dynamism is the most obvious aspect; a KBS operating in a process environment must be capable of maintaining a view of its world which is consistent with reality. This requires that the knowledge base must be updated at a frequency defined by the application, and that either a sampling approach must be adopted or that an interrupt facility must be provided. It should be noted that very little work has been done on KBSs operating in an asynchronous environment.

To maintain a consistent view of its world a real-time KBS must realise when its data is out of date and when it is still required. It must know when an assertion can be replaced by a later assertion or an actual measurement and where and when that assertion must be retained (and time stamped) for the purpose of reasoning about, for example, trends. It is also necessary to know when a given piece of information is irrelevant or suspect because of the time difference between assertion time and knowledge use time. These requirements imply a need for "memory" and the ability to "forget".

The treatment of uncertainty is a general requirement within KBSs. Indeed, a fundamental advantage of a KBS is its ability to handle uncertainty, and this requirement is not particular to continuous systems. It is clear, however, that a special factor in industrial process related systems is that they will almost invariably use data collected from sensors and hence must incorporate mechanisms, either knowledge or statistically based, for sensor validation. Other ways in which uncertainty can be present in a KBS involve imprecision, incompleteness and inconsistency. Imprecision can arise either from the quality of sensor data, where it can be mitigated by knowledge based validation techniques such as the employment of 'belief' factors; or from the quality of the knowledge embodied in the KB itself. This can arise, in a rule based system, from missing, conflicting, or redundant rules. These problems can be mitigated by the use of conventional software engineering methods such as network checking and, to an extent, by the use of some form of deep knowledge or causal model.

Deep models can also assit in the handling of incomplete and inconsistent data. The whole area of uncertainty is currently a very active one in AI research and this activity has given rise to the sets of techniques known as Truth Maintenance Systems (TMS). Such systems are able to reason with multiple hypotheses whilst maintaining a record of support for each hypothesis. Other main techniques currently employed for representing and reasoning about uncertainty are Bayesian Inference, Fuzzy Set Theory and the approach using certainty factors originally developed in MYCIN (1).

There is a further aspect of real-time KBS design which, whilst
it is more environmental than intrinsic, is fundamental to success in
the real world. This is the need for the system to interface to human
operators in a 'co-operative' manner and one with which operators feel
comfortable and confident. This implies a critical need for a
properly engineered and purpose designed HCI and a 'justification'
rather than a mere 'explanation' system.

In summary, a real-time KBS needs the ability to operate in a
dynamic, time constrained environment; it must be able to maintain a
consistent set of beliefs about itself and its world; it must be able
to reason with and about time; it must be able to reason with and
about inconsistent, uncertain and incomplete information; it must
interface with its human 'colleagues'. These factors are not
particular to RESCU, they must be handled in any real time KBS. The
next section describes how some of these aspects were covered within
RESCU.

Analysis of the RESCU Technology

Within RESCU the KBS process is one of a number of major
sub-systems. The KBS process itself, consisting of knowledge based
and inference mechanisms is overviewed in this section. A further and
substantial, part of the total system consists of conventional
software components handling such areas as external communications,
logging, message monitoring and operator interfaces. These areas are
not further detailed in this paper; however it is worth noting that
the ability to mix AI routines with conventional procedural programs
is a useful approach when developing practical systems. This approach
is well supported by POPLOG, the AI development environment used in
the project. An early project activity was to review the then (1984)
available commercial expert systems. It became clear that none met
the requirements and the decision was made to specify and build a KRL
suitable for real-time continuous operation.

Knowledge Representation

Knowledge representation in RESCU is entirely rule-based. This
resulted from a conscious decision to adopt an established and well
understood technology rather than the then emerging techniques of,
say, frame based representation or object oriented programming. These
techniques would certainly be incorporated in some areas at least,
were the project starting now (June 1987).

The KBS process consists of two major components; the first is
the knowledge base itself, developed in the RESCU KRL and consisting
of active and passive knowledge. The other component is a set of
utilities, written in POP11, these include reasoning mechanisms, a
tracker or executive and other routines for manipulation of the
knowledge base. Overall control of the knowledge base activities is
maintained by a knowledge based scheduler, itself written in the RESCU
KRL.

The passive knowledge sources are declarative in nature and are
used to provide knowledge about plant variables and their relationship
to each other. They represent process knowledge recording the facts
and relationships assumed true in a given process and include
knowledge about the basic chemistry of the process and engineering
knowledge about the plant. This presents an explicit model of the

process under observation; the knowledge represented was mainly
obtained from design documentation, plant chemists and engineers.
     An example of a passive rule follows. This type of rule
indicates a product specification (in a real example XXXX and YYYY
would be replaced by chemical data).

     RULE Spec_derived_requirements_for_feedstock_synprol

        IF Spec_feedstock_code = Spec_XXXX_code THEN

             Spec_uses_XXXX   IS TRUE;

             Spec_XXXX   IS Spec_feedstock;

             Spec_molar   IS

                 (Qual_YYYY_to_molar_A_series(Spec_final_YYYY_max) +

                 (Qual_YYYY_to_molar_A_series(Spec_final_YYYY_min))

                 /2;

        END_IF

     END_RULE

     This knowledge source operates on a data base consisting of
both asserted facts and of current facts to give a description of the
current plant state. Uncertainty is handled by each state having
associated with it a 'degree of confidence' in the current value of
that parameter. This 'degree of confidence' is a decimal value in the
range 0-1 and expresses the likelihood of the value of the state
variable being correct. These values are updated as evidence
increasing or decreasing confidence is measured or inferred. In the
case of rules with compound antecedents a max-min formulation, as in
fuzzy logic, is employed. Uncertainty is also propagated within the
KRL using rule conditions in accordance with conventional probability
theory.
     The KRL also allows for the explicit representation of time.
Both antecedents and consequents of rules can be qualified by a scan
number, which can be related to absolute time, and by a time validity
value. These temporal qualifiers are used by the inferencing
mechanisms to determine the value of consequent or antecedent for
forward or backward reasoning at a given scan number. These
mechanisms are clearly necessary given the requirement to reason both
with and about time.
     Active knowledge sources are procedural in nature and are used
to represent the main knowledge elicited from the plant operators,
the heuristics for how they go about their job. Active sources
utilise the passive knowledge previously discussed and specify the
actions necessary to carry out a particular task. In the actual ICI
system there are five active knowledge sources covering such tasks as
process monitoring and batch quality assessment. The active knowledge
sources are closely coupled to the external world as, in general, they
either receive information from the plant or present it, as advice to
the operators. They are typically of the form: ON condition, DO

action as in the example (again in reality ZZZZ is replaced by chemical data):-

    from: ACTION Reconcile_formulate_conclusions

    ON analysis_and_stoichiometric_close AND

       (NOT analysis_and_ZZZZ_cutoff_close) DO

       ;;; reconcile analysis and stoich - update ZZZZ_cutoff

       reconcile_code = 2

       do_update_ZZZZ_cutoff = True;

    END ON

Inferencing Mechanism

A central component of the RESCU KBS is the inference engine which provides four standard inference mechanisms: single and multiple backward chaining and single and multiple forward chaining. These mechanisms are invoked by the active knowledge sources to manipulate the passive knowledge sources and draw inferences. The inference engine also co-ordinates the flow of information between knowledge bases via a shared working memory or 'blackboard'. This blackboard maintains the current set of values and their associated likelihoods and also records how a value was generated and whether it was measured or inferred. An inferred value will be updated when a measurement is available. An entry on the blackboard consists of a structured data record supporting dynamic values for the attribute, its current confidence factor, temporal information and pointers to associated values. These entities allow the inference engine to handle uncertainty and to reason with time.

Entries on the blackboard include the following fields:-

NAME	VALUE TYPE	VALUE	CONFIDENCE
TIME STAMP	TIME VALIDITY	PARENT	DEPENDENTS

The parent and dependent entries are used in the generation of explanation and justification messages. A typical blackboard entry, in this case a value frame, appears as:-

```
        Value type:       REAST_attribute
        item - name:      <Attribute vol_in>
        timevalidity:     8
        timestamp:        8
        value:            28
        reason:           REASR_inferred
        parent:           <Definition - anonymous>
        usedlist:         [<*REAST_attribute-<Attribute
                             vol_recommended>AT8=28*>]
        dependantlist:    []
        assertionid:      <false>
```

Real Time Control

An essential difference between conventional and real-time KBSs is that in the latter explicit control over the progress of the reasoning process is a requirement. Real-time control of knowledge base activities is still an open issue and so far most systems define the complete KBS as a single activity under a real time scheduler. The approach within RESCU was to define a number of competing KBS activities each of which can be separately scheduled and allowed to run to completion. This approach avoids problems of inconsistency within the working memory of the KBS but can imply limitations in the time allowable for an activity. In the case of RESCU it was possible to so partition the Knowledge Base that it was able to stay consistent with the plant. The tracker monitors the time taken for each reasoning activity and ensures that it remains compatible with the overall process. All activities within the knowledge based process are under the control of a scheduler designed specifically for managing the KBS activities and itself written in rule form, using the RESCU KRL. Within each system cycle the scheduler, which is itself an active knowledge source, initiates a KBS activity consisting of a concatenation of active knowledge sources. These activity initiations are the consequents of rules of which the antecedents are, for example, another activity being completed or a specified time having elapsed.

The RESCU KRL in Use

The objective within RESCU is to offer advice and recommendations such that a consistent product quality is attained. This implies identifying the purity of certain components of the process of which the state variables are inaccessible. This is done by inferring these values from variables which can be measured. It is also necessary to estimate the errors of measuring instruments. The task strategy centres upon a model based state identification procedure in which active knowledge sources are defined to implement sub-procedures for process monitoring, quality estimation and so on. These active sub-systems are interconnected through the activity of the inference mechanism. Starting from a set of hypotheses the RESCU system estimates the quality of the current batch. In doing this the passive knowledge of the process chemistry is used. On detection of a discrepancy between estimate of quality hypotheses are generated and tested to find a most plausible explanation and the system state updated accordingly. This new state variable will be inferred using the levels of confidentce factors previously described and the new variable will itself be assigned a certainty factor.

A major advantage of the RESCU KRL is its capability to represent time in both the conditions and consequences of rules. This is necessary to model the changing behaviour of a plant or process over time. The ICI application, whilst requiring that time stamps and scan numbers were recorded, made little use of the ability to relate conditions and conclusions at different times. However this facility has been demonstrated using simulation and found to be both expressive and general.

RESCU in Comparison with Other Prototypes

      In this section the techniques used in RESCU to approach the
special problems of real time systems are compared with other systems
where results have been published. The systems considered are:-

      ESCORT - the real time shell developed by Pactel(2)

      EXTASE - an alarm processing expert system developed by CGE
                (France) (3)

      REACTOR - operators assistant for nuclear powerplants, E.G. &
                G. Idaho (4)

      PROP   - an expert system for monitoring water pollution in
                power plants developed by CISE s.p.a. of Milan (5)

      This list, and the comparison section itself, is necessarily
brief, a more detailed treatment will appear in a further paper by one
of the authors (Leitch).
      As previously discussed, a RT KBS must be able to cope with
dynamism, with temporal memory and with uncertainty. RESCU handles
the first of these by so structuring the KBS process that each task
can run to completion. So far all reported RT systems have adopted
this approach. The more comprehensive alternative, of providing a
real time interrupt handling system is extremely difficult with a KBS
where reasoning is not a simple progression.
      To cope with the problems of memory and the temporal nature of
process information RESCU provides time stamped data items and is able
to refer both to the specific time of an event's occurence and to the
interval of time for which that event may be valid. ESCORT provides a
similar mechanims, associating time intervals with hypotheses to
enable the system to reason with historical data. PROP recognises the
need for temporal information handling but the mechanisms it uses are
unclear from published material.
      The problem of reasoning over time is handled within RESCU by
the modular reasoning approach previously discussed. ESCORT uses a
graceful degradation approach where events are assigned a priority
rating and only high priority events processed when time becomes a
constraint. EXTASE uses best first conflict resolution to investigate
the most important hypotheses first and has a number of criteria for
implementing the scheme.
      RESCU handles uncertainty by associating 'confidence factors'
with both facts and rules in the knowledge base. Most reported
systems provide some sort of uncertainty handling mechanism. PROP
keeps a 'credibility value' for each hypothesis considered at the
control level whilst EXTASE attaches factors to causal couplings (of
an explicit model) which give a validity rating for that link.
ESCORT, for its part, uses a three valued logic with an explicit
'unknown' value.
      It is of interest that different systems have taken different
approaches to knowledge representation. RESCU, ESCORT and EXTASE all
use explicit models of the process under observation, these models are
faily shallow in the case of ESCORT and RESCU, rather deeper for
EXTASE. By way of contrast PROP's model is implicit within the
event-graph formalism used by the system. Another factor is that

RESCU's knowledge representation is entirely rule based. Other
systems use mixed strategies including 'causal couplings' in EXTASE,
rules and event graphs in PROP and frames and rules in ESCORT.
REACTOR uses 'event-oriented' rules for diagnosis and
'function-oriented' response trees for representation of the way in
which plant components combine to perform a given task. Most reported
systems, including RESCU, use both backward and forward chaining
inferencing mechanims.

Conclusions

As the RESCU project concludes it is possible to draw certain
conclusions from the work done. Firstly, and most important, that it
is practicable to build real-time KBSs which will carry out a real
world task. The level of performance has been measured and is
comparable with that of experienced human operators, and superior to a
conventional algorithmic process control system. The approach of
building a KBS to work with and through a conventional system (in this
case a Foxboro system) is, we believe, the right one and the one we
would recommend. A second lesson is that such systems can be
developed on conventional hardware (in this case a DEC VAX) using
conventional project life cycle methods. There are two points worth
making in this context. Firstly RESCU is not demanding in the
real-time sense, a more demanding context would require much more
processing power at run time. Secondly, we feel that a prototyping
environment would have been very beneficial in the earlier stages of
knowledge acquisition. We did not build a prototype but would almost
certainly do so in a future development. A third major lesson, not
specifically addressed in this paper, is the vital importance of a
properly designed and engineered HCI. This was not an area which was
seriously addressed using specialist human factors expertise. In
retrospect this was a failing; the HCI was not as good as it could,
and should, have been.

At the more technical level we felt the lack of a frame based
knowledge representation, which would have been of great use during
systems development if having little effect on actual performance. We
would also, in a future development, devote more attention and effort
to the 'deeper' models. We feel that deep models are essential for
improving the performance of real-time KBSs. A further technique
offering a possible performance improvement would have been the
adoption of an ESCORT or EXTASE like approach to prioritising
hypotheses.

Overall, the major achievement of RESCU was to develop in the
context of an Alvey club, and using only fairly conventional AI
techniques, a system which stands comparison with other reported
real-time KBS. The intention is to carry the work forward to produce
a fully engineered and general purpose system. Plans include:-

the incorporation of additional knowledge representation
formalisms such as frames or object oriented methods;

attention to deeper knowledge modelling;

possibly the inclusion of qualitative models;

a focussing method to speed the dynamic response of the system.

Acknowledgements

The authors wish to express their thanks to:-

The managers and staff of ICI Wilton

The chairman and members of the RESCU club

The staff of the Alvey Directorate

Without their active participation and support, the project, far from being successful, would not have been possible.

References

1)   Shortliffe, E.H. (1976). Computer Based Medical Consultation: MYCIN, Elsevier.

2)   Sacks, P.H., Paterson, A.M. and Turnes, M.H.M., (1986). ESCORT: An expert system for complex operations in real time, Expert Systems, Vol 3, No. 1.

3)   Jakob, F, Suslenschi, P. and Vernet, D. (1986). EXTASE: An expert system for alarm processing in process control, Proceedings at the 7th European Conference on Artificial Intelligence, Vol 2, pp. 103-108.

4)   Nelson, W.R. (1982). REACTOR: An expert system for diagnosis and treatment of nuclear reactor accidents. Proceedings of national Conference on Artificial Intelligence (AAA1), pp. 296-301.

5)   Gallanti, M., Guida, G., Spampinato L. and Stefanini, A,. (1985). Representing Procedural Knolwedge in Expert Systems: An Application to Process control. Proceedings of 9th International Joint conference on Artificial Intelligence pp. 345-352.

THE WATER INDUSTRY EXPERT SYSTEMS SUPPORT ENVIRONMENT

C.P.W. Hornsby, P.R. Holmes-Higgin and K.Ahmad,
Computing Unit, University of Surrey, Guildford, Surrey.

Abstract

The Water Industry Expert Systems Support Environment (WIESSE) was developed as part of the Water Industry Expert Systems Club. It was designed to support two applications for the UK water industry; an advisor to assist in the rehabilitation of sewer networks, and an offline monitoring system for the control of water distribution networks. WIESSE, written in Prolog, makes use of a variety of knowledge representation schemata, including frames and rules, and contains a procedural facility which enables its user to structure knowledge in a task-oriented fashion. It is primarily an executive system, maintaining a model of the real-world problem to be solved, and carrying out operations on this model as well as providing advice. WIESSE includes facilities to explain and justify its reasoning and to interface with external programs.

1. Introduction and Overview

The Water Industry Expert Systems Support Environment (WIESSE) was developed to support two applications. The Sewerage Rehabilitation Planning Expert System (SERPES) mimics an expert engineer by providing advice and assistance on the repair ('rehabilitation') of large sewer networks. The Water Distribution Network Control Expert System (WADNES) emulates an experienced operator monitoring and controlling a medium-sized water distribution network.

SERPES and WADNES were developed as part of a two-year project to demonstrate the relevance of expert systems to the U.K. water industry. They were funded under the Alvey IKBS Comunity Club programme by the Water Industry Expert Systems Club (WIESC). This is a consortium of 17 organisations including water authorities, private engineering consultants, water companies and government and research bodies. Further details of the club can be found in the Alvey Conference Poster Supplements for 1986 and 1987. SERPES, WADNES and WIESSE were developed by the University of Surrey with assistance from the joint contractor Software Sciences PLC.

The WIESC project plan specified the use of the cascade model of software development, augmented by provision for rapid prototyping (WIESC Project Plan,

1986). The decision to develop an environment was a product of the definition phase for the two sub-projects (Hornsby et al, 1986 and Holmes-Higgin et al, 1986). This phase helped the collaborators and domain experts to determine the scope of the problems to be solved, to identify and organise access to knowledge sources, and to outline the project's hardware and software requirements. An initial prototyping stage was used to refine the design of the two systems, leading to the development of the 'final' prototype in phase two of the project. The final phase relates to project debriefing.

The principal objective of this paper is to discuss the specification and development of the environment for expert systems which emerged from the design and development phases. We begin by briefly describing the SERPES and WADNES application areas. The next section outlines the origins of WIESSE, and is followed by a description of its architecture and significant features. We then discuss some implementation issues, and conclude by describing some lessons learnt from the project, and by mentioning future extentions to WIESSE.

2. An Outline of SERPES and WADNES

The WIESC projects are concerned with a broad spectrum of problems typical of the water industry. An important feature of both is the need to integrate expert systems with large (FORTRAN) simulation models, in the sewerage case the WASSP-SIM package (Wallingford Procedure, 1981), in the water distribution case the WATNET system (Stimson, 1986). Both systems thus rely on quantitative analysis as the basis of many decisions.

SERPES follows the procedure laid down in the Sewerage Rehabilitation Manual, focusing particularly upon the Manual's Phase 2b; building, verifying and using a hydraulic simulation model of the existing sewer network, and Manual Phase 3; applying hydraulic and structural information to prepare a plan for the rehabilitation of the sewers in an entire drainage area. The knowledge has been obtained from many different experts, verified, clarified and expanded by a single principal domain expert. Two drainage areas were chosen as representative of current problems, and these have been used for verification and validation purposes.

WADNES supports a distribution network controller by providing procedures to operate the network during a failure and to specify the repair actions required to restore the network to its normal operation. These procedures are complex and depend heavily on the current and expected behaviour of the network. An abstract representation of the network status has been developed, which is used with a simulation program to provide 'templates' to represent this behaviour under various conditions. Poole in Dorset is the reference site. The knowledge was acquired from water distribution experts in a manner similar to that of SERPES.

3. The Origins of WIESSE

The decision to develop an environment for water industry expert systems work, rather than to make use of a commercial shell or development environment, or to code directly in an artificial intelligence language, stemmed from a variety of factors. The complexity of the problems to be tackled indicated that an expert system shell would not provide the variety of knowledge representation and reasoning techniques. In addition, at the time of procurement, the large systems such as KEE, ART and KnowledgeCraft were beyond the hardware and software budget of £70,000, and involved a long learning curve. In addition, the use of a programming language such as Prolog (Clocksin & Mellish, 1984), with which the applications team had substantial experience, would allow incremental development of the tool, as facilities were required. It was unclear whether the existing tools would provide the precise facilities needed by the applications, and it was felt appropriate to develop a system in harness with the applications, in order to focus it upon the particular problems encountered. It was also considered important that the rules be directly comprehensible to the domain experts involved. The experts' time was scarce, so the reduction of the

domain expert --> knowledge engineer --> rule base

interaction time was important. Experts also felt more comfortable with the knowledge when expressed in an external language, and then compiled in to Prolog and run. Since the overall strategy of SERPES and WADNES is procedural, it was also felt that adopting a system which provided an explicit procedural element was important.

The technical origins of WIESSE lie primarily in structured object-based systems (Nilsson, 1980) such as OPS5, and in commercial development environments such as Inference ART. They also reflect the weaknesses of Prolog alone as a high-level language for implementing large-scale applications, and the need to develop additional features appropriate for such work.

4. The Structure of WIESSE

WIESSE is a conceptually-unified object-based system, allowing the manipulation of large bodies of information in a structured manner, and in addition making possible the development of control and explanation facilities within the system itself. It is an executive system as well as an advisor, executing operations on simulation packages, and maintaining a model of the real world problem within its memory.

4.1. Knowledge Representation Techniques

WIESSE uses several basic techniques for the representation of knowledge and of facts about a particular application (see figure 1):

4.1.1 Defining the Domain

There are three forms of knowledge-representation schemata used to define the domain:

WIESSE **object types**, which are analogous to *frames* or *schemata*, define the kinds of entities within the application, and the basic relationships between them. Thus for example

> *there is an object type named sewer,*
> *an object type named concrete sewer is a class of the object type*
> *named sewer.*

Attributes define the properties which an object type can possess. WIESSE treats them as objects in their own right, related to other objects. Thus for example

> *an attribute named length is part of object type named sewer.*

All facts must **set** values for an object attribute, and rules test and modify them. It is possible to state a variety of restrictions upon the values of an attribute, and to state the access mechanisms used to obtain such a fact when needed. In the case where the values can be fully enumerated (e.g. small, medium,large), the system can then use this, in combination with reasoning using negative facts, to deduce by elimination that if the size is not small, and not large, then it must be medium.

Relationships in WIESSE are similar to attributes, except that they state that an object of a specified type has a certain relationship to another object in the system. Thus

> *sewer s1 is represented by pipe p1.*

The standard inheritance system through *class, isa* or *a kind of* relations was initially implemented as a hard-coded special case, but was reimplemented as a commonly-used and thus pre-defined relationship. In cases of multiple inheritance, values are inherited on a simple depth-first left-to-right basis. This should be integrated with the truth maintenance system to allow the expansion of different equally valid inherited default values as assumptions (Touretzky, 1986).

4.1.2. Tasks.

Tasks are the mechanism in WIESSE by which the procedure for problem-solving is represented and traversed, and by which the rule base is structured. Tasks describe the natural structure of a problem-solving strategy in a large real-world application, with top-level tasks such as 'simplification of network model' being additionally sudivided into sub-tasks such as 'merging simplification'. They are linked together as a directed (possibly cyclic) and-or graph. Each task contain a statement of the inference technique appropriate to the particular problem. During execution, outstanding tasks are held on an agenda, which can be applied sequentially or on an 'any first' basis. This allows both a procedural and a blackboard-like interpretation of tasks.

4.1.3. Deductions

Rules are the most common knowledge-representation structure in WIESSE. They test and modify facts about attributes and relationships, and also call external functions. The rules are written directly in a natural-language style allowing the expert to examine and understand them, and making the process of knowledge engineering easier. The rule-base is partitioned by task, which is important for simplicity and efficiency (there are usually no more than 40 rules under consideration at one time). For most inference engines, the ordering of the rule-base is significant.

In addition, **demons** can be attached to individual attributes or relationships. They allow the global testing or modification of the data-base, to obtain a value (*if needed*) or to carry out operations if a condition holds (*if added*, *if deleted*, *if changed*), whether alterations to the data-base or external functions. Such demons have respectively the form of rule antecedents and consequents.

4.1.4. Statements of Fact

WIESSE provides two basic tructures within which factual information may be stored; object instances and tables.

Object instances group the information so far available during a consultation about individual objects. In contrast to Prolog, WIESSE makes use of the open-world assumption, allowing explicitly reasoning on the basis of true, false and unknown information. Facts about the value of an object's attribute may thus record values to be positive, negative or unknown. If the attribute is defined as such, then it may simultaneously hold several values (e.g. a model object may have several pipes as members).

Tables are a specialised form of WIESSE data structure which are used by the knowledge engineer to store static information for fast lookup for large tables of data in engineering applications. They can be used to replace several similar rules manipulating the same objects; in such circumstances a four by four table could replace 16 rules.

4.1.5. Predicates.

WIESSE also allows predicates to be used to test the values of particular object attributes, such as *if a pipe has diameter large...*

Predicates correspond to a form of global backward-chaining rule, called when a value is obtained and a test of it required. They may be used as functions, to return a result, and may be interfaced to external procedures.

4.1.6. External Functions.

It also proved necessary from the first to provide functions to interface with the outside world, to call routines in other languages such as C, and to read and write files. These are written in Prolog, with their interface to rules and tasks specified within the object definitions. The aim is to minimise their use by knowledge engineers by providing with the system a set of basic functions which may be called directly, as well as the facility for knowledge engineers to define their own.

4.2 Inference Strategies

A variety of inference engines have been developed, all variations of forward or backward chaining strategies, These include forward chainers which inference object by object or rule by rule, cycle iteratively or use one-pass only, and do or do not recompute values which are already known. Access mechanisms, which are speicified for each attribute definition, control the order in which the system initiates database access, looking for default information, asking the user and backward chaining.

4.3 The User and Knowlege Engineer Interface

WIESSE contains failities to explain and justify decisions and advice, including the ability to display the rule used to obtain a value in a form close to that in which it was initially input, and the current task, rule and goal under consideration. In addition, rules may be linked to help objects which contain relevant information and which may be accessed and browsed through in response to a help query. The system also contains tracing and debugging facilities, including the ability to insert break-points on rules and to examine the rules fired during the run, plus the ability to view the database and the knowledge base in both internal and external language forms.

5. Implementation Issues

WIESSE has been developed and currently runs on a SUN-3/160 workstation, under Quintus Prolog. The main body of code is relatively compact, taking less than 200K bytes of memory. When running, WIESSE applications are processor-

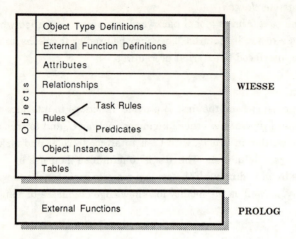

Figure 1: Knowledge Representation Schemata in WIESSE

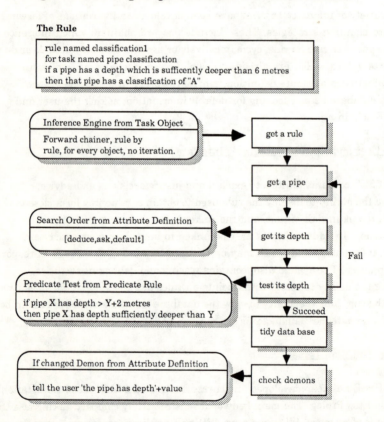

Figure 2: A WIESSE Rule and the Execution Strategy Used

intensive, and large applications require several megabytes of memory, since the number of facts expands rapidly with time. The largest application at present uses over 500 rules, with about 100 tasks and 60 object type definitions, and over 2000 facts about objects.

The core of WIESSE is an **incremental compiler** that compiles statements in the external language into Prolog code. This code can then be compiled by Prolog for fast execution or interpreted for ease of development. The compiler has been implemented as three separate modules: a *lexical analyser*, *object parser* and *code generator*. The lexical analyser produces a list of lexical elements, such as *atom(pipe)*, which are passed to the object parser to produce a generalised intermediate structure. This is then transformed by the code generator into the appropriate Prolog code. The control of the execution of the code generated by the compiler is performed by the inference engines and access mechanisms (see the example in figure 2). Since the basic knowledge representation schemata are described as objects, alterations to these require only the inclusion of their new definitions and modifications to a small portion of the object analyser.

Human-computer interaction proved to be a more complex problem than originally anticipated. Three different user interface systems were implemented and tested for WIESSE on the Sun workstation; (i) using Sunview and C, (ii) simply opening windows as Unix-files for reading and writing, and (iii) making use of PCE-Prolog (Anjewierden 1986). All had disadvantages, and work is continuing on the most appropriate techniques.

6. Lessons Learnt from the Project

There are several important lessons which can be learnt from the development of WIESSE and from the applications which rest upon it:

i. The experience of work with the FORTRAN simulation models demonstrated that is both possible and appropriate to integrate an expert system with existing conventional programs as an executive as well as an advisor. The applications have successfully used WIESSE, with a set of external functions, to create input files, run models, analyse output files to deduce results, and present them to the user in a comprehensible form.

ii. During the project, the need became apparent within the applications for a number of sophisticated features to be provided by WIESSE, reflecting the fact that such features are important to any large project. The facilities which thus evolved included demons, relationships and a number of variants upon the basic forward and backward chaining systems.

iii. Frame-based executive systems such as WIESSE require the knowledge engineer not only to identify the agents that are operating in the problem domain and their relationships to each other, but also the precise nature of the operations which must be carried out. An enormous quantity of information about **how** to execute operations is left implicit in the text strings of an advisory system, and these systems thus ignore major issues both in knowledge representation and application.

iv. The need for expertise in problem analysis and decomposition is even greater than in a simple advisory system, since knowledge representation and application is more complex. In practice, it might well have been of value to adopt more structured knowledge elicitation and software development methodologies early on.

v. As a manifestation of the complexity of the domain, WIESSE has sometimes proved hard to use, due to the interrelationships between the different knowledge representation structures, and the need to understand the more sophisticated facilities available.

vi. The lack of sophisticated debugging tools in WIESSE has been a serious handicap in the applications work, and it is recommended that these be a high priority in any future exercise of this kind.

vii. The development of WIESSE was resource-intensive and it would be difficult to develop such a system without the investment of substantial time and expertise. The design of the inference engines has proved particularly complex, with three different techniques for representing their nature and activities used at various times. However, the 'do it yourself' approach has proved of value in extending the skills of the applications team in the techniques of artificial intelligence.

viii. In practice, the use of pure *class* inheritance and default values alone proved to be a weak technique, when the domain hierarchy covers such entities as geographical areas, which are specific to the case-study. This led to the implementation of a more general mechanism allowing values to be inherited across all types of relationships.

ix. The ability in WIESSE to specify facts to be true, false or unknown proved a crucial feature, requiring additional complexity in the fact-base access and modification routines, but producing high returns in reducing unnecessary user-interaction.

x. Human-computer interaction considerations proved very resource-intensive. Few practical guidelines were available for constructing user interfaces and the basis still appears to be *ad hoc*. All the available software tools that were examined for developing user interfaces on the configuration of hardware and software had serious drawbacks.

xi. The incremental debugging and development of WIESSE had both positive and negative aspects. It allowed the team members working on the specific systems to target features they desired and the system to be altered accordingly, but required modifications to the application to be made when the environment changed.

xii. The choice whether to structure knowledge acquisition around the tool on which the system will be built, or to attempt system-independent acquisition remains unresolved. System-independent knowledge is complete but unfocussed; tool-dependent acquisition allows specific progress to be made, but makes the knowledge itself less useful in translation to another system, and makes it more complex to alter and improve the tool itself.

7. Extensions to WIESSE

Several important issues remain the subject of future study.

We have designed two substantial additional features: uncertainty and a truth-maintenance system. However, we have decided not to implement them at present, since they are not crucial to the particular applications. The basic structure of the uncertainty system is to make use of 'piles' of *uncertainty modulations* as suggested by Duval and Kordatroff (Duval, 1986), in which symbolic representations of uncertainty are stored when deduced, but not evaluated until the end of the deductive process. Added to this was the facility for the knowledge engineer to define in tabular form the interpretation of and relationships between modulations.

The truth maintenance system is very much more complex, with the facilities envisaged resting upon de Kleer's work on assumption-based truth maintenance systems. The goal was to design a form of *views*, which would be automatically generated when information was known to be missing, or to be uncertain. The views would be implemented by the 'tagging' of facts.

Parallelism remains an interesting issue for all Prolog systems, and particularly for an expert system which repeatedly applies the same rules to a set of objects (i.e. All-solutions AND-parallelism), or applies a series of rules to the same object (OR-parallelism). The efficiency increase from implementing these forms of parallelism in particular would be very great.

The needs of the applications chosen, and the practicalities of real world commercial work strongly suggest that built-in interfaces to relational database systems be developed for WIESSE, allowing access to existing records, and replacing the use of the Prolog internal database.

8. Conclusions

The WIESSE language and environment has been accepted by many of its prospective users in both application areas as a tool with which they could readily create complex expert systems, despite some performance problems both with the hardware and software chosen, and the need to improve the user interface. We feel the development of WIESSE was justified within the circumstances of the WIESC project, since a complex prototype was required, finance was limited, and full rights to the source code were important. The result is a sophisticated tool for implementing knowledge-based systems, which combines several techniques for knowledge representation and inference in an integrated manner.

References

Ahmad K., Holmes-Higgin P, Hornsby C, Hakami B (1986) Water Industry Expert Systems Club Design Specification Part I. University of Surrey (Restricted Circulation).

Anjewierden A., (1986). PCE-Prolog Reference Manual, University of Amsterdam.

Clocksin W.F., Mellish C.S., (1984). Programming in Prolog Second Edition. Berlin: Springer-Verlag.

Duval B., Kordatroff Y.,(1986). 'Automated Deduction in an Uncertain and Inconsistent Data Basis'. In Proceedings Seventh European Conference on Artificial Intelligence, pp 101-8.

Holmes-Higgin P.R., Ahmad K., Hakami B., (1986). Water Industry Expert Systems Club Water Distribution Network Expert System (WADNES) Requirement Specification. University of Surrey (Restricted Circulation).

Holmes-Higgin P.R, Hornsby C.P.W., (1987). Knowledge Representation Schemata for WIESC University of Surrey (Restricted Circulation).

Hornsby C.P.W., Ahmad K., Hakami B., Bolland J., (1986). Water Industry Expert Systems Club Sewerage Rehabilitation Planning Expert System (SERPES) Requirement Specification. University of Surrey (Restricted Circulation).

Nilsson N. J., (1980) Principles of Artificial Intelligence. Palo Alto. California: Tioga.

Stimson K.R., (1986) Analysis and Simulation of Water Networks: A Guide to the Watnet Simulation Computer Program. Engineering T.R 237. Swindon:Water Research Centre,

Touretzky D.S., (1986) The Mathematics of Inheritance Systems. London: Pitman.

(1981) Wallingford Procedure 'Design and Analysis of Urban Storm Drainage - The Wallingford Procedure' Vols. 1-5 Department of Environment, National Water Council, Standing Technical Committee Report No. 29.

(1985) Water Industry Expert Systems Club Project Plan . University of Surrey.

ROLE OF INTERMEDIATE REPRESENTATIONS IN KNOWLEDGE ELICITATION

Richard M. Young
MRC Applied Psychology Unit, 15 Chaucer Road,
Cambridge CB2 2EF

Abstract

The traditional, informal approach to expert system construction involves the elicitor in chatting with the expert and then trying to build some of what was said directly into machine-executable rules. Progress thereafter relies upon having the expert iteratively comment on and help debug a "prototype" system. Such an approach may be adequate for certain limited tasks, but its fundamental inadequacy lies at the root of the common complaints voiced about the difficulties of knowledge elicitation. The approach suffers from a number of drawbacks, including (a) the fact that it is unsystematic, and (b) the coding of elicited knowledge directly into rules.

The first problem, the reliance on informal interviews, can be overcome by the use of systematic techniques developed in psychology (Gammack, 1987). Expertise is made up from knowledge of different kinds, each of which is best elicited with different techniques. The basic concepts and structure of a domain, for example, can be elicited by investigating pairwise similarities between objects in the domain or by the use of Repertory Grid. The resulting data can be analysed in various ways, such as by multidimensional scaling, cluster analysis, or pathfinder, to yield maps of the domain at different scales. The validity of the knowledge elicited can be checked by using it to predict the expert's performance on further, secondary tasks known as validation tasks. This approach is particularly appropriate in the early stages of elicitation, where there is otherwise little guidance available. These systematic techniques are quick, can be used with one or more experts, include convergent procedures for validation, and produce visualisable representations for which the traditional procedure offers no equivalent.

Among the characteristics of these psychological techniques are that they yield non-executable representations intended for use by human as much as by computer, and that they produce several such representations. They thereby solve the second problem with the traditional approach by providing an alternative to the direct coding into rules, in the form of intermediate representations mediating between the human expert and the final expert system. Other examples of intermediate representations are diagrams of various sorts (e.g. circuit diagrams), systemic grammar networks, "semantic nets", influence diagrams, and so on.

Using such intermediate representations in the process of knowledge elicitation has a number of advantages. First, intermediate representations serve as a record of the elicited knowledge that is independent of the current technology (such as a particular expert system shell), and so can act as a source for re-implementing a system later, using improved technology, without having to repeat the whole elicitation procedure. Second, intermediate representations can act as a medium of knowledge communication shareable by the expert and the elicitor. Third, use of a variety of intermediate representations can provide a more complete record of the knowledge than can be captured solely in a machine-executable representation. Fourth, the knowledge recorded in the intermediate representations can be used for purposes other than building an expert system, such as for explanation, for training, and as a basis for system documentation.

In order to understand more about the properties of intermediate representations, it is necessary to deal with a couple of preliminary issues. One is the notion that the implicit assumptions made by traditional practice in knowledge engineering and the metaphors used to describe knowledge are seriously misleading. Whatever it is, knowledge is not a substance, and it cannot be quarried from experts' heads. Knowledge elicitation has to be viewed as an enterprise, not in which little nuggets of knowledge are successively extracted from the expert, but in which evidence provided by the expert's behaviour is used to infer what the knowledge must be. Another issue is the somewhat unfamiliar view of expert systems as being media for communicating knowledge rather than engines for solving problems. From this alternative view follow some important consequences for knowledge engineering. One is a reminder that representations can "contain knowledge" only by virtue of the information that an interpreter brings to bear on them. A second is the incoherence of the aim of capturing "all" the knowledge relevant to a domain of expertise.

Intermediate representations can be thought of as lying along a spectrum, ranging between the human-like at one end and the computer-like at the other. It is worth trying to understand the systematic changes that occur as one moves along the spectrum. Among these gradations are: (1) A loss of completeness. There are many kinds of information which can be elicited from experts, and which we can perfectly well understand and notate, but which lie beyond the state of the art for representation in a computer. (2) A gain in self-sufficiency. The more human-oriented representations require semantic interpretation by the reader. By contrast representations at the computer-oriented end of the spectrum are more self-contained, and require only syntactic interpretation. (3) A loss of cognitive compatibility with the human users. Representations at the human end are intelligible to the expert, and can act as a shared medium of communication between the expert and the elicitor.

A number of miscellaneous issues arise from this discussion. The standard claim that "knowledge elicitation is the bottleneck" in building expert systems can be seen to be doubtful at best. The alternative analysis is that the constraining factor is the lack of a range of good techniques for representing knowledge in the computer. The initially confusing issue of selecting among the medley of techniques and notations on offer can be clarified by understanding the nature of different "schools" which approach questions of knowledge elicitation and notation in different ways. Choosing between them has to be seen as a more subtle matter than simply asking which is "best". Finally, some unreasonable expectations current in the field about what knowledge elicitation techniques could plausibly be expected to deliver need to be confronted.

Reference

Gammack, J. G. (1987). Modelling expert knowledge using cognitively compatible structures. Proceedings of 3rd International Conference on Expert Systems, pp. 191-200. London: Learned Information.